Groove Theory

Groove Theory

THE BLUES FOUNDATION OF FUNK

Tony Bolden

UNIVERSITY PRESS OF MISSISSIPPI / JACKSON

The University Press of Mississippi is the scholarly publishing agency of the Mississippi Institutions of Higher Learning: Alcorn State University, Delta State University, Jackson State University, Mississippi State University, Mississippi University for Women, Mississippi Valley State University, University of Mississippi, and University of Southern Mississippi.

www.upress.state.ms.us

Designed by Peter D. Halverson

The University Press of Mississippi is a member of the Association of University Presses.

First printing 2020
∞

Library of Congress Cataloging-in-Publication Data available

LCCN 2020030543
ISBN 9781496830524 (hardback)
ISBN 9781496830609 (trade paperback)
ISBN 9781496830616 (epub single)
ISBN 9781496830623 (epub institutional)
ISBN 9781496830630 (pdf single)
ISBN 9781496830593 (pdf institutional)

British Library Cataloging-in-Publication Data available

Contents

Side A—Groove Theory
CONCEPTUAL FOUNDATIONS OF BLUE FUNK

Side B—Devotion
BLUE FUNK AND THE BLACK FANTASTIC

Side A

Groove Theory
CONCEPTUAL FOUNDATIONS OF BLUE FUNK

Intro

One afternoon many years ago, I stopped by my father's house for one of our daily listening sessions on jazz. I was fresh out of the Army, and my experiences during my thirteen-month tour in South Korea had transformed my worldview. While overseas I had become fascinated with jazz, literature, and the world of ideas. I was taking classes at Merritt College in Oakland, but my real passion was jazz; and since my father was an aficionado of modern jazz, I shared my new interest with him. Dad regarded Charlie Parker, Dizzy Gillespie, and Thelonious Monk as models of intellect, artistic ingenuity, and self-development. So we began our sessions with bebop recordings such as Parker's "Confirmation," "Yardbird Suite," "Scrapple from the Apple"; Gillespie's "Salt Peanuts"; and Monk's "In Walked Bud," and we later discussed the 1949 and 1950 recordings of Miles Davis's 1957 album *Birth of the Cool*. But on this particular afternoon, Dad said it was time to focus on the next period. He called it hard bop, and introduced me to Horace Silver. "Horace," he said, "was a bebopper, but he played funky." And sure enough, we listened to Silver's standards like "Opus de Funk" (1953), "Doodlin'" (1954), "Señor Blues" (1956), and "Song for My Father" (1964), arguably the funkiest hard bop composition ever recorded.

Dad's explanation had a bingo-like effect on me. It was perfectly clear, and we went on listening to the music and talking as we normally did. Many years later, though, I wondered what made Dad feel so confident that I would understand him. Neither of us had ever used "funky" in previous conversations, so why would he think the word would be so clarifying to me? And since I now understood that hard bop was part of the blues tradition, I became curious about the relationship between blues and funk. Silver's recordings suggested that the concept of funk preceded the musical genre, and that both are related to blues. Yet there was not much scholarship on funk, particularly the concept. Writers as varied as Ralph Ellison and Gayl Jones engaged funk in fiction, but most scholars ignored it. So I read musicians' memoirs and quickly realized that artists demonstrated tremendous insight on the concept. In retrospect, of course, this makes perfect sense. Since funk is a vernacular concept, who would understand it better than the artists themselves? *Groove Theory: The Blues Foundation of Funk* represents musicians as organic intellectuals. D'Angelo is a prime example. In an interview with Nelson George a few months before the release of his Grammy Award–winning 2014 album *Black Messiah*, George asked the virtuoso singer and multi-instrumentalist about his new sound, noting that the music seemed to have "more rock and more funk." D'Angelo underscored blues in his response:

> The thing with me—about rock and all of that . . . Through years and years of crate digging, listening to old music, you kinda start to connect the dots. And I was seeing the thread that was connecting everything together. Which is pretty much *the blues*. And everything— soul or funk—kinda starts with that. That's kinda like the nucleus of everything.[1]

D'Angelo encapsulates my central argument—that blues and funk are not just musical forms; they are interrelated concepts. And blues is "like the nucleus" of rock as well as rhythm and blues, which includes soul and funk. As we'll see, his statement is evidenced by numerous writers and fellow artists. For instance, Greg Tate, a founding member of the Black Rock Coalition, offers the following perspective on Miles Davis's forays into funk: "What Miles heard in the musics of P-Funk progenitors, James Brown, Jimi Hendrix, and Sly Stone was the blues impulse transferred, masked, and retooled for the Space Age through a lowdown act of possession."[2] Similarly, when pioneering funk scholar Rickey Vincent states that "[f]unk is actually the *last* form of black popular music played by musicians trained in the jazz arena,"[3] he situates funk in the blues tradition.

Groove Theory traces the concept of funk from the beginning of the blues era around 1890 to its manifestation as a full-fledged genre in the 1970s. But since "blues" and "funk" also reference dissimilar musical forms, some historical background may be helpful. Beginning in the 1950s, early rhythm and blues musicians began developing cyclical, riff-based styles of music that culminated with funk. Richard J. Ripani writes: "Rhythm and blues . . . overlaps to a great extent with the blues genre, so much so that the border between the two seems impossible to define exactly."[4] Moreover, James Brown's "Papa's Got a Brand New Bag" (1965) "showed the way to a whole generation of R&B artists who wanted to interpret blues in a more modern way."[5] Thus

Ripani identifies a conceptual relationship between blues and funk. Analyzing Maceo Parker's saxophone solo on "New Bag," he asks:

> Why would the blues scale be the preferred vehicle for solos of this sort, played over extended cyclic sections of R&B grooves? The answer seems to be that when musicians performing in this style want to communicate a certain "deep-soul," the blues scale is usually the language used to express it. [Charlie] Parker's "dirty" tone, like Brown's vocal timbre, is also part of the style and transmission of a desired feeling.[6]

Ripani's comments corroborate D'Angelo's premise while raising an important question: How are blues and funk musically related, especially since they sound so dissimilar? The answer lies in the flexibility of the blues scale. Few saxophonists differ as much as modern jazz musician Charlie Parker and rhythm and blues musician Maceo Parker.[7] The former played an intricate style known as bebop in the 1940s. The latter achieved notoriety as James Brown's featured soloist in the 1960s. Yet both saxophonists played variations of the blues scale.

Funk is a percussive form of rhythm and blues that emphasizes the groove. Listeners get in sync with the melody and rhythmic pulse of the music. They become enthralled or immersed psychologically, and express joy through dancing and other forms of body movement. Most discussions of rhythm and blues focus on soul music, which blended elements of blues, gospel, and jazz.[8] Funk musicians extended this fusion, but changed the overall sound quality by incorporating James Brown's rhythmic innovations and elements of rock. In Brown's new concept, the drummer emphasized the first beat in a four-bar measure—generally known as the "One"—whereas rock contributed musical technology, especially electronic devices like amplifiers, wah-wah pedals, synthesizers, and so forth. These changes placed more significance to rhythm players. Previously, bass guitarists were relegated to the background as accompanists for singers and soloists; however, funk bassists Larry Graham and Bootsy Collins whose slap-bass techniques influenced younger musicians, performed in the limelight. Electric guitarists were also important. Guitarist Kelvyn Bell provides a helpful explanation in an interview with Maureen Mahon:

> Funk put even more emphasis . . . on heavy rhythms [than R&B]. . . . It's all based on the power of the electric guitar and the overdrive and the distortion. When you get like wah wah wah [he imitates a scream-

ing guitar], you play one note and it's waaaah. . . . When you use that kind of sound to create rhythm, especially syncopated rhythm, everything's exaggerated because of the volume. . . . You play that rhythm with all the distortion on an electric guitar [and] it's going to be a much bigger, more powerful rhythm.[9]

At the same time, funk musicians envisioned rock as a new approach to blues. As George Clinton, spokesman for the Parliament-Funkadelic collective, put it, "[W]e saw Cream and Vanilla Fudge and all them take the music that my mother liked, flip it around and make it loud and it became cool," said Clinton. "We realized that blues was the key to that music. We just speeded blues up and called it 'funk' cause we knew it was a bad word to a lot of people."[10] Clinton's characterization of blues and rock is nearly identical to D'Angelo's statement. Equally important, his allusion to funk as a "bad word" highlights the contrarian disposition that funk inherited from blues and rock. The predilection for bohemianism in rock was related to broader social issues, though. As Mahon observes:

> The hard rock associated with the 1960s counterculture incorporated calls for social, personal, and sexual liberation with political critique—especially of the war in Vietnam. The presence of these ideas and the challenge that the rock scene presented to the mainstream helped forge a link between rock music and freedom from individually and socially imposed strictures. Performers like Bob Dylan, Janis Joplin, the Grateful Dead, and Jimi Hendrix communicated this spirit in their lyrics, music, dress, and performance styles.[11]

Occasionally called black rock, funk coextensively promoted and implicitly critiqued contradictory aspects of black nationalism. The Black Power Movement provided much of the impetus for funk. Activists encouraged black youth to reexamine their African ancestry, especially stigmas related to skin color, hair texture, and vernacular expressions associated with funkiness that were previously objects of shame. But while radical black writers often represented Africa as an idealized "Motherland," Brown and other funk artists, including Sly and the Family Stone, played rhythms that didn't exactly "match those regions of West Africa and the Caribbean for sheer rhythmic complexity, [but did] seem to be following some of the same basic rules of that music, including the dense, overlapping and interlocking rhythms in a setting of limited harmonic functionality in the Western sense."[12] As such, funk highlighted African-derived aspects of African American culture.

The new form was mostly a black street phenomenon that reflected party themes, social commentary, and vernacular idioms, while projecting cultural values at variance with the status quo. But notably, "street" didn't mean anti-white. Funk exemplified African-derived concepts of music making without promoting racial exclusion. Greg Errico, the drummer who played "overlapping and interlocking rhythms" for Sly and the Family Stone, is white. So is guitarist Dennis Coffey, one of Motown's famous Funk Brothers, who introduced the wah-wah pedal into Motown's sound and thus helped change the direction of its music. Both Rufus and Tower of Power were leading funk bands with interracial lineups, and Average White Band, a stellar band based in Scotland, was quite popular with black audiences. To the extent that funk artists recognized social demarcations at all, they generally cited the groove as a main criterion. Bassist George Porter Jr. of the Meters typified funk artists' emphasis on performative talent when he said, "We became sort of like musicians' musicians . . ."[13] Clinton was more explicit in a 1978 interview: "The whole black/white thing . . . it's all bulls—t put out as propaganda to keep the people away from each other."[14]

Funk also created opportunities for women instrumentalists. Rose Stone played organ and tambourine for Sly and the Family Stone, and singer Maxayn played piano with her husband Mandré (né Michael Andre Lewis) in the eponymous band Maxayn. There was also Klymaxx, an all-women's band founded by drummer and vocalist Bernadette Cooper. For instance, in 1984 alone Klymaxx released such hits as "The Meeting in the Ladies Room," "I Miss You," and "The Men All Pause." At various points the band included Cooper, keyboardists Lynn Malsby and Robbin Grider, bassist and vocalist Joyce "Fenderella" Irby, guitarist Cheryl Cooley, and vocalist Lorena Porter. And finally, singer and keyboardist Patrice Rushen, who jumpstarted her career as a dancer on Don Cornelius's nationally syndicated television show *Soul Train*, wrote and recorded jazz-funk tunes such as "Let There Be Funk" (1976) and "The Funk Won't Let You Down" (1980).

Yet the construction of funk entailed a fascinating irony. Black radicals expanded the parameters of expression with their strident assertions and celebrations of vernacular culture. The freer atmosphere enabled young dancers and musicians to reimagine "funk" as a metaphor for unapologetic blackness. However, funk artists often interpreted freedom in ways that activists never imagined. As I've written elsewhere:

The repositioning of funkiness as a leading cultural aesthetics was coterminous with widespread activism among black youth during the period. Indeed, one could reasonably argue that funk was a discursive child of the Black Power movement; and yet it wasn't necessarily a reflection of its politics. Since funk [was] suffused with blues, it tended to emphasize independence which was often expressed in irony, alterity, and contrarianism. Thus, while funk was a child of the civil rights movement, it was indubitably a wayward child.[15]

The broad spectrum of contrarian sensibilities included freakish theatrical styles that represented what Francesca T. Royster calls a resistive "fugitive identity" that responded to "white privilege and power . . ."[16] We can observe a perfect example Bruce W. Talamon's classic photo of Bootsy Collins (see fig. 0.1). Performing in full regalia as a member of Parliament-Funkadelic, the acclaimed bassist is knee-deep in the funk as he delights the audience. Such "eccentricity," "outsized personae . . . [and] invented characters,"[17] writes Royster, typified a predilection for unconventional expression. Deviating from "respectable" models of blackness, funk encouraged people "to see around corners, push the edges of the present to create . . . new sounds, new dances, new configurations of self—the makings of a black utopia."[18]

Royster's notion of a "black utopia" is what political scientist Richard Iton has called the search for the black fantastic. For Iton, the black fantastic references black artistry that "transcend[s] the prevailing notions of the aesthetic and the predominance of the state as the sole frame of subject formation and progressive and transformative discourse and mobilization."[19] Such expression deviates from prevailing ideologies, values, styles, and sensibilities. The black fantastic reflects cultural standards and perspectives of "minor-key sensibilities generated from the experiences of the underground, the *vagabond*, and those constituencies marked deviant . . ."[20] Both components of Iton's two-pronged definition coincide with funk aesthetics. After all, black youth were considered America's primary deviants. Clinton remarks: "We're all about opening up people's minds to what's going on and through our stage show, we attack a lot of taboos and hang-ups that have been around for years. We teach people that you [shouldn't] be afraid to be different."[21] Jimi Hendrix was a prototypical example. Before he became the famous bandleader of the Jimi Hendrix Experience in 1966, his migratory lifestyle, economic challenges, and bohemian sensibility were legendary among fellow musicians. To cite one of many examples, saxophonist Lonnie Youngblood,

Figure 0.1. Bootsy Collins The Forum, Inglewood, California, 1978. Photo by Bruce W. Talamon.

who played with Hendrix before he left for Britain, once said, "Jimmy . . . he was a vagabond, man."[22]

In the following chapters, then, we'll examine the development of blue funk in a multidimensional discussion that will engage songs, fiction, memoirs, interviews, scholarship, and more. The discussion proceeds in two parts. Side A presents a conceptual introduction to funk aesthetics, an historical overview of funk during the blues era, and a chapter on Sly Stone that examines his foundational role as an architect of funk. Side B includes chapters on Chaka Khan, Gil Scott-Heron, and Betty Davis, whose recordings and aesthetics exemplify distinct variations of blue funk and the black fantastic.

Chapter One

Groove Theory

LINER NOTES ON FUNK AESTHETICS

When asked to define funk, George Clinton once said, "If it makes you shake your rump, it's the funk."[1] At the most basic level, the term "funk" signifies honesty and beauty of expression at the depths of human emotion. As such, funk comprises the secular counterpart of "the spirit"—what Albert Murray calls "paroxysms of ecstasy"—in black church worship. Writing about James Brown, musicologist Teresa L. Reed makes an observation that's applicable to funk music generally. She states that the music "captures the soulful spontaneity of the Sanctified church and the animated exhortation of the Sanctified preacher. [The music] also emulates and incites an emotional intensity parallel to the Holy Spirit possession that is a trademark of the Sanctified worship service."[2] Teddy Pendergrass makes a similar point in his memoir *Truly Blessed*. Recalling his childhood experiences in what he described as a "rock-'em, sock-'em, sanctified, feel-the-Spirit church," Pendergrass said, "We talk today about the innovations in rhythm made by great jazz musicians and pioneers like James Brown, but the truth is, they had nothing on a congregation going full force in praise of the Lord."[3] The musician and musicologist Guthrie P. Ramsey Jr. echoes Pendergrass's statement in his recollection of his experiences as a member of the Sanctified Band in Chicago in the mid-1980s. According to Ramsey, "*Funky* was the watchword . . . God liked funky. Funky ministered to the people."[4]

Of course, black churches have always functioned as training repositories for black musicians, but the frenzy and kinetic expression associated with holiness churches played a disproportionate role in funk music. These churches emphasized African-derived worship styles, and funk music showcased many of the aesthetic sensibilities and epistemological principles that were central to their worship styles. Hence jazz/funk guitarist James

"Blood" Ulmer entitled his 1980 composition "Jazz Is the Teacher (Funk Is the Preacher)."[5] Similarly, on the initial recording of "Papa's Got a Brand New Bag," the Godfather of Soul can be heard saying that he feels "like preaching."[6] And Lyn Collins, who sang with Brown, was nicknamed Mama Feelgood *and* the female preacher. Her comments regarding the conceptual approach to "Think (About It)," which was a funkified womanist manifesto, typify the spirituality of funk music. Seconds before Collins's recording, Brown told her, "[W]ait, Miss Collins. . . . [W]hen you're talkin' to the women, I don't want you to just talk. I want you to do that gospel thang. You know, I want you to tell 'em, I want you to *preach* to 'em. . . ."[7]

KINESIS, COGNITION, AND CONSTRUCTIONS OF FUNK

Many discussions of funk music emphasize ideological relationships with the Black Power Movement and musical innovations that influenced Afro beat and hip hop. But while such approaches are vital to understanding the larger significance of the funk genre, they often overshadow the psychosomatic construct known as the funk. In this chapter, we'll observe how the funk/spirit—or, more simply, the funk—operates as a distinct form of black vernacular epistemology. Though often mischaracterized as a *lack* of rationality, the quasi-electric sensation that Clinton calls the pleasure principle should be understood as an alternative *form* of rationality. Nathaniel Mackey touches on this point in an interview with Paul Taylor. Responding to a question about the importance of mystical traditions in his writings, Mackey states: "by juxtaposing the mystical to reason as you do you're giving it the status and the scope of an alternative reason, much the same way in which Pascal, in that famous formulation of his, writes of the heart having reasons that reason knows nothing about. So we're talking about a recognition, even within the Western tradition, of the limits of reason, a recognition of other ways of knowing, multiple ways of knowing."[8] Naturally, conventional notions of epistemology, which are based on the Cartesian mind-body split, foreclose the possibility that sensuality is involved in the production of knowledge, that thinking can be both "sensual and abstract."[9] However, Funkadelic's 1970 album *Free Your Mind . . . And Your Ass Will Follow* belies the very premise of such foreclosure, as does the subtitle of Funkadelic's "Lunchmeataphobia ('Think! It Ain't Illegal Yet')" (1978). In fact, the funk is typically constructed by the interplay between motion and emotion. John Miller Chernoff refers to this driving dynamism as "a basic funk energy source."[10] Likewise, the pioneering funk scholar Rickey Vincent has argued that the funk (as distinct from funk music) is actually an impulse. He states that it is "much more than a *style*[;] it is a *means* to a style."[11] Dance scholar Jonathan David Jackson describes this phenomenon as "sensing." In his analysis of improvisation in black vernacular dancing, Jackson defines sensing as "the valorization of emotion as intelligent knowing. Sensing also signifies a heightened, in-the-moment" form of logic.[12] The acclaimed novelist Leon Forrest made a similar observation in his analysis of dance and spirituality in black churches in Chicago. In the following passage, Forrest speculates on the extent to which holy dances have prefigured black social dances:

> During these seizures, the anklebone and the hipbone, the hipbone and the backbone seem almost disconnected, so violent is the shock of the rhythm. . . . And one can't help but reflect on how these holy dances have influenced popular dance patterns. For under the cover of church and in the name of God, you might act out steps that you might not show at home, nor even think to attempt. But here the creative juices are up; you are encouraged to let the mind and spirit romp, roam, and reinvent. And if you are high in the ecstasy for Jesus, who knows what the body might tell the soul to reveal?[13]

Contrary to conventional wisdom, Forrest suggests that the frenzied atmosphere of many black churches has been as conducive to choreographic experimentation as house parties, juke houses, and night clubs. This emotional fervor and choreographic display, which has long been the subject of ridicule and derision, became an important aesthetic barometer in funk.

Several scholars and artists have examined the pivotal role of the body in black music. Funk is especially notable in this regard. Bruce W. Talamon's photo (see fig. 1.1) of the late bassist Louis Johnson's blistered thumb graphically illustrates the physical demands and emotional intensity required to play funk. As Talamon explains, "This is one of those moments where we see exactly what the artist has to give to get that great performance."[14] Research suggests that, by and large, the body functions as the primary instrument in black music, and that all other instruments function as appendages to the body.[15] This is precisely ethnomusicologist Kyra D. Gaunt's argument in her groundbreaking analysis of black girls' double-dutch games. She argues: "[T]he body is a *technology* of black musical communication and identity. . . . Extra somatic instruments (drums, flutes, violins, steel pans, and, arguably, in some circles, turntables) are acceptable media of *artistic* technology."[16] Thus,

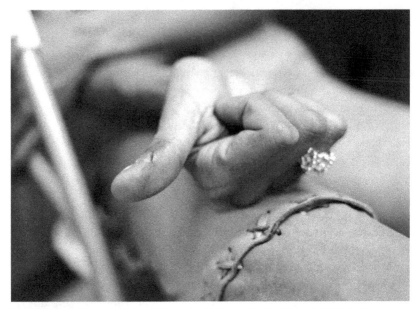

Figure 1.1. Louis Johnson's Blistered Thumb. Funk Fest, Los Angeles Coliseum, 1977. Photo by Bruce W. Talamon.

black vernacular thinkers tend to privilege corporeal communication over abstract analysis, and their ideas are often reflected in various types of artistic expression, especially self-reflexive performances methods that merge with meaning.[17] As Thomas F. DeFrantz observes, "In general, black expressive cultures value the process of signification over the signified, the performance of spirituality over scriptural exegesis, talking by dancing over talking about dancing."[18] Though black dancing is typically regarded as pure entertainment, that is, devoid of meaning, DeFrantz suggests that kinesis comprises dynamic captions of black organic intellectualism: "Dance movements convey speech-like qualities which contain meaning beyond the formal, aesthetic shapes and sequences of movement of the body in motion. African diaspora dance conveys the sense of performative utterances like those cultural theorist Eve Sedgewick cites, 'that do not merely describe, but actually perform the actions they name. . . .'"[19] Gaunt corroborates DeFrantz's observation when she writes, "Through these games, girls learn to play with the convergence of oral-vernacular conventions from speech to song, and the 'grammatical syntax' or logic of embodied musical language—coded gesture, movement, and dance."[20] Likewise, in "Bodies Talking," a section of the book *Go-Go Live: The Life and Death of a Chocolate City*, Natalie Hopkinson writes, "Bodies are also used to tell stories through dances such as the Beat Your Feet."[21]

Although the meanings of these three-dimensional utterances aren't always capable of being translated into words, meanings do exist.[22] Gaunt addresses this critical problem by creating the term somatic onomatopoeia in her discussion of a children's game called shimmy shimmy coke-ca-pop! which riffs on Little Anthony and the Imperials' "Shimmy Shimmy Ko-Ko-Bop" (1960), and reappears as a "sampled" phrase in Nelly's "Country Grammer" (2000). According to Gaunt, somatic onomatopoeia involves "the naming of a thing or action by a vocal imitation" combined with "the rhythmic accents internally associated and felt by embodying such movement."[23] At times, though, the inscriptions within these choreographic captions are sufficiently translucent to lend themselves to narrative analysis. The best example of this is Michael Jackson's famous Moonwalk. Naturally, I'm not suggesting that Jackson *intended* to create any sort of legible iteration. On the contrary, I'm arguing that Jackson's body-talk bespeaks a narrative that Jackson himself may not have surmised. A postmodern revision of earlier versions of the dance,[24] the Moonwalk can be read as a choreographic narrative of political economy, revealing the contradictions between black vernacular creativity and the alienation and marginalization of black workers under American capitalism. To put it differently, the Moonwalk (choreo)graphs the increasing amounts of labor that blacks must produce in exchange for decreasing amounts of dollars and benefits amid deteriorating working conditions and declining job security. Jackson (re)presents the black artist-laborer as an everyman who personifies coolness and panache. He is the expressive embodiment of the Blackbyrds' 1975 jazz-funk hit "Walking in Rhythm." Indeed, the King of Pop dances so fluidly that he creates the illusion of effortlessness—this despite the fact that the dance is the result of countless hours of practicing.[25] The black everyman expends a considerable amount of energy, while *literally* moving backwards. In the context of political economy, the import of this retral motion is comparable to putting money into an empty pocket with a gaping hole at the bottom.

In her research on street funk in Dayton, Ohio, Portia Maultsby demonstrates that dance was a crucial aspect of funk musicianship. In her interview with bassist Marshall Jones of the Ohio Players, Jones suggests that he "read" black dances as choreographs. He says, "I'd always find somebody on the dance floor and I would watch how they moved. I would watch them flowing with the hips and then move. And I would get in sync with that pattern."[26] Jones's statement that he got "in sync" with the dancers' movements epitomizes actionality as a cognitive device. But it's important to understand that this approach to music making was not peculiar to funk, but was part of the legacy that blues and jazz artists bequeathed. Jones's comments are nearly identical to those of drummer Dannie Richmond, who played with the legendary jazz bassist Charles Mingus. For Richmond, Baby Laurence's tap dancing provided a repository of rhythmic inscriptions expressed as body-talk. Richmond recalls:

> The band would play the head on the theme and Baby Laurence played the breaks. Little by little we worked it where at first I was just doing stop-time, fours, so that I'd memorized every lick of his. I learned that it wasn't just single strokes involved in the drums. My concept was that if you had the single strokes down, you could play anything. It's not true. It's almost true, but not totally. And the way Laurence would paradiddles along with single strokes. He could do all of that with his feet. It got to where we're doing fours together. He'd dance four, then we played threes, twos, one bar apiece, but I was copying him. I'd more or less play what he danced. I was trying to keep it in the context of melody dance and, mind you, to me that was the same as a saxophone player trying to play like Charlie Parker. . . . It was a gas for me to duplicate what Laurence danced. When he switched up on me and changed the time, there was no way I could play that.[27]

The comments by Jones and Laurence are highly instructive. They point up black vernacular concepts of music making, and call into question the normative presumption that sound is more important than dance by suggesting that the rhythmic complexity of black dancing can exceed that of accomplished drummers such as Richmond. Note that Richmond "copies" Laurence, just as Jones gets "in sync with [a dancer's] pattern." Although this concept of music making has existed as long as the black presence in America,[28] it was highlighted during the funk era in a perhaps unprecedented manner. Similarly, the low-down dirty blues licks and unabashedly sensual bodily movements were essential parts of blues and jazz cultures,[29] but because they were considered obscene by white cultural standards and bourgeois black tastes, dancers and musicians usually confined these expressions to places such as rent parties, dives, and churches where blues people felt free to express their feelings according to their own dictates.

Of course, no artist has theorized and practiced funk aesthetics more substantively than the Godfather of Soul. But part of Brown's uniqueness was that he led his band as a dancer—which is to say, he used body talk to communicate with his band. Bootsy Collins's remembrance of his first performance with the Godfather is instructive here. "If you noticed," he said, "it wasn't so much about his singing and screaming, it was all about his body. His moves. You had to pay attention!"[30] Collins's experience with Brown was like playing in a funk conservatory. That he later became recognized as the premier bassist in funk as a prominent member of the Parliament-Funkadelic collective, widely regarded as the premier band in funk, suggests the profundity of Brown's kinesthetic concepts of music making. Alan Leeds, Brown's tour manager, reached a similar conclusion after watching old videotapes, stating that a lot of his movements "were code[s] for the drummers—a certain hand signal, a certain move of the foot. Every move of the foot demanded a rim shot. Or a kick. And there certain moves of the hand that said, I want a hit here; I wanna break this down."[31] The comments by Bootsy and Leeds recall Zora Neale Hurston's suggestion that black social dances function as distinct forms of ideography: They signify "dynamic suggestion . . . [and] compelling insinuation."[32]

Brown's 1965 breakthrough recording "Papa's Got a Brand New Bag" provides an exemplary illustration of the role of kinesthesia in funk aesthetics. For Brown, the song choreographed the feelings of pride and frustration that fueled the Civil Rights Movement. But when he introduced the song to his band members, Brown's concept of the "One," the first hard beat of a four-beat measure, was so avant-garde that it caused cognitive dissonance. Brown recalls, "The drummers couldn't move their sticks in their hands to the *ONE two THREE four* progression I asked for as a replacement to the *one TWO three FOUR* they had always played . . . [which was] the basic rhythm of rock and roll that stretched all the way back to Chuck Berry."[33] That Brown was fully cognizant of the innovative nature of "New Bag" is not only indicated in the title, but also his exclamatory statement that prefaces the song: "This is a hit!" Yet when King Records owner Syd Nathan asked him to explain the meaning of the apparently nonsensical song, Brown confessed that he, too, was unable to explain it in words, and attributed its inspiration to a spiritual feeling.[34] On the surface, Brown's confession casts suspicion on my claim about the Godfather's self-conscious artistry. But given his statement that all of his music "begins with *feeling*,"[35] it becomes clear that emotion (read: the funk) was the key ingredient of Brown's artistic method. And since "New Bag" concerns the relationship between the funk/spirit and its representation in various dances, it's understandable that he was unable to provide an analysis in abstract terms. The meaning of the song is synonymous with its methods and effects. In order to demonstrate the power of the funk, Brown had to construct it and render it in full effect.

Interestingly enough, though, Brown doesn't use the word "funk" in the song. Instead the persona opens the song with an invitation to a female partner to join him on the dance floor, telling her that his new bag of music generates a "swing[ing]" sensation that compels him to dance. Using black street lingo that was current at the time, the singer-persona calls attention to himself, appealing to his would-be partner to check out his innovative style. He catalogues the dances that he performs, including the Fly, Jerk, Alligator, Mashed Potatoes, and Twist. Immediately following the latter allusion, he calls attention to his performance style once again ("just like this") to demonstrate the unique nature of his art. In live performances, Brown briefly performs the Twist as he alludes to the dance in the song. But perhaps the most important line of the song occurs when Brown engages in a subtle form of signification and braggadocio.

Much has been made about boasting in black popular culture. Whereas conventional Western philosophy has normalized the notion that the mind and body are polar opposites, boasting is usually considered crude in mainstream American culture. But sensuality is intrinsic to the epistemology of funk, and braggadocio and hyperbole are often viewed as endemic to black performance, particularly insofar as they accentuate individual talents and styles which, in turn, are typically reflected in various forms of adornment. That Lyn Collins was also known as Mama Feelgood is an indication of how highly regarded are braggadocio and show(wo)manship in black vernacular culture. At the pinnacle of a given performance, an artist demonstrates a superlative level of creativity that highlights their special talents. When this happens, the artist's distinctive flair elicits responses from audiences, and the responses inspire the artists to experiment even more demonstratively. According to the late composer and musicologist Olly Wilson, "These are moments when the artist performs a particularly unique phrase in which rhythmic, timbral, melodic, or harmonic displacement is ingenious. It is these moments that reveal the quality of the artist's musical imagination."[36] Thus in Brown's "New Bag," the line "Jump back, Jack, see you later, Alligator," is actually Brown's proclamation that he has achieved an incomparable level of creativity. He aptly engages in one-upmanship with his rivals. Using the sound-image of the dance, which was performed with both hands and feet simultaneously, Brown "samples" lines from Cajun artist Bobby Charles's 1956 recording "See You Later, Alligator," which included the popular rhyme: "See you later, alligator / after 'while, crocodile." Ostensibly directed to his dance partner, the line is an indirect but stinging critique of other popular band leaders. Basically, Brown is serving notice that he reigns supreme in rhythm and blues.

Brown followed "New Bag" two years later with his 1967 recording of "Cold Sweat," which many musicians and critics hailed as an important formal breakthrough in the history of funk music. However, the epistemological implications of his oxymoronic title are more pertinent to our discussion. Though the image of cold sweat refers specifically to the feeling that the persona's lover gives to him, Brown's emotive quasi-religious delivery foreshadowed numerous funk songs thereafter. In a manner and intensity heretofore inconceivable, funk artists paid homage to the funk/spirit. Sly and the Family Stone, Parliament-Funkadelic, Ohio Players, Earth, Wind & Fire—to name a few—recorded a plethora of songs that were self-referential to the funk. Even lesser known artists such as Tom Browne recorded songs that heralded the unabashed celebration of the funk/spirit. In his 1980 hit recording "Funkin' for Jamaica," singer and songwriter Tonni Smith repeatedly identifies the psychosomatic sensation that she calls Jamaica funk, while imploring listeners to open themselves up and "let it come" into their bodies. But while the pleasure principle was endemic to funk, the funk/spirit is hardly peculiar to funk music as such.

Stevie Wonder's 1976 recording of "Sir Duke" provides a case in point. A ringing tribute to the musicianship of such artists as Louis Armstrong, Count Basie, Glenn Miller, Ella Fitzgerald, and, naturally, Duke Ellington, "Sir Duke" demonstrates the fallacy of confining our concepts of funk to the genre of funk music. With the notable exception of Armstrong, who adroitly engages the pleasure principle in his classic 1926 recording of "Heebie Jeebies," all of the musicians who are cited are associated with swing music of the 1930s and early 1940s. Yet Wonder suggests that these very musicians became models for him precisely because of their ability to construct what Clinton would later coin the pleasure principle, that is, pure, uncut funk. Moreover, the psychosomatic effect that Wonder ascribes to the swing of Ellington and Basie ("you can feel it all over") is synonymous with the funkiness of his own composition. Naturally, most people think of swing and funk as dissimilar genres of music. But while the two *styles* of music differed as markedly as their respective historical periods, the emotional referents of "swing" and "funk" are as synonymous as the words "red" and "crimson."[37] For instance, Hopkinson considers Chuck Brown's hit "Go-Go Swing" "a funked-up version of the Duke Ellington's classic" "It Don't Mean a Thing (If It Ain't Got That Swing)." Preston Love, who began playing alto saxophone in Basie's band in the early 1940s, underscores this point in his recollection of lead trumpeter Ed Lewis. According to Love:

> Much of the Basie sound was Ed Lewis. He "grew up" with the original Basie style from Kansas City and captured the essence of the Basie feeling and the Kansas City charm. . . . Basie's was the greatest swing band with the most relaxed feeling in jazz history, and Ed always swung like no other lead trumpet probably did. We always referred to his lead as "funky," far before the word came into common usage in connection with rhythm and blues.[38]

At the same time, Wonder suggests that music and movement aren't necessarily related. Punning on the word "groove," he sings that success in recording ("in the groove") isn't synonymous with rhythmic success, which means putting people "in a groove." In other words, Wonder suggests that body movement is the ultimate sign of a funky groove. Not surprisingly, his concept is nearly identical to Ellington's concept of swing. Ellington says, "No *notes* represent swing. You can't *write* swing because swing is the emotional element in the audience and there is no swing until you hear the notes. Swing is *liquid*,[39] and though the same group of musicians may play the same tune fourteen times, they may not swing until the fifteenth time."[40] Whereas Clinton posits motion as the primary signification of funk, Ellington theorizes swing as the sensory undercurrent—"the emotional element in the audience"—that triggers or energizes what Clinton and Ellington respectively call funk and swing. It's also worth mentioning incidentally that Ellington prefigures the concept of flow in hip hop—the indescribable formula of syllabic rhythms and sick rhymes that compel audiences to nod their heads to the beats.

Ellington's concept of swing also prefigured Brown's foregrounding of sensuality. But where Ellington stresses emotion as the defining ingredient of a swinging groove, Brown emphasizes the epistemic significance of the pleasure principle. In his song "Super Bad," the speaker boasts that not only does he have this unique "emotional element" but that it feels so good he wants to shout with joy. Then the Godfather sings that the feeling (Brown calls it soul) isn't confined to the body. Quite the contrary, as a kinetically oriented cognitive mechanism, the funk is integrally related to cerebral activity. Hence Brown's "*move*[s] tell [him] what to do." Saxophonist Maceo Parker, who achieved fame playing with Brown, reveals the dynamics of Brown's theory of music making. When asked to account for his former band leader's powerful effect on his audiences, Parker coextensively analyzed and demonstrated a core precept of funk aesthetics. Having learned that he could use melodic instruments to accentuate rhythm, Brown virtually turned his whole band into a drum kit. The effect was immediate. "Right away," said Parker, "your attitude is better, your attitude is lighter. You get this happy, I-wanna-dance feeling and your neck, it gets to movin'. . . and . . . with that in mind you go . . .".[41] Caught up with emotion, Parker begins to play his saxophone to express his ideas. That Parker says "mind" *before* he plays is telling. His word choice and subsequent performance suggest that, in this context, he could convey ideas most effectively in music. Parker's sudden shift from explanation to demonstration sheds light on Brown's statement that funk is "a physically performed, roots-derived configuration of music that comes straight from the heart."[42] Consequently, he says, "You can't tell yourself how to funk onstage; it is your musical child that takes you and the rest of the audience to another place through the delivery of a song and a dance, combing the joy that they produce together."[43]

BALANCE: CONTRARIETY AS AESTHETIC AND PHILOSOPHICAL INSCRIPTION

In an interview with Tavis Smiley and Cornel West, Clinton responded to a question about the "One" by saying that when everyone in the band is on the one the rhythmic effect is much stronger. But as he continued he ventured into metaphysics. The energy created largely by that first hard beat tends to resolve oppositions and dichotomies. Not only do audiences become performers through dance, but social constructs such as race, class, gender, creed, and so forth are dismantled to some extent for fleeting moments when "we're all together as one. A lifeform. I'm for you and you for me; we for trees and we for the planet."[44] Clinton's logic is almost identical to the Yoruba concept of *Ase*. The term literally means "So be it,"[45] and refers to the moment when spirits enter human bodies in religious ceremonies—what Amiri Baraka calls the unity of opposites. During live performances, dancers enact this principle by conjoining the body with the spirit and reaffirming (and extending) through improvised choreography the affective phrases of the music. Thus they serve a role that is analogous to witnesses in church services who testify to the powerful presence of the Holy Spirit.

So steeped is funk music in contrariety that the Ohio Players followed their hit album *Honey* with an album entitled *Contradiction* (1976). Situated in the context of romantic love as envisioned by black working-class men, the title track, sung by lead singer and guitarist Sugarfoot Bonner, is ostensibly an appeal to the speaker's lover to maintain her belief in him and the love that they share, despite the painful rumors that have circulated regarding his infidelity. Notwithstanding the masculine hegemony the song naturalizes, "Contradiction" is a scintillating illustration of axiology as well, a paralinguistic reading of the nature of dialectics. The opening line of the song establishes its fundamental premise—that contradictions constitute the very essence of life. The speaker then proceeds to enumerate a string of contradictions that form the basis of his life: his religious convictions keep his soul in doubt; his intention to lead a healthy life is at variance with his street lifestyle; his commitment to his relationship conflicts with his sexual attraction to other women; and his purported infidelity has lacerated his lover's feelings, so the love she feels for him is now mingled with anger and hatred. This places him in a precarious position. He's insecure, but fearful of acknowledging this because it confutes his image of cool machismo, and yet he clearly expresses his insecurity in the very act of his soulful appeal.

Contrariety is a trademark of funk, one of the qualities it inherited from blues. Beginning with "What is Soul," which appears on Funkadelic's 1970 debut album *Funkadelic*, we can observe the manner in which the Funk Mob used contrariety by inverting black cultural alienation and orthodox American values.[46] In the opening line the persona (Clinton) identifies himself as Funkadelic and tells us in a mock-harrowing voice that he "is not of your world." He defines goodness as a state of nastiness, and defines soul as "a joint rolled in toilet paper." Oxymoronic songs such as "Free Your Mind . . . and Your Ass Will Follow" (1970), "Balance" (1972), "Miss Lucifer's Love" (1972), and "March to the Witch's Castle" (1973) are additional early recordings that illustrate funk's sheer delight in defying cultural norms and aesthetic conventions, including those among blacks.[47] Even the dances moves that young African Americans performed during the period exemplified contrariety. The Funky Four Corners, the Penguin, the Breakdown, the Good Foot, the Bump, the Freak, and other dances consisted of antiphonal movements.[48]

Several funk musicians have mentioned Jimi Hendrix as an important influence on their music. Like many of the musicians who admired him, contrariety was crucial to his aesthetic. Born in 1942 in Seattle, Washington, Hendrix was enamored as a youth by country-born blues singers. He listened assiduously to blues stalwarts such as Robert Johnson, Howling Wolf, and Muddy Waters during a period when increasing numbers of black youth conceptualized hipness in terms of black urban experiences, especially the soulful sounds of rhythm and blues, not to mention the dances and fashion that accompanied it. By the early 1960s, many blacks in large urban areas not only considered the blues "country" but also politically reactionary. Moreover, many blacks wrongfully envisioned rock as an expression of whiteness. Yet Hendrix flouted social conventions by commingling musical forms and cultural styles that many people misread as mutually exclusive. For Hendrix the ultimate challenge was reconfiguring the blues and creating what he called "a today's type of blues,"[49] a postmodern form that illustrated kaleidoscopes of contrasting sentiments and shifting points of view in American society. By injecting large doses of dirty blues stank into the acid rhythms of rock, Hendrix succeeded in his efforts to blue-funk rock music, while rocking the blues into the stratosphere like an electric sky church. He showcased the various techniques he learned on the chitlin circuit, and spawned a form of blues-rock whose apotheosis was registered indelibly in songs such as "Purple Haze," "Foxy Lady," and "Hey Joe" with the Jimi Hendrix Experience; "Who Knows," "Changes," "Earth Blues," and "Machine Gun" with Band of Gypsys; and his renegade performance of "Star Spangled Banner" at Woodstock in 1969 with Gypsy Sun & Rainbows. Having developed his craft as a journeyman while playing with rhythm and blues artists such as Little Richard, King Curtis, and the Isley Brothers, Hendrix delighted his audiences with blues-style showmanship. He humped his guitar, played it with his teeth, and plucked it behind his neck, while engaging in many other antics. He also adopted a psychedelic image that was consistent with the free-love and free-drugs sensibilities of his predominantly white audience. Such a sharp deviation from the resplendence of the crystal-clean, ghetto-fabulous fashion that prevailed at neighborhood house parties and clubs compelled some blacks to misinterpret Hendrix's music in terms of racial apostasy. Although his music had strong appeal within innumerable interstices of black youth culture, many blacks reacted to Hendrix's music with an indifference they might have shown the Grateful Dead. This was especially true during his Jimi Hendrix Experience days, when he played with British musicians Noel Redding and Mitch Mitchell. As Hendrix's former girlfriend, Fayne Pridgeon, recalls, "I've been on the scene a couple of times when people would say, 'Hey, you know Hendrix is playing . . . down in the Village.' And they'd say, 'Oh yeah, that's nice.' You know, just shine it on, like it ain't no big thing."[50]

But while Hendrix's pre-futuristic, blues-rock virtuosity may have nonplussed some people, he foregrounded the electric guitar in a manner heretofore inconceivable, and in the process he developed a novel approach to the instrument. The drummer Frank "Kash" Waddy, who played with James

Brown along with Bootsy and his brother, guitarist Catfish Collins, before joining Parliament/Funkadelic with the Collins brothers in 1972, describes Hendrix's playing as an exceedingly rare combination of "[b]ass, rhythm, [and] lead [guitar] all into one."[51] A consummate organic intellectual, Hendrix created a methodological formula for transmitting impulses of emotional color through musical sound. According to Hendrix's brother, Leon Hendrix, it was "a concept called Energy Sound Color Dynamics—which he playfully sometimes referred to as $E=sc^2$ [raised 2, i.e., squared] to borrow a little style from Einstein's $E=mc^2$ [raised 2, i.e., squared] theory."[52] According to Tate, "Not until hip hop moved the sound of electronically altered drums to the fore would a single instrument sound so flatten all other elements, including vocals, in a pop context. Not until technology provided a mechanism for digitized drum tracks to outshout guitars in the mix was the supremacy of the lead guitar solo as the voice of god in pop music sent packing."[53] Thus, Hendrix's artistic breakthroughs, black hippie persona, and penchant for flaunting presumed contradictions provided younger musicians such as Collins with a new model for avant-garde aesthetics. Collins recollects, "[B]ack in that day, brothas wasn't cool with being freaky and . . . bein' out there like that."[54] For Collins, Clinton, and members of other funk groups, Hendrix's artistic experiments and outrageous stage persona were expressions of creative freedom that constituted an utter refusal to genuflect to societal norms.

Hendrix's representation of black-blues-rock personae as cultural outlaws were especially influential. The politicized contrariness of "If 6 Were 9" anticipated a similar gesture in Funkadelic's "Mommy, What's a Funkadelic" (*Funkadelic* 1970), and his line "play on drummer" prefigures Funkadelic's line "Fly on" in its song. Hendrix's emphatic transformation of cultural marginality into a psychic location of autonomy and creativity ("got my own world") served as a springboard for Funkadelic's flight-metaphor in "Mommy, What's a Funkadelic." The words "Fly on" highlight the speaker's geopolitical departure from earth, the resultant freedoms and pleasures this affords him ("feels good to me"), and the nascent theme of Afrofuturism that foreshadows P-Funk's later treatments of the topic. Similarly, the Isley Brothers' "Ohio/ Machine Gun" is a groove-oriented cover of Hendrix's "Machine Gun" and a critique of the Vietnam War that Hendrix recorded live with his blues funk group Band of Gypsys on New Year's Eve in 1969, a performance that writer and musician Greg Tate claims "changed the sound of soul music forever."[55]

Funk musicians routinely employed contrariety to express nonconformity while formulating rhetorical strategies and fashioning aesthetic ideas. As with blues singers, a common rhetorical strategy involved various sorts of irony, particularly the use of parody. Commenting on his habit of wearing a blue Ku Klux Klan robe, for instance, singer Calvin Simon of Parliament-Funkadelic said, "It was a mockery, really."[56] Clinton explained, "We said, 'We gonna be the blackest, we gonna be the funkiest, we gonna be dirty.'"[57] This strategy facilitated the expression of a raucous, rebellious sensibility that allowed many musicians to question a wide range of presumptions and mythologies associated with the status quo. For instance, singer and songwriter Betty Davis recorded songs such "Whorey Angel" and Nasty Gal," satirizing conventional terms and points of view to address gender politics in sexual relationships.

Funk artists also used contrast for experimental purposes. Commenting on his decision to invite child prodigy Worrell into the band, Clinton said: "Bernie Worrell could take any groove and make it Beethoven, Bach, or any jazz thing you want it to be, right within the groove. . . . So the *contradiction* was done on purpose—the classical things against the real simple-minded, silly, basic."[58] Funkadelic's 1978 recording of "Who Says a Funk Band Can't Play Rock?!" serves as a case in point. The song foregrounds rhetorical questions regarding accepted taboos in musicianship. For instance, according to accepted norms, funk and rock, like jazz and dancing, are mutually exclusive. But like Hendrix, Funkadelic relished in flouting this view. The song elaborates on a theme that the band had laid down seven years earlier in its freaky, psychedelic classic "Maggot Brain." But where "Maggot Brain" blended the contrasting sounds of hippies and hoods in Eddie Hazel's amazing nine-minute guitar solo, on "Who Says a Funk Band Can't Play Rock?!" Clinton layers his falsetto over the guitar sounds of (black) rock guitar to add more flavor to the texture of the song. Announcing his intention to funk the rock so nasty that people can't help but move to the groove, Clinton re-energizes the term "rock and roll," employing rhythm and blues semantics that reflect black speakers' preference for verbs ("rocking" and "rolling"), while bragging about his skills: "Watch them dance."

The capacity to accommodate contradictions, then, was essential to the philosophy of funk, which was largely resistant to either/or logic and therefore skeptical of arbitrary privileges and hierarchies related to Manichean logic. Perhaps the most striking example of contrariety in funk is Funkadelic's "Cosmic Slop" (1973). The song focuses on a woman who has turned to prostitution in order to support her five children. That the band addressed this topic illustrates one of the unique aspects of funk—its commitment to depict the realities and reaffirm the values, sensibilities, and aesthetics of blacks who lived in urban ghettos. The thematic complexity of "Cosmic Slop" involves its simultaneous engagement with several contradictions: male/ female, rich/poor, holy/heathen, God/devil. And since Garry Shider sings the narrative in autobiographical form, there are racial implications as well.

Reminiscent of blues singers' penchant for composing songs in first person while addressing other people's situations, Clinton utilized Shider's maternal memory when he composed the lyrics of "Cosmic Slop." Having known Shider since he was a youngster who snuck away from his mother to indulge in mischief at his local barber shop, Clinton encouraged the young musician to approach the song as the protagonist. "[I]t was almost like he was telling my story," said Shider. "There were seven of us, we were in foster homes, and all kinda shit. My mother, I remember her out hustling to get the cash to feed us. So I could relate to it."[59] The flip-side of Shider's comments, though, is that they invoke the mother/whore dyad. As with many hip hop artists today, the circumstances and conditioning of many young black men compel them to envision their own mothers as black/brown Madonnas while simultaneously categorizing other women, including mothers, as "hoes" who are fit for exploitation and differential treatment. This is not to suggest that "Cosmic Slop" *promotes* misogyny. Quite the contrary: it points up the fact that black music is always already implicated in the contradictions it names. In other words, "Cosmic Slop" is a beautifully rendered sonic painting of the dialectics between Africanist perspectives of the pleasure principle and the hard-core realities and racial conditioning that constrict the spatial and conceptual contexts in which black women express pleasure. Though the song reflects a masculinist perspective, "Cosmic Slop" underscores the role of black women as primary producers of free and/or cheap labor in the United States. In so doing, it posits the idea that black women have comprised a disproportionate share of the labor base for capitalist hegemony.

The song opens with drummer Tyrone Lampkin creating a funk-laden vibe, which sets the tone for an infectious vamp that features the rock-fla-vored guitars of Shider and Ron Bykowski as well as a chorus of background vocalists who invoke the plaintive calls of the singer-narrator's mother. An-chored by Bootsy Collins's bass line, the vamp establishes a groove that is maintained throughout the song. But while the instrumentalists construct the quasi-electric sensation of the funk, Shider's gospel-style singing is un-fathomable. The texture of his sound establishes a poignant yet festive mood, intermingling beauty and pain as he prefaces the narrative with a captivating onomatopoeic falsetto. As the autobiographical narrator, Shider becomes the sensitive son who tells his mother's story, and the story *he* tells is mark-edly different from the ones typically circulated in the mass media. For the anonymous son, his mother is the walking embodiment of heroism. Though her life is a living hell, she manages to maintain an uplifting disposition and a sense of grace, while attempting to shield her children from the horrors of her life. But since the community is a collective witness, she is ultimately unable to conceal the labor that produces her wages, and, consequently, her children bear the shame and ignominy that accompany prostitution. Like the black prostitutes in Toni Morrison's novel *The Bluest Eye*, she is stigmatized as a jezebel by other inhabitants of the ghetto who have internalized repressive aspects of Christian morality. That there is silence regarding men's complicity in her actions—both as contraband businessmen (pimps) and consumers (johns)—is quite telling regarding the pervasiveness of misogyny in the community.

The mother's ambivalence is also noteworthy. On the one hand, she feels the bitter wages of sin. On the other hand, she's sufficiently rewarded by the acts of hustling to endure the potential risks and exigencies of selling her body, not to mention the disrepute that attends it. So she prays passionately to God, beseeching His forgiveness, assuring Him that she only turned tricks for her kids, and that she intended no wrongdoing. At which point, the devil enters the narrative. He whispers in her ear, tempting her to dance the cosmic slop. The dance represents a lifestyle—cards, dice, and dominoes, not to mention parties, alcohol, and perhaps even illicit drugs and sex—which is not, on its own terms, amoral. But because race and repression are twin constructs in conventional Christian morality, these activities have been framed so that viewers misread them in pejorative terms. Blacks' refusal to abide by these dictates has often resulted in caricature, castigation, and confinement. To make matter worse, the people own and/or control relatively few cultural institutions, and therefore exercise minimal influence over social and economic policies. While they create and/or contribute to new linguistic, choreographic, and musical forms from which certain African Americans and the larger society profit, they're constantly depicted as incapable of creating anything of value. The devil figure in "Cosmic Slop" isn't so much the red Christian devil who reigns the underworld of Hell with a pitchfork. He's closer to the devil figure that Zora Neale Hurston represented in black southern folktales during the blues era. Unlike the biblical devil, the devil in black folklore was a counterbalancing figure capable of offsetting power imbalances that affected weaker characters who appealed to him for moral redress.[60] In "Cosmic Slop," the devil's association with dancing and sexuality symbolizes the stigmatization of black women's sexuality and black people's sensuality in American society. Having been conditioned by missionaries' association of sensual pleasure, trickster antics, and brazen sexuality with evil, many modern black Christians considered secular deviations from white cultural norms as sinful.

Even so, the contradictions of race don't erase the contradictions of gender in the male narrator's male gaze. As Lyn Collins "preaches" in her recording of "Think (About It)," men can never represent women's experiences as well as women they can themselves. The ugly contradiction latent in "Cosmic Slop" is that agency often hinges on privilege—at least to some degree—and the nameless mother is marginalized to such an extent that she never acquires the empowerment of authorship. We never hear *her* call. And yet in spite of the contradictory gender politics, the harrowing timbre and tones of Shider's voice bear such a tremendous resonance that his representation of the mother becomes nonetheless primal and evocative. As he sings the line "I can hear my mother call," his emotions intensify with each repetition until he can only sing "mother," eliding and collapsing the remaining words into a reverberating fluctuation of sound, bordering on liquidity and glossolalia. The latter term, of course, refers to a form of tonal semantics that signifies a crescendo of spirituality which in turn influences aesthetics. "The singer—as caught up spiritual performer—is in control and then loosens control over his spirit. The moment that he appears to be losing control, he is actually opening himself to be taken over by the Holy Spirit."[61]

THE COSMOLOGY OF FUNK: OR, FUNKLORE AS POLITICAL ALLEGORY

The contrariety in funk established the conceptual ground for the creation of lyrical narratives that reaffirmed black vernacular styles and sensibilities. Combining the fashion and language of black street culture with disparate elements of mainstream popular culture, especially comic strips and sci-fi television shows, Clinton created and extended an Afrofuturistic narrative that elaborated on the themes of alterity and alienation that Funkadelic had expressed as early as in "What is Soul" in 1970. This theme, which harkens back to the antebellum spirituals when blacks imagined flying chariots capable of transporting them out of the hellish realms of slavery, became the basis for Clinton's funk operas (this historicity is accentuated in the 1975 title track of *Mothership Connection*, where the hook of "Swing Low Sweet Chariot" is riffed-sampled in the line, "Swing down sweet chariot / stop and let me ride"). Beginning with the *Mothership Connection*, then, Clinton transposed *Star Trek* narratives into allegories of funk. But while alterity was associated with evil in *Star Trek*, otherness constituted goodness in Clinton's narratives, just as X-Men did in comic strips. Moreover, funkateers wield the all-powerful (life)force in funklore, whereas in traditional sci-fi settings the force belongs to hegemonic representatives. Thus on the *Mothership* album Dr. Funkenstein descends from a spaceship to restore p-funk, that is, the *pure* funk to humans, especially black people. His primary funkateer, Star Child, functions as an intermediary between humans and Dr. Funkenstein, providing the former with a "mothership connection" with the funk. Not surprisingly, the people are compelled to dance; and in turn their ability to dance on the funk enables them to levitate metaphysically. To put it differently, dancing becomes a conduit for transcendence in the form of psychic and emotional release from the mendacity of everyday life for African Americans in the inner cities. Singer Jeanette Washington's remembrance of the Mothership's landing in live performances is an excellent example. In the universe of P-Funk, the music engendered such an ecstatic sense of joy and rapture that the funk/spirit transported dancers into metaphysical realms of existence. But what's intriguing about Washington's comment is that it's simultaneously descriptive and emblematic of the power of funk music: "to hear those people just go out of their minds . . ."[62] That Washington was unable to complete her sentence regarding her own observation is a testimony to the indescribable nature of the funk in full effect.

According to Clinton's funklore, ancient Afronauts had not only danced on the funk throughout entire galaxies; they also had the capacity to infuse and suffuse the funk into infinite locations and aspects of life. But because humans chose to abuse the funk and confuse it with negativity, it was mysteriously repossessed and deposited inside Egyptian pyramids along with pharaohs and kings until humans acquired a more amenable attitude toward the wondrous virtues of the funk—at which time funkativity would be restored to humans in the personification of Dr. Funkenstein. But as with all sci-fi narratives, Dr. Funkenstein is counterpoised by a villain: He and his funkateers must wage battle with Sir Nose D'Voidoffunk, an archenemy who opposes the (life)force of the groove with such resolve that he wages an incessant battle with Star Child and the Children of Production who are clones of Dr. Funkenstein.

That Clinton's funklore is filled with signifying parody and ribald humor should come as no surprise since these characteristics are trademarks of blues and black vernacular expression generally. But since "vernacular" is usually interpreted in opposition to intellectualism, it's important to point out that the ideas in Clinton's funklore are conversant with some of the most influential writings in African American literature. For instance, in *The Bluest Eye* Toni Morrison employs funk in much the same way that Clinton does with Sir Nose. Published in 1970, the same year *Funkadelic* was released, Morrison employs funk as a metaphor for the black vernacular sensuality from which the middle-class black women characters of Lorain, Ohio, steadfastly recoil. In one of her most telling passages, Morrison writes:

> Wherever it erupts, this Funk, they wipe it away; where it crusts, they dissolve it; wherever it drips, flowers, or clings, they find it and fight it until it dies. They fight this battle all they way to the grave. The laugh that is a little too loud; the enunciation a little too round; the gesture a little too generous. They hold their behind in for fear of a sway too free; when they wear lipstick, they never cover the entire mouth for fear of lips too thick, and worry, worry, worry about the edges of their hair.[63]

Likewise, scholars generally regard Ishmael Reed's novel *Mumbo Jumbo* as one of the most complex works of fiction in the history of Western literature. Scholars also agree that Reed challenges Eurocentric epistemology in the novel. Seldom discussed, however, is the striking similarity between the tropes that Clinton and Reed employ, not to mention the critical problems they engage. This similarity isn't coincidental. When asked about his inspiration for his narrative, Clinton replied, "Have you ever read *Mumbo Jumbo*?"[64] Reed uses the ironic term Jes Grew as a trope to represent the funk principle. Early in the novel, which is set in the 1920s, the Mayor of New Orleans rushes to St. Louis Cathedral to inquire about what appears to be a "*psychic epidemic*";[65] he finds twenty-two people lying on carts, and is given the following report: "[P]eople were doing 'stupid sensual things,' were in a state of 'uncontrollable frenzy,' were wriggling like fish, doing something called the 'Eagle Rock' and the 'Sassy Bump'; were cutting a mean 'Mooche,' and 'lusting after relevance.'" For the Mayor's cohorts, the "epidemic" is a plague that they decode as a "coon Mumbo Jumbo."[66] However, as black poet Nathan Brown says later in the novel, most blacks "are trying their best to catch"[67] Jes Grew because, according to the protagonist Papa LaBas, it's an anti-plague. Both Reed and Clinton satirize the binary logic of Christian philosophy by suggesting that somatic illustrations of the pleasure principle comprise consummate signs of civility.

Like Reed, Clinton engages Egyptian mythology. He revises the conflict between the benevolent sun god Ra and his archnemesis Set, and recasts

Set, a symbol of evil and foreign control, as the comedic villain Sir Nose who dwells in the vapid zone of zero funkativity. For Clinton, Sir Nose is a symbolic representation of blacks who associate vernacular dancing with unintelligence because they have adopted racialized views toward black vernacular expression, particularly dancing. And inasmuch as Sir Nose's nasal voice is reminiscent of earlier black comedians' parodies of white speakers, we could also argue that Clinton's representation of social conditioning is compatible with W. E. B. Du Bois's famous double-consciousness theory: "It is a peculiar sensation, this double-consciousness, this sense of always looking at one's self through the eyes of others . . . who look on in amused contempt and pity." So while Clinton worked within the discursive space of popular music, his position in relation to black vernacular epistemology is commensurate with some of the most complex thinkers in black cultural history.[68]

Dr. Funkenstein's mission, then, is manifold: to disrupt constructed normality; to reeducate black people; to redefine and redirect the racialized joke that Du Bois references; and to lampoon the logic inherent in the caricatures that blacks have historically internalized. Of the numerous art forms in African American culture, dancing has almost certainly been most ridiculed and stereotyped. Such derision has been particularly injurious to African Americans not only because dancing has been an effective diversion from dead-end jobs, joblessness, and other forms of alienation, but also because dominant narratives in American culture tend to frame black dancing as indications of mental ineptitude, despite the fact that kinetic expression was historically related to spiritual faith, and indicated ingenuity and creativity in black vernacular expression. As Gaunt points out, "African Americans, male and female, are constantly contending with imposed stereotypes about our social and musical bodies, our somebodiness, as well as the internalized assumptions we carry and impose upon ourselves and other black bodies."[69] That funk has received so little critical attention seems to underline Gaunt's statement.

We can observe a satirical critique of this mindset in Parliament's "Flash Light," which appeared on the 1977 album *Funkentelechy Vs. the Placebo Syndrome*. Having invented the bop gun to zap potential funkateers with quasi-electric beams of the funk,[70] Dr. Funkenstein commissions Star Child to shoot Sir Nose until he experiences an irresistible urge to dance. But Sir Nose remains steadfast in his refusal. As the song opens, he declares his intention to go to sleep. In Clinton's funklore, sleep symbolizes such a state of *un*funkiness that Sir Nose is unable to feel the beat. However, in spite of Sir Nose's preparation to count his sheep and thereby avoid kinesis, Star Child is determined to zap him. And when he does, he commands Sir Nose to "[d]ance sucker," while Parlet and the Brides of Funkenstein sing the chorus: "Most of all he needs the funk / help him find the funk." Naturally, Sir Nose's resolve begins to weaken: "Oh funk me!" There are also assorted light-images—neon light, flash light, spot light—which suggest the multitudinous tones of emotional color imbued within p-funk. And though Sir Nose represses his desire to funk after this point, he finally does succumb to its power, proclaiming that he, too, has found pure funk. Sir Nose's proclamations and conflations of his mind, body, and spirit reflect the premise of the song—that the funk is real. Its medicinal qualities are tangible. As Clinton says in "P. Funk (Wants to Get Funked Up)," funk can move and *re*move, and thereby improve the quality of people's everyday existence. This notion is clearly imprinted in the album title. Since "entelechy" refers to "a vital force" that drives "the actualization of the potential form or function of a substance," the term "funkentelechy" is synonymous with the funk principle. It means to manifest the funk in 3-D. Tate describes this state of mind as "hav[ing] your funk low in the saddle and eat[ing]-it-cum-intellectualiz[ing] too."[71] Thus funk music conveyed worldviews and values that enabled people to realize their full potential. And while the cultural allusions and metaphors relate to specific aspects of black working-class culture in the cities, the premise of the song is that repression is a Eurocentric construct because all humans have the kinetic desire symbolized by the stimulating rays of Star Child's flashlight. In other words, *every*one is blessed with a few flickers of "light under the sun."

Sir Nose reappears in "Alpha Boogie (A Psychoalphadiscobetabioaquadooloop)," which is included on the album *Motor Booty Affair* (1978). But where "Flash Light" uses an electricity-trope, "Aqua Boogie" features water as a primary metaphor. Featuring the legendary multi-instrumentalist and singer Junie Morrison, "Aqua Boogie" is replete with aquatic tropes. And while the water-trope recalls Ellington's trope of liquidity, not to mention the Greek legend of Atlantis, "Aqua Boogie" is also a rhetorical reprisal of the Swim, a dance that was popular during the early 1960s. Created by Bobby Freeman in 1961, the Swim became so popular that Tina Turner performed it with Ike Turner and the Ikettes. The Swim also served as inspiration for a twenty-one-year-old songwriter who later achieved international acclaim as Sly Stone to compose "C'mon and Swim," which became a hit recording three years later in 1964. Clinton elaborates on the works of Freeman and Stone, extending the swim-metaphor to create a funk(y) suite.

"Aqua Boogie," then, memorializes the fluid nature of black vernacular dancing. Exemplifying funk's predilection for hyperbole, the title boasts of rhythms so fly and fluid that believers of the funk could dance underwater without getting wet. Just as water assumes the form of its host, the dancers shape the contours of their body movements according to the rhythms and the sensations they feel at a given moment's notice. The song title, which is reminiscent of jazz musician Yusef Lateef's term "autophysiopsychic music," defies easy interpretation. However, the multiple affixes provide some clues. Besides referencing water, "alpha" is the first letter of the Greek alphabet. It suggests the proverbial "one" in funk music. That "Psycho" precedes "alpha" in the subtitle suggests that the mind is indelibly linked to the sensations of the body, and that funk is the cognitive conduit for this fusion. The latter section of the subtitle is even less transparent. The combination of the words "disco" and "beta," which typically connotes testing, suggest a critique of disco music. To put it differently, since Dr. Funkenstein's mission is to reprogram other-wise funkateers, the beta-image implies that disco constituted a discursive faking of the funk. Insofar as its aesthetic imagery and rhythms were squeaky clean and antiseptic, disco was utterly devoid of rhythmic stank. According to Nelson George, "Disco's movers and shakers" felt that funk "was too raw and unsophisticated, and one thing dear to the hearts of disco fans . . . was a feeling of pseudosophistication."[72] Thus Clinton likens disco to an unwaver-ing computer programming system which encoded a mechanistic logic and lifestyle that he associates with the dominant superstructure. Likewise, the affixes fusing "bio" (life), "aqua" (funk), and dooloop (repetitive program-ming) imply that the olfactory chords of the aqua boogie are designed to reprogram unfunky subjects, allowing them to adopt an alternate vision of normality, so that people can learn to accept swimming, that is, funking, as natural. As Anne Danielsen states, "According to Clinton, the funk grooves were nothing less than a means of arriving at a spiritual focus while also providing bodily release to an afflicted audience."[73]

"Aqua Boogie" illustrates the absurdity of the narrow parameters in which blackness is defined. The song mocks the notion of a mind-body split as a self-defeating method of responding to black disfranchisement. More funda-mentally, though, "Aqua Boogie" foregrounds agency, while positing dancing and musicianship as related channels of expression. In other words, the song constructs the funk in order to engage the deplorable living conditions that African Americans experience as direct consequences of racial politics. The contrariety becomes particularly evident in Morrison's solo ("with the rhythm it takes to dance to what we have to live through") where the singer references choreography in relation to disfranchisement. Thus, "Aqua Boogie" exemplifies how funk reaffirmed cultural values and sensibilities of working-class black people in the 1970s. Here again, the narrative revolves around the arid wallflower Sir Nose who adamantly refuses to learn how swim because he's too cool to get wet. His limited olfactory perception, which is reflected in the nasal timbre of his voice, suggests more broadly his acceptance of standardized definitions of the word "funk," not to mention hegemonic framings of blackness as well. Consequently, he experiences a cognitive dysfunktion when he interfaces the funk—he "can't catch the rhythm of the stroke." But since the meaning of the funk is synonymous with its subcutaneous amelioration, Sir Nose must be rescued from the blahs. As with small children who must be forced to bathe, Nose is physically placed into the water—presumably by Star Child. And much to his surprise, he discovers that he enjoys swimming in water and thereby dancing on the funk: "Oh it feels good." Thus, the band creates superlative doses of funky music that engages self-reflexively the problem that it names, while instantiating an ethos and sense of insouciance which enkindle dancers to jam on the good foot.

THINK! IT AIN'T ILLEGAL YET

Funk artists occasionally expressed overt radicalism. But even when they didn't transpose black power ideology into a philosophy of funk, their music was jam-packed with political significance. After Brown helped transform previous meanings of blackness to beautification in 1968, singing "I'm black and I'm proud," Funkadelic took it to the stage seven years later, proclaiming "I'm funky and I'm proud." Whereas black activists concentrated on political changes that could be measured concretely (e.g., numerical representations of blacks in corporate, educational, and political institutions), funk artists revolted against staidness and artificiality in American culture at large. Many African Americans had been conditioned to misread black vernacular mannerisms, fashion, and performances—both sacred and profane—as uncouth, uncivilized, and unintelligent, and they were often repulsed by such expression. The terms "sanctified" and "holy roller," for instance, which referred to black people who attended Pentecostal churches, carried a stigma well into the 1990s. Ramsey echoes this point when he recalls the mistreatment of sanctified churchgoers during his youth. "When I was growing up," writes Ramsey, "we whispered, 'She's sanctified' behind someone's back with disinterested pity. It was a suitable explanation for why someone who came from a religious family would dress out of date, or otherwise seem a little out of sync with the time."[74] Yet groups such as Sly and the Family Stone, Parliament-Funkadelic, the Ohio Players, Lakeside, the Bar-Kays, and others accentuated the very characteristics that people had displayed previously in the relative obscurity of churches, clubs, dives, and so forth.

Funk artists' preoccupation with pleasure probably overshadowed the political implications of their music to some degree, primarily because people often confuse artistic politics with protest. This is a somewhat reductive approach, though. What distinguishes funk aesthetics from other paradigms is its insistence that body movement and sensuality are essential to a broader approach to music making. In this context, feeling is essential to knowledge and expertise. As noted earlier, Brown led his band as a dancer, and Mingus's former drummer Richmond was influenced by tap dancer Baby Laurence. But it's important to understand that these aren't isolated cases. Nor are they limited to funk music as such. Numerous musicians who have received wide acclaim for their vision and virtuosity, including Ellington and jazz saxophonist Lester Young, have attested to the vital contributions that black vernacular dancers have made in black music.

Ellington is quite pointed about this in his commentary on swing drummer and bandleader Chick Webb. Webb's band, which included a young Ella Fitzgerald, was the house band at the Savoy Ballroom, and one of the highlights of the Savoy was the famous battle of the bands which often included Ellington's band. In the following passage, the Duke explains why he admired Webb. In doing so, he dispels the myth that thoughts and feelings exist in mutual exclusion. Notable also are Ellington's remarks on composer and arranger extraordinaire Billy Strayhorn:

> Some musicians are dancers, and Chick Webb was. You can dance with a lot of things besides your feet. Billy Strayhorn was another dancer—in his mind. He was a dancer-writer. Chick Webb was a dancer-drummer who painted pictures of dances with his drums. . . . If you listen to the figures in some of Strayhorn's pieces, like "U.M.M.G.," those are dances—tap dances maybe—and you can't mistake what they essentially are.[75]

Naturally, some readers might object to using an example from swing to substantiate an argument about funk. But the point here is that black dancers' sensing techniques have been central—not marginal—to innovations throughout much of black musical history. What was so distinctive about

funk was its brazen defiance of social conventions and its insistence on expressing that defiance in black vernacular *terms*—even if this meant resisting
taboos in African American culture.

Funk music challenged normative presumptions about the role of human
emotion in the production of knowledge. That funk was created by two dancers, Brown and Stone, simply underscores this point. Noting the discrepancy
between the music that represented black culture and the young civil rights
activists' defiant spirit, Brown wrote "New Bag" as "a way to choreograph the
burgeoning pride that could be felt everywhere."[76] Notwithstanding Brown's
1968 recording "Say It Loud—I'm Black and I'm Proud," his reputation as a
political conservative rests largely on his support of Richard Nixon, black
capitalism, and his refusal to support violent means of resisting state violence. Brown never claimed to be a political theorist. He was a quintessential
scientist of sound, and the rhythm nation that he affirmed in his dance-beat
aesthetics shaped Nigerian musician and activist Fela Kuti's blueprint for
Afrobeat, which is widely recognized today as an international musical genre.
That he did so is an indelible testimony to the agency lodged deep within
the sediments of funk.

Chapter Two

Blue Funk

THE UGLY BEAUTY OF STANK

Notwithstanding the "Stanky Leg" dance craze that swept the nation a roughly decade ago, most people today associate funk with virtuoso performances of James Brown, Tina Turner, Sly and the Family Stone, Betty Davis, Parliament-Funkadelic, Labelle, the Ohio Players, Chaka Khan, Earth, Wind & Fire, Prince, and many others. Such was the power of funk music. Yet when we acknowledge the fact that funk is a concept, blues dancers and musicians were, retroactively speaking, early funkateers near the turn of the twentieth century. Consider New Orleans bassist Pops Foster's characterization of the legendary Buddy Bolden: "He played nothing but the blues and all that *stink* music, and he played it very loud."[1] Beginning in the mid-twentieth century, explicit references to funk began to appear in blues culture. In the late 1940s and early 1950s, pianist Henry Roeland Byrd, better known as Professor Longhair, created a new musical sound in New Orleans. An important influence on the premier New Orleans funk band, the Meters, Professor Longhair described his "sound [as] completely different than rhythm & blues, or calypso or any of that. It's just deep-down funk."[2]

In modern jazz, Horace Silver's composition "Opus de Funk" (1953) marked the beginning of the hard bop era, arguably the first funk movement in American music. Artists even discussed the concept in public. Notable recordings include Cannonball Adderley's "Blue Funk" (1958), Wes Montgomery's "Montgomeryland Funk" (1958), and Donald Byrd's "Pure D. Funk" (1960). It was the same concept that P-Funk exemplified a decade later. The new gospel and blues–based jazz emphasized traditional black musical values. Writing in 1961, historian Lerone Bennett Jr. described the music as "militantly protestant," stating that initially "the qualities deemed soulful (earthiness, emotional, spiritual vigor) were canonized under the general term—funky. One of the best indications of the thrust of this move-ment is that this word, originally disreputable, quickly became acceptable in journalistic circles. . . . Young musicians who had shunned the so-called emotionalism of the Negro church began to discourse learnedly on the poly-rhythms of the ring shout."[3]

However, the most notable statement on funk during the blues era was Bessie Smith's comment in 1925. Smith had been invited to an after-party in her honor at a private home located in a predominantly black section of her hometown of Chattanooga, Tennessee. The evening was off to a great start. The party featured collard greens and other black southern cuisine treats; but while the aroma of the food was delicious, the bluesy flavor of the bar-relhouse pianist's syncopation captured her full attention. As she entered the party with her girlfriends, Smith remarked in memorable fashion, "The funk is flyin'."[4] Her invocation of the funk principle is essentially synonymous with the figurative language that funk artists used a half-century later.

Blues musicians envisioned funk as a vital concept in music making, whereas many funk musicians have credited blues as the foundation of their development. Leroy "Sugarfoot" Bonner, lead singer and guitarist for the Ohio Players, one of the most influential bands in funk history, was enthralled by Delta blues during his formative years. "That's how I got started is copying Jimmy Reed," says Bonner.[5] Born in Hamilton, Ohio, in 1943, Bonner and his much younger friend, Roger Troutman, snuck into clubs in Dayton to watch blues singer and guitarist Robert Ward who led a band named the Ohio Untouchables. And as luck would have it, Bonner eventually replaced Ward, and that group became the Ohio Players. Betty Davis has also emphasized her debt to the blues. And though the Godfather of Soul was unequivocal about his utter distaste for blues, stating flatly, "I still don't like the blues,"[6] he's admitted that he was influenced by saxophonist Louis Jordan who pioneered a style of rhythm and blues that became known as jump blues during the late 1940s and early 1950s. Likewise, Brown considered "Papa's Got a Brand New Bag" as his first funk song, but his former saxophonist Maceo Parker refers to it as "a simple blues."[7] And, finally, Roger Troutman, a multi-instrumentalist whose artistic achievements with the talk box prefigured hip hop artists T-Pain's and Kanye West's experiments with Auto-Tune, once described his music as "blues for the eighties."[8]

This chapter examines the development of funk in the blues era. Bennett's statement that "funk" was "originally disreputable" raises several interrelated questions that we'll explore. Why was funk "disreputable"? How did it become a significant concept among black musicians? And how did the word become a metaphor for beauty, artistic integrity, and cultural affirmation? Writer

Albert Murray touches on all three questions, although somewhat ironically. Murray expressed disdain for the word "funky," stating that "the use of the word *funky* to mean earthy and soulful" is "even more exasperating than ludicrous."[9] Yet his writings illuminate the role of funk in blues aesthetics—he simply used different terminology to explain the concept. Murray's notion of "the blues counteragent" is unmistakably similar to Rickey Vincent's notion of the funk: that it isn't merely the name of a genre; it's "a means to a genre" as well. Murray correlates blues with the funk principle when he writes: "The blues counteragent that is so much a part of many people's equipment for living that they hardly ever think about it as such anymore is that artful and sometimes seemingly magical combination of idiomatic incantation and percussion that creates the dance-oriented good-time music also known as the blues."[10] Murray uses the words "incantation" and "percussion" to argue that surges of sensual pleasure helped create the music "known as the blues." My term for "incantation and percussion" in blues is the funk principle.

FILTHY McNASTY: THE STIGMATIZATION OF FUNK

Ralph Ellison's essay "The Little Man at Chehaw Station" serves as our point of departure. Writing in 1978, Ellison, Murray's longtime friend, offers an insightful perspective on interconnections of blues and funk, while paying a backhanded compliment to funk: "If we put the blues, bluegrass music, English folk songs, et cetera, together with Afro-American rhythms and gospel shouts, we have, God help us, first rock and now 'funk,' that most odiferous of musical(?) styles."[11] Ellison's question mark is revealing. Admired by scholars and fellow writers for his meticulous prose and predilection for satire, Ellison's punctuation after "musical" is as demeaning as "most odiferous." In addition to implying that funk defied conventional standards of decency and good taste, he snobbishly suggests that the music is deficient in artistic intelligence and creative imagination—which is to say, anti-intellectual. Yet Ellison's elitist attitude is instructive in understanding earlier stigmas of funk. Though he brilliantly illustrates the proclivity for hybridity and the funk principle in blues aesthetics, his conflation of odor and ignorance invokes Charles R. Johnson's analysis of racial stigmas of blackness in his essay "A Phenomenology of the Black Body."

According to Johnson, the Western construct of race was founded on René Descartes's premise that the mind and body are separated, and that intellectualism and sensuality are necessarily mutually exclusive. In this schema, race was constructed as a castigating stain on the black body. Descartes previously associated irrationality with sensuality among Europeans, especially women. White supremacist ideologues transfigured his conflation of sensuality and irrationality into a racialized paradigm of blackness. Herein blackness was portrayed as *phenotypically* irrational and unintelligent, and Johnson argues that much of black cultural philosophy has recapitulated aspects of white supremacist ideology by privileging physical prowess and emotive expression at the expense of intellectualism. So when Ellison questions funk musicians' artistic intelligence, he affirms a cornerstone of Manichean logic: that blackness signifies evil, ignorance, and irrationality and must therefore be controlled. Thus Johnson's essay provides an apt framework to explore why funk was "disreputable." Since black sensuality was stigmatized as evil and ignorant, white authorities often condemned it as a civic contaminant. In racial mythology, black dancers' trancelike performances of the Ring Shout during slavery were transmuted into racially disfigured exemplifications of nastiness and sin. To the extent that authorities envisioned black sacred and secular performances as social contaminants, they were discursively marked as taboo.

Such caricaturing of black vernacular expression characterized the Manichean frameworks in which "funk" signified the utmost stain on black bodies. Johnson writes: "Stain recalls defilement, guilt, sin, corpses that contaminate, menstruating women; and with them come the theological meanings of punishment, ostracism, and the need to be 'cleansed.'"[12] Since the meaning of "stain" is related to "smudge" and "smut," "funk" is arguably an olfactory manifestation of "stain." The stereotyped image of the reeking black body is a by-product of the castigating stain of race in Johnson's analysis. And, as the Brothers Johnson signified in the popular song "Get the Funk Out Ma Face" (1976), the words "funk" and "fuck" were closely related, so the term connoted licentiousness. Insofar as blues songs and dances met criteria that people considered funky, their performances were considered morally and intellectually suspect by conventional standards. Indeed, blues-based performance styles were routinely stigmatized as rude, crude, and anti-intellectual throughout much of the twentieth century. Consequently, exploring interconnections between blues, funk, and racial stigmas can elucidate the process in which "funk" became a blues metaphor and ultimately, in the late 1960s, a leading metaphor for black cultural aesthetics.

Writing at the height of the funk era in 1975, Johnson engages two narratives in his essay. The first one is brief and folkloric. It recapitulates principles of Manichean logic by conflating black masculinity with hyper-virility. In the story, white men praise a black man for the comparatively huge size of his penis and pay him twenty dollars for his presumed sexual virility. Johnson

posits this story as an example of how black cultural philosophy has reiter-
ated racial ideology by promoting physical prowess and sensuality at the
expense of intellectualism. Johnson's second narrative is more pertinent to
our discussion. Reminiscent of black elegance and fashion in the mid-1970s,
the second narrative can be interpreted as a historical allegory of funk. Set
in Manhattan, Johnson's character—let's call him Blue—is clad in the fashionable, urban gear of the period. As he strolls down Broadway, a bright
marquee catches his attention. Blue steps inside the bar to quench his thirst
and immediately senses hostility: "Their look, an intending beam focusing my
way, suddenly realizes something larval in me. . . . Epidermalization spreads
throughout the body like an *odor*, like an echoing sound."[13] Note Johnson's
images: larval, odor, sound. These interrelated images represent central tenets
of racial ideology. The first, larval, establishes the premise for the next two:
odor and sound. The larval image suggests that African Americans have
animalistic *genetic* structures which dovetail with the emission of bestial
odors and sounds. As we'll see shortly, such racialized views toward African
Americans' physical characteristics and vernacular expression were directly
related to stigmas associated with blues music and dancing near the outset
of the twentieth century.

Johnson's analysis of Manichean logic coincides with political theorist
Frantz Fanon's writings on colonial situations. Fanon notes that in colonial
narratives nonwhite people are depicted as "the negation of values," "the
corrosive element," and "the deforming element, disfiguring all that has to
do with beauty and morality. . . ."[14] Thus, when coupled with Descartes's
representation of sensuality as irrational and anti-intellectual, racial ideology
promoted the myth that African Americans were biologically, and therefore
culturally, incapable of mental development. As a result of such a devastating
stain on black character, Johnson argues, black cultural philosophy tended
to reproduce Descartes's logic in several ways, including a variation of false
consciousness in which black people interpreted empowerment and positiv-
ity in opposition to black vernacular epistemology and expression. Outlining
what contemporary scholars call respectability politics, Johnson represents
this mindset satirically: "I police my actions, and take precautions against
myself so the myth of stain, evil, and physicality . . . does not appear in
me."[15] In this compartment of racial ideology, young MCs, black Baptist and
Pentecostal worshippers, and black women who twerk are rendered morally
suspect and intellectually inferior.

However, Johnson directs most of his criticism to black expression that
represents sensuality and intellectualism as mutually exclusive and thereby
reasserts the mind-body split. According to this logic, "real" blackness is

physical, and intellectualism is a metaphor for whiteness. In practical terms, this mindset projected performance (music, dancing, sports, etc.) as attributes and definitive manifestations of blackness, whereas intellectual predilections and mental development (science, technology, philosophy, etc.) are interpreted as "white" liabilities and therefore impediments to expressing "real" blackness. Johnson posits Eldridge Cleaver's essay "The Primeval Mitosis" as an example: "The . . . sundering of man and the world into mental and physical substances by Descartes in the *Meditations* throws light on the issue Cleaver is trying to bring to clarity—consciousness is experienced as being identical with, yet curiously distinct from the body."[16] During his tenure with the Black Panther Party for Self Defense, Cleaver attempted to foment armed confrontation with the American state. And since he presumed that successful confrontation could only be achieved by men who were physically virile and aggressive, Cleaver inverted Descartes's mind-body split by privileging the body over the mind. That his inversion repeated the stereotype of black inferiority evidently didn't occur to Cleaver. He represents black masculinity as Supermasculine Menial, and white masculinity as the Omnipotent Administrator: "The body is tropical . . . Muscles are strength."[17] Not surprisingly, Johnson reads Cleaver's inverted reproduction of racial mythology as emblematic of Fanon's statement that there are times when blackness is locked into the black body.[18]

But while Cleaver's contradictions seem laughable in hindsight, the bifurcated logic in his writing formed the basis for many criticisms of the Ring Shout and blues. The exhilaration that dancers experienced in the Shout resembles how blues affected audiences when musicians played lowdown and dirty. The central experience in the Shout was the moment of ecstasy when the Holy Spirit entered the dancer's body. For slaves and their descendants who performed the dance, the experience was so spiritual that it constituted the sublime. Participants were compelled to sing, shout, or otherwise testify and express their deepest emotions in the dramaturgy of the frenzy. But since missionaries and other authorities considered bodily restraint a prerequisite for morality, performances of the Shout often ran afoul of prevailing moral codes. Eyewitness accounts of the Shout include terms such as "lewd" and "lascivious"—in a word, *nasty*. Yet countless dancers ignored these criticisms. During slavery, many of the dance movements and styles of music making that provoked the ire and confusion of white eyewitnesses actually expressed what the dancers envisioned as the sublime: their freest and most spiritual expression.

We can observe how African-influenced styles of worshiping God, which were often characterized by emotive, kinetic expression, became stigmatized as vulgar and vile when we examine white writers' representations of early Afro-Christianity. In these writings, the altered state of consciousness, which occurs in most black musical forms, was often racially caricatured. The Swedish writer Fredrika Bremer's description of a black camp meeting during slavery is an excellent example. During her visit to America in the mid-nineteenth century, Bremer observed a religious ceremony wherein black congregants caught the spirit, and her account demonstrates how vernacular conceptualizations of spirituality became associated with nastiness, crudeness, and ignorance. She writes, "In the camp of the blacks is heard a great tumult and a loud cry. Men roar and bawl out; women screech like pigs about to be killed; many, having fallen into convulsions, leap and strike about them, so that they are obliged to be held down. It looks here and there like a regular *fight*. . . . During all this tumult, the singing continues *loud and beautiful*, and the thunder joins in with its pealing kettle-drum."[19] What Bremer actually witnessed were expressions of peace and spirituality.

What Bremer misreads as violence was, in fact, an act of care and kindness. The worshippers who "held down" some of the others were protecting them from hurting themselves because they were embodied by the Spirit, and therefore not "conscious" in the normal sense of the term. But from Bremer's viewpoint, the expression was frightening—it seemed mindless and purely emotive, chaotic and tinged with violence. Thus her depiction of slaves' exultations of spirituality is instructive because it prefigured similar criticisms of blues singers. The great blues musician B.B. King once confided to Charles Keil: "When I go to a jazz club, sometimes the leader or the M.C. will say 'B.B. King, the well-known blues singer, is in the audience tonight,' and the way he says 'blues' you know he really means 'nasty.'"[20]

Discursive projections of stink onto black bodies in early American popular culture were part of a broader ideological assault that rationalized black disfranchisement under the guise of Jim Crow codes and customs. Depictions of odorous African Americans coalesced several racial stereotypes. The notion that African Americans were *naturally* malodorous suggested that blackness ipso facto engendered contamination, and that black people were intellectually inferior because the inability to understand simple hygiene suggested an analogous inability to understand basic aspects of civilization. Both Thomas Dixon's novel *The Clansman* (1905)[21] and D. W. Griffiths's film *The Birth of a Nation* (1915) represented African Americans as odorous and hopelessly irresponsible, while strongly suggesting that the two traits were interrelated. In addition, both narratives implied that blackness necessarily corrupts and contaminates the (white) commonweal. These depictions of African Americans appeased the aesthetic tastes, ideologies, and presumptions of entitlement in white Americans' imaginaries. In *The Birth of a Nation*, for instance, a black congressman removes his shoes and wriggles his toes during a legislative session, stinking up the entire room. Griffiths represents his fumes with smoke-like images that waft toward the ceiling; and after a white congressman objects, the Speaker of the House is obliged to state for the record that congressmen must keep their shoes on at all times. Racialized funk-images symbolized moral and civic contamination, stoked whites' resentment, and enflamed their indignation.

At the same time, stigmas of black sensuality seeped into black expressive culture. The demonizing of black expression was an effort to besmirch African Americans, and thus stigmatize black vernacular concepts and artistry. That such attitudes persisted well into the twentieth century is evidenced by Grammy Award winner Quincy Jones's comment: "The word 'funky' always embarrasses me," said Jones, who won critical acclaim writing jazz-funk tunes. "For me, it means a form of sincerity. But it's extremely difficult to define . . . I prefer to say 'soulful.'"[22] Whereas Jones's preference for "soul" affirms Bennett's suggestion that the word was a euphemism for "funky," his embarrassment recalls Johnson's statement: "Stain recalls defilement, *guilt, sin*, corpses that contaminate, menstruating women; and with them come the theological meanings of punishment, ostracism, and the need to be 'cleansed.'"[23]

But ironically, what Johnson posits as a method of engaging the mind-body split, that is, conceptualizing sensuality as an essential element of the *cerebral* process, was actually a foundational aspect of blues musicianship. Although Johnson only devotes a small portion of his essay to this idea, he outlines the parameters for an alternative cultural philosophy that merges mind and body. Similar to blues aesthetics, Johnson's epistemological framework emphasizes assimilative reasoning and deemphasizes compartmentalization. Herein mind and body interconnect, and bodies extend into objects: "[I]f I am 'downcast,'" writes Johnson, "the body gestures accordingly with a drooping posture. . . . The blind man's stick is no longer alien to him, not a mere object, but his bodily extension; the woman with a feather in her hat keeps a safe distance between it and things that might snap it off, but without looking: she *feels* these distances."[24] Johnson recognized few viable alternatives to Descartes's schema in black expressive culture; however, funk artists were exemplifying his premise at the time of his writing. Singer Betty Davis created an approach that was unmistakably psychosomatic. In an interview, the pioneering funk bassist Larry Graham emphasizes this point when he describes her approach:

[Betty] didn't play, but her mind, her body, her spirit would become an instrument that she used to get across to us what she was feeling, how she was flowing, and we'd catch that and roll with that. And then we'd tell from her reaction if we were on the right track or not. If something hit her and she was feeling it, you would immediately see it. So our job was to try to move her. We were feeding off each other in that sense.[25]

Of course, Graham mainly focuses on situating Davis in the history of funk, but his description of her method coincides with Johnson's thesis that feeling and thinking shouldn't be thought of as separate entities. Likewise, the term "funkentelechy" in Parliament's 1977 album title *Funkentelechy Vs. the Placebo Syndrome* combines the words "funk" and "entelechy," and arguably puns on "intellectual" which also suggests that funk expressed a black cultural philosophy.

Nonetheless, there were also traces of racial ideology in blue funk, especially in social commentaries. For instance, when Horace Silver introduced his 1961 composition "Filthy McNasty" at the Village Gate in New York, he told the audience the song was "about a mythical young man of rather dubious character." Silver's anecdote was meant to be lighthearted, of course, but both his song title and comments affirm Johnson's argument on some level. Similar connotations in the phrase "'down in the alley' . . . have always been with blues."[26] That some rappers recently boasted about the size of their penises also underscores Johnson's argument. Physicality thus emerged as a superior attribute in much of black expressive culture, especially venues in which social standing hinged on performance or other physical acts. Inasmuch as black expression was associated with African-derived performative styles, it was typically interpreted as *racial*, as opposed to cultural, expression. Consequently, even when black artists exceeded vernacular criteria for innovation, their expressions were often interpreted as indications of "natural" (read: phenotypical) talent rather than manifestations of creative processes wherein artists developed unique styles in specific historical and regional contexts.

But as we'll see, the epistemology of blue funk was predicated on contrariety. Though blues and funk were popular forms, the artists who created them managed to merge the mind and body in precisely the manner that Johnson advocates. The technique called voice extension became a trademark of blues musicianship. Conceptualizing their instruments as appendages of their bodies or vice versa, artists created previously unimaginable styles and sound qualities that activated the pleasure principle and made the funk fly.

WHERE'D YOU GET YOUR FUNK FROM?

Research suggests that "funk" has multiple etymologies. According to *A New Dictionary of the English Language*, published in 1846, the first citation of "funk" in English occurs circa 1330 in two passages written by R. Brunne. One reads: "Be beten alle fonkes," which means "be beat all to funks, or until they stink again . . ." Another one reads: "Now of this olde & this new king, / That was not worth a fonk." In this denotation, there's a clear correlation between stink and diminished value. The word "funk" was also used widely at Oxford University: "to be in a funk," and in old Flemish, *fonck* denoted "turba, perturbation."[27] In 1623 another reference to "funk" appears in a letter written by a man in Virginia: "Betwixt the decks there can hardly a man fetch his breath by reason there ariseth such a funke in the night that it causes putrefaction of bloud."[28] Although the letter wasn't about a slave ship—the passengers weren't black—it provides a possible clue as to how "funk" became racialized when we consider the subsequent history of slavery.

Meanwhile, according to art historian Robert Farris Thompson and poet-scholar Clarence Major, African etymologies coexisted with the English etymology. In *Juba to Jive: A Dictionary of African American Slang*, Major dates the etymology of "funk" to the 1640s, tracing it to a Central African term *"lu-funki,"* which denoted "bad body odor." Major notes that the word has evolved to mean "down to earth, in touch with the essence of being human." So "funk" can refer to "body odor" or "an offensive or unpleasant smell or thing," and it can also reference a style or expression that is "attractive or beautiful." Similarly, Thompson traces "funk" to the Ki-Kongo term *lu-fuki*. In both instances, the word denotes body odor. However, Thompson's definition of *lu-fuki* is more nuanced. He states: "[T]he Ki-Kongo word is closer to the jazz word 'funky' in form and meaning, as both jazzmen and Bakongo use 'funky' and *lu-fuki* to praise persons for the integrity of their art, for having 'worked out' to achieve their aims."[29]

African Americans across the Atlantic formulated a remarkably similar concept that became a central component of their cultural philosophy. Considering the joy and jubilation that characterized the Shout, it seems fitting that musicians who inherited that legacy would reimagine "funk" as the direct opposite of torment and resignation. The obvious question, though, is whether similarities between the Ki-Kongo and black vernacular terminologies are merely happenstance. Ned Sublette surmises that the languages coalesced at some point: "It appears that in the polyglot linguistic environment of early colonial slavery, a word was more likely to be taken up if it could be identified with a meaning in both European and African languages. . . . Since the word *funk* was in use in Virginia as of 1623, we can pretty well assume it has been part of the African American vocabulary ever since."[30] Sublette's reasoning seems plausible. By the eighteenth century, white ideologues had conflated blackness with malodor; and since these attitudes were pervasive, it seems reasonable that Bakongo speakers or their descendants eventually ascertained the meaning of "funk" and its racist connotations. But by the same token, it's difficult to ascertain when or even whether such syncretism occurred. Yet both scenarios posit far-reaching implications. On the one hand, African Americans' transfigurations of Ki-Kongo terminology would demonstrate an interconnection between a traditional African language and black vernacular expression. On the other hand, vernacular constructions of "funk" that bear no etymological relation to *lu-fuki* suggest that African Americans configured a concept that was virtually an African facsimile.

All the same, an exploration into blues aesthetics reveals valuable insight into the etymology of "funk." Even the words "blues" and "funk" are inter-related, and the historical connection extends back to Europe. The phrase "in a funk" is similar to a British definition of "'blues,' [which] in its original sense, seems to have come from the despondent mood associated with having a fit of 'blue devils' that anyone could experience. The phrase 'blue devils' was employed in Elizabethan England, and during the nineteenth century, people such as Lord Byron, Washington Irving, and Thomas Jefferson used the words 'blues' and 'blue devils' in their writings."[31] Similarly, at least one British dictionary defines "funk" in a manner that corresponds with the older sense of blues: "*Also called* **blue funk**. a state of nervousness, fear, or depression (esp. in the phrase **in a funk**)."[32] This correlation between "blues" and "funk" filtered into African American expression. Although the two words reference distinctly different musical genres, their definitions overlap in blues lexicon. As Silver explains, "The term 'funky' in jazz vocabulary means bluesy or down-to-earth."[33] Likewise, Larry Neal writes: "To be 'mean' in the lexicon of the blues is to express one's emotional experiences in the most profound, in the most intense manner possible. It means daring to be, to feel, to see."[34] Neal's characterization of "mean blues" corresponds favorably with the core meaning of "funk": integrity and honesty of expression.

Still, the evolutions that led to the modern definition of "funk" took place over several generations. In early blues culture, the word was often related to sex. B.B. King recollects: "[W]e'd never even use the word 'sex.' Even 'funky' was far too crude an expression. Church kept us in line."[35] King's conflation of "funky" and "crude" recalls Johnson's references to stain and contamination related to racial ideology. The impact was that many black parents believed that blues threatened their children's souls. Ruth Brown, otherwise known as "Miss Rhythm," recalls: "In my household, the attitude towards the blues was the same as it was in nearly every household. You just did not do it. It was called the Devil's music—whatever that meant, and I often questioned that. . . ."[36] Brown's comment clarifies the perilous stakes involved in performing blues-based music, not to mention expressing its unruly attitude in extraordinarily proscriptive environments.

Buddy Bolden's performance of "Funky Butt" was therefore a watershed moment in blues culture because it occurred during its foundational stages. The preeminent crowd pleaser in New Orleans between 1897 and 1905, Bolden had little interest in linguistic experimentation when he played the song alternately titled "I Thought I Heard Buddy Bolden Say" and "Buddy Bolden's Blues." From all indications, the song was a lament about working conditions—namely body odor. According to a newspaper account, several band members complained about a foul odor during a performance one evening, and trombonist Willie Cornish went home and wrote lyrics which included the line: "Open up the windows and let the foul air out" and "Funky butt, funky butt, take it away." The next night the band played it; the crowd went wild, and "Funky Butt" ultimately became Bolden's theme song.[37] Figurative interpretations of the lyrics were likely serendipitous. The crowd may have responded, in part, to the bawdiness of Bolden's X-rated blues. At the time, "funk" was strictly taboo in most public and private settings. "The police put you in jail if they heard you singing that song," said Sidney Bechet. "I was just starting out on clarinet, six or seven years old, Bolden had a tailgate contest with Imperial Band. Bolden started his theme song, police began whipping heads. The Eagle Band [played "Funky Butt"] every Saturday night . . . but they did not sing any words to it."[38] The Eagle Band's omission of Bolden's lyrics adds meaningful context to his expert musicianship and brooding. Since "funk" and "fuck" rhyme almost perfectly, the proscription likely was motivated by racialized attitudes toward sexuality that shaped authorities' notions of propriety in matters concerning black people.

In all probability, "Funky Butt" registered on both literal *and* figurative levels. Steatopygia was a focal point of eroticism in black southern culture, and at least some of the people who heard Bolden's initial performance probably interpreted the hook sexually. Such imagery would have almost certainly signified sexuality regardless of the singer's intentions. It's also possible that Bolden expressed erotic effects with his horn. As we'll see shortly, blues musicians often communicated paradoxical ideas as a matter of course.

Musicians were also adept at using instruments to convey ideas via tonal collages that represented emotions and experiences with distinct sounds that listeners understood. The idea that there were erotic implications in the band's performance is supported by a key eyewitness. As Dude Bottley recollects, "Funky Butt" was the last song the band would play during a gig. The "tune would last about *forty minutes* and if you had your woman with you, you and her was supposed to do that last dance."[39]

The Funky Butt dance was also popular during this period, and though it seems likely that the song inspired the dance, it's uncertain whether they were related. Blues singer and guitarist Coot Grant, who was born in 1893 and began dancing professionally in 1901, remembered watching the Funky Butt as a preadolescent in her father's honky-tonk in Birmingham, Alabama. When asked to describe the dance, she initially hesitated and then said that "women sometimes pulled up their dresses and showed their petticoats."[40] At which point, Grant recalled a woman who was known for her performances of the dance, and said,

> I remember a tall, powerful woman who worked in the mills pulling coke from a furnace—a man's job. And I can call her name, too. It was Sue, and she loved men. When Sue arrived at my father's tonk, people would yell "Here come Big Sue! Do the Funky Butt, Baby!" As soon as she got high and happy, that's what she'd do, pulling up her skirts and grinding her rear end like an alligator crawling up a bank.[41]

It's clear from Grant's initial hesitation, her reference to women pulling up their dresses, and Big Sue's performance *after* she "got high and happy" that, in this context, "funky" denoted motion and connoted sexuality. Interviewed in her golden years—a stage in life when many blues singers joined churches and renounced the blues—Grant's tone and alligator metaphor suggest that there were conflicting attitudes among African Americans toward blues, dancing, and public displays of sexuality, black women's in particular, at the beginning of the twentieth century. Blues artists' indifference toward social norms anticipated the nonconformity that later characterized funk music, and the popularity of the risqué dance ensured that figurative definitions of "funky" became part of blues lingo. Also, in a rather elaborate process the provocative gestures of "Funky Butt" contributed to a preexisting stockpile of dance vocabularies that future dancers reinterpreted.

Blues people expanded the meaning of "funk" to signify the pleasurable sensation that compelled people to dance. Blind Sid Hemphill, a fiddle and fife player born in 1876, is a case in point. When Alan Lomax interviewed him in the backwoods of Mississippi in the 1940s, Hemphill was still playing a "driving rhythm that made local dancers hop and shake"[42] in a picnic area called the Funky Fives where the music was "harsh and crude and vital and *rank* as milkweed."[43] The blues construction of "funk" was therefore more nuanced than the Standard English word. It excised most of the explicitly racist connotations, and signified honesty of expression and artistic excellence. Yet it also retained its reference to smell, including sex, and, to some extent, unsavory character. Earlier we discussed Quincy Jones's embarrassment about "funky." Tina Turner's sister, Aillene Bullock, conveyed a similar meaning when she wrote Ike and Tina Turner's B-side single "Funkier Than a Mosquito's Tweeter" (1970). In the song, the persona lambasts her "dirty old" lover's religious hypocrisy: "You're funkier than a mosquito's tweeter." The contrasting meanings within "funky" exemplify the contrariety in the blues tradition. The ethnomusicologist Portia K. Maultsby, who has written extensively on funk, encapsulates the multiple meanings of "funk" in her examination of the music in 1970s: "The term 'funk' captured both the complex, and often contradictory, feelings of optimism, ambivalence, disillusionment, and despair that accompanied the transition from a segregated society to a post-civil rights society."[44] Blues artists created a variegated concept that enhanced their creativity and assimilative modes of thinking. The ability to subsume dissimilar styles and points of view evinced an epistemological dexterity uniquely suited to the traumatic conditions that young African Americans encountered in the post-Reconstruction period. In the new art form, funkiness emerged as an important criterion that lent contrapuntal logic, barrelhouse bawdiness, and boundless resiliency to blue funk aesthetics.

Funk artists who grew up in the 1950s and early 1960s were part of the last generation of American youth who witnessed blues as popular music. These musicians incorporated important elements of blues philosophy, especially imagination and determination, into their sensibilities at crucial stages of their development. Consider Bootsy Collins's explanation. When Michel Martin asked him to define "funk," he said:

> Give you a perfect example. I played guitar when I first got started because of my brother, Catfish. I wanted to be just like him. So the opportunity came where he needed a bass player. And I said, "I'm the man, I can do it." [Catfish said,] "You don't even have a bass." I said, "Well, if you give me four strings, if you can get four strings, I

will have a bass." And I made a bass out of that guitar. And that same bass that I played with him that night was the same bass that I played all the way up until we got with James Brown. That's funk, making something out of nothing.[45]

Collins's recollection of the makeshift bass he used as a teenager exemplifies the innovation and determination that characterizes blue funk. In addition to other adjustments, he removed his six guitar strings, replaced them with four bass strings, and became so proficient and distinctive as a bass player that James Brown hired him while he was still in his teens. Brown's only stipulation was that he buy a new bass. Such is the essence of blue funk. Renowned for his trademark space bass, Collins later revolutionized musicians' understanding of the instrument's possibilities. And his achievement is probably due, in some measure, to having met the challenges of fulfilling, and ultimately exceeding, the uncompromising expectations of audiences and band members while playing a makeshift bass.[46]

Still, it's important to acknowledge Richard Iton's skepticism about the agency that marginalized people achieve when they redefine denigrating words. He states that "in the language game staked out by the modern, blacks are uniquely locked into a relationship that allows few possibilities for agency, autonomy, or substantive negotiation."[47] Quoting Walter Ong, Iton writes: "Concepts have a way of carrying their etymologies with them forever."[48] He states further that "modernism's language game" posed considerable challenges to black agency, and that "there is some validity" to the argument "that no word in and of itself has a fixed connotation and that the meanings attached to certain terms can be challenged or revised—witness Savion Glover's efforts to redefine tap dancing and free it from any embedded minstrel subtexts."[49] In blues culture, the discursive latitude afforded by artists' ingenuity was circumscribed by America's political economy, which supported "modernism's language game." A 1941 "study of black class structure reveals that the very terms used to classify and evaluate particular kinds of blues [were] used by upper and middle class blacks to describe and refer to lower class black society. These terms include 'dirty,' 'nasty,' 'unclean,' and 'common alley niggers.'"[50] A generation later, in 1974, Michael Haralambos found similar attitudes when he conducted interviews for his book on soul music. Many black informants conflated musical styles with varying levels of cosmopolitanism, which they praised or criticized as smoothness or crudeness, depending on their musical tastes and worldviews: "blues in the style of [B.B. King's] Memphis synthesis are described as 'modern' and 'clean' in contrast to the 'dirty,' 'gutbucket,' 'lowdown' and 'downhome' blues of Chicago and the Delta. . . . When fans of B.B. King call Chicago blues 'dirty' or 'gutbucket,' they often use the terms in a pejorative manner meaning crude, unsophisticated, unpolished."[51] That these tropes virtually replicate Johnson's language shows how thoroughly racial ideology permeated American society.

However, inversions can be substantive in certain situations. The blues homonym "funky" constituted an act of *symbolic* inversion. According to Barbara Babcock, symbolic inversion refers to "any act of expressive behavior which inverts, contradicts, abrogates, or in some fashion presents an alternative to commonly held cultural codes, values, and norms, be they linguistic, literary, or artistic, religious, social, and political."[52] There are numerous instances of symbolic inversion in American culture. The term queer theory comes immediately to mind. Queer theory has clearly become a term for resistive scholarship in LGBTQ social media and milieus. We can observe a prime example of symbolic inversion in Amiri Baraka's classic 1963 study *Blues People: Negro Music in White America*.[53] In a discussion of hard bop, Baraka stated, "Even the adjective *funky* which once meant to many Negroes merely a stink (usually associated with sex), was used to qualify the music as meaningful . . . The social implications, then, was that even the old stereotype of a distinctive Negro smell that white America subscribed to could be turned against white America. For this smell now, real or not, was made a valuable characteristic of "Negro-ness."[54] Similarly, the title of Louis Armstrong's "Gut Bucket Blues" (1925) is an allusion to the foul air that permeated the fish markets he remembered from his boyhood days in New Orleans. In this context, "Gut Bucket" literally referred to the buckets wherein fish guts were thrown. Likewise, in his recollection of jazz in New Orleans during the 1920s, multi-instrumentalist Garvin Bushell stated, "You could only hear the real blues and jazz in the gutbucket cabarets where the lower class went. The term 'gutbucket' came from the chitterlings bucket. . . . [T]he practice used to be to take a bucket to the slaughterhouse and a get a bucket of guts. Therefore, anything real low down was called gutbucket."[55] Zora Neale Hurston corroborates Bushell's point in her writing about the role of jook joints in early blues culture. Hurston writes, "[T]he Jook is the most important place in America. For in its smelly, shoddy confines has been born the secular music as blues, and on blues has been founded jazz."[56]

Tanya Ballard Brown also points up symbolic inversion in her article "The Origin (And Hot 'Stank') of the Chitlin Circuit."[57] The term "Chitlin Circuit" referenced a loose assemblage of varied black performance venues that showcased black talent and served as primary sources of entertainment for black audiences for nearly half a century beginning circa 1930 until approximately 1980. In her discussion, Brown quotes Preston Lauterbach: "The Chitlin' Circuit was African-Americans making something beautiful out of something ugly, whether it's making cuisine out of hog intestines or making world-class entertainment despite being excluded from all of the world-class venues, all of the fancy white clubs and all the first-rate white theaters." Naturally, the term "stank," like "gut bucket," "lowdown," "dirty," and other terms were euphemisms to circumvent the pervasive proscriptions in places where the blues were birthed.[58] Yet the very act of creating "funk" anew constituted a type of inversion.

Given the extensive irony in blues, it seems natural that vernacular intellectuals reinterpreted Standard English with appreciable irony. Homophones of "funk" correspond with homophones of "blues," so that "having the blues" meant being "in a funk." Both phrases referenced angst and anxiety that people could defer or diminish by playing blues and invoking the funk principle. Blues singer Willie King drives this point home in his remembrance of an older musician who said, "I'ma tell you what the blues is really all about. You got to participate in the blues. Sing the blues. Dance the blues. Play the blues on any instrument you wanna play. And this will keep the blues off of you. [But] now, if you don't want to participate in the blues, then the blues gonna be on you."[59] Similar to Collins, King emphasizes agency while distinguishing between blues music and having the blues as such. The latter is what Robert Johnson alternately referred to as "a low-down achin' chill" and an "achin' old heart disease," whereas blues music and dancing functioned as momentary salves—all of which prefigured the premise of Collins's co-authored song "P-Funk (Wants to Get Funked Up): "Funk not only moves, it can re-move, dig?"

The symbiosis between "blues" and "funk" becomes more evident when we compare meditations on their meanings. Reverend Rubin Lacy, a former blues singer, once asked: "What is the blues, then? It's a worried mind. It boils down to worry. Sometimes you worry so, it cause you to jump off the Frisco bridge up here, worry you so it cause you to stick a gun in you. . . ."[60] By contrast, Clinton essentially described funk as a lifesaver: "Anything you need it to be, when you're about ready to end your life—that's what funk is. . . . You know when . . . it's like you can't take it no more? Funk is that excuse that gives you [something] positive to live on."[61] The interconnection between these commentaries is undeniable. Though Lacy and Clinton are separated by musical genres and historical generations, their statements complement each other like red beans and rice. If the essence of blues is trouble, the essence of funk is alleviating trouble.

History demonstrates that ideological contestation is seldom cut-and-dried. All in all, the blues construction of "funk" marked a rare instance in which disfranchised people effectively negotiated the politics of "modernism's language game." When Iton says that funk bands like Sly and the Family Stone and Parliament-Funkadelic were "important and symbolic discursive formations in and of themselves," he suggests that blues musicians' cumulative impact was momentous, if not transformative. Despite being unlettered and caricatured as biologically odorous and cerebrally inept in white supremacist narratives, the creators of blue funk were inventive organic intellectuals. As the people's poets, they "sampled" the very term that referenced the most repulsive castigations of blackness imaginable, while affirming the psychosomatic phenomenon that writers such as Bremer previously racialized as crude, violent, and animalistic. That black southerners achieved such a profound ontological triumph under such dire economic conditions and political circumstances is nearly as comical and ironic as many blues songs themselves.

(PRE-)FUNK: CONTRARIETY AS PRECEPT IN BLUES AESTHETICS

Contrast was essential to the philosophy of blue funk. The funk principle melded mind and body, while emphasizing contrariety in the process. The blues scholar David Evans's commentary on stylistic elements of Delta blues singers reflects how thoroughly blues artists incorporated contrast into their techniques:

> a great many of these features of form, style, and content serve to create contrasts, tension and release of tension, and a sense of ambiguity and uncertainty, and that [blues singers] do this within an extremely compact form. Ambiguity and compactness are undoubtedly responsible much of the appeal of the blues to performers and listeners alike. The call and response principle provides several forms of tension and contrast in the blues. There is the "blues logic" of the B line "answering" the A line. The accompaniment also "answers" the singing at the end of each line and "comments" on individual notes and phrases within the line.[62]

Evan's analysis of form is illuminating, yet it's only the tip of the iceberg. His reference to "blues logic" is noteworthy. Contrast was indispensable to blues aesthetics and directly related to the funk principle.

The concept of funk accentuated dialectics in blues aesthetics. Amiri Baraka discusses this key point in one of his later essays titled "The 'Blues Aesthetic' and the 'Black Aesthetic': Aesthetics as the Continuing Political History of a Culture." Writing in his signature style of poetic prose, Baraka posits funk as a philosophical core of blues aesthetics: "Any and Every—All are related to the *one*, part of a whole, whole of a part. The hole and what goes in and out, the creatinginginging . . . What is *funky* is history, what comes goes."[63] Baraka's comment on blues echoes Evans's observations, and corroborates an argument I've made elsewhere: "[T]he blues are characterized by both subsumption and infusion. In fact, the blues are themselves products of hybridization. In addition to the ballads' capacity to resolve contradictions (God/Devil, bad/good), which stemmed from the spirituals, the blues absorbed other forms, including 'fables, metaphors, and melodies.'"[64] Spencer makes a similar point when he writes, "Once integrated into the wholeness of the Self, what may otherwise be evil is evil no longer."[65] Thus even the guitar, once considered evil, became a staple of performance in blues venues,[66] the Church of God in Christ, and other holiness denominations. Sister Rosetta Tharpe, who recorded her first gospel hit "This Train" in 1939, played guitar in both sacred and secular music, and many churches featured guitarists and other instrumentalists before her emergence.

Blues artists delighted in various types of contrast as a matter of course, including paradox, parody, irony, satire, signifying, and so forth. But the most momentous conflict for blues artists involved their opposition to church dogma. "The blues," writes Angela Davis, "were part of a cultural continuum that disputed the binary constructions associated with Christianity."[67] At issue was blues singers' insistence on addressing the full spectrum of human emotions, including sexual excitement. "Wait until you see me do my big black bottom / It'll put you in a trance," Ma Rainey sings in "Ma Rainey's Black Bottom" (1927). That the song was based on a preexisting dance is further indication of unabashed pleasure in blues. As Davis points out, "Sexuality after Emancipation could not be adequately expressed or addressed through the musical forms (e.g., shout, spirituals) existing under slavery."[68] Blues artists challenged church authorities on both moral and epistemological grounds.[69] They mocked the premise of the mind-body split and the resultant vilification of blackness and blues with remarkable clarity and humor. Doing so, they fashioned a new aesthetic framework by "sampling" both familiar and unfamiliar resources: musical sounds, performance idioms, contrasting viewpoints, and available terminologies.

Early blues musicians who matured during the post-Reconstruction period were amazingly resourceful. The very terms that missionaries and other authorities used previously to condemn the Shout (e.g., lewd, lascivious) furnished significant discursive material.[70] As Charles Keil points out, shifts and creative exchanges between blues and gospel often generated "repercussions in the [other]. This mutual malleability has been a constant factor—even a deciding feature—in" African American music.[71] Two related precepts were decisive factors in the artists' revisions of church music: the altered state of consciousness[72] and contrariety. In fact, using contrast was a common tool of the trade. Keil touches on this point when he notes that "there are many stock phrases in the blues tradition . . . that can be *played off against each other* to illustrate a particular theme or create a general mood."[73]

We can develop a clearer understanding of blues logic and its relationship to the funk principle by considering Brenda Dixon Gottschild's critical insights. Her research focuses on contrariety in dance movements, including "blues, jazz, rhythm and blues, hip hop,"[74] in African diasporic cultures, but her findings are also useful for understanding blues musicians' use of contrast. Gottschild demonstrates that black dancers have used contrariety as a guiding principle to facilitate expression and experimentation. She writes, "In a broad sense, the Africanist aesthetic can be described as a precept of contrariety, or an encounter of opposites. The conflict inherent in and implied by difference, discord, and irregularity is encompassed rather than erased or necessarily resolved. . . . The conflicts are *paired* opposites."[75] Gottschild acknowledges[76] that "All traditions use contrast in the arts,"[77] but she contends nonetheless that the degree of emphasis on contrapuntal styles and viewpoints in African diasporic cultures was "heightened beyond the contrast that is within the range of accepted standards in the Europeanist academic canon."[78] Likewise, blue musicians envisioned contrariety as a common tool of the trade. Rather than avoiding the stigmatization and "conflict inherent" in the Standard English term "funk," musicians "encompassed" the "difference." They "sampled" the word-sound, spelling, and certain aspects of its meaning to create a new homonym that gave expression to a new cultural concept. And they used a similar approach in their revisions of church aesthetics. Using church hymns as a musical foundation, blues singers composed songs about the most profane human experiences imaginable.

The blues definition of "funk" affirmed the quasi-trance impulse that was previously the central feature of the Shout. Hurston's description of the infinite joy that worshippers experienced when they "shouted" epitomized the emotional fever that blues musicians strived to create. "Broadly speaking," Hurston writes, "shouting is an emotional explosion, responsive to rhythm. It is called forth by: (1) sung rhythm; (2) spoken rhythm; (3) humming rhythm; (4) the foot patting or hand-clapping that imitates very closely the tom-tom."[79] Baptist and Pentecostal churchgoers considered these bursts of emotion as kinetic manifestations of the sublime. Blues artists studied church musicians' techniques and reinterpreted innumerable codes and customs in church settings. The fact that gospel singers were praising God mattered little to blues singers. Their concerns were purely artistic when they transmuted "religious ecstasy" into blue funk. Thomas A. Dorsey, known as the father of black gospel music, provides a stellar example in his recollection of Ma Rainey during his tenure as her pianist under the name Georgia Tom.

> When she started singing, the gold in her teeth would sparkle. She was in the spotlight. She possessed her listeners; they swayed, they rocked, they moaned and groaned, as they felt the blues with her. A woman swooned who had lost her man. Men groaned who had given their week's pay to some woman promised to be nice, but slipped away and couldn't be found ...[80]

Notice Dorsey's language: "possessed," "swayed," "rocked," "moaned," "groaned," etc. These verbs pertain specifically to psychosomatic phenomena in Baptist and Holiness churches, particularly congregants' altered states of consciousness. Yet he praises Rainey's ability to "possess" listeners with her blues.

We can develop a more detailed understanding of the reciprocity between blues and gospel by considering churchgoer Camille Roberts's commentary. Having grown up in the Church of God in Christ, Roberts offers a vernacular intellectual's perspective on the psychosomatic relationship between gospel and blues. She emphasizes ecstatic kinetic expression as a foundational aspect of spirituality, and her notion of spirituality parallels the funk principle. According to Roberts, sanctified church members

> expressed joy, the same as if you were to hear a man sing a record or blues or something, and you would express it with the body, and that's the way [my mother] would. . . . She'd come home and [through] her prayers she would express joy. . . . I really didn't understand it until I came to Chicago Fortieth, and I began to understand that the spirit was within you; you expressed it. If a song inspired you or you felt anything, you express it, the same as a dance floor.[81]

Roberts asserts that church members believed that, reminiscent of the Shout, "the spirit" was within you" and "you would express it with the body." The contemporary gospel duo Mary Mary's hit single "God in Me" (2008) is arguably a contemporary R&B variation of this idea.

Notably, Roberts doesn't distinguish between secular (blues) and sacred (gospel) genres of music in her explanation of the inner workings of the "spirit." Rather, in her thinking, the Holy Spirit interfaced with and communicated *through* body movements of parishioners who were in sync with the music regardless of whether the style was sacred or profane. Roberts's explanation of music and spirituality recalls Craig Werner's observation of the funk principle. He states that "it really doesn't matter whether you call it jazz or blues," gospel or soul, jazz or funk. "As long as the bass holds the groove (present or implied), maintains a heartbeat . . . and keep[s] the spirits on the dance floor moving, you can layer anything on top of it" because "funk speaks in all possible tongues. . . ."[82] In Roberts's model, the relationship between the "spirit" and body movement parallels the relationship between motion and emotion in blues and funk. Indeed, she mentions "blues" in her prefatory comments. Naturally, Baptist churches maintained stricter standards toward body movement, but their congregations witnessed and participated in "hand-clapping and foot-shuffling and rocking and rolling"[83] every Sunday God sent. So even though churchgoers imagined music as a gospel-train to the Lord, their spiritual ethos and joyous interactions with preachers and singers established a conceptual model for blues-oriented musicians.

There were very practical reasons why blues artists transmuted church aesthetics. Since most of them grew up in Baptist churches, it was the most soulful music they knew. Murray observes:

[M]any of the elements of blues music seem to have been derived from the downhome church in the first place. After all, such is the nature of the blues musician's development that even when he or she did not begin as a church musician, he or she is likely to have been conditioned by church music from infancy to a far greater extent than by blues music as such. There are, it should be remembered, no age limits on church attendance or church music. Whereas during the childhood of all the musicians whose work now represents the classics of the idiom, blues music was considered to be so specifically adult that as a rule children were not even permitted to listen to it freely, and for the most part were absolutely forbidden to go anywhere near the festivities of the Saturday Night Function until they were of age.[84]

Thrust into a contradictory world of brutal confinement and more freedom than they had ever known, blues artists fashioned an amazingly flexible aesthetic framework with the meager resources at their disposal.

Pianist Clarence Williams's commentary demonstrates the ideological tensions between blues and gospel music, while hinting at similarities between the two forms. Williams was born near New Orleans in 1893 and spent much of his youth in New Orleans during the period when trumpeters Bolden, King Oliver, and Louis Armstrong were living there. Williams recorded with Armstrong, Bessie Smith, blues singer Sippie Wallace, Sidney Bechet, the pioneer of the soprano saxophone, and many others. So his perspective on blues musicianship is highly informed. In comparing the attitude of blues with that of church music, Williams implies that while the forms expressed contrasting semantics and attitudes toward life, the peculiarities of their soundscapes were somewhat comparable. Commenting on blues, he says, "It's the mood. . . . That's the carry-over from slavery—nothing but trouble in sight for everyone. . . . A blue mood—since prayers often seemed futile the words were made to fit present situations that were much more real and certainly more urgent."[85] Williams clearly emphasizes lyrical and thematic divergences between blues and gospel rather than stylistic dissimilarities between the two forms.

But Williams's omission of contrasting stylistic elements of blues and gospel suggests that musical elements of these forms (e.g., timbres, tonalities, techniques) probably weren't as dissimilar as many people might assume. For instance, Duke Ellington once told Roebuck "Pops" Staples, bandleader and guitarist of the Staple Singers, "You play gospel in a blues key."[86] So even though Williams doesn't address Murray's specific point that blues musicians elaborated on the approaches of black church musicians, his focus on contrasting *lyrics* in blues and gospel, rather than sound quality, suggests that vocal and instrumental techniques were fairly similar. "Everyone wants to know where I got that funky style," vibraphonist Milt Jackson once said. "Well, it came from the church."[87] The featured soloist for the acclaimed Modern Jazz Quartet for many years, Jackson collaborated with another gospel-trained musician, Ray Charles, on the 1958 album *Soul Brothers*, which included Charles's composition "Blue Funk."

But long before Tharpe, Dorsey, Charles, and untold others, Bolden personified the holy profane.[88] The trombonist Bill Matthews recalls, "On those old, slow, low down blues, he had a moan in his cornet that went all through you, just like you were in church or something."[89] From all accounts, Bolden had an amazing ability to blend disparate musical styles—ragtime, blues, and hymns—into a coherent sound that "allowed seeming opposites to be unified into a synchronous whole: the spiritual and the sensual together, spirit and body together, good and evil together, heaven and hell together."[90] The pianist Jelly Roll Morton described him as "the most powerful trumpet in history" whose boldness was such that he "never wore a collar and a tie, had his shirt busted open so all the girls to see [his] red flannel undershirt."[91] Yet religious overtones are palpable in Morton's recollection of Bolden:

> I remember we'd be hanging around some corner, wouldn't know that there was going to be a dance out at Lincoln Park. Then we'd hear old Buddy's trumpet coming on and we'd all start. Any time it was quiet at night at Lincoln Park because maybe the affair hadn't been well publicized, Buddy Bolden would publicize it! He'd turn his trumpet around toward the city and blow his blues, calling his children home, as he used to say.[92]

Note the preacher-poet metaphor in Morton's remembrance. Born in 1877, Bolden grew up as a proverbial church boy. Though he came of age after the Ring Shout, Bamboula, and other dances and rituals were prohibited at Congo Square, the preachers who served as his models inherited the legacy of those performance styles.[93] In Baptist churches that he attended, preachers were expected to preach with such emotional power that congregants were moved to respond viscerally. New Orleans musician Harrison Barnes recalls: "Sometimes the sisters would begin to shout. . . . They'd be shouting, it wasn't dancing, but it was so near dancing."[94] Likewise, Kid Ory remembers Bolden leaving church with his wife Nora: "They were swinging."[95] Of course, many congregants may have objected to the word "swinging" as a description of their religious services. But Bolden's transformation to a purveyor of dirty blues provided a blueprint for countless musicians thereafter. While Jim Crow policies were successful in thwarting African Americans' pursuits of economic and political autonomy, Jim Crow writers' projections of funk onto black bodies proved to be less effective as a discursive strategy.

THE UGLY BEAUTY OF STANK

According to the late composer and musicologist Olly Wilson, analyzing African American musical history reveals that cultural values inscribed in music have been evident in other black expressive forms. Writing in the latter stages of his career, in 2001, Wilson observes:

> Earlier I mentioned predispositions in African American music. These predispositions also reflect basic values in the culture. It is the reaffirmation of these values that forms the basis of "aesthetics" in African American music. I define "aesthetics" broadly, by which I mean the full range of attitudes, values, and assumptions about the fundamental nature of the musical experience; the criteria by which a culture assesses quality, and assigns meaning to music, and the relationship of the musical experience to the overall system of reality.[96]

Wilson highlights the principles of music making and posits them at the core of an aesthetic framework. His commentary provides a potential outline for a multifaceted discussion of blues culture, notwithstanding his omission of specific genres. The notion that "predispositions" in the music "also reflect basic values in the culture" invokes an approach that detects and inspects precepts such as contrariety in multiple forms of expression related to blues and black vernacular culture.

As Wilson noted in a 1985 essay, much of the critical focus on blues-based music centered on such stylistic elements as call-and-response, off-beat phrasing, pentatonic scales—what he calls "foreground aspects." Though these characteristics were certainly important, he contends that scholars' overemphasis on "foreground aspects" tended to ignore the principles or "basic values" that comprised the conceptual foundations of the music. Wilson calls these values "the guiding background factors . . . [that] determine the presence of these foreground features."[97] So his notion of cultural aesthetics consists of two interrelated components that function as guiding factors of musical performance.[98] One component is the ethos, that is, "the full range of attitudes, values, and assumptions about the fundamental nature of the musical [and lived] experience." The other component is epistemological. Wilson's statement that the existence of "*criteria* by which a culture assesses quality and assigns meaning to music" presupposes the existence of corresponding standards and techniques and thus self-consciousness and know-how. For instance, Bessie Smith's criterion was to make the funk fly. Insofar as the funk principle embodied a "means to a style," it was certainly among the "guiding background factors" of the music, and constituted a "basic value" in blues culture. But since the assimilative reasoning of blue funk permeated black vernacular culture, we'll discuss various blues-based art forms.

If Wilson's model is viable, examples of irony, paradox, and contrast should become noticeable in a variety of artistic media, including visual art and literature. As we'll see, balance and complementarity were part and parcel of blues culture. Scholars familiar with Wilson's writings would point out, for instance, that his concept of the heterogeneous sound ideal epitomizes contrariety. Writing in 1992, he states that black musical history revealed a distinct preference for clashing sounds: "a kaleidoscopic range of dramatically contrasting qualities of sound (timbre) is sought after in both vocal and instrumental music. . . ."[99] Wilson's statement corresponds with Evans's discussion of contrasts in blues lyrics and Spencer's notions of synchronous duplicity and a "unity of apparent opposites."[100] But we might also consider two notable commentaries about modern jazz pianist Thelonious Monk. In a brief essay on Monk, whose composition "Ugly Beauty" was recorded in 1968, poet Yusef Komunyakaa writes, "Thelonious Monk was interested in how things struggle with opposites . . . A synthesis of conflict and beauty."[101] Likewise, Thelonious Monk's biographer, Robin D. G. Kelley, stated in an interview that "Monk's radical idea was not to add more notes to chords but rather take them away, creating much more dissonance. He'd often play two-note chords—for instance taking the third and the fifth out of a major seventh chord and playing just the root and major seventh—and wham, there's Monk's sound. It's the right chord, yet he makes it sound like a completely bizarre choice."[102]

However, evidence suggests that Monk's approach was prefigured by black singers during slavery. In his *Narrative of the Life of Frederick Douglass*, Frederick Douglass depicts an early example of the heterogeneous sound ideal. In one scene, a slave has been selected to run the monthly errand to Colonel Lloyd's plantation. And though such a privilege may seem somewhat trivial by contemporary standards, these errands not only signified favor with one's master; they also provided a temporary reprieve from the grueling labor conditions, including the horror of the overseer's lash, which were routine experiences of American slavery. Consequently, it's understandable that individuals "chosen" in these instances were often overcome with emotion. Though these respites were brief, they probably felt like interventions from the Lord. The slaves thanked Sweet Jesus and praised his Holy name. Douglass writes:

The slaves selected to go to the Great House Farm . . . were pecu-
liarly enthusiastic. While on their way they would make the dense old
woods for miles around, reverberate with their wild songs, revealing
at once the highest joy and the deepest sadness. They would compose
and sing as they went along, consulting neither time nor tune. The
thought that came up, came out—if not in the word, in the sound—
and as frequently in the one as in the other. They would sometimes
sing the most pathetic sentiment in the most rapturous tone, and the
most rapturous sentiment in the most pathetic tone. Into all of their
songs they would manage to weave something of the Great House
Farm.[103]

Douglass's passage is important for several reasons. We'll discuss his depiction of the heterogenous sound ideal momentarily, but it's important to note
that he highlights a psychosomatic approach to music making that became
prominent in black music in the modern period. When Douglass writes, "The
thought that came up, came out—if not in the word, in the *sound*—and as
frequently in the one as in the other," he describes a version of the voice-
instrument dynamic. This precept is manifested as beatboxing in hip hop;
in jazz singing, it's called scatting, and we'll discuss it later as voice extension
among blues instrumentalists. Similarly, jazz aficionados tend to associate
Monk's blues-oriented approach to the piano with his tendency to pound
his elbows on the keys. But black instrumentalists used similar forms of
corporeal percussion during slavery, and in the 1920s, a blind pianist named
Arizona Juanita Dranes developed a corporeal "Sanctified piano style" while
playing in the Church of God in Christ.[104] Relatively unknown to the outside
world, Dranes was classically trained; and according to Camille Roberts, she
"could make the piano talk, and she'd get so good she'd hit it with her elbows,
she could *perform* with it."[105]

But Douglass's description of slave music is also instructive because it
provides an opportunity to demonstrate the potential of blue funk as a critical model. As Gottschild acknowledges, "All traditions use contrast in the
arts,"[106] but the degree of emphasis on contrapuntal styles and viewpoints in
African diasporic cultures was "heightened beyond the contrast that is within
the range of accepted standards in the Europeanist academic canon."[107] As
a result, the deliberate pairing of apparent opposites "may be considered
naïve and extreme . . . flashy and loud, lowly and ludicrous, or just plain bad
taste" when writers interpret such expression in conventional frameworks.
At least one scholar has interpreted the singers' sonic dissonance as evidence

of *cognitive* dissonance. According to Lenore Kitts, Douglass's depiction reveals the slaves' confusion about the songs they composed. Kitts states, "Frederick Douglass famously observed that slaves themselves had difficulty interpreting their music, and conveyed 'the most pathetic sentiment in the most rapturous tones.'"[108] But the notion that the *singers* were confused seems a bit far-fetched. Such a reading directly contradicts Douglass's suggestion that slave songs revealed the contradictions of the political economy of slavery more effectively than "volumes of philosophy."

Since he spent over twenty years as a slave, it's safe to assume that Douglass heard many black musical performances. His description is therefore a synopsis of his memory of early African American singing styles. But to Kitts, the simultaneous articulation of joy and pain seem illogical (one wonders what soul singer Frankie Beverly, lead vocalist and co-writer of Maze's hit single "Joy and Pain" [1980], might say about this). As Gottschild observes, "Africanist contrasts may be considered naïve and extreme" from a Manichean perspective. However, when we situate Douglass's passage within the framework of (blue) funk, the contrariety that bewilders Kitts becomes more intelligible. The clashing tone colors exemplify what Gottschild describes as "balancing the ludic and tragic"[109] and, of course, Wilson's heterogeneous sound ideal. But it's also notable that the singers' blending of sadness and delight parallel Gottschild's findings that black dancers often emphasized movements as "paired opposites."[110] Approximately a century later, Ralph Ellison used contrast in narrative imagery, song lyrics, and thematic scenes while depicting blues culture in his novel *Invisible Man*.

Ellison's portrayal of a blues-singing street vendor analogizes Douglass's portrayal of slave singers. Douglass represents black song as a commingling of joy and pain; Ellison underscores paradox in blues lyrics. In the novel, the narrator encounters a bluesman named Peetie Wheatstraw who sells his wares on the street. Wheatstraw is a self-described Devil's-son-in-law just like his real-life counterpart, Peetie Wheatstraw himself. As many scholars have pointed out, the song that the fictional Wheatstraw sings is an allusion to Jimmy Rushing's 1937 recording "Boogie Woogie (I May Be Wrong)" wherein Rushing sings, "She got ways like a devil, she shaped like a frog / Starts a-lovin' me, I holler 'Ooh, hot dog!'" In the comedic spirit of blues irony and signification, Ellison displays his parodic talents to poke fun at the narrator's befuddlement, which reflects the parochial nature of his binary logic. The narrator asks, "What does it mean . . . Certainly his woman, *no* woman fitted that description. And why describe anyone in such *contradictory* terms?"[111] Beneath Ellison's lighthearted humor lies a philosophical question: What sort of logic informs Wheatstraw's song? Perhaps the most immediate response is that, in this specific instance, Wheatstraw is distinguishing erotic pleasure from physical beauty. In other words, the sensual power of touching exceeds the gratification derived from physical beauty. So even though the woman has unattractive physical features, he loves her deeply because she thrills him to the core and functions as his muse.

More significantly, though, the limitations of either-or logic was one of Ellison's central concerns. Since he considered assimilative reasoning a crucial component of blues aesthetics, he used fiction as a method to illustrate the impact of the narrator's Manichean conditioning. Ellison clarifies this point in an essay on visual artist Romare Bearden, stating that his "combination of technique is in itself eloquent of the sharp breaks, leaps in consciousness, distortions, *paradoxes*, reversals, telescoping of time and *surreal blending of styles, values, hopes and dreams* which characterize much of Negro American history."[112] Ellison wasn't alone in his interpretation of Bearden. The acclaimed jazz musician Wynton Marsalis makes a similar observation about Bearden's blues-based aesthetic in an interview. According to Marsalis, Bearden's penchant for contrapuntal imagery reflected his concern for "balance." Bearden will "do one thing and then there'll be something else down on the page that *balances* that. . . . You're always dealing with call and response with figures, colors, and . . . a call and response of ideas. And then ultimately, a call and response between him and the viewer."[113] Thus the narrator's question is actually a pretext for Ellison's elucidation of blues aesthetics.

But in the context of blues people's everyday lives, Rushing's song functioned as a variant of symbolic inversion. Ironic humor and grotesque imagery in blues songs were counterpoints to stigmas associated with blackness; and to some degree, they were allegorical. Living in a world in which beauty and whiteness were synonyms for virtue and value, blues artists developed alternative concepts of beauty that tended to emphasize interiority. This construction affirmed the value of their own humanity without negating the value and/or beauty of others. Since blues singers represented large segments of black communities in their roles as folk poets, such imagery tended to engender compassion—or at least tolerance—for people who were outliers or social pariahs: gays and lesbians, vagabonds and drifters, outcasts and prisoners, and so forth. In this conceptual framework, no individual was considered so high and mighty that he and/or she was beyond the pale of ridicule. Underlying the apparently nonsensical contradictions in the blues was brutal honesty and a quest for rock-bottom truth. Perhaps Langston Hughes characterized the ugly beauty of stank most poignantly when he stated, in the conclusion of his 1926 manifesto "The Negro Artist and the Racial Mountain," "We know we are beautiful. And ugly too."[114] In this sense, blue funk was a fundamentally democratizing aesthetic framework. The legendary comedienne Moms Mabley, a butch lesbian who dressed in dapper men's suits offstage, once signified, "My husband was so ugly, he used to stand outside the doctor's office and make people sick."

Such songs and comedy routines challenged the normative notion of equating beauty and value with phenotypes, while positing the contrarian premise that wit, sensuality, and compassion are far better barometers of beauty and virtue. We can observe a prime example in Memphis Minnie's "Killer Diller Blues" (1946). Ostensibly a song about ugliness, "Killer Diller Blues" is a lighthearted affirmation of the value of people who were routinely degraded and disrespected in American society. As such, the song is a comedic statement about the value of cultural diversity. An early innovator of the electric guitar, Minnie sings about an outrageously grotesque, homeless man who saunters into town, observing people and places while looking for a new home. Everywhere he goes—stores, hotels, and the like—people scatter at the mere sight of him. Minnie describes Killer Diller (whose name means "devastating effect") as an ugly sucker; and, like Ellison, Minnie uses animalistic imagery to dramatize his deformity—his face resembles a crying cat. Yet in the conclusion of the song, Killer Diller peers into a mirror and smiles at his own ugly beauty, stating proudly in blues-infused humor, "I'm a awful lil creature, I'm a killer diller from the South." The self-pride that Killer Diller demonstrates highlights the premise of the song: the arbitrariness of American beauty standards. In characteristic blues fashion, Minnie uses irony to illustrate the canards and contradictions of a hierarchical system based on the construct of race. Doing so, she prefigured the Temptations' 1967 hit single "Beauty Is Only Skin Deep."

Apart from blues singers' use of irony in social commentary, counterstatement was essential to the musical form. This feature of the blues was evident in the lyrics, sound textures, and listeners' responses. Murray states that "sometimes the lyrics mock and signify even as they pretend to weep. . . ."[115] Blues instrumentalists also demonstrated a penchant for counterstatement. Murray notes, "Even when what the instrumentation represents is the all but literal effect of the most miserable moaning and groaning, the most excruciating screaming and howling, the most pathetic sighing, sobbing, and whimpering[,]" the irony is that ". . . the more lowdown, dirty, and mean the music, the more instantaneously and pervasively sensual the dance gestures it engenders."[116] Succinctly stated, Murray is describing the funk principle as it was envisioned during the blues era. Note his reference to "dirty," "mean," and "sensual." He suggests that the blues' ratio of stank—or soul, to use Quincy Jones's term—is proportionate to the sensuality infused into a listener's dance movements. The day-to-day struggle of making ends meet, of robbing Peter to pay Paul, so to speak, from sunup to sundown, six days a week and sometimes seven took an emotional toll on people. Consequently, the simulated cries of a bottleneck guitar or the falsetto scream of a good blues singer performing at a neighborhood bar on Saturday night often struck an inner chord among audience members. Blues singers reflected fundamental truths of their listeners' everyday lives; and when such truths were expressed with artistic virtuosity, audiences typically responded with kinetic expression.

Critical writings on black dancers during the blues era indicate that vernacular dances were also characterized by contrariety. In Zora Neale Hurston's 1934 essay "Characteristics of Negro Expression," she underscores asymmetry in black vernacular dance movements. Citing Bill "Bo Jangles" Robinson and Earl "Snake Hips" Tucker as exemplars, Hurston observes "the lack of symmetry" and "abrupt and sudden changes. The presence of rhythm and lack of symmetry are *paradoxical*, but there they are."[117] Hurston's work not only prefigures Gottschild's writings but Jacqui Malone's as well. Both these later scholars provide more detailed analyses of contrariety in black dancers' movements. In her book *Steppin' on the Blues: The Visible Rhythms of African American Dance* (1996), Malone observes an isomorphic relationship between dancing and music making in blues culture: "'Multiple meter' refers to the use of *cross rhythms*. Musicians create tension in the music by playing several different rhythms at the same time. Dancers articulate some of the rhythms in different parts of their bodies."[118] Similarly, in her research on dance movements in African diasporic cultures, Gottschild writes: "From an Africanist standpoint, movement may emanate from any part of the body, and two or three centers may operate simultaneously. . . . Africanist movement is also polyrhythmic. For example, the feet may maintain one rhythm while the arms, head, or torso dance to different drums."[119] Gottschild and Malone published their books in 1996. That both dance scholars came to nearly identical conclusions during the same period suggests that the dancers they examined conceptualized their styles within strikingly similar aesthetic frameworks.

But before Gottschild and Malone, Marshall and Jean Stearns examined African American dancers during the blues era. Like Hurston, the Stearns posit "Snakehips" Tucker as a model of blues-based dancing, and highlight contrariety as a defining characteristic of his style. In the pioneering study

Jazz Dance: The Story of American Vernacular Dance (1968), the Stearns provide a detailed description of Tucker performing his signature dance known as "Spanking the Baby":

> The combination was part of a routine known in Harlem as Spanking the Baby. . . . Using shock tactics, he then went directly into the basic Snake hips movements, which he paced superbly, starting out innocently enough, with one knee crossing over behind the other, while the toe of one foot touched the arch of the other. At first, it looked simultaneously pigeon-toed and knock-kneed.[120]

Needless to say, Tucker's style was inimitable. He not only delights in paradox; he seems to project it as braggadocio. Indeed, Tucker expresses contrariety as the pinnacle of his performance. He begins with snake-hip movements, and builds energy while creating tension in the audience. That Tucker waited until his final dance move to emphasize paradox in his routine suggests that he considered this gesture as his most profound artistic statement. Viewed from this perspective, the ability to infuse paradox into a seamless flow of performance is an important barometer of a dancer's level of talent and virtuosity. We can even think of Tucker's blues-era dance move as a precursor to MC Hammer's famous boast: "Can't touch this." More fundamentally, though, the fact that Hurston, Malone, Gottschild, and the Stearns all highlight paradox and cross rhythms in black dance movements in roughly the same period demonstrates that contrariety in blues culture extended beyond the realm of music making.

The funk principle established the conceptual foundation for a broader cultural aesthetics wherein complementarity and balance were evident in multiple art forms. Kalamu ya Salaam, a New Orleans–based Black Arts writer, poignantly summarizes the dualities of blue funk when he states that in blues, "life is both sweet and sour. . . . good and evil eaten off the same plate."[121] Likewise, contemporary producer Dâm-Funk recently said, "To me, funk is like a smile with a tear—and that's the kind of funk that I make."[122] The comments by Salaam and Dâm-Funk coincide with those of the late visual artist Houston Conwill, whose sculpture *Juju Funk* includes what he calls a "gutbucket."[123] Conwill described his creative process in terms that are unquestionably paradoxical: "'High Funk' is a deliberate contradiction in terms. [I]t conjugates the high (the transcendent-metaphorically, the ancestral plane) with the low (the working, the functional)."[124] Thus in the cultural aesthetics of blue funk, artists in multiple media have used contrariety to enhance their representations of life's experiences.

As a final note, analyzing contrast in numerous aspects of blues culture illuminates important principles and perspectives that have gone largely unexamined. Notwithstanding Ellison's elitist attitude toward funk music as such, the theme of funk in *Invisible Man* is especially pertinent. Obviously, the novel has drawn attention from countless writers and scholars, yet little has been written about Ellison's treatment of funk. Writing in 1952, when "funk" was still taboo in most social settings, he engages the concept while avoiding the actual word, and he addresses conflicting meanings of "funk" by depicting contrasting views toward the topic. In the first treatment, Ellison satirizes the stereotype of the funky black body. The narrator ponders a migration to the North after his expulsion from a historically black college modeled after Tuskegee University. After his exit interview with Dr. Bledsoe, the college president, the narrator naively anticipates job opportunities with rich, white employers. However, Bledsoe has deceived him by writing letters to the men, imploring them not to hire him. The narrator is therefore blissfully unaware of his predicament. He muses, "My shoes would be polished, my suit pressed, my hair dressed (not so much grease) and parted on the side; my nails would be clean and my armpits well deodorized—you had to watch that last item. You couldn't allow them to think *all* of us smelled bad."[125] Needless to say, the protagonist's attitude demonstrates that stigmas associated with blackness and funk are interrelated.

Ellison revisits his stank-theme in the final scene of *Invisible Man*. But in his second treatment, he associates stank with blues musicianship, and posits Louis Armstrong as an exemplar of blue funk phraseology. Ellison's premise is that funk was an invaluable ingredient of the blues aesthetic. Indeed, he affirms Hubert Sumlin's statement that "[s]oul is the foundation" of the blues. In his closing statement on Armstrong's music and legacy, the narrator says,

> With Louis Armstrong one half of me says, "Open up the windows and let the foul air out," while the other half says, "It was good green corn before the harvest." Of course Louis was only kidding, he wouldn't have thrown old Bad Air out, because it would have broken up the music and the dance, when it was the good music that came from the bell of old Bad Air's horn that counted. Old Bad Air is still around with his music and his dancing and diversity, and I'll be up and around with mine.[126]

Ellison's passage is one of the finest in American literary history, and many scholars have examined it as the apotheosis of musical depictions in black writing. However, a closer reading reveals that the passage also represents the funk principle—hence Ellison's allusions to dancing. Writing a year before Silver released "Opus de Funk" in 1953, Ellison arguably presages the first funk era in American music, when many younger jazz players envisioned their music as "Blues de Funk," as trombonist Curtis Fuller titled his 1960 composition. The corn image in the narrator's line "it was good green corn *before* the harvest" prefigures the cuisine tropes that black musicians later used for funk. Lee Morgan's 1967 album *Corn Bread* is one of many examples. In Ellison's treatment of stank, he uses personification and euphemism. "Bad Air" is obviously a euphemistic allusion to funk, but Ellison's capitalization of the term personifies it, and suggests that the funk principle was a crucial element of Armstrong's virtuosity.

The line that Armstrong sings in *Invisible Man* is probably an allusion to Jelly Roll Morton's 1947 recording "Buddy Bolden's Blues," which includes Bolden's famous line: "Open up *them* windows and let the foul air out." But though Armstrong recorded a concise version of the song under the same title for the soundtrack of the Hollywood film *New Orleans* (1947), it's unlikely that he recorded a version that included these lyrics. Ellison seems to have created a fictional illustration of Armstrong's performance, especially since he represents Armstrong as the walking embodiment of blues aesthetics. To the extent that funk was essential to Armstrong's music, the iconic trumpeter envisioned blues in terms of lowdown dirty stank. Yet Bolden is conspicuously absent in *Invisible Man*; and since invisibility is a metaphor for the erasure of black achievement, Ellison's omission of the funkmaster Bolden is ironic indeed.

BLUE FUNK AS KINETIC AESTHETICS

A cursory list of musicians who were dancers before or during the beginnings of their careers includes Ma Rainey, Bessie Smith, Louis Armstrong, Ethel Waters, Duke Ellington, Lionel Hampton, Dizzy Gillespie, Ella Fitzgerald, Philly Joe Jones, T-Bone Walker, Little Richard, Patrice Rushen, Jodie Watley—to name a few. That such groundbreaking artists danced *before* they achieved musical acclaim illustrates the importance of kinesthesia (dancing, finger-popping, head-nodding, nondescript bodily movements, etc.) in blue funk. Occasionally, dancers were so extraordinary that they anticipated new genres. Writing about tap dancer John W. Bubbles, of the duo Buck and Bubbles, for instance, Marshall and Jean Stearns state: "Approximately fourteen years before the Basie band came east, Bubbles was dancing to the kind of rhythm that Count Basie called four heavy beats to a bar and no cheating."[127] Likewise, Duke Ellington's "The Mooche" (1928) was a daring musical experiment, but the composition was preceded by a dance called the Mooche, a sort of slow loose-jointed grind that served as Bert Williams's signature routine at least as early as 1898.[128] Finally, in his remembrances of Saturday night square dances in Centerville, Texas, blues guitarist Lightnin' Hopkins calls attention to a major principle of blue funk aesthetics when he suggests that the dancing and music were interrelated: "Near about everybody you see around them dances could near about play for them."[129]

These examples beg the question: Why was kinesthesia so essential to blues musicianship? Perhaps the most basic response is that dances were visualized rhythms.[130] That is, dances functioned as three-dimensional captions of sound that both dancers and musicians responded to and reinterpreted. Of course, the music functioned as easy listening; but even in these situations, danceable rhythms and melodies were key factors in capturing audiences' attention.[131] As artistic counterparts to instrumentalists and singers, then, dancers were both barometers and interpreters of musicians' artistry. Murray states:

> what is at issue is the primordial cultural conditioning of the people for whom blues music was created in the first place. They are dance-beat oriented people. They refine all movement in the direction of dance-beat elegance. Their work movements become dance movements and so do their play movements; and so, indeed, do all the movements they use every day, including the way they walk, stand, turn, wave, shake hands, reach, or make any gesture at all. So, if the preponderance of their most talented musicians has been almost exclusively preoccupied with the composition and performance of dance music, it is altogether consistent with their most fundamental conceptions of and responses to existence itself.[132]

Murray's comments on blues and dancing coincide with Wilson's model of cultural aesthetics. Although Murray never uses the word aesthetics in his study, he still anticipates Wilson's concept. When Murray states that dancing reflects the "cultural conditioning" of African American people, and that it's only natural that blues music inspired "dance-beat elegance," he prefigures Wilson's statement that a cultural aesthetics highlights "the criteria by which a culture assesses quality and assigns meaning to music...."[133]

For Bessie Smith, blues music should make the funk fly, and her criterion wasn't anomalous. The Slow Drag, which was considered a salacious dance, was also referred to as "the blues"—thus the centrality of the funk principle.[134] As musician John Cephas says, "[F]irst you have to feel the music yourself. . . . If you really get down, they will feel it too. . . . They'll feel that and be dancing or clapping in the aisles."[135] The atmosphere in dives and juke houses got so festive that sometimes the floors sounded like drums.

Blues at the Juke House

> knee bones bent, black bodies low
> ebony eyes bass and bow
> saxophones and jimmy mack
> slant black stetson hats
> painted nails and tail feather suits
> lipstick and juicy fruits
> thick chocolate cherry spread
> over a duck, then pluck him
> on the table with his legs propped up
> wang dang doodle, snake hips quiver
> boogie down and rump roll shiver
> snatch it back and hold it tight
> prance and dance till broad daylight
> rainwater muddy, the hawk
> steady biting but listen at
> that timber wolf howl
> he files his teeth on guitar strings
> goin' down slow jookin' todalo
> way down the bottom
> on the killin' room flo'[136]

But while dancing contributed to the excitement in blues performances, dance gestures often informed musical ideas. In an article about Texas blues singer Mance Lipscomb, who was born in 1895, Mack McCormick, a Texas blues collector, suggests that early Texas blues musicians thought of specific styles and genres in terms of specific dances and rhythms:

These men did not think of themselves as blues singers. They were singers whose employment was often to provide music for dancers and thus they thought of its rhythms, not its poetic structure. Thus, to Mance, the ballad Ella Speed is a breakdown; the bawdy Bout a Spoonful is a slow drag. For the most part he thinks of "blues" as a particular slow-tempoed dance that became fashionable around World War I.[137]

For many blues instrumentalists, it was sometimes difficult to create the tone color they desired without creating an inner dynamics of body movement, particularly in ways that movement and positioning can affect sound quality during performances. Of course, the irony is that many people have long presumed that the sensuality of blues musicianship suggested a *lack* of intelligence.

In his autobiography *Music Is My Mistress*, Duke Ellington exposes such thinking as fallacy. Ellington personified organic intellectualism, and his remembrance of Bubber Miley provides keen insight regarding the significance of kinesthesia. For Ellington, Miley was a paragon of blues musicianship. An extraordinary instrumentalist, Miley co-wrote and played the defining solo on Ellington's first theme song, "East St. Louis Toodle-oo,"[138] which was originally recorded in 1926. In the comments below, he describes Miley's artistic philosophy, emphasizing his soulfulness and swing "credo" as critical factors underlying his monumental achievement as a musician. Ellington's allusion to two signature recordings in his remembrance of Miley suggests the trumpeter's vast influence:

> Every note he played was soul filled with the pulse of compulsion. It don't mean a thing if it ain't got that swing was his credo. Before he played his choruses, he would tell his story . . . such as, "This is an old man, tired from working in the field since sunup, coming up the road in the sunset on his way home to dinner. He's tired but strong, and humming in time with his broken gait—or vice versa." That was how he pictured "East St. Louis Toodle-o."[139]

Ellington posits soul as "the foundation" of Miley's aesthetics. During his heyday, kinesthesia and storytelling were essential to the epistemological process in which blues instrumentalists gestated ideas. To put it differently, body movement not only shaped Miley's topics; it also informed his techniques. In his approach, the ability to swing the blues was proportionate to the ability to read, translate, and elaborate on various aspects of body-talk. As poet Kevin Young muses, "We call this transmission, this memory as history, this changing same, *the groove.*[140] Miley's reference to the man's "broken gait" corresponds with the meaning of the song title. In a 1962 interview in Toronto, Ellington explains,

> What actually happened, we started out calling it the "Todalo," and of course, the printer obviously made a mistake and put another "o" in it or something. I never spelled it for him, actually. "Todalo," you know, is a broken walk.
>
> In those days—well, now we do the same thing—practically everything we wrote was supposed to be a picture of something, or it represented a character of something. . . . We were walking up Broadway one night after playing the Kentucky Club, and we were talking about this old man, after a hard day's work in the field, where he and his broken walk [are] coming up the road. But he's strong, in spite of being so tired, because he's headed [home] to get his feet under the table and to get that hot dinner that's waiting for him. And that's the *East St. Louis Todalo*, actually, but since it was misspelled we've been compromising it, and we call it *Todalo, Toodle-Oo*. . . .[141]

For Ellington, "East St. Louis Toodle-Oo" was an improvised sculpture of sound, a musical story about the conflicting moods and attitudes of a fictional old man walking home from work, humming to the syncopated rhythms of his own footsteps. Miley's story about the man's broken walk highlights the psychosomatic nature of blue funk.

Again, the widespread perception was that blues singers were backward and ignorant, but their countrified grammar bore little reflection on the complexity of their musical ideas. Muddy Waters, who dominated the blues scene in Chicago, was unequivocal about the complexity of his music, and he underscored the role of sensuality. "See," he says, "my blues is not as easy to play as most people think they are. I makes my blues in different numbers, sometimes thirteen, fifteen, fourteen, just the way I *feel.*"[142] Waters, an early influence on Hendrix, dispels any misconceptions about the presumptions that blues was a simplistic musical form. Guitarist Hubert Sumlin elaborates on this point in an interview. Known for his musicianship as Howlin' Wolf's longtime sideman, Sumlin was also a model for Hendrix. Speaking in his colorful Mississippi vernacular, he uses the word "soul," and explains that the difficulty in playing blues is because they *require* emotional honesty. That is, the ability to play well hinged largely on people's ability to explore depths of their emotions when they interpreted a song. Note Sumlin's emphatic tone:

"Blues is the most hardest thing in the world for anybody to play. Everybody can't play the blues. *You* think they can, *they* think they can, but . . . Ain't no soul there. Soul is the foundation of this whole thang, man. And what you say is your bond."[143]

Herein Sumlin epitomizes what black folks once called signifying. He satirically distinguishes between playing prescribed notes and playing blues "sho nuff." He states that the degree of soul that musicians infuse into their sounds determines the scale or caliber of the blues they play, suggesting that blues without stank is oxymoronic. Musicians had to interpret the keys in conjunction with their feelings in that specific time and space because the songs were personal statements in which artists confronted and ultimately interpreted their most profound emotional realities—this was a touchstone of blues aesthetics. Even today, the phrase "Keep it funky" in black urban parlance means complete honesty and unvarnished truth. Sumlin's emphasis on soul recalls Murray's statement that the "seemingly magical combination of idiomatic incantation and percussion . . . creates the dance-oriented good-time music also known as the blues." That is, the "incantation and percussion" or funk principle "is a means to a [musical] style." For all practical purposes, good blues were virtually inconceivable without considerable infusions of stank.

The acclaimed modern jazz trumpeter Dizzy Gillespie made a similar point about the importance of funk and kinesthesia in music making. Recollecting the hard bop era of the 1950s, Gillespie said that funk "reasserted the primacy of rhythm and blues in our music and made you get funky with sweat to play it. . . ."[144] Of course, some readers may dismiss Gillespie's statement as hyperbole. But when he elaborated on the topic, Gillespie shifted the focus to his own music, and further emphasized a strong connection between music making and body movement: "A feeling for dancing was always a part of my music; to play it right, you've got to move. If a guy doesn't *move properly* when he's playing my music, he ain't got the feeling. Thelonious Monk, Illinois Jacquet, and all those instrumentalists who move a lot, are playing just what they're doing with their bodies."[145] Gillespie's comments elaborate on Murray's notion of "dance-beat elegance." But where Murray references the dancers who respond to the music, Gillespie emphasizes having "[a] feeling for dancing" during performances. For Gillespie, it wasn't only important for musicians to move; they had to "move properly," which suggests that in addition to understanding musical concepts, not to mention the history and capacity of specific instruments, studying dance vocabularies and other aspects of kinesthetic semantics were also essential to blue-funk apprenticeship.

Blues musicians routinely envisioned instruments as extensions of their bodies. In blue funk aesthetics, the body and object (e.g., instrument) are joined together. B.B. King articulates this concept clearly when he states, "I tried to connect my singing voice to my guitar an' my guitar to my singing voice. Like the two was talking to one another."[146] Tharpe's biographer, Gayle F. Wald, explains that when people said that Sister Rosetta Tharpe made "her guitar talk," it "convey[ed] how Rosetta transformed the guitar into an extension of her body, how she could let her instrument speak through and for her." All of these statements correspond with Cephas's belief that ideally blues music is "an expression of your mind, of your inner self. And the guitars or harmonicas or other instruments are like added voices, an extension of yourself to make the expression more deep."[147] Of course, most blues musicians had little interest in philosophizing—they wanted a partying good time. But Cephas's statement that blues musicians used instruments for the express purpose of amplifying and extending their own voices exemplifies Johnson's notion of "bodily extension" nonetheless. Their approach intensified the music's depth and resonance, which magnified the emotional effect on the audience.

Blues musicians often used voice extensions to activate the funk principle. Lucky Cordell, a disc-jockey at WVON radio station in Chicago in the 1960s, underlined this point in an interview: "When I say, 'Ain't that the truth,' it means you're playing the way I feel, you hit me right in the bag, the music you're playing is the truth, it's the blues."[148] Cordell's commentary on blues instrumentalists evokes Neal's definition of "mean blues." His bag metaphor and references to truth correspond with core meanings of "funk" and "blues" respectively. Murray elaborates on this aspect of blues aesthetics when he states: "Blues music . . . is not always song in the conventional sense of the word. Sometimes if not most times the incantation is instrumental, and while it is true that blues instrumentation is derived from voice extension, it is equally true that much vocalization is now derived from instrumentation."[149] For "incantation," read funk principle. The parallel between Johnson's essay and Murray's analysis of the blues aesthetic is notable. It's almost as though Murray is responding directly to Johnson's basic claim that black cultural philosophy hasn't formulated or (re)presented viable alternatives to the either-or logic of the mind-body split. Implicit in Murray's comments is that when blues instrumentalists used voice extension, both their techniques and objectives (e.g., funk) were viable alternatives to the either-or logic of the mind-body split.

The unique qualities of blue funk facilitated the melding of mind and body that we examined at the outset of our discussion. Recall Johnson's

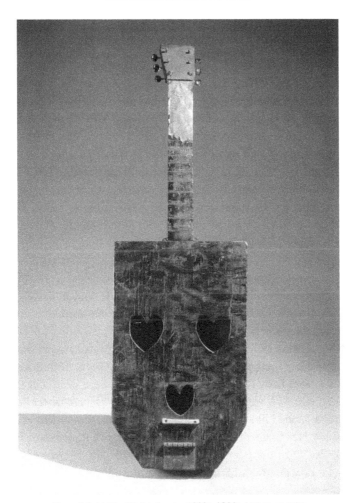

Figure 2.1. Unidentified guitar, ca. 1920s–1930s. Unknown artist.

passage: "The blind man's stick is no longer alien to him, not a mere object, but his bodily extension; the woman with a feather in her hat keeps a safe distance between it and things that might snap it off, but without looking: she *feels* these distances."[150] Unlike the mind-body split that Johnson criticizes, *feeling* is crucial to blue funk because musicians used kinesthesia to generate artistic ideas. This principle is exemplified beautifully in the photo of a homemade guitar made by a black southern musician in the early twentieth century (see fig. 2.1). The exquisitely crafted instrument has a dark blue hue and heart-shaped sound holes that evoke a human face,[151] which illustrate the soulfulness Cephas emphasizes when he references the "inner self." In the epistemological vortex of blue funk, the body was miraculously extended so that it subsumed the instrument. Guthrie P. Ramsey Jr. makes a similar point when he observes:

> When singer Sarah Vaughan recalled her apprenticeship in early be-
> bop ensembles, she deconstructed one of the earmarks of the mod-
> ernist mind-body split by collapsing (in classic Afro-modernist fash-
> ion) the divide separating mental "education" and bodily celebration:
>   "Oh listen, I was going to school. I really didn't have to go to Juil-
> liard, I was right there in it. . . . I just learned a lot. Lots and lots. I used
> to stare at them in amazement. But I used to *feel* it; you know, both of
> us used to sit on the stand and we'd get to swinging so much, Dizzy
> would come down and grab me and start jitterbugging all over the
> place. It was swinging."[152]

For "school," read organic intellectualism. In Vaughan's recollection, the word "swinging" is synonymous with the funk principle, and her reference to "feeling" is virtually identical to Johnson's usage of the word.

Other notable singers also used kinesthetic methods. Billie Holiday, once a member of Count Basie's orchestra, was widely respected among jazz musicians because her method of "singing [w]as synonymous with horn blowing."[153] But before Lady Day arrived on the scene, Bessie Smith developed a kinetic aesthetic. As is widely known, Smith's voice was full of sheer beauty—deep blues seasoned like soul food. Yet Smith's aesthetic was just as kinetic as Gillespie's. Her "stage gestures" were often "as much dance movement as anything else."[154] In the poem "Bessie on my wall," Sherley Anne Williams creates a literary portrait of Smith singing a mean blues:

> in the deep brown
> face nostrils
> flared on a last
> long hummmmmmmmmm.[155]

The poet clearly represents Smith's body as an instrument. Her depiction of Smith recalls Gillespie's comments about the importance of body movement. Note the images: Smith's chocolate brown skin and flared nostrils accentuate Williams's suggestion that Smith infused pyrotechnics into her approach to lyricism. Alluding to Smith's humming in her famous 1927 recording of "Back-Water Blues," which many people believed was about the Great Mississippi Flood of 1927 (the song was recorded about two months before the levees broke), the poet captures Smith's vision as an artist, while exemplifying the majesty of the blues. The persona becomes so distraught that words can't express the depths of her emotions, so she hums: "Mmmmmm, I can't move no mo."

The blues were tonal illustrations of the pains and pleasures that African Americans experienced in everyday life. To the extent that the voice/instrument accentuated the hypocrisy they encountered, it became a technical device that helped activate the funk/spirit. Eventually, this feature became somewhat clichéd in the music of avant-garde artists like Anthony Braxton. But in the old days, many musicians, especially horn players, simulated a wide variety of sounds, including cries, moans, laughter, and other human emotions.[156] Likewise, jug bands often used kazoos when they performed risqué songs, while blues singers like Tampa Red used the kazoo as a voice extender or disguiser (mask). Some musicians were so adept at voice extension that they simulated animals' sounds. Smith's trombonist Charles "Cholly" Green was such a musician, and she celebrates his innovative talents in her 1927 recording "Trombone Cholly." Several of Smith's songs memorialized "unsung black musicians who, by the prevailing white musical standards, were refused recognition as the brilliant instrumentalists they were."[157] Written by George Brooks, "Trombone Cholly" showcases Green as a bona fide scientist of sound. Smith brags about his talents, and pokes fun at the limitations of the white establishment's musical theories. She sings, "Nobody else can do his stuff 'cause he won't teach 'em how."

Green's sound quality on "Trombone Cholly" is lowdown and dirty. He transforms his instrument into an anatomical appendage, using it as a narrative device to convey thoughts and feelings through the medium of sound: wails, moans, grunts, groans. These sounds simulated scenes from, and evoked memories of, everyday black southern life in early twentieth century. Green's ability to tell a story in sound is reminiscent of Miley's solo in Ellington's "East St. Louis Toodle-oo." We can gain further insight into Green's aesthetics by looking briefly at an analogous commentary by Ellington. When asked to explain his reasoning for using Harlem in several of his titles, Ellington articulated a unique method of reading and recreating sound that correlates with Green's technique. If music was a language for Ellington, as he said it was, then we can read his following comments as a guide for analyzing blues instrumentalists during his heyday:

You get the full essence of Harlem in an air shaft. You hear fights, you smell dinner, you hear people making love. You hear intimate gossip floating down. You hear the radio. An air shaft is one great big loudspeaker. You see your neighbor's laundry. You hear the janitor's dogs. The man upstairs' aerial falls down and breaks your window. You smell coffee. . . . An air shaft has got every contrast. You hear people praying, fighting, snoring. . . . I tried to put all that in my "Harlem Airshaft."[158]

Ellington's allusions to mundane experiences in Harlem suggest that he interpreted sounds as units of meaning just as painters and poets interpret images and symbols in visual art and literature.

Green's trombone playing evidences a similar approach. Accompanied by Smith on vocals, Fletcher Henderson on piano, and Joe Smith on cornet, Green displays many of the signature sounds and unique approaches that became trademark features of blues musicianship. Just as black southern dancers created extemporized choreographs of their experiences in social dances such as Pitchin' Hay and the Buzzard Lope, Green approximates the sounds of cattle and other farm animals. When Smith sings that he "moans like a cow," Green intersperses growls of various sound qualities, creating an incantatory effect that borders on eroticism. It's important to bear in mind that many of Smith's fans lived in the South. Others were black southern migrants who trekked to large cities like New York, Philadelphia, Chicago, and Detroit. As Jeff Titon argues, "A downhome blues song locates downhome as a feeling in the listener's mental landscape. . . . In the city, downhome blues . . . remind listeners of the feeling of life down home."[159] Likewise, bluesman Baby Doo Caston muses, "Blues is a sound. . . . it's a feeling that a sound would put you into."[160] Many of Smith's fans probably responded to Green in much the same way that Cordell responded to blues instrumentalists—the music was "the truth" and hit them right "in the bag." The impulse that Caston describes is hot stank—the pleasure principle. Green evoked this feeling on slide trombone, and Smith sings the verb "swing" to accentuate his aphrodisiac effect: women swinging their hips from side to side, doing the shim-sham-shimmy as the funk begins to rise.

Musicians such as Bolden, Smith, Miley, Tharpe, and legions of other artists made important contributions to the development of funk as an influential concept in American music and culture. If we recall Larry Graham's explanation of Betty Davis's artistic method, blues musicians' contributions to funk becomes readily apparent. Though preoccupied with questions that concerned the nature of music and performance, their foregrounding of contrariety enabled them to express viable alternatives to the mind-body

split. That most blues musicians had little knowledge of Western philosophy is less important than the fact that their music expressed an alternative
cultural philosophy.

By the 1970s the sounds blues instrumentalists used to activate the funk
were outmoded, but the assimilative logic they used to simulate the human
voice was foundational for funk musicians. In his book *Midnight Lightning:
Jimi Hendrix and the Black Experience*, Tate points out that Hendrix elaborated on the musical approaches of Delta blues musicians such as Charley
Patton and Robert Johnson:

> In country blues especially, the guitar's lingo evolved into a stun-
> ningly complex, shaded, vocal that could sing and solo with weight
> and authority in designated spots and sustain a piece without any
> vocals at all. What Hendrix did was effect a marriage or ménage a
> trois between the various strains of blues, modern soul, avant-garde
> jazz, and the English rock and roll derivatives of same that pushed
> the guitar to the fore in a frightening way.[161]

Tate's passage emblematizes blue funk aesthetics. The two points he outlines
recall two important issues we discussed earlier. Tate's first statement that
country blues guitarists transmuted the guitar into a singing voice evokes
blues' use of voice extension. Tate's second point underscores the assimilative nature of Hendrix's aesthetic. But what's interesting here is that Tate's
description of Hendrix's use of contrariety is virtually identical to Ellison's
characterization of funk's blending of multiple musical styles. But where
Ellison implies that funk's artistic hybridity demonstrated limited creative
aptitude, Tate argues that Hendrix's musical multilingualism was the foundation of his unparalleled achievements as a guitarist.

Hendrix's use of his body is also reminiscent of older blues instrumentalists. Writing for the *Seattle Post-Intelligencer* in 1969, journalist Janie Gres-
sel offered an impressionistic representation of Hendrix: "Hendrix's guitar
seemed to be an extension of his body; the peculiar positions from which he
sometimes played seemed a result of emotion. . . . The impression was that
if Hendrix were to have put down his guitar, the music would have to come
from his body—that the instrument was entirely superfluous."[162]

Still, the most striking example of bodily extension in funk was arguably
Roger Troutman's experiments with the talkbox. Troutman's sound was literally an amalgam of his own voice and the voice modulator of his keyboard,
which he connected to a tube he placed into his mouth. More fundamentally,

though, Troutman's approach to the talkbox was amazingly similar to that of blues guitarists and horn players. For instance, when television talk show host Donny Simpson asked Troutman why he used the talkbox, he essentially repeated Murray's correlation between voice extension and incantation in the audience. Troutman says, "When I started using it [people] would look up like, it would seem to hypnotize them in a way."[163] In another interview recorded in Tokyo in the early 1990s, Troutman emphasized voice extension. Before using the talkbox, the multi-instrumentalist also sang in the conventional sense of the term. But his new "instrument" expanded his range. He could even go "so high like a female screaming." Troutman explains, "What I try to do is, instead of using my own voice, I'm using the sounds of a keyboard, and the sound of the keyboard comes through this tube. But then the special part is, I try to imitate what a human singer does."[164] Troutman's statement recalls Murray's observation that blues musicians approximated the human voice. It therefore seems even more fitting that Troutman characterized his music as "blues for the eighties."

The jazz-funk innovator Herbie Hancock, who played piano in Miles Davis's Second Great Quintet, also deserves mention. Hancock grew up playing classical music, and though his background and tastes were much different from those of blues musicians, his notion of the audience's role during performances is distinctly blues-inflected. Hancock recounts a pivotal experience in his early twenties. In 1962 he was playing a gig at a supper club with Afro-Cuban percussionist Mongo Santamaria, and trumpeter Donald Byrd was his roommate and "older surrogate brother." Byrd had released over twenty albums as a leader, so he was considerably more experienced than Hancock, who recollects that during an intermission:

> Donald had a conversation with Mongo something about, "What are the examples of the common thread between Afro-Cuban or Afro-Latin music and African-American jazz?" And Mongo said he hadn't really heard a thing that really links it together, he was still searching for it. And I wasn't paying that much attention to that conversation, it was a little too heavy for me at the time. But then all of a sudden Donald Byrd says, "Herbie, why don't you play *Watermelon Man* for Mongo? And I'm thinking, "What does that have to do with the conversation that they're talking about?" I thought it was a little funky jazz tune.
>
> So I started playing it, and then Mongo, he got up and he said, "Keep playing it!" And he went on the stage, and started playing his

congas, and it fit like a glove fits on a hand . . . And then one by one the other musicians got up and started playing the tune. The bass player looked at my left hand for the bass line, and he learned that, and he started playing it, and then the saxophone player, the trumpet player, pretty soon the whole band [was] playing it. And also little by little the audience was getting up from their tables, and they all got on the dance floor. Pretty soon the dance floor was filled with people, laughing and shrieking, and having a great time, and they were saying, "This is a hit! This is fantastic."[165]

Hancock's backstory not only demonstrates how thoroughly he learned the importance of the audience as a young musician. It also suggests that the funk principle comprised a "common" intergenerational and diasporic "thread" that connected Hancock with Santamaria, Byrd, and presumably earlier musicians as well. Roughly ten years later, Hancock rearranged "Watermelon Man" for his breakthrough jazz-funk album *Head Hunters* in 1973. During the same year, he offered the following perspective on energy and feedback from the audience:

The audience doesn't play a physical part in what goes on the same way the musician does, but there is feedback that the audience gives in vibes. The audience puts energy in the air. I'm not talking applause, really. The true measure of the accuracy of a musical performance is the energy in the air that's produced by the vibes of the listeners and the players.[166]

For "feedback" and "energy," read "funk." Reminiscent of Ellison's statement that blues audiences engaged in "antagonistic cooperation"[167] with musicians, Hancock elucidates the dynamism that Smith invoked in her proclamation: "The funk is flyin'." Though Hancock came of age long after Smith's reign as the Empress of the Blues, his comments invoke blues singers' objective to compel listeners to sing, swing, shake, shout, shimmy, and so forth.

Funk music was an urban manifestation of blues aesthetics that flourished in the rebellious period of the late 1960s and 1970s. As such, funk was an elaborate expression of the concept that blues dancers and musicians developed near the turn of the twentieth century—what Amiri Baraka called "the blues impulse transferred." Whereas Delta blues musicians such as Waters, King, and Koko Taylor worked on farms in the rural South during their youth and migrated to cities later as adults, most funk musicians grew up in cities. So when blues singer Bobby "Blue" Bland released "Ain't No Love in the Heart of the City" in 1974, the premise of the song was an age-old maxim to most funk artists. Of course, there were notable exceptions. James Brown exuded black southern culture in his sensibilities and speech patterns, but even he grew up in a city. Augusta, Georgia wasn't a metropolis, but Brown didn't plow mules or pick cotton like legions of blues musicians. Similarly, Chaka Kahn was born Yvette Marie Stevens, but changed her name as a youth activist in the Chicago chapter of the Black Panther Party. And Sheila E grew up playing drums in Oakland, California, while watching her father, Pete Escovedo, perform as a drummer and bandleader in the Bay Area.

These vast geographical contrasts led to experiential differences and therefore new perspectives toward music and life itself. Hendrix's birthplace of Seattle was thousands of miles away from the Mississippi Delta, and seemed like a different world. Hendrix said that he was frightened the first time he heard Muddy Waters playing the guitar: "[I]t scared me to death because I heard all those sounds. Wow! What was all that about?"[168] But it was precisely these vast regional and generational differences that created the impetus for musicians like Sly Stone to reinterpret blue funk aesthetics in a previously inconceivable manner.

Chapter Three

Sly Stone and the Gospel of Funk

Perhaps more than any other artist of his generation, Sly Stone was singularly responsible for the contrarian attitudes and bohemian sensibilities that characterized funk music. Born in 1943 in Denton, Texas, and baptized Sylvester Stewart, Stone grew up in Vallejo, California, a multi-ethnic community located on the outskirts of the San Francisco Bay Area. A child prodigy, Stone began performing in church around the age of four. As is often the case in black musical history, the Stewarts were a musical family. His mother, Alpha, sang and played piano and guitar. His father, K.C., played a self-made violin and juice harp, and he accompanied the singing and tambourine playing with a percussion instrument he made out of baking pans, tin cans, and a washboard.[1] In Denton, the Stewarts had belonged to St. Andrew church, but before the building was constructed the congregation worshipped the Holy Spirit outside. The divisive contradictions of class and creed that existed in black communities were reflected in the stigmas that accompanied membership in Sanctified churches back then. Referred to derisively as "holy rollers," Sanctified congregants were more exuberant in their praise styles than Methodists and Baptists. "Consciously or not," writes Robin D. G. Kelley, they shared spiritual beliefs that resembled traditional African concepts of spirituality, which posited an "essential relationship be-tween music and dance—music is supposed to move the body and touch the soul."[2] And given the racialization of Africanist expression, St. Andrew church-goers provoked consternation from others in their community.[3] Ac-cording to Stone's biographer Jeff Kaliss, "passersby would throw things at the 'hollering' parishioners."[4] This appalling treatment notwithstanding, the church persisted in praising the Spirit, exemplifying musicologist Guthrie P.

Ramsey Jr.'s idea that churches and other black spaces and institutions have functioned as community theaters wherein black performers learn distinctive styles, sensibilities, and cultural values that not only become models for younger artists but points of reference for contemporaries as well.

During Stone's youth, church members were enthralled wherever he sang. Such was the affective intensity of Stone's singing that grown adults wanted to touch the boy-genius physically. Alpha Stewart recalls, "They'd stand this bitty five-year-old on a table and he'd sing 'You Got to Move' . . . You'd have to hold [the parishioners] back sometime."[5] Not surprisingly, Stone identified a church musician named Blind Daniel as his mentor during his youth. Stone said, "He was a man of the Lord who used to visit our church and sing and play."[6] In his approach to music making, then, Stone drew heavily from the aesthetic concepts and moral values that he developed in the Sanctified church. As part of the Stewart Four, which included his brother, Freddy, and his sisters, Rose and Vaetta, Stone performed regularly as a child. At age nine, in 1952, he recorded the songs "On the Battlefield" and "Walking in Jesus' Name." Listening to the precocious pre-adolescent singing, Stone's immense talent and unshakeable confidence are already quite evident. "Walking in Jesus' Name" foreshadows the emotive power that would became a trademark feature of Sly and the Family Stone in later years. The song is a moving act of testifying to his devotion to a life in Christ, a testimony that is eerily in conversation with the ignominy imposed on Sanctified black churchgoers in black communities. It is as though the young singer's praise for Jesus as Lord and Savior is a defiant rejoinder to the hostility that church members routinely experienced. And though it goes without saying that Stone eventually penned some of the most profane songs imaginable, the contrast between the songs he sang as a child and the secular songs he performed before thousands of people as an adult isn't especially stark. In fact, the unabated pride that young Sylvester Stewart expresses as devout Christian becomes a foundation for Sly Stone's credo that both artists and audiences should take pride in expressing the funk/spirit.

The intense nature of the spirituality that informed Stone's aesthetic framework was invariably expressed in hand claps, finger snaps, toe taps, shrieks, shakes, shouts, quivering shivers, moans, hums, chants, cries, and falsetto diphthongs of onomatopoeia. Such was the invigorating energy that Stone channeled into the infinitely pleasurable stimuli that he referred to as "the fonk."[7] Within its epistemological vortex, dancers visualize backbeat rhythms of the music. Whether listeners danced the Popcorn, the Boogaloo, or the Funky Four Corners, their dances functioned as three-dimensional

significations of sound, dynamic captions of motion and emotion. As a manifestation of call and response, the dances were extemporized reflections of
the funk/spirit that symbolized the resolution of opposites, the pinnacle
of black vernacular performance: God-human, preacher-congregation,
musician-audience. This psychic ascension into communal, participatory
cultural experiences, which Stone developed in church, is also discernible in
secular performances. Singer Patryce "Choc'Let" Banks, lead female vocalist
of Graham Central Station, characterizes her first time listening to Stone's
song "I Want to Take You Higher" (1969) as a transformative, quasi-religious
experience. She recalls: "I thought I had found my musical niche . . . [But]
[t]his brotha sang with so much feeling and the music was so captivating,
I had to stop in my tracks, sit down, and listen. When the song was over, I
felt I had just had a religious experience."[8] Trumpeter Cynthia Robinson, a
founding member of the Family Stone, strikes a similar tone in her recollection of a live performance. According to Robinson, Stone performed a
version of the Hambone, a percussive dance based on the juba pat that was
popular during the nineteenth century. Robinson recollects:

> [Larry Graham, Freddie Stone, and Sly] started doing the Hambone.
> . . . They jumped off the stage and went down the aisle and the crowd
> was going wild. They went down the side and went out the door. The
> whole place ended up getting out of their seats and following them
> out the exit and around the front and through the entrance and back
> to their seats. Amazing. . . . [Then] they got back up on stage and
> grabbed their instruments and . . . the people went wild.[9]

The emotive, call-and-response interaction that Robinson describes was a
central component of the musical values that were prevalent in Pentecostal
churches. As musicologist Teresa L. Reed observes, "In a black Holiness/Pente-
costal church, it is not at all unusual to find the entire congregation—old and
young alike—overtaken in the 'holy dance' and speaking in tongues. These
impromptu expressions are welcome features of the worship experience."[10]

The unique forms of expression that are common in black holiness
churches often confound normative models of cultural criticism, particularly notions of genre, media, and disciplines. As Mark Anthony Neal points
out, "Stone functions as a conflation of the musician and the preacher—not
unusual in African American musical idioms—with the desired goal being
that of transcendence."[11] Likewise, Dalton Anthony states that Stone "learned
to approach sound as an extension of prayer" while "[g]rowing up in the

Church of God in Christ."[12] But while Neal and Anthony provide important insight into Stone's aesthetic, it should be noted that dance was also a crucial aspect of Stone's aesthetic and a foundational element of his spiritual ethos. In the performative spaces that he experienced during his childhood, "motion [was] an inextricable aspect of the music."[13] "Given their particular cultural bias toward merging motion and music," members of the Church of God in Christ were "particularly attracted to this mode of music-making."[14] However, Stone not only referred to himself as a poet in his song "Poet" (1971); he also personified the holy profane. Stone played expertly what churchgoers considered "worldly" music, especially blues. Recollecting his earliest songs, he said, "When I look back on it, I realize I was writing *blues*. But I had a rock and roll attitude."[15] Stone's gospel of funk "transcended the blues, yet captured its intimate essence."[16]

An important characteristic of funk aesthetics was its unadulterated blend of pleasure and social consciousness. Stone was an exemplar in this respect. While he prompted partygoers to slip, slide, and shake loose booties on the funk, he evinced a social vision that was often as bright as leading poets of his era. But since his music was so effusive, some of his most profound ideas have been largely overlooked. As Nikki Giovanni muses in "Revolutionary Music," "you've just got to dig sly . . . damn the words / you gonna be dancing to the music."[17] Thus Stone's approach to music making coincided with two principal tenets of the spiritual ethos that Olly Wilson observed: "a belief in the affective power of music, a view of music as a force that is capable of making something happen"[18] and the belief that "movement is part of the music-making process and therefore intrinsic to the process."[19] As a preacher-poet par excellence, Stone divulged the troubles of everyday life, and testified to the promise of redemption imbued in the possibilities of social change. At the same time, he refused to confine himself to sanctimonious themes and points of view. After all, he wrote and recorded "Sex Machine," which we'll examine a bit later.

Stone's politics were complex. Rather than advocating a radical politics, he espoused a notion of spirituality that was ineluctably rebellious. As Nelson George contends, "Sly . . . rebelled against the narrow-mindedness in which [he] grew up. It is not coincidental that [he] blossomed in [an environ-ment] removed from the traditions of black America."[20] But underneath his black hippie accoutrement, deep inside the glaze of cocaine, Stone was still his mother's son. The major difference now was that he led a *new* church. It was a tie-dyed, multi-ethnic sky-temple[21] of peace, love, and harmony, a spirit-house rejoicing in the very freedoms proscribed in the Sanctified church: free drugs, free sex, and free-fashion clothes. And though many black activists equated Christianity with the status quo after the murder of Martin Luther King Jr., the reality was that spirituality and resistance weren't mutually exclusive. As Angela Davis argues, "Karl Marx comments on religion as the 'opium of the people' notwithstanding . . . religious consciousness can itself play a transformative role."[22] Given its nonconformity and interracial composition, the sky-temple might have etched an outline for a class-based coalition that anticipated #BlackLivesMatter. But neither Stone nor his flower power congregants believed in the value of organized struggle.

Like blues-oriented musicians before him, Stone conveyed his ideas in stylistic terms. And though he would almost certainly phrase it differently, the critical problem he understood quite clearly was the prevailing Western concept of rationality, particularly the normalization of repression, which demonizes sensuality by reproducing an either/or logic, which in turn engenders a mythic dichotomy of the mind and body. Stone tended to avoid material aspects of social change. He seemed to believe that the power of his music could assist in a widespread conversion of funkified believers in love and peace. Such thinking was politically naïve; but so was the idea, held by some black cultural nationalists, that they could actually create a separate black state inside the continental United States.[23] So despite Stone's political contradictions, his music made a significant contribution to a history of anti-hegemonic ideas. His spiritually based communal vision reflected an urgent desire for social democracy in the immediate aftermath of the second black reconstruction period. As a co-creator of funk, Stone imagined an American collectivity that resolved political contradictions of class, creed, gender, and race. At the core of his songwriting is an abiding message of love that was often expressed as infinite pleasure: love of thyself, thy neighbor, and even thine enemies before he became disillusioned and fell victim to drug addiction in the 1970s.

INSIDE THE FUNKSHOP

According to singer-guitarist Garry Shider, a mainstay of P-Funk, funk is a combination of "gospel, R&B, blues [and], jazz—all of it just mixed up."[24] If we add elements of rock to Shider's definition, Sly and the Family Stone was an exemplary funk band. Part of the group's novelty was that it introduced elements of rock into rhythm and blues. As George Clinton points out, the Family Stone "was the bridge between Motown and the psychedelic

[rock] world."[25] Recollecting his first time seeing Sly and the Family Stone at the Electric Circus in New York, Clinton says, "They had the clarity of Motown but the volume of Jimi Hendrix or the Who. They literally turned this motherfucker out."[26] It's important to bear in mind, however, that when Sly and the Family Stone signed with Epic Records in 1967, "funk" had little meaning as a referent to musical genres. But during live performances, Stone proselytized the gospel of funk. Banks, who observed numerous Family Stone concerts during her six-year relationship with bass guitarist and singer Larry Graham, recalls: "When Sly was making us dance, he said, 'The fonk will do you no harm.'"[27] Indeed, Stone was the first major rhythm and blues artist to posit "funky" as a criterion of music making. In the liner notes to *Dance to the Music*, he foregrounds the concept. Praising Graham, Stone says that Graham's sound is as "funky as nine cans of wet magic shave."[28] Again, Stone isn't referring to any genre here; he's expressing an artistic ideal. For Stone, "funky" signified a superlative reference to Graham's innovative style that influenced legions of funk and jazz bass players thereafter.

Whereas James Brown is rightly credited for revolutionizing rhythmic structures in music, Stone expanded preexisting models of sensibility and expressive parameters in American popular music. As Vincent remarks, "James Brown cracked open the door to the funk—that's true. But Sly let everybody else in."[29] Stone projected the sort of irreverent, contrarian attitudes that typified funk. Prefiguring what Richard Iton subsequently termed the black fantastic, Vincent writes: "In so many ways, funk represented doing what you're *not* supposed to do. . . . 'funk is the conscious adoption of value systems previously considered antithetical to one's social position.'"[30] Stone outlined a gospel blues-hued aesthetics whose principles defied prevailing musical theories. He reportedly said, "My music is like the devil's music. . . ."[31] Paul Shaffer, longtime musical director for television host David Letterman, explains Stone's unconventionality in his recollection of a class on aesthetics at University of Toronto where the music professor, a jazz aficionado, characterized "Dance to the Music" as an example of crudeness and artlessness in music: "Listen to this record. . . . There's no accent on two and four . . . And after this guy has the nerve to put an accent on all four beats of the bar, he has the absolute—he *dares* to say to the audience, 'Dance to the music.'"[32] Stone personified musical audacity in his prime, and his audacity belied the musical knowledge that shaped his apparently eccentric approach to music making. Although he remained an ardent exponent of the spiritual ethos, Stone studied music theory at Vallejo Junior College, so his unconventionality exemplified the self-consciousness of blue funk.

Between 1967 and 1969, Sly and the Family Stone was at its apex. Stone's construction of funk was shaped largely by his experiences of growing up in the Bay Area, where there was a potpourri of live music. In addition to the conga rhythms of Latin American music and psychedelic hippie rock, many venues in San Francisco and Oakland featured jazz and blues, respectively. In San Francisco's Fillmore district, predominantly African American, the Black Hawk attracted such jazz musicians as Thelonious Monk, Ahmad Jamal, and Miles Davis, who all recorded live albums there. By contrast, Seventh Street in West Oakland was a "proving ground" for blues artists. Clubs such as Slim Jenkins' Place featured Big Joe Turner, Ray Charles, Aretha Franklin, Ike and Tina Turner, and Bobby "Blue" Bland—to name a few. The sonic heterogeneity of the region "created space for musical fusions not imagined or attempted anywhere else."[33] Based in the Haight-Ashbury district in San Francisco, where hippies listened to rock and protested against the Vietnam War, Stone was conversant with black working-class culture in Oakland, which is located across the bay. The ability to code switch proved invaluable to Stone who, like Jimi Hendrix, strived to achieve wide popularity across racial and ethnic lines while avoiding Motown's crossover formula. Stone fashioned an aesthetic that was considerably broader than soul music. As a songwriter, he blended music and social perspectives that resonated equally with white rock fans and black working-class youth who listened to Oakland's KDIA radio station, where Stone once worked as a disc jockey. Even Stone's flamboyant fashion—white, tasseled, psychedelic suits, purple vests, large silver chain, and space glasses—was envied by black musicians and street hustlers, and considered groovy by white rockers. For instance, Charlie Wilson, lead singer for the Gap Band, said that in addition to patterning some of his bodily movements after Stone, Wilson sported fur boots, tight knitted pants, and a knitted cap like the ones Stone wore on stage.[34] Meanwhile, Parliament-Funkadelic elaborated on the Family Stone's image by parodying the very notion of style, donning outrageous costumes that accentuated their portrayals of specific personas in Clinton's funk operas.

Interestingly enough, Stone's social vision of uniting disparate social groups was compatible with the contrariety of funk. In fact, Stone's multifaceted cultural literacy was indispensable to his approach to music making. Nourished by the Bay Area's diverse musical culture, Stone drew from a variety of musical styles, and exhilarated audiences wherever the Family Stone performed. Invariably, Stone's music induced an altered state of consciousness that became known as the funk. Gospel-style singing, steady, syncopated drum beats, percussive bass lines, blues- and rock-flavored guitars, percussive ensemble horn riffs, riff-like organ and keyboard accompaniments, jazz-style improvisations, individualized dances in sync with the music—all of these elements were staples of Sly and the Family Stone performances. When asked to explain his ability to captivate both white rock fans and black soul aficionados simultaneously, Stone said, "I think it has to do with songs that involve everybody and a message that involves everybody. Everybody wants to be happy, and the songs that we do are songs that I feel should make everybody happy, you know, and I think that's basically it."[35] Stone's statement is a distillation of his credo as an artist. As suggested in his reference to "message," many of the Family Stone's early recordings emphasize love and communal values.

Thus young Sylvester Stewart who aspired to be a preacher became the visionary artist Sly Stone who wrote invigorating songs for throngs of people from various backgrounds. Stone not only posited a visual image of racial and gender diversity with his band; he created rich textures of sounds with inspirational lyrics that amplified the funk. Doing so, he articulated a spiritually based liberationist ethos. Like the legions of gospel and blues musicians who helped shape his musical sensibilities, he functioned as a secular priest, that is, a preacher-poet whose ultimate mission was to affect audiences subcutaneously. When Sly and the Family Stone was at its best, in both live performances and studio recordings, the group imbued audiences with democratic impulses that were expressed in kinetic expression. In fact, Cynthia Robinson danced the Boogaloo in the early days of the Family Stone. Cornel West touches on this point when he says, "Sly created a music that became a place we can go and have a foretaste of that freedom of that democratic experience even though we couldn't live it on the ground, because white supremacy is still operated. . . . Let's say, you're living on the vanilla side of town, I'm on the chocolate side of town; we listen to Sly, we're in the same place."[36]

Stone's gospel of funk was the fruition of artistic experimentation that began on the group's debut album *A Whole New Thing* (1967). For most critics, the album never measured up to its title. And while it's true that Stone had yet to find his groove as a songwriter, the album hinted toward his search for a new sound; and even after the Family Stone's commercial success, some band members still considered the album a profound musical statement. When Freddie Stone was interviewed nearly fifty years later, in 2014, he said, "our first album was one of those things where Sly did what he wanted to do with it and not to say he didn't do it with the others, but that first album was great."[37] Much of the instrumentation sounds like dance-beat fluctuations between gospel, soul, jazz, and rhythm and blues. And though the band was still "honing [its] ability to communicate with each other (and Sly),"[38] *A*

Whole New Thing demonstrates that Stone's aesthetic stood at variance with conventions of the music industry. In contradistinction to the polished image of James Brown and the Famous Flames and the prissiness of the Supremes, Sly and the Family Stone projected sounds and images that foreshadowed the bohemianism of P-Funk, Betty Davis, Chaka Khan, the Bar-Kays, and many others. Clive Davis, President of CBS Records which owned Epic, was taken aback by Stone's image and attire. Davis recalls,

> I had asked to have lunch with Sly. I remember . . . feeling hesitant, but still it was my place to ask him because he had such vivid cos-tuming and that was a concern to me. Did he consider the fact that all the satin and platinum wigs could risk that he would not be taken seriously . . . which would have been injurious to his career as a new pioneering musician?[39]

Even David Henderson, an influential poet who co-founded the famous Umbra Writers' Workshop, stated, "I could not tell whether the brothers wore marcels or wigs but the effects were strikingly strange."[40] Thus *A Whole New Thing* reflected Stone's new model of experimental black popular music. The album documented Stone's departure from and implicit critique of prevailing models of pop, especially Motown. As KDIA Lucky 13 radio personality John Hardy says in his liner notes, Sly was "an entertainer who refused to restrict himself to time and temperature one-liners," which he defined as formulaic love songs with lines such as "'my baby loves me' or 'my baby doesn't love me,' as the case may be."[41]

Perhaps the most exemplary song that indicates Stone's musicianship during this period is "Turn Me Loose," especially live versions. A revision of Otis Redding's 1965 love song "I Can't Turn You Loose," Stone transposes Redding's ecstatic expression of romantic love into a praise song about the interrelationship between music and ecstatic sensations—hence the con-trasting pronouns in the respective titles. And where Redding's song has a mid-tempo beat, "Turn Me Loose" has a blistering, up-tempo gospel-like rhythm. However, the tune is overlaid with riff-percussive horn arrangements that typified rhythm and blues during the period. A sonic mélange including Stone's high-pitch falsetto onomatopoeia ("whoo!"), ensemble handclaps, and pithy intermittent guitar solos by Freddie Stone, "Turn Me Loose" is a musical depiction of listeners' thoughts and emotions when they're mesmer-ized by music. As such, the song is a testimony to the funk/spirit. Prefiguring Funkadelic's "(not just) Knee Deep" (1979), Stone personifies this pleasurable phenomenon as a woman ("She got my heart, I'm out of control") whose power compels him to lie down on the ground and confess conflicting emotions: his need to keep moving and his distaste for grooving. At the conclusion of the song, Stone breathes audibly to accentuate the effect, and says, "Whew!" Likewise, the previously unreleased instrumental "You Better Help Yourself" defies categorization even by contemporary standards. The composition sounds like a blue-streak hybrid of soul jazz and rhythm and blues seasoned with olfactory dance rhythms. The band routinely blended impromptu dancing with a riff-laden medleys that allowed each artist to improvise. Saxophonist Jerry Martini remembers, "We did a thing called jazz riffs that blew people's minds—an eight minute song of all these different riffs that we linked together."[42]

Nonetheless, few people bought *A Whole New Thing*, and Stone re-examined his approach shortly after a meeting with CBS Records executives, who urged him to be more conscious of radio playlists in his songwriting.[43] Davis reportedly gave him a few recordings and said, "This is what you should listen to."[44] Not surprisingly, Stone repudiated what he interpreted as an infringement on his artistic freedom; however, the meeting was nonetheless momentous. Martini recalls, "[Sly] looked at me and said, 'Okay, I'll give them something.'"[45] For Stone, the next album, *Dance To The Music* (1968), represented a compromise that enabled him to present his ideas in a more accessible format—no small feat given the dictates of the music industry and whimsical tastes of record buyers. As Dalton Anthony cogently observes, "The cornerstone of Sly's genius . . . was his ability to organize the untamed elements that were seeping out as alternatives to . . . commercial sounds into a product that was commodifiable without losing its rugged honesty and emotional integrity."[46] Indeed, the tension between the commercial demands of the record industry and Stone's concern for "honesty and emotional integrity," that is, expressing the funk/spirit became a source of disillusionment and a deciding factor in his decision to ultimately leave the music scene in the 1970s.

Nonetheless, Stone's creative juices flowed during this early period. He collaborated extensively with other band members, tapping into the communal values that characterized the participatory nature of church performances he witnessed as a child. So instead of being dictatorial, Stone sought input from members of the group. As trailblazing funk bassist Larry Graham recollects:

> Sly was the songwriter, but part of his genius, in addition to the
> great songs he created, is [that] he allowed each player, especially the

rhythm section . . . to contribute what we do. He didn't try to make me play the way he might play a bass line or try to make Freddie play a guitar the way he would play a guitar line, cause he played guitar as well—Sly did. But he let us contribute what we would do. Same thing with Greg Errico with some of those great beats like "Dance to the Music" and things like that. [Sly] would write the songs, but he let us contribute our style of playing whatever bass line, the drum line, or guitar line we'd come up with. . . . We were never credited as writers, but we did get a chance to contribute.[47]

Similarly, drummer Greg Errico remembers debating Stone: "Sly and I would sometimes clash and argue if one of us felt strongly about something. Sometimes I would lose and sometimes he would lose [*laughs*]. Therein lies the honesty of the music."[48] Errico's statement is telling. Since "funk" signifies honesty, his comment about Stone's method of music making demonstrates why so many young musicians envisioned his music as the quintessence of funk aesthetics. Stone's democratic approach was a welcome departure from the conventional rhythm and blues format in which soul singers stood exclusively in the limelight. Stone's egalitarianism established an important precedent for funk bands. As Vincent points out, Parliament-Funkadelic, Earth, Wind & Fire, Labelle, the Ohio Players, Rufus, War, and many other funk bands were collectives that de-emphasized individual stardom in the 1970s.[49]

In "Dance to the Music," the Family Stone not only boasts about its array of musical sounds but the band's affective power as well. For the first time on record, Graham can be heard using two of his innovations: the fuzzbox and his slap-bass technique, which occurs in the first few notes of the song. The fuzzbox is a form of technology that had been popularized by rock groups like the Beatles. Fuzz enabled Graham to amplify the "bottom" sound, and thereby administer the funk in full effect. As Clinton recollects, "I had never heard bass like this before, and one of our bass players, Billy Bass Nelson, would have eight cabinets, so I knew what bass sounded like! Larry Graham was loud as hell!"[50] If the criterion for commercial success was dance floor activation, Sly and the Family Stone was uniquely qualified. Using an approach typically associated with jazz combos, Stone showcased everyone in the band except Rose with a brief solo. In fact, Stone himself doesn't sing until midway through the song. Instead, Freddie and Graham display their singing and playing talents. More fundamentally, though, the success of "Dance to the Music" marked a pivotal moment in black music making. Earlier I mentioned

Brown's rhythmic innovations, but predilections for percussive concepts of music making were widespread among funk artists, and Stone's selection of Graham demonstrates his prescience in this regard. Graham has described his now famous technique as "kinda like playing drums on bass."[51] His style became a prerequisite for would-be funk and jazz bass players. But before Sly and the Family Stone became a household name in American culture, few people outside the Bay Area recognized Graham's name, and even local musicians weren't always sold on his talent. For instance, Robinson admitted that she didn't immediately recognize Graham's potential the first time she saw him play: "Sly said, 'What do you think of this guy?' And I thought nothing special. But Syl always had another ear and another eye."[52]

Graham's impact on aspiring funk and jazz bass players is immeasurable. As pianist and musicologist Tammy Kernodle explains, the electric bass was indispensable to funk because it "articulat[ed] . . . the riff or melodic idea that all of the other instruments either responded to or worked with to achieve rhythmic symmetry."[53] But before 1968, many musicians were reluctant to play bass because it connoted anonymity. Alan Leeds, who worked as a tour manager for James Brown and Prince, recollects, "Bass had been the afterthought [of rhythm and blues]. I mean, you had to have a bass player to give you the bottom, and he was always this anonymous guy who kinda stood like a wooden whatever in the background just playing the changes."[54] In fact, Graham initially avoided playing bass himself: "I wanted to be the out-front lead guitar player."[55] But ironically, albeit serendipitously, it was precisely because Graham was set on playing guitar that he developed his innovative technique.

Like Stone and scores of black musicians, Graham was born in a musical family. After starting out as a tap dancer at age five, he began playing piano during preadolescence, and played drums, clarinet, and saxophone in secondary school. At age eleven his father, Larry Graham Sr., gave him his first guitar; and when he reached fifteen, he began performing in Bay Area clubs with his mother, Dell Graham, a well-known singer and pianist, and drummer Ruben Kerr who was in Graham's first band. At some point, Graham and his mother began working in a club that had an organ, which intrigued Graham. So he "played the bass pedals and the guitar at the same time." But eventually the organ broke down and, since Graham had developed an affinity for the "bottom," he rented a bass temporarily to compensate for the void. He didn't even study bass players. And when he and Dell began working without Kerr, he was troubled by the lack of percussion. Consequently, he "thump[ed] the strings to make up for not having a bass drum, and pluck[ed] the strings because [he] didn't have that snare drum backbeat."[56] And though Graham wasn't especially excited about his style,[57] younger musicians thought differently. Marcus Miller, a two-time Grammy Award winner known primarily as a bassist who "was the last primary collaborator of jazz legend Miles Davis," offers an insightful perspective in his recollection:

> When I began playing the bass in the 1970s in New York, everyone played the bass pretty much based on James Jamerson's style. James Jamerson was the bass player who played for Motown. Then all of a sudden we heard Larry Graham . . . and he wasn't playing with the traditional bass guitar sound. He was thumping it and hitting it with his thumb and plucking it. And we were like, "Whoa, what is that, man?" You know; and like, everyone that I knew—every bass player was like, "Man, I gotta learn how to do that." Cause that's the coolest sound, especially to a young ear. You know what I mean? Because it was very dynamic: boom, bap! You know, it really got your atten-tion. So, uh, I was like everybody else . . . Larry Graham was such a huge influence. . . . I think he influenced a lotta bass players. I think Stanley Clarke was influenced by Larry Graham. Bootsy [Collins] was influenced by Larry Graham, and his personality was so huge, we all got swept up.[58]

Miller's allusions to James Jamerson and Graham indicate the transition from soul to funk. *Dance to the Music* galvanized musicians and fans alike in disparate enclaves of rock, jazz, and rhythm and blues. The album became the de facto "new thing" for the Family Stone, and established Stone as a visionary songwriter who wrote poetic lyrics that resonated with joy and social consciousness. The cataclysmic upheavals created by the Vietnam War and the Civil Rights Movement sparked a growing awareness of societal contradictions. But while activists expressed their opposition to variants of bourgeois ideology and related public policies, Stone personified the promise of social change. Through a rare combination of poetic lyrics, sonorous singing, psychedelic fashion, freestyle dancing, and magnificent musician-ship, Sly and the Family Stone soothed listeners' souls. The band's aesthetic exemplified the cultural values and styles of life that Stone advocated in his songwriting. In the process, he sharpened his thinking as a preacher-poet, while crafting a foundation for funk as a liberating dance-beat aesthetic that reflected a spiritual ethos.

Like many funk songs, the meaning of "Dance to the Music" is synonymous with its ecstatic effects. The entire song exemplifies irresistible funk. Shortly before Stone sent the recording to Epic executives for its release, he made an ostensibly mundane edit that contributed immensely to the song's appeal. Robinson's raucous chant ("Get on up and dance to the music") initially occurred in the middle of the song, but Stone shifted her lines to the beginning. Another notable alteration occurred fortuitously. During a rehearsal, Stone forgot to sing his part, so he extemporized with onomatopoeia. "The next time it would come around," recalls Robinson, "Freddie would fall in and do it in harmony, and then Larry would fall in with his harmony part. The next group of songs that Syl wrote, he added those 'boom booms' as part of the song."[59] Thus "Dance to the Music" features Sly, Freddie, and Graham scat-singing choruses of neo doo-wop onomatopoeia (boom-boom, doom-doom, boom-boom-boom) with staccato interjections of syllabic improvisation accompanied by Rose Stone's rhythmic tambourine. Then the trio of singers harmonize the song's title several times—all while Freddie riffs on guitar, Graham funks on the bass, and Errico drops stank bombs into the beat.

"Dance to the Music" celebrates and activates the medicinal qualities of the funk principle. Stone revises the sacred-profane dialectic in conventional Christian philosophy, transforming the heathen-holy opposition into a conflict concerning the politics of pleasure: hipness versus unhipness. The tension between the conflicting sensibilities is accentuated when Robinson shouts in her blues-tinged timbre: "All the squares go home!" Though realities of race and generational division are factored into this opposition, Stone conceptualized the chasm primarily in terms of contrasting notions of morality and aesthetics. And since he considered style as a reflection of ethos and intellect, there are important implications associated with his critique of the "squares." Stone's vision is all-embracing: myriad shapes, shades, and hues of soulful people in cooperative collectives and coalitions. Such people were believers in intrinsic values of spiritual love, psychosomatic joy, social awareness, emotional honesty, and idiosyncratic expression. By contrast, he associated soulless people with proscription, parochialism, and so forth.

Even so, Stone was hardly immune to contradictions himself. Despite his rebellious personality and revolutionary ideas about music making, his thoughts about race-related issues tend to reflect a bourgeois ideology of self-help and uplift advocated by many black conservatives.[60] At times, he conceptualized politics in reductive terms. Stone abhorred black radicalism, singing, "Don't burn baby, burn," and urged youth to "learn" as if

enlightenment and highly developed skill sets preclude the necessity to address problems created by inequities of systemic wealth and power. In this
respect, Stone subscribed to a politics of respectability. His idea of self-help
was closer to Father Divine's philosophy than Malcolm X's sermons on self-
determination for black people. Stone's public stances on racial matters and
the interracial composition of his band probably enhanced his crossover
appeal to white rockers.

As a songwriter, Stone tended to shun political views of black radicals.
Instead, he focused on commonplace themes, reinterpreting them in ways
that resonated with a broad spectrum of people. Stone's lyrics were relatively
moderate compared to songwriters like Curtis Mayfield, but his songs were
so effusive that radicals interpreted them as affirmations of their objectives.
Since he represented social crises as a moral conflict between funky people
and squares, activists recognized an analogy that described their political
conflicts with police. Consequently, even though Stone's political views were
nearly antithetical to Huey P. Newton's philosophy of revolutionary nationalism, the cadre of the Black Panther Party for Self-Defense in Oakland found
the Family Stone's recordings effective as recruiting measures. In 1970, for
instance, a multi-racial band known as the Freedom Messengers performed
a rendition of "Dance to the Music" at a Black Panther Party rally at Merritt
College. Where Robinson chanted to urge listeners to get up and dance,
"Sister Candace" chanted, "Hey, get up! And make revolution / Get on up!
And make revolution!"[61] to promote the Panthers' political philosophy. Stone's
staunch opposition to political uprisings notwithstanding, the resistive energy of black power lent significant impetus to the defiant carefree attitude
that characterized funk.

FUNKIN' THE BLUES

In the 1960s the Black Power Movement generated a heightened sense of
cultural awareness, and young black dancers and musicians transfigured
the word "funky" into an aesthetic metaphor that not only encompassed
music but also dancing (e.g., Funky Broadway, Funky Four Corners), literature, and visual art. As such, funkiness became synonymous with the word
"fly" (read: dope, cool, [super]fly, etc.). By contrast, many young African
Americans considered blues outdated. Cultural nationalists such as Maulana
Karenga and Haki Madhubuti condemned the blues as reactionary. Yet blues
principles were nearly as significant to Stone as they were to John Coltrane,

the patron saint of black cultural nationalism. Although the Family Stone's studio recordings achieved wide popularity on the soul and pop charts, early performances demonstrate that the band was fundamentally a rhythm and blues band. Indeed, recordings tend to obscure the extent of the influence of blues on the group. But if we recall Shider's statement that funk encompasses blues, this shouldn't be surprising. As mentioned earlier, Stone acknowledged his debt to the blues, but Robinson also had an extensive blues background. She states, "I used to play with Jimmy McCracklin and Lowell Fulson. I used to hear all these guys on 78s at my mother's [house] when I was a teenager. When my friends came in with these 45s, I said I didn't even want to hear about it. . . . I used to daydream that I was onstage playing . . . with B.B. King and I'm playing with Lowell Fulson, with Jimmy McCracklin. And I literally ended up being in a band that backed them up at different clubs."[62]

Robinson's distinction between 78s and 45s is notable. During a period when singers such as Sam Cooke, Etta James, and Solomon Burke were favorites among young black music fans, she listened closely to blues musicians, which enabled her to become a pioneering artist as a female instrumentalist in rhythm and blues. Her blues-inflected approach is evident in the live recording of the Family Stone's rendition of "St. James Infirmary" at the Fillmore East in 1968. Recorded by Louis Armstrong and Cassandra Wilson in 1928 and 2010 respectively, "St. James Infirmary" is an instrumental slow jam that showcases Robinson's blues-tinged trumpet. An exquisite dancer, she embellished her live solos with extemporized choreographs and infused so much stank into her horn that audience members were compelled to shout: "Play!" At the outset of "St. James Infirmary," Robinson riffs staccato-style while Stone comps on the organ intermittently. Then she begins her solo, playing with a mute and growling magnificently. Like the brass blues artists she studied assiduously, Robinson "growls" and simulates slurs and wah-wah blues cries that evoke images of belly rub dancers in southern juke joints and soft-shoe dancers in backstreet city dives in the early twentieth century. Her sound is reminiscent of blues musicians like James "Bubber" Miley and Oran "Hot Lips" Page, who played trumpet for bandleaders Duke Ellington and Count Basie, respectively. Henderson echoes this point in his review of the band's performance at the Electric Circus in New York in 1967. He states, "In Sly's tunes I hear James Johnson, Jelly Roll Morton, and some James Cleveland too. Rural black lands and the southern crossings of freight trains, the transcended peoples of Africa tuning their symphony banjos of Euro-America to the pitch of their voice, their rap. Voices like instruments, instruments like voices."[63]

Henderson's reference to the voice-instrument dynamic recalls our discussion of blues aesthetics in chapter 2. His characterization of Robinson's style and sound is unmistakably blues-inflected: "She blows a *hot lip* trumpet (the only female player of trumpet I've seen in any group) and comes forth with a sensual gutsy blues wail as well."[64] Note the imagery here. Henderson's term "hot lip" is an allusion to "Hot Lips" Page and therefore a notable tribute to Robinson's musicianship. But his underlining this approach in his overall discussion of the band also demonstrates the centrality of blues aesthetics in Stone's conceptualization of funk. Midway through the performance of "St. James Infirmary," the tempo changes. The rhythm is decidedly upbeat, and Errico plays a powerful drum solo, igniting a veritable fire under the band. Robinson rides on top of the energy, playing trumpet without the mute. And after a brief period, the band slows the tempo again, and Robinson returns to her bluesy sound on the mute. In the final minute of the song, the band shifts fleetingly into a modern jazz mode in which Graham picks nimble licks on bass guitar as the band closes out the tune.

Shortly before her death, Robinson was asked why the Family Stone imparted a more "gospel/blue" sound during live performances than in studio recordings. She replied, "We were free to adlib things. . . . Sly would cut things off in a different way than the real recordings; he'd just stop it and go into something else."[65] Robinson's comment is intriguing. While implying that record executives tended to excise blues from Epic's marketing strategy, she also suggests that Stone and his executives had contrasting views toward blues, and that the festive atmosphere of live performances lent him more latitude to explore "gospel/blue" elements of sound. Stone's tendency to "adlib" the blues is especially noticeable in the Family Stone's live performance of "We Love All (Freedom)." Recorded in the studio as "We Love All" in 1967, the song was curiously excised from *Dance to the Music* when it was initially released. And though the studio recording is certainly memorable, the live version titled "We Love All (Freedom)" is one of the most notable recordings in the Family Stone songbook. The performance not only demonstrates the emotive power the band exuded at its zenith; it also reflects the group's versatility and highlights Stone's spirituality as a songwriter. The premise of the song is reminiscent of the biblical concept of loving thine enemies. As such, "We Love All (Freedom)" is a funkified expression of peaceful coexistence, a dynamic expression of Stone's belief that love is the most effective antidote for resolving societal conflicts. Of course, the idea of loving our antagonists might strike many people as incredibly naïve, certainly as paradoxical as black beauty in America. However, as Martin Luther King demonstrated in his often neglected speeches against the Vietnam War in 1967 and 1968, loving and contesting one's political opponents aren't mutually exclusive.

Similarly, "We Love All (Freedom)" balances the egalitarian principles of love against the normative tendency in the United States to (mis)interpret cultural differences in Manichean terms, especially since either/or logic typically informs scapegoating and other forms of objectification. At its core, "We Love All (Freedom)" is a secular distillation of black gospel love. Stone attempts to defuse racial discord by suggesting that prejudices fluctuate according to people's biases. Singing beautifully in tenor, he intones, "People don't like what they don't understand." He accentuates "don't," and elongates "understand," while promoting universal love as a corrective value before Freddie and Graham join Sly, singing the hook ensemble: "We love *all* y'all," underscoring the word "all" in their individual phrasings of the line that delivers the song's fundamental message: that love requires us to embrace the good with the bad. Of course, this perspective reflects the contrariety of funk aesthetics. Stone gives a nod to the fuzz (i.e., police) and their weapons, and expresses love for a litany of other authority figures (e.g., judges and colonels) and functionaries such as parking meter operators. All these figures symbolize repression. The criminal justice system and military establishment were reviled by black activists and anti–Vietnam War protesters alike, and Stone's allusion to meter operators illustrates how repressive power is often executed and normalized as mundane aspects of life. Thus Stone alludes to small-town restrictions and old ladies' vans.

Clearly, Stone had a unique perspective, especially in this early period before drugs and disillusionment sapped his creative energies. Writing with the concision of poets, he demonstrates a lucid understanding of the dynamics of repression, particularly the roles of institutions and individuals in executing horrendous policies. But despite the naïveté of his communal vision of America and his belief that love, ipso facto, could counteract institutional power, Stone never endorsed the police or the sanctity of the state. He simply disagreed with the notion that outright rebellion was an effective solution to social problems. He represents police officers as fellow human beings who coexist in civil society, and he believed that love shouldn't be predicated on ideological precepts. Besides, as a secular priest, he may have presumed that sectors of the flock would always evince waywardness, and that he needed to tailor his song-sermons more effectively. In order to sing a gospel of love, Stone had to feel it himself—an all-embracing love: good, bad, ugly. He uses melisma when he sings the word "love" and elongates the word "all" to emphasize his conviction and thus intensify the emotional effect: "We love *all* / y'all." The phrase epitomizes Afro-Christian morality, particularly the somewhat controversial tenet, in many black enclaves, of expressing genuine compassion for white Americans who perpetrate evils against African Americans. While Stone was firmly positioned in the glitz and glamour of the entertainment industry, his gospel-blue vision of love is nonetheless commensurate with Audre Lorde's analysis of societal discord: "It is not our differences that divide us. It is our inability to recognize, accept, and celebrate those differences."[66]

The next section of "We Love All (Freedom)" commences after Stone sings "We," and Freddie and Graham sing the word "all." Robinson and saxophonist Jerry Martini create a brief horn ensemble before Stone repeats the hook twice, the background singing fades out, and Freddie commences one of the nastiest riffs in the history of funk. His electric guitar riff is accented by Robinson's call-and-response interjections on trumpet, and provides the melodic foundation of the song. Thus, when Stone chimes in on vocals the affective resonance that the Stone brothers create is nearly indescribable. Such is the enthrallment of the Stone brothers' funk that the lyrics seem nearly illegible—not because Stone's singing is indecipherable but because the combination of his singing with Freddie's guitar licks produces such an exhilarating sound that one is inclined to submit to the pleasure of the funk. Indeed, ascertaining the specificity of the lyrics requires considerably attentive listening. Given the premise of the song, it's plausible that the tingling *feelings* the Stone brothers generate accrue from tonal semantics whereby meaning—in this case, universal love—is conveyed primarily through affect. In other words, the Stones' expression of love is the funk that listeners experience. Once people come down from their natural highs, so to speak, and focus on the meanings, it's even more evident that "We Love All (Freedom)" testifies to the power of love.

The song gets even funkier when it becomes an instrumental. Graham anchors the ensemble, riffing on bass while Errico plays a staccato version of the riff on drums. The Family Stone is playing a new style of finger-snap music that inspired jazz musicians like Miles Davis and many others to create a new genre of music that became known as jazz funk. Stone and sister Rose add color on organ and keyboards, respectively, and both Freddie and Graham embark on freestyle solos. Yet shortly after the group settles into a soulful groove, Stone "adlibs" and launches into a downhome blues on harmonica. Though brief, his solo is significant. He plays a mean, howling, stank-infested blues, accentuated by Errico and Graham who add light touches of color on drums and guitar, respectively, before the rest of the band chimes in to close out the song.

Yet Stone's most daring blues experiment was recorded in the studio. "Sex Machine," a groove-oriented blues-rock instrumental that extends for nearly fourteen minutes, appeared on Sly and the Family Stone's album *Stand!* (1969). Stone plays a Farfisa organ on the tune, but he used some sort of additional contraption to make it sound more like a Hammond B-3, the coveted instrument in traditional black gospel music. Suitably titled, the song is a tonal illustration of erotica, but there are conflicting if fairly similar explanations of Stone's approach. One reviewer, Alec Dubro, stated in *Rolling Stone* that Stone connected a wah-wah pedal to a microphone, and scatted into it. By contrast, British music critic Barney Hoskyns, who wrote the liner notes to a 2006 reissue of *Stand!*, says that Stone, who also plays rhythm guitar on the tune, put a microphone in his mouth to approximate the sound of a harmonica. Because of the numerous slurp-sounds in the solo, the latter method seems more likely. But either way, Stone's voice-instrument approach is a variation of a long line of blues-oriented instrumentalists. As we observed in chapter two, legions of musicians, including Jimi Hendrix and lesser-known musicians like Slam Stewart used variations of this approach. Stewart created distinctive sounds by simultaneously humming and playing his acoustic bass with a bow. He even simulated laughter in his composition "Laff, Sam, Laff" (1945). Like his predecessors, Stone uses his body as his primary instrument in "Sex Machine," which means that his harmonica functioned as a technological appendage. Amiri Baraka made a similar point in his characterization of Charlie Parker's technique: "Parker . . . literally imitate[d] the human voice with his cries, swoops, squawks, and slurs . . . Parker did not admit that there was any separation between himself and the agent he had chosen as his means of self-expression."[67]

But while Stone elaborated on blues principles, he prefigured a significant development in funk. His harmonica solo in "Sex Machine" is probably best described as an early version of a talk box, foreshadowing the pioneering efforts of Stevie Wonder and Roger Troutman who used the talk box in the 1970s, paving the way for hip hop artists like T-Pain and Kanye West. "Sex Machine" is thus popular avant-garde music. In its stylistic experimentation and expert musicianship, including Freddie Stone's bluesy improvised solo on guitar and Rose Stone's gospel-style tambourine playing, "Sex Machine" is yet another realization of the Family Stone's whole new thing. The tune exudes the deliciously licentious sensuality of a psychedelic shack. Crammed with guitar vamps, keyboard accents, and dance-beat-oriented drumming, "Sex Machine" is a variegated collage of sound, a pulsating sound painting of the pleasure principle. Stone's electronic, pre-futuristic, wah-wah scat vocals are sonic depictions of an (almost) anything-goes freakish sensibility that defies codes and customs of constructed normality.

"Sex Machine," then, emblematizes funk aesthetics in its thematic import as well—which is to say, the tune exudes the attitudinal unruliness that blues bequeathed to funk. Of course, most contemporary readers conceptualize music as lyrics; but even though "Sex Machine" is wordless, it signifies the delights of corporeal pleasure in a manner that made the blues so controversial. If we briefly recall the proscription of "funk" and its taboo related to its slant rhyme "fuck," "Sex Machine" highlights the denotative relationship between the f-words, and flouts social conventions designed to repress such expression in the process. Essentially, Stone used a musical style that exemplified the former term in order to represent human experiences referenced in the latter—without singing a word. Such irony is the very stuff of the blues. Even the closing passage of the song suggests coitus. Errico plays his drum solo at an increasingly slower pace until he drums the very last lick, suggesting orgasm. And for a finale, the musicians laugh immediately afterwards, and issue an anonymous statement: "We blew your mind."[68]

THE GOSPEL OF FUNK

When Mark Anthony Neal characterizes "Sing a Simple Song" (1968) as "an unreconstructed piece of funk,"[69] he suggests that the song generates a level of ecstasy that approximates black congregants' experiences in Pentecostal churches. Singer Marva Whitney's commentary affirms and contextualizes Neal's observation. Dubbed Soul Sister #1 by James Brown, Whitney performed in Brown's band from 1967 to 1969, and grew up singing in the Church of God in Christ in Kansas City before she sang rhythm and blues. Whitney said, "Church [music] is about reaching the soul of a person and letting them feel free and heal from all the negativity. You're able to go within your inner self and feel good *if only for a moment.* And if I haven't done that for my audience, I don't feel too good."[70] Note Whitney's phrase "only for a moment." Her description of the basic function, objective, and criterion of sanctified music is nearly identical to a line that conveys the meaning of "Sing A Simple Song"—that music, as Olly Wilson puts it, should demonstrate "a belief in the affective power of music, a view of music as a force that is capable of making something happen."[71] Thus "Sing a Simple Song" is a "worldly" song that channels the spirituality in Stone's gospel of funk. For George Clinton, "Sing a Simple Song" was a jaw-dropping experience: "It was the funkiest thing I had ever heard in my life, from Motown, to James Brown, to the Beatles."[72] Needless to say, Clinton's statement is high praise given his allusions to Brown and the Beatles, not to mention his own stature as a funkmaster.

Still, relatively few scholars have examined "Sing a Simple Song" in detail. That the lyrics seem nonsensical and nonconsequential is a possible explanation. Nonetheless, the song is quite meaningful. Considering Stone's belief that music has healing qualities, perhaps no other song in his songbook reflects his philosophy of music making more clearly than this recording. The fact that the lyrics *are* apparently meaningless is part of the point—to demonstrate the potential to engender emotional release. Exemplifying Teresa Reed's notion of the holy profane, Stone's narrative resembles the Scriptures so closely that it paraphrases the book of Samuel: When the evil spirit is present, the harpist "shall play with his hand, and thou shalt be well."[73] A fanciful story composed in first person, "Sing a Simple Song" is replete with colorful choruses and contrasting solos. At its core, though, the song engages the immediacy of agency through the medium of music.

Robinson opens the song by repeating the title, chant-singing the words as an infectious directive; then Rose, in one of her few solos, sings the word "yeah" eight times in descending notes. Beginning in high soprano, she ends with a timbre that can only be described as pure funk. The theme of medicinal music recurs throughout the song. Various members of the band sing solfege syllables (do rey me fah soh lah ti do), but their voices transform the syllables into onomatopoeic phrases. The personae (sung by Graham, Freddie, and Sly) are gripped with confusion, standing on the brink of despair. Consequently, they sleepwalk and talk in their sleep. As a rejoinder to their resignation—what Robert Johnson had called the blues and Clinton later called "the blahs"—Stone posits funky music as a pyrotechnic antidote. "Sing a Simple Song" is a brilliant example of self-reflexivity—its meaning and effect are synonymous. In other words, the band renders the musical therapy that Stone invokes in his lyrics. As in the Sanctified church, "Sing a Simple Song" not only invites a participatory atmosphere; it induces kinetic participation, which in turn facilitates a pleasurable intervention. Stone doesn't represent dance as a panacea. He offers it as temporary respite—a natural high to soothe the pain "for a little while," just as Whitney describes "Church [music]." Stone's falsetto screams illustrate the joy of the funk/spirit while urging people to partake in it. But his falsetto can also be interpreted figuratively as tonal expressions that call on groove-oriented people to resist resignation by asserting themselves as agents of the holy profane.

In "Thank You (Falettinme Be Mice Elf Agin)," Stone revisits the holy profane, while simultaneously exemplifying funk's propensity for multiple significations. For instance, the song expresses gratitude to fans and family members for supporting the young musicians. The persona cites several Family Stone hit recordings: "Dance to the Music," "Sing a Simple Song," and "Everyday People." Then he alludes to his parents' love and support, specifically his mother's joy and his father's encouragement and instruction regarding the value of persistence. But as in "Dance to the Music," the central conflict involves groove-oriented people versus haters of the groove. In "Thank You," hipness is synonymous with morality, that is, a live-and-let-live sensibility. The lack of hipness is therefore associated with evil and intolerance. As such, Stone's rhetorical strategy prefigures the conflict in Parliament's song "Flash Light" (1977). In "Thank You," prudishness is personified as a devil-policeman who is defeated by the persona-poet in a physical confrontation that culminates in a shooting: "Lookin' at the devil grinnin' at his gun." Released as a hit single in 1969, "Thank You" is an extended vamp that reflects the tenor of its time. The devil figure is a derisive rebuke of America's cultural establishment. Thus, the word "lettin[g]" in the title-hook is tongue in cheek. That is, the persona's personality is a character that refuses to bow down. Rather than "lettin[g]" the devil-policeman grant him agency, he *assumes* power by confronting this figure and, hence, everything he symbolizes (e.g., violence, hypocrisy, and greed) victoriously. Later in the song, Stone sings "thank you" ironically again. After he portrays oligarchical figures as thoroughly pretentious (stiff collars, meaningless chit chatter), the persona extricates himself from the gathering: "Thank you for the party / but I could never stay." The stuffy atmosphere inhibits the blue funk sensibility that "Thank You" reflects and reaffirms.

"Thank You" is also reminiscent of "Dance to the Music" in the way it represents political differences in terms of mindsets and values rather than skin color and ethnicities. In the years following Stone's departure from the music world, conflicting ideals of American culture have intensified into dichotomies: urban-rural, male-female, white-nonwhite, rich-poor, queer-straight, etc. Nonetheless, the spiritual import of "Thank You" resonated with multiple communities in Stone's figurative sky-temple. As Neal shrewdly points out, one of Stone's unique abilities as a songwriter was his ability "to create a context for spiritual transcendence without . . . responding to specific political realities."[74] Stone's avoidance of specific racial experiences enabled him to minister to large numbers of people who probably had conflicting views on racial and economic issues. But since the spirit of rebellion pulsated through various sectors of American youth and activism, the song's anti-authoritarian theme and imagery were sufficiently intelligible and ambiguous for disparate groups of listeners to interpret "Thank You" as a reaffirmation of their various viewpoints. While Vietnam War protesters could interpret the song as a poetic rendering of their experiences with police officers, so could the Black Panthers. Indeed, it's difficult to ignore the revolutionary implications of Stone's song given the close proximity between his base in San Francisco and the Panthers' headquarters across the Bay in Oakland, where Huey P. Newton, Bobby Seale, and Elaine Brown were cultural heroes for multitudes of black youth.[75] Although Stone was staunchly opposed to the Panthers' political philosophy of revolutionary nationalism, his vision wasn't altogether dissimilar from the Panthers' Marxist-inspired dreams of a liberated future characterized by multiethnic egalitarianism. In fact, the cultural diversity for which Stone has been lauded was precisely what Chairman Fred Hampton had in mind when he founded the Rainbow Coalition. The contrast between Stone and the Panthers was their conflicting beliefs about appropriate methods to achieve a liberated future. Yet Stone's music was rebellious despite his conservatism because he was committed to the funk and unvarnished truth.[76] For instance, Stone's political allegory foreshadowed the conflicts between Black Lives Matter activists and police officers regardless of his intentions.

Apart from the political implications, "Thank You" proved to be a pivotal recording in musical history. Whereas "Dance to the Music" introduced Graham's slap-bass technique and his use of the fuzzbox, "Thank You" features Graham thumping *and* plucking his bass. Stellar musicians took notice, including pianist Herbie Hancock. A child prodigy who performed with the Chicago Symphony Orchestra as a preadolescent, Hancock rose to fame in jazz as a member of Miles Davis's band in the mid-1960s. Hancock was still only twenty-nine years old when "Thank You" was released in 1969, but he was undecided about the direction of his music. His own jazz sextet had "reached its peak," and he wanted to play music that was "more spiritual," "more earthy," and "more grounded," but he couldn't pinpoint the sound that conveyed these qualities. And since terms like "spiritual," "earthy," and "grounded" often referenced a heightened degree of funkiness, there were racial stigmas associated with the style Hancock wanted to play. As it happens, he realized that he had internalized these stereotypes. Then one day he began to chant; and as he did so, he thought about "Thank You." Hancock recalls, "I was hearing ["Thank You (falettin me be mice elf again)"] over and over again. Then I had this mental image of me playing in Sly's band playing something funky like that. Then the next image . . . was about my own band

SLY STONE AND THE GOSPEL OF FUNK

playing in Sly Stone's musical direction. My unconscious reaction was, 'No, I don't want to do that.'"[77] That such a sensitive artist as Hancock held reservations about the funk demonstrates the depth with which racial stigmas were ingrained. His comments help explain why so few writers have devoted critical attention to funk music. Of course, Hancock eventually came to terms with his contradictions. Stone's music inspired Hancock to experiment with funk, which led to his landmark album *Head Hunters* (1973). Listed as one of the 500 greatest albums of all time by *Rolling Stone* magazine, *Head Hunters* established him as a trendsetter in the new genre of jazz-funk. As a token of gratitude, Hancock composed "Sly" and included the tune on *Head Hunters* as his tribute to Stone.

In 1969 Stone was at the apex of his career. He was a preacher-poet who offered spiritual uplift to throngs of people by delivering messages through music with political overtones. Few musicians before or after Stone have achieved such critical acclaim and wide popularity while recording songs of social awareness. In the title track of the Family Stone's album *Stand!* (1969), Stone addresses freedom, agency, and justice. The sermonic overtones are unmistakable: "There's a permanent crease in your right and wrong." The precision and concision of Stone's imagery in "Stand!" reflect his poetic talents as a songwriter. His central method was using biblical imagery. The image of a teetering giant next to a stately midget, for instance, is reminiscent of David and Goliath. Also, Stone testifies to the importance of truth and evokes the Crucifixion when he alludes to bearing the cross. He sings, "It's the truth that the truth makes them so uptight." Stone's repetition of "truth," coupled with the alliteration of /t/ sounds in "uptight," epitomizes the music inherent in poetic language. But the line is also notable for its political acumen. The social contract between citizens and the state is based, by and large, on morality. Insofar as deceit contributes to corruption, truth functions as a bulwark against wrongdoing. Thus people intent on deceit get "uptight" when truth is exposed.

What is intriguing about "Stand!" is that Stone's sermonizing didn't alienate his fans. Such didacticism might have fallen flat in the hands of most songwriters. But the instrumentation and Stone's voice are so invigorating that the lyrics blend with the melodies and rhythms. Perhaps more than any other song, "Stand!" reflects Stone's social vision. The song is a poetic sketch of a new American ideal, a dream deferred of a world without divisions of race, class, creed, gender, or sexuality. And while it's easy to criticize Stone's utopian vision, the song performs a fundamental function of art: to imagine points of view and styles of life that haven't been normalized, much less codified. For instance, Stone and reggae legend Bob Marley were worlds apart ideologically, but his advocacy for integrity prefigured Marley's political anthem "Get Up, Stand Up" (1973). Stone's repetition enhanced the affective power of the song by accentuating the music of his lyrics. Similar to riffing in the blues tradition, the repetition of the word "stand" is a poetic device commonly found in black sermons, blues songs, and blues poems.

But riffing is also a mnemonic device that serves an epistemological purpose. To the extent that repetition induces people to listen more closely, it facilitates a greater "sense of understanding through memory."[78] Gerald Davis's analysis of the poetics of black sermons is helpful here. According to Davis, "The power of the performance moves beyond the walls of the auditorium. . . . As in church, the spiritual essence . . . of the performance may well be carried into the days and weeks following the actual performance as those who experienced [it], or those who have reports of [it], discuss it, evaluate it, and relive it."[79] And, of course, there is the aural appeal of the riff to consider as well. While Errico provides a rhythmic foundation with his mid-tempo backbeat, the Stone brothers' blend their tenor voices with Graham's baritone as Robinson plays a single high note on trumpet that creates a soprano-like effect just above their voices. At the same time, band members perform syncopated handclaps to accompany the ensemble singing of "stand."

Thus the dynamism of "Stand!" compels dance floor activation. In addition to Stone's falsetto screams and deep, guttural vocables, guitarist Freddie Stone's falsetto interpolations and rhythm guitar licks throughout the song lends color to its tonal tapestry. Stone elevates the funk to a feverish pitch at the conclusion of the song. Having already written the song, he played a demo version in a club. But since he was dissatisfied with the effect, he decided to add a vamp that the band had been playing outside the studio,[80] and it turned out to be the funkiest part of the song. Encompassing an array of sounds—Errico's propulsive rhythms on the high hat,[81] choral-alliteration, keyboard riffs, and frenetic double-beat, hand-clapped percussion—the vamp was a defining moment in funk. Live footage of this part of the song shows people dancing ecstatically.

Even so, the most important event for Sly and the Family Stone was its appearance at the Woodstock Festival in 1969. Unquestionably, the Woodstock performance demonstrated the band's ability to enthrall audiences in dire conditions. Scheduled to perform at eight in the evening, the band didn't begin to play until after three o'clock in the morning. To make matters worse, it had rained throughout the night, and the audience had been up for more than twenty-four hours. Errico recalls, "People were sleeping, it was the middle of the night . . . They were spent."[82] Yet the general consensus is that the Family Stone was the most powerful band at Woodstock—no small feat given the star-studded lineup, including Jimi Hendrix, Canned Heat, Grateful Dead, Janis Joplin, and Richie Havens. *Rolling Stone* magazine reported that Sly and the Family Stone "won the battle" of the bands.[83] Though the chemistry and musicianship of the band were superb, much of the success can be attributed to Stone's charismatic interaction with the audience. Recollecting Stone's performance, Robinson muses, "Sly was like a preacher."[84]

Although Robinson is probably alluding to Stone's use of call and response, video footage of the concert allows us to closely examine the multidimensional nature of his approach. His objective was to induce the audience into an altered state of consciousness. The exhilaration of the psychosomatic experience is such that audiences become participants in the performance through varied forms of audible and/or kinetic responses. But since the audience was "spent," few people initially responded to the music. So Stone stopped abruptly in the middle of "Music Lover," and approached the microphone. Resplendent in his purple-and-white tasseled psychedelic suit with matching boots, he appealed to the audience for its participation. And while the rhythm section of Errico, Freddie, and Graham played lightly behind him, he asked people to raise the peace while repeating the word "higher" after him. Stone's utterance of "higher" signaled band members to transition to the song "I Want to Take You Higher," a sure bet to arouse people's attention. Such was the emotive power of "Take You Higher" that Neal playfully speculates whether it was "taken directly from the Holy Ghost's most cherished songbook."[85] Indeed, the song celebrates the spiritual ethos and musical values that Stone learned in church. He even says in the song that music should stimulate moving and grooving.

But Stone's invocation of audience participation was also an age-old rhetorical method that remains a common feature in many black churches today. At certain points in the service, preachers often direct their congregations to turn to the person sitting next to them and express fellowship to their neighbors. But instead of reading the scriptures, Stone ministered the gospel of funk. The premise of his text was twofold: that phenomena related to altered states of consciousness have been misrepresented by mythology; and that the funk is medicinal. He says,

> Most of us need approval . . . from our neighbors before we can actually let it all hang down. Now, what is happening here is that we're gonna try to do a sing along. . . . [A] lot of people don't like to do it

because they feel that it might be old fashioned. But you must dig that it is not a fashion in the first place. It is a feeling. If it was good in the past, it's still good. . . . What I'd like you to do, is say "higher" and throw the peace sign up, it'll do you no harm. Still again, some people feel that they shouldn't. Because there are situations where you need approval to get in on something that could do you some good.[86]

Stone's sermonic commentary included a pointed critique of constructed normality and conventional notions of propriety in relation to bodily expression of the funk/spirit, particularly inasmuch as it's associated with social deviance. Naturally, Stone was particularly troubled by this viewpoint toward sensual expression because minimal audience participation would impact the quality of his performance.

Given the participatory nature of Stone's aesthetic, audience participation was a crucial measure of his effectiveness as a musician. He was therefore compelled to address the critical problem underlying the audience's tepid responses. Doing so, Stone demonstrated his wisdom as an organic intellectual. He shrewdly distinguishes between the historicity of funkentelechy as a phenomenon and the perpetuation of arbitrary norms that tend to repress manifestations of it. And having established this premise, Stone points up psychological consequences of repression: people's senses are dulled, and their communication is restricted. Thus Stone functioned as performer and theorist at Woodstock. The hybrid nature of his appearance points up an important principle within the broader concept of funk. Just as the word "funk" encompasses contrasting and conflicting definitions, the concept of funk recognizes no fundamental division between the workings of the mind and body. L. H. Stallings writes, "With funk, there is no definitive separation of mind and body that intends to disembody imagination or represent reality. . . ."[87]

When the Family Stone resumes its performance of "I Want to Take You Higher," Stone works the crowd to a frenzy,[88] calling on people to stand up for peace because "it'll do you no harm." He sings variations of the song's title "I Want to Take You Higher" nine times, increasing his intensity with each repetition until he concludes with a falsetto scream. After which, the band plays another fragment of "Music Lover"—except this time Robinson and Martini perform a percussive riff-chorus whose ensemble substitutes vocals. The funk is in full effect as Sly, Freddie, Rose, and Graham perform various dances before Freddie and Graham dance in unison in one-legged, horizontal skips on the beat, and begin accentuating the rhythmic effect of the music by jumping up and down, while playing their instruments. Then Rose breaks out into syncopated polyrhythms; and Stone, who had jumped along with Freddie and Graham, begins a solo dance to the crowd's hand claps without any music from the band. The Family Stone's foregrounding of dance emblematized the funk aesthetic as it was conceptualized in black vernacular culture in the late 1960s. The dancers' variegated swings, jerks, bends, and bounces bespeak black vernacular body-talk that was conversant in house parties, clubs, and perhaps even some churches at the time. The dances can therefore be interpreted as extemporized choreographs of the funk/spirit—what Clinton later called the funk in 3-D. Equally important, though, the Family Stone's performance demonstrated that "unreconstructed funk" not only appealed to black audiences but white audiences as well. The question concerned marketing and accessibility, not the music and performances themselves.

IF YOU WANT ME TO STAY

The ambiguity of Sly and the Family Stone's hit recording "If You Want Me to Stay" (1973) characterizes Stone's songwriting. Reminiscent of "Thank You (Falettinme Be Mice Elf Agin)," the addressee and nature of the conflict remain unclear throughout the song. On the one hand, Stone's references to his "woman" could be interpreted as an appeal to his future wife, Kathleen Silva. On the other hand, when he sings "How could I ever be late?" he's probably sneering at promoters and journalists who criticized him for no-shows and late arrivals to concerts. But regardless of Stone's signification, "If You Want Me to Stay" expressed a salient funk credo—always be true to yourself. In retrospect, the persona's announcement of his departure coincided with Stone's departure from the music industry. In just a few short years, he was generally regarded as the mystery man of funk. The nucleus of Stone's original band had disintegrated by 1973. Graham, Errico, Freddie, and Rose had all left the band. His second version included drummer Andy Newmark and bass guitarist Rustee Allen. Meanwhile, Stone had moved to Los Angeles. His decision not only created tension among the original band members but also coincided with Stone's drug abuse. Previously, the band had dabbled with wine and marijuana, but Stone began using cocaine and other hardcore drugs with more frequency after he moved to Los Angeles. Drug abuse was ultimately a cancer to his career. Drug abuse plagued his performances, clouded his judgment, and compromised his musical talent.

He missed concerts; and according to one musician, he didn't even know his own lyrics by the late 1970s.[89]

Nevertheless, Stone's creative genius is unquestionable. His legacy rests on his vast influence on musicians in several genres. Betty Davis has acknowledged Stone as an important influence, and I've mentioned his impact on Hancock's jazz-funk. But Stone influenced other notable artists, including Miles Davis and James Mtume. "When I first heard Sly," says Davis, "I almost wore out those first two or three records."[90] Davis's foray into funk is evident on his album *On the Corner* (1972), which features the percussionist Mtume, who later ventured into R&B and became a Grammy Award–winning songwriter. Donny Hathaway, Phyllis Hyman, Teddy Pendergrass, and Mary J. Blige are among the artists that Mtume has produced. But most people today know his music via sampling. He wrote the 1987 single "Juicy Fruit" that the Notorious B.I.G. sampled in his famous first single "Juicy" on his debut album *Ready to Die* (1994). So Mtume's assessments bear significance, and he cites Stone as "one of the three geniuses" he's known in life.[91] Maurice White, founder and bandleader of Earth, Wind & Fire, summarizes Stone's momentous influence when he states:

> The music world of the late 1960s and early '70s can be largely described as before and after Sly. Sly and the Family Stone came with a whole new bag. . . . All of the bands that came into prominence in the early 1970s, including Earth, Wind & Fire, are indebted to Sly. There would be no Mandrill, Kool & the Gang, Ohio Players, War, Commodores, New Birth, or later even Prince without Sly Stone.[92]

Indeed, Stone was the foundational poet of funk. Prominent themes such as Afrofuturism, universal love, integrity, bohemianism, and several others were implicit or explicit in his songwriting. He established much of the conceptual ground for Clinton's theory of funk. For instance, in Stone's song "I Want to Take You Higher," the word "flashing" signifies the funk (spirit), and thus prefigures the central message and metaphor in Parliament's song "Flash Light."[93] Of course, Clinton is rightly regarded as a trendsetter in Afrofuturism, having created such Afronaut characters as Dr. Funkenstein, Star Child, and the Children of Production while addressing social concerns that were especially pertinent to black youth. But again, it's important to acknowledge Stone's contributions. Bands such as P-Funk, Labelle, Earth, Wind & Fire, and Lakeside elaborated on Stone's ideas. As Vincent puts it,

"Sly wanted to take you higher . . . Well, [Clinton] said[,] 'I got a space ship here. I'll take you higher."[94]

The question, then, is what made Stone's music so resonant? Perhaps Errico offers the most accurate explanation. He states that "our music still lives today because that honesty is so strong. . . . Some of those songs have been sampled more times than I can count. I think it really has to do with the honesty that was present when we created the music."[95] Errico's emphasis on honesty epitomizes the foundational meaning of "funk," and demonstrates why the music of Sly and the Family Stone was so invigorating and influential. During a period when "funk" was largely taboo in public discourse, Stone imagined an irreverent attitude and liberationist aesthetics as foundational aspects of his gospel of funk.

Side B

Devotion

BLUE FUNK AND THE BLACK FANTASTIC

Chapter Four

Songbird

CHAKA KHAN AS FUNK QUEEN

rguably the most talented singer of the funk era, Chaka Khan was born Yvette Marie Stevens in 1953 in Great Lakes, Illinois, and rose to fame as the exhilarating lead singer of the interracial funk band Rufus. During a career that has spanned four decades to date, Khan has won ten Grammy Awards. She joined Rufus at age eighteen in 1972 and catapulted the band into prominence. Between 1974 and 1979, Rufus released seven studio albums that included four #1 hits. Promoted as the Wild Child by ABC Records, Khan captivated audiences with her incredible voice, stunning beauty, and electrifying stage presence. She became an iconic figure in American culture. People with varying musical palates flocked to Rufus's concerts. They bought albums, listened to radio stations, and watched performances when Khan appeared on nationally syndicated shows such as Don Cornelius's *Soul Train* and Dick Clark's *American Bandstand*. But while she exemplified the virtuoso flair of black feminine funk, Khan developed a unique variation of the concept, and Rufus deviated thematically from other funk bands. Sly and the Family Stone, Parliament-Funkadelic, War, and other bands routinely addressed social concerns; and though Earth, Wind & Fire didn't foreground blackness, their songs and performances reflected a sense of style and cultural awareness that resonated black consciousness. But in Rufus's songs, prominent topics in funk—nagging unemployment, distressing labor conditions, social justice, partying, the funk principle—seldom appear. Yet young black audiences, who comprised the largest segment of rhythm and blues fans, were nonetheless enthralled.

This chapter examines Khan's development into a powerhouse singer and talented songwriter as the frontwoman of Rufus. We'll observe how Khan's musical philosophy and contrarian sensibility reflected a distinct version of funk aesthetics. But since Rufus downplayed social themes to a greater degree than most funk bands, a central question related to Khan's appeal is, how did she become a symbol of artistic integrity? A pat answer would argue that she was apolitical, and that audiences simply ignored this because they focused on her singing and her band members' musicianship. There's some truth to this explanation. Rufus definitely brought the funk. As Rickey Vincent observes, "The band's rhythm chops often pulsed in stuttering precision. . . ."[1] But while Vincent accounts for Rufus's appeal on a purely stylistic basis, his statement doesn't explain why Khan became a symbol of integrity.

Khan's status as a funk queen is related to her jazz-influenced musical philosophy, which emphasized the capacity of nonverbal sound to convey emotion. Even so, Khan didn't completely avoid social topics. Her maturation as an artist was coextensive with the feminist movement; and though she mostly co-wrote love songs that typified conventions of the music industry, she forthrightly addressed women's concerns. In addition, her performance style, which elaborated to some degree on Tina Turner's, was unquestionably daring. Like Turner, Khan used her beauty and talents as a singer, songwriter, and dancer to project a powerful combination of insight and eroticism that maximized the agency in the love songs she sang. Arguably, Khan's artistic ideals coincide with Richard Iton's notion of the black fantastic: black art that "transcend[s] the prevailing notions of the aesthetic and the predominance of the state as the sole frame of subject formation and progressive and transformative discourse and mobilization."[2]

Khan's incomparable sound and nonconformity reflected the sensibility and aesthetic she developed while growing up in Chicago. Her career was preceded by a youthful flirtation with black revolutionary nationalism; and though she categorically renounced this political philosophy, her involvement foreshadowed her rebellious spirit. Like such trailblazing artists as Jimi Hendrix, Sly Stone, and George Clinton, Khan had a black-hippie attitude that approximated Francesca Royster's notion of an "eccentric" artist. "By 'eccentric,'" writes Royster, "I mean not only out of the ordinary or unconventional performances but also those that are ambiguous, uncanny, or difficult to read."[3] Khan's outlook was certainly "out of the ordinary." In her memoir *Chaka: Through the Fire* (2003),[4] she recollects her seventeen-year-old mindset, and credits Black Arts feminist writer Toni Cade Bambara retroactively for encapsulating her worldview in her groundbreaking her anthology *The Black Woman* (1970). Quoting Bambara, Khan writes: "'We are involved in a struggle for liberation . . . liberation from the constrictive norms of 'mainstream culture. . . .'"[5] But in the core of her personality there was an impulse for nonconformity that prevented Khan from abiding by the regimentation of activist organizations.

The artistic freedom Khan searched for had unexpected limitations, though. The discursive latitude in funk aesthetics was fraught with double standards. Given the longstanding stigmas and proscriptions of black sensuality and the consequent repression that had lasted for generations, it's only natural that young artists expressed the new sensibility in uninhibited fashion styles, dances, and other bodily representations. What Francesca T. Royster observes in Parliament-Funkadelic's performances and recordings— "rejection of fear, loathing, and shame of the black body and the embrace of sexual and imaginative freedom"[6]—characterized most funk collectives on some level. P-Funk simply represented the extreme. As Garry Shider recalled, "Funkadelic was selling sex—hardcore sex. In fact, they used to call us X-rated. We'd go to some cities, and on the marquee, it would [read] 'X-rated.' George would walk out there in the middle of the people's food on the table; started jerkin off on the bone."[7] Even the band's album covers represented hardcore sex. Amy Nathan Wright notes that beginning with the album *Free Your Mind . . . And Your Ass Will Follow* (1970), Funkadelic's albums "picture[d] a naked, black woman . . . on the album cover . . . in new and more imagined forms."[8]

However, Khan's manifestation of sexual freedom was rather tame. For instance, the back cover of *Rufusized* (1974) pictures her lying on a mattress covered with rumpled white sheets. She's wearing a casual top, bellbottomed jeans, and she's barefoot; her head is propped up against a pillow, and her face is filled with laughter. But the central image is connected to her elevated left pant leg: the grimy bottom of her left foot and splayed toes. This composite image is emblematic of Khan's nonconformity. It's difficult to imagine soul singers doing anything of this sort. But again, the photo was innocuous by comparison. And yet, when Khan performed onstage, the combination of her skimpy outfits and sensual performance style provoked stereotypical reactions from men. At times, she experienced overt misogyny.

To complicate matters further, Khan's experience as a woman in the world of funk was somewhat atypical. For instance, singers Marva Whitney and Patryce "Choc'Let" also published memoirs about their careers with James Brown and Larry Graham, respectively. Brown dubbed Whitney Soul Sister #1. Banks played the Funk Box as the lead woman singer in Graham Central Station. And both women detail brutish misogyny that ended their careers prematurely. But Khan slipped through the cracks. Her narrative exemplifies artistic longevity despite conflicts with record executives and band members, not to mention personal problems she exacerbated herself. Her musical background was also unique. Khan listened to a comparatively broader variety of genres, observing the peculiar configurations of their soundscapes as well as implicit sensibilities they inscribed. She even taught herself how to play drums. And though the entirety of her musical rolodex isn't recognizable in her sound quality, the long hours she spent listening to music closely influenced various aspects of her sound, sensibility, and performance style.

Like many funk artists, Khan envisioned rock as a channel of rebellion. Hendrix, Led Zeppelin, and Bob Dylan were among the artists she enjoyed. In addition to rhythm and blues, she also listened to modern jazz. Saxophonist Charlie Parker and multi-reed player Yusef Lateef were among her favorites. There was also a local soul jazz band called the Pharaohs that caught her attention. A few years later, a much different version of the Pharaohs became widely known as Earth, Wind & Fire. Thus Khan developed an affinity for jazz and incorporated key elements into her vocal style. The long hours she spent listening to this music ultimately shaped the foundation of her musical philosophy. Instead of addressing social issues explicitly in the lyrics of a song, she chose a different approach. Khan envisioned herself a musical healer and emphasized ethereal themes. She aspired to affect listeners like jazz instrumentalists did, that is, to eviscerate people's torments and anxieties with exhilarating musical pleasure. Just as blues-oriented musicians functioned as secular priests, Khan sought to administer joy.

For Khan, a singer's ultimate achievement is to "touch" people beneath their skin, and thereby enhance their sense of value and self-assurance. She told David Nathan in a 1975 interview: "It's very important to me to put over through my music some of the ideas that I feel should be expressed. There is so much wrong in the world that, yes, I do want to see changes."[9] Accordingly, Khan developed a distinctive way to engender the funk. Using her four-octave voice as an instrument, she induced "an altered state of consciousness" that simultaneously conveyed her signification. The music critic Vernon Gibbs makes a similar observation in a 1975 article in *Crawdaddy!* He writes: "As a band, Rufus chooses material from other songwriters with far more attention to how the emotion expressed works its way into their image than do any of the funk bands. Like their own material, the songs they choose don't have heavy messages, yet they speak to the human condition in a language that is universal."[10] Gibbs rightly points up universality in Rufus's songs, but Khan's ability to "speak to the human condition" was predicated on her signature sound, which raises another question. Since Khan's family members weren't musicians, and she didn't grow up singing in Baptist or Pentecostal churches like most rhythm and blues singers, how did she develop her sound?

Part of the answer can be attributed to growing up in Chicago, which was a hub of innovation for musicians in several genres, including blues, jazz, rhythm and blues, and gospel. Singers such as Mahalia Jackson, the Staple Singers, and the Soul Stirrers, including a young Sam Cooke, shaped the soundscape. In jazz, the critically acclaimed Association for the Advancement of Creative Musicians (AACM) was founded in 1965 on the South Side of Chicago, where Khan grew up, by jazz musicians Muhal Richard Abrams, Jodie Christian, Steve McCall, and Phil Cohran, who founded the Affro-Arts Theater, which in turn played a significant role in Khan's development. But there were also blues legends like Muddy Waters, Koko Taylor, Howlin' Wolf, and many others who contributed to Chicago's musical potpourri. And then there was soul. Etta James, Jackie Wilson, Gene Chandler, Fontella Bass, Jerry Butler, and Curtis Mayfield were trendsetters in rhythm and blues. Collectively, these artists established standards of excellence that enhanced young artists' musical development regardless of their musical preferences. Khan's artistic development epitomizes the rich cultural tapestry in Chicago during this period. It's not surprising, for instance, that Joyce "Baby Jean" Kennedy and Minnie Riperton, who was trained as an opera singer and had a five-octave voice, also grew up in Chicago during this period. Nonetheless, Khan's family played the most significant role in her development.

EARLY BEGINNINGS: BLACK COMMUNITY THEATER AS CRITICAL MODEL

Few people would question the idea that Khan has an untraditional background as a singer. She had no formal training and never imagined a career as a singer.[11] But a careful consideration of her family background reveals an exemplary model of artistic development in black vernacular culture. In an interview filmed in the mid-1980s, she recalls, "I was raised around music. My dad was a bebopper, and my mother was veteran opera, Barbra Streisand type. And um, I always had music around. There was always music. In fact, I was named after a Max Roach song called 'Yvette.' I think I started out singing around the house with my mother. We'd harmonize standards when I was a kid."[12] Khan's recollection typifies developmental processes in blue funk aesthetics. If we think of musicianship as a form of reading and writing in sound, Khan's remembrance reflects the beginnings of *aural* literacy at a very early age. She not only emphasizes her exposure to diverse

musical styles but also a participatory learning process that involved singing "standards" as a child. Khan's experience exemplifies Guthrie P. Ramsey
Jr.'s analysis of developmental processes in African American performance.
He points out that participatory approaches have been instrumental for
countless musicians. Louisa "Blu Lu" Barker once said that singing blues
with her mother was invaluable to her success as a blues artist.[13] Khan's early
immersion into music while singing with her mother, Sandra Naomi Sallie
Coleman, epitomizes Ramsey's concept of black community theater. Ramsey
points out that legions of black artists have developed their talents in vernacular venues (churches, house parties, night clubs, etc.) and transformed
them into community theaters:

> The communal rituals in the church and the underdocumented
> house party culture, the intergenerational exchange of musical hab-
> its and appreciation, the importance of dance and the centrality of
> the celebratory black body, the always-already oral declamation in
> each tableau, the irreverent attitude toward the boundaries set by mu-
> sical marketing categories, the same intensive, inventive, and joyful
> engagement with both mass-mediated texts and live music making,
> the private performances of class-status and gender, the fusion of
> northern and southern performance codes, the memories of food,
> sights, smells, and the ritualized spaces of what the old folks called
> drylongso, or everyday blackness—all these combine to form living
> photographs, rich pools of experiences, and a cultural poetics upon
> which theoretical and analytical principles can be based.[14]

As a matter of course, the communal rituals expressed as "living photographs"—the steps, stamps, shrieks, shivers, shouts, moans, and groans—are
re-photographed, so to speak, in new expressions that form the basis of future
art forms. Black community theaters were tutorial infrastructures wherein
varied melodies, rhythms, timbres, gestures, steps, and styles were remixed
into fragments of new dances and musical styles.

Khan's living room served as a theatrical space for countless hours of
practice and rehearsals for her autodidactic development. "We were always
singing around the house," recalls Khan, "singing for family, singing for Mama's friends at her card parties."[15] The cumulative effect of being "immersed
in song" was that listening to music and performing felt natural to her as a
child—as perfunctory as eating or breathing.[16] "Singing was just a natural
thing to do," she says. "I thought everybody sang and played music during

Saturday morning chores."[17] In this way, Khan developed a singular sound quality as well as a critical understanding of musicianship. Her remembrance of a conversation with her grandmother about the album cover of Billie Holiday's *Lady in Satin* is emblematic of the process. When she asked Gramma Maude about Holiday's photo, she responded in a manner that typified black elders of her generation. She interpreted the question literally, and merely told her Holiday's name. Khan recalls comically, "I could read. But who was she beyond her name?"[18] Given the racy details of Lady Day's persona, not to mention blues lyrics, it's hardly surprising that Gramma Maude withheld information about Holiday. But her decision to evade Khan's question had an ironic effect. Curious and deprived of factual data, Khan "let [her] imagination run amok about the life of this pretty lady . . . singing in pain."[19] In the process, she learned to listen with a critical ear: "I heard so many things in her voice. Vulnerability, sadness, and a strain of the tragic. . . ."[20] The women who shaped her life, especially Gramma Maude, surrounded her with multiple styles of music, including symphony, opera, blues, rhythm and blues, and jazz.[21] Her constant exposure to a wide variety of music at an early age enabled her to attain a high level of musical fluency.

Khan formed her first band, the Crystalettes, with her sister, Yvonne, when she was eleven years old. The group participated in talent shows in precisely the sort of venues that Ramsey outlines: youth centers, clubs, and the like.[22] Not surprisingly, the Crystalettes won their competitions quite often. That the Crystalettes' chief rival was a gospel group of sisters known as the Heavenly Sunbeams, and later the Hutchinson Sunbeams, demonstrates the pivotal role of community theaters in Chicago. Eventually, Wanda Hutchinson, Sheila Hutchinson, and Jeanette Hutchinson became the Emotions, who won a Grammy Award for the 1977 single "Best of My Love." That Khan and Yvonne were neither Baptist nor Pentecostal points up the viability of secular black community theaters, especially in Chicago.[23] Yet the fact that the Emotions were Khan and Yvonne's "chief rivals" also suggests the significance of gospel sounds and techniques in the judges' criteria. So even though Khan didn't attend Baptist church services, she was well aware of gospel techniques at a crucial stage of her development.

In their early teens, Khan and Yvonne transformed the Crystalettes into an Afrocentric group called Shades of Black. They sang songs similar to those recorded by Miriam Makeba, the great South African singer. Also during this period, Khan and Yvonne became active in the Affro-Arts Theater in Chicago, which Khan describes as "an old movie house transformed into a cultural center."[24] Ramsey's notion of black community theater is especially useful in understanding this pivotal stage of Khan's development. Naturally, as a musicologist, Ramsey is primarily concerned with providing a critical framework that enhances our understanding of the music-making process in black vernacular venues. He uses "black community theater" as a figurative phrase, but his insight is highlighted by the fact that an actual community theater shaped Khan's cultural politics and her approach to music making. Remembering the theater fondly, she states, "I will forever cherish my Affro-Arts days, which were so important in my becoming me. . . ."[25] The theater provided both a regular space to perform and her first opportunities to perform away from home. Though Cohran envisioned the theater, it was eventually run by "the Pharaohs."[26] According to Maurice White, "The Afro-Arts [sic] Theater on the South Side was a hip place of non-conformity, filled with Afrocentric thinkers teaching yoga, music, and everything else artistic. The theater was a hub of 'new thought' and a new kind of consciousness, which was being born in centers like that all over America."[27]

For Khan, the theater functioned as a training ground. She had already begun listening to modern jazz,[28] so it must have been fascinating to see Rahsaan Roland Kirk,[29] an outspoken jazz musician who often played two saxophones and several other instruments simultaneously. The Affro-Arts Theater also sponsored African-style dancing and literary events. Gwendolyn Brooks, the first African American poet to win the Pulitzer Prize, read her poetry at the theater. Accomplished writers affiliated with the Organization of Black American Culture (OBAC) were also featured there: Haki Madhubuti, Carolyn Rodgers, Johari Amini, Angela Jackson, Sterling Plumpp, Sam Greenlee, and others. These writers were notable figures of the Black Arts Movement in Chicago, and their influence on Khan demonstrates how the movement contributed to funk. In fact, Khan met the Yoruba priest who bestowed her new name at the Affro-Arts Theater in a naming ceremony:

Chaka—"Woman of Fire"
Adunne—"Loves to Touch"
Aduffe—"Someone Others Love to Touch"
Yemoja—"Mother of the Waters"
Hodarhi—"Woman of Nature"
Karifi—"Strength"[30]

At this time, Khan lived with her father Charles Alexander "Buddy" Stevens, whom she credits as nurturing her free spirit and intellectual development. Through him, she developed an interest in nineteenth-century philosophers Fyodor Dostoevsky and Friedrich Nietzsche. An avid listener to Jimi Hendrix, Khan also developed a passion for black poetry. She read Brooks, and Amiri Baraka's poem "SOS" became her virtual calling card.[31] However, it was Maya Angelou's memoir *I Know Why the Caged Bird Sings* (1970) that captured her full attention. "[L]ooking back," she says, "I now know what it did for me: It held out hope while it told truth. Tough, rough times will be, but so too the overcoming."[32] The artistic equilibrium that Khan discovered in Angelou's writing prefigured a similar balance that became prominent in her music.

DEVOTION: TRANSPOSING BLACK POWER TO BLUE FUNK

Khan's study of African American poetry and jazz epitomizes the intellectual predilections in funk and the genre's relationship to the black consciousness movement. Her exposure to these art forms as a teenager sparked an interest in activism. Inspired by Fred Hampton, founder and chairman of the Illinois chapter of the Black Panther Party, Khan did volunteer work. She sold the *Black Panther* newspaper and directed a free breakfast program for children. Her sense of fashion also reflected her radicalism. She wore "combat boots and talked about the plight of the Black Nation"[33] before dropping out of school. Khan states that she was "down with the BPP Ten-Point Program," which called for "employment, education, decent housing, the power to shape black communities, and an end to police brutality."[34]

But like most funk artists, Khan had contrarian proclivities. Hers engendered disillusionment with the Panthers, and her subsequent separation from the organization initiated an abrupt and absolute rejection of nationalist politics altogether. As the Panthers' contradictions became more glaring, she became an advocate for humanity without regard to specific ideologies, ethnicities, or national borders. And like funk artists generally, she grew resentful of social categories. Consequently, Khan reflected her aversion to conventional social constructions, including racial identity, in the lyrics she wrote and sang. And one night after a gig with a local band known as the Babysitters, Khan went to see another band she had heard about. Ask Rufus was a band of white musicians that featured a dazzling black woman singer named Paulette McWilliams.

Initially dubbed the Nite Lites, Rufus was founded by guitarist Gary Loizzo, drummer Lee Graziano, bassist Chuck Colbert, and guitarist Al Ciner in 1966.[35] Shortly afterward they changed their name to the American Breed, which became Ask Rufus in 1970.[36] Like legions of artists during this period, the young white musicians envisioned Sly and the Family Stone as a model, and decided to recruit McWilliams to front their band. As it happened, the singer was dating a friend of Khan's husband. She and McWilliams became good friends. Khan recollects, "What a stunning creature Paulette was—top of the line black leather pants, fishnet tops . . . monster Afro, eyelashes doing the Betty Boop. Guys came from miles away just to see her big boobs. And what a voice!—beautiful, strong. A very Sagittarius singer, and quite experienced."[37] McWilliams became an invaluable model for Khan, and when she decided to leave the band, she recommended Khan as her replacement. The musicians were initially skeptical, but they agreed to give her a chance after they heard Khan sing.[38]

Khan's sound is exceptionally unique, and her relationship to blues is complex. In a 1975 interview, she said, "I have to admit it, I don't really care for the Blues—it brings me down and depresses me. I can appreciate the guitar playing but I don't relate to the lyrics."[39] Khan's comment isn't surprising. Most urban African Americans of her generation considered blues singers outdated and countrified. But rhythm and blues, their preferred style of music, blended elements of blues, gospel, and jazz,[40] so Khan's style is nonetheless related to blues. As D'Angelo stated in the Outro, blues is "the nucleus" of soul and funk. Rhythm and blues singers revised "older models of [gospel] and the blues" to create "a stylistic mode adaptive to the urban" experience.[41] In many ways, Khan's Chicago-based sound is largely a modernized elaboration of southern-derived gospel-textured soundscapes and tone colors of earlier rhythm and blues. Studying jazz thus enabled Khan to create a classic sound. So when she posits jazz as her artistic ideal, as she does below, she effectively positions herself in the blues tradition, while highlighting the artistic integrity of blue funk. Khan states,

> I guess that my own personal ambition for myself is to get deeper into jazz—whether it be with the group or without. The type of jazz that people like Phoebe Snow are into right now. They are singing about the truth and it doesn't have to all revolve around the man-woman love thing. I'd like to get to the point where I don't have to think about being commercial.[42]

For Khan, jazz is the apotheosis of musicianship because of its proclivity for emotional truth and skepticism toward commercialism. "That's what jazz, the thinking person's music, is all about: *listening*," states Khan. "You don't need pyrotechnics. You don't need razzle-dazzle."[43] Of course, early jazz musicians like Louis Armstrong held slightly different views. All forms of American expression are enmeshed in capitalist production, but there are varying degrees to which art defies, questions, or perpetuates commercial values. What Zora Neale Hurston called adornment was essential to vernacular notions of style, and the theatricality that characterized funk bands such as Parliament-Funkadelic, Labelle, Earth, Wind & Fire, and, to some degree, Khan herself epitomized Olly Wilson's concept of cultural aesthetics. The flair or "razzle-dazzle" was part of the criteria that people used to evaluate beauty in various forms of expression. But what's ironic about Khan's comment is that her concern for "emotional truth" emblematizes blue funk. Her criterion for valorizing jazz is equally applicable to her magnificent singing with Rufus. Khan's aversion to "being commercial" exemplifies an artistic criterion compatible with Iton's notion of the black fantastic: art that "transcend[s] prevailing notions of the aesthetic and predominance of the state as the sole frame of reference for subject formation and progressive and transformative discourse and mobilization."[44]

We can develop a clearer understanding of Khan's jazz-based funk by examining her 2007 interview with LaShanda Katrice Barnett. During the conversation, Khan commented on a previous interview in which she cited Sarah Vaughan, Ella Fitzgerald, and Peggy Lee as some of the earliest singers she heard. When Barnett asked what she learned from them, Khan acknowledged her admiration for the singers, but stated, "I think that I learned about vocalizations from horn players. Charlie Parker and Miles Davis were my teachers."[45] From a conceptual standpoint, then, Khan's closest analogue among singers is arguably Billie Holiday. Both artists have been lauded by jazz musicians, and both likened their singing to blowing a horn. Holiday said, "I feel like I am playing a horn. I try to improvise like Les Young or Louis Armstrong. What comes out is what I feel."[46] Khan makes an eerily similar statement while recollecting a conversation with Davis who gave her "the biggest compliment" when he said, "You sing like my horn."[47] Khan was thrilled because Davis "confirmed something I'd long felt: that I was never really singing, but playing my voice, which I saw as a horn, an alto sax."[48]

Khan's comment exemplifies the voice-instrument dynamic in the blues tradition. Perhaps Kathy Dobie best describes Khan's approach when she writes, "Sometimes she sang funky . . . her voice blasting and receding like she was part of the horn section. I always listened to Chaka for those moments where she said the hell with words, cast them off, and flew—"Love me now or ahhhhhhhhh . . ."[49] Khan's and Kobie's comments are emblematic of funk aesthetics, particularly the use of the body as a primary instrument. More fundamentally, though, her notion of "playing [her] voice" helps explain how she endeavored to provide audiences with "empowering message[s]" that simultaneously served as musical healing that soothed people's souls. As Kobie observes, "Sometimes she gave a kind of spacey, keep-your-head-to-the-sky encouragement."[50] Thus, if Parliament-Funkadelic's music can be characterized as electronic jazz, as Greg Tate has recently suggested, Khan's singing was a significant jazz-inflected contribution to funk.

Khan's musical philosophy coincides with salient aspects of the funk ethos. Her representation of Rufus in the early years typifies the egalitarian-ism that characterized many funk bands. Khan states, "Ask Rufus wasn't an autocracy like the Babysitters. Ask Rufus was a real *democratic* band—ev-eryone had a say. . . . I had longed to be part of the group but never had the gumption to lobby for inclusion."[51] Once again, Khan's rejection of autoc-racy and underscoring of democracy epitomizes the black fantastic. In fact, Khan has often invoked truth and honesty as hallmarks of musicianship. In a televised interview in the mid-1980s, she stated: "I'm tapping pure emo-tion. I really am. Honest, pure emotion."[52] Similarly, when Barnett asks her to pinpoint the prerequisites for communicating with audiences in various sorts of songs, Khan replies, "Honesty always. Honesty in everything, because believe me, people can see when you're faking the funk."[53] Khan's admiration for jazz should therefore be interpreted as an index to her peculiar brand of funk. Just as blues-oriented musicians related moods and sensations through sound, Khan sculpted "messages" through resplendent tone colors—what L. H. Stallings calls "affective technology."[54] The cultural ambiguity in her lyrics complemented her cultural politics. Though the Panthers impressed Khan with their work in black communities, especially their empowerment of black youth, she chose music as a more effective medium to promote black agency. In the interview with Barnett, she elaborates on her decision, and articulates her musical philosophy:

> I thought to myself, I need to find another way of reaching people aware of the plights of the black nation, the injustices of black life, but also the beauty of it. I was inspired by how the Panthers had empow-ered me and I wanted to be able to do that—to empower people. I de-cided I would use music as a vehicle to get to people. And I wouldn't necessarily put the message in the music. . . . So what I'm saying is that my identity as a singer helped me to get an empowering message out there sometimes without even having to put it in my lyrics.[55]

What's notable in Khan's recollection is that her view of art and politics is similar to Duke Ellington's. In *Music Is My Mistress*, Ellington writes, "I think a statement of protest in the theater should made without saying it, and this calls for the real craftsman."[56] Like Ellington, Khan avoided singing about black people's cutthroat experiences in urban America, as Stevie Wonder does in "Living for the City" (1973). Instead, she imbued audiences with sonic beauty, and sang about common experiences in a performance style shaped ineluctably by her informal training in community theaters. For Khan, musical meaning was nearly indistinguishable from its psychosomatic effects. To the extent that joy constituted her criterion *and* objective, it functioned as a measure of her signification as well.

CHAKA KHAN AS FUNK QUEEN AND LYRICIST

Music fans exalted Khan as a funk queen because she captivated audiences with her incomparable sound. Bruce W. Talamon's photo, taken in 1977 at a packed football stadium, captures her appeal (see fig. 4.1). Khan's mouth is a gaping smile. Her head is slightly tilted, eyes closed as she rocks the mic with her right hand, while stretching her left arm into the air, her fingers curled in passion. In addition to her soaring sounds and invigorating wail, Khan's four-octave vocal range, swivel-hip dance moves, and exhilarating performance style embodied funk aesthetics. As such, her avoidance of racial themes was irrelevant. Rufus's commitment to the pleasure principle exemplified a major funk precept—that musical pleasure has intrinsic value, and that its medicinal impact was invigorating and somewhat comparable to loving, which Iton describes as "an important public good, and . . . a significant political act, particularly among those stigmatized and marked unworthy of love."[57] Khan muses, "I've always seen myself as a healer, with my songs, with my singing. Of course, I'm not claiming to have healed diseases, but so many people have told me that my songs have made them feel better."[58] Herein Khan characterizes herself as a modern-day secular priest. Her notion of singing as a medicinal force recalls Sly and the Family Stone's "Sing a Simple Song."

Khan used her talent to counteract, and occasionally philosophize, people's trials and tribulations in everyday life. The effect was electrifying. Her singing, combined with Rufus's musicianship, transported listeners into ecstatic realms of semi-consciousness, ephemeral spheres of life that exist largely beyond the constructs of racial ideology. Khan's emphasis on creating this sort of psychological impact demonstrates the power of Rufus's

Figure 4.1. Chaka Khan. Funk Fest, Los Angeles Coliseum, 1977. Photo by Bruce W. Talamon.

funk, especially in the early days. She posits Rufus mainstay Tony Maiden's term "krudde" as an apt description of Rufus's grooves: "'Music that is below the belt, way down, real deep." In an interview recorded many years later, Maiden explained that even the superlative term "funky" was insufficient to describe the band's level of stank. "It wasn't funky," he said. "It went beyond funky—it was krudde."[59] In her memoir, Khan accentuates Maiden's point by quoting drummer Andre Fischer's characterization of Rufus: "We're minstrels, so to speak. We carry a message, not a supreme message, but simply a means of expressing ourselves to others. After all, music is communication. We don't like unhappy songs. We don't like unhappy things. We like songs that make people happy, because we're reflecting in our music how we *want* things to be."[60]

By 1973 the group had shortened its name to Rufus, and recorded its eponymously titled first album *Rufus*. Although it didn't produce any hits, the album included a cover of Stevie Wonder's song "Maybe Your Baby" that impressed Wonder enough to write a new song for Khan, and he surprised the group by showing up unexpectedly in the studio. But according to Khan, the song ("Come and Get This Stuff") fell on deaf ears. The young singer blurted out what older band members may have thought, but dared not say aloud: "Got anything else?" When Wonder played chords to another next song, Khan reportedly said, "Now *that* I like."[61] The song turned out to be

"Tell Me Something Good." Although Wonder is credited as the songwriter, Khan claims she co-wrote the song. Having been inspired to write poetry by Gwendolyn Brooks and other poets at the Affro-Arts Theater, she had curtailed her efforts at literary poetry. But her music career presented an opportunity to use her poetic talents in songwriting. "Tell Me Something Good" was released on Rufus's second album *Rags to Rufus*, and the song won a Grammy Award in 1974.[62]

Though funk singers' poetic talents are seldom discussed, it's important to bear in mind that songwriters played key roles in distinguishing funk from soul. In fact, the transfiguration of "funk" into a preeminent cultural metaphor couldn't have occurred without imaginative songwriting. In a real sense, funk lyricists were vernacular poets. Khan's approach parallels those of Sly Stone, Curtis Mayfield, and Gil Scott-Heron—which is to say, these artists envisioned songwriting as a poetic form. Discussing her early attempts at songwriting, she told Barnett: "To me it was just poetry. . . . And it's still the same way. My songs start out as poems."[63] Maiden also marveled at Khan's poetic talents as a songwriter. He said, "The way she came up with melodies, she was such a great poet."[64] "Tell Me Something Good" is a traditional love song. It opens with a contrapuntal beat—a single-note bass line offset by stank-filled sounds of wah-wah guitar. Fischer embellishes the rhythm with staccato beats on drums, and Khan begins to sing. Using a slow-paced phraseology with a hint of melisma, she sings a musical narrative filled with sensual critique and erotic braggadocio. On a basic level, the song reinforces traditional views of gender in heterosexual relationships. The persona is a sultry woman who boasts about her erotic power in a way that normalizes traditional views of sexual relationships: that she can dissipate his pride, make him yearn for longer days, and penetrate his impassivity. But while the lyrics reflected traditional views, Khan asserted independence in her appearance onstage, and eventually adopted a somewhat eccentric image that reflected funk's nonconformity during the period.

Khan's stylization of "Tell Me Something Good" epitomized black feminine funk. The lyrics aren't especially eye-opening, but Khan's interpretation added spice to the flavor. Singing in black vernacular, the soulfulness of her sound quality epitomized classic funk: "You ain't got no kind of feelin' inside." In addition to the term "ain't," the double negatives ("ain't got no") and elision of the /g/ sound demonstrate that, her distaste for blues notwithstanding, Khan's notion of what constituted funkiness was nonetheless shaped, to some degree, by the black southern migrants who sang and listened to Chicago blues and gospel. For funk fans, "Tell Me Something Good" was like a taste of honey whetting their appetites for future songs. Khan projected an image of beauty and blackness replete with sensuality that had rarely been showcased in mainstream culture. In 1974, for instance, Khan appeared with Rufus on *Soul Train*, Don Cornelius's nationally syndicated television show. Wearing a short, sexy top that showed her mid-section and bare shoulders, she lip-synced the song, exemplifying what Stallings calls funky erotixxx.[65] Her fluidity as a dancer was icing on the proverbial cake.

Khan's first hit as a credited songwriter is "You Got the Love," which also appeared on *Rags to Rufus*. Co-written with singer-guitarist Ray Parker Jr., the song soared to #1 on the R&B charts in 1974. Reminiscing about how she and Parker came up with the song, Khan's description coincides with the epistemology of funk: "That song just happened . . . When [Ray Parker Jr.] started that guitar line, the words flowed like water. The whole thing must have been written in all of ten minutes."[66] Khan's statement that "the words flowed like water" exemplifies the psychosomatic nature of funk aesthetics. The stank-encrusted guitar riff at the outset of the song sets the mood and lays the foundation of the entire soundscape. Like her first hit, "You Got the Love" is a prototypical pop song about unrequited love. Khan sings "Love me right," accentuating the tension in the relationship with her phrasing. She sings "love me" in a silky, smooth high note that oozes sexy sweetness; then, after a slight pause, the last word "right" is delivered in a lower, full-bodied register, and Khan intones the long /i/ sound with melismatic texture. This vocalized simulation of call and response establishes a pattern of tonal fluctuations that highlight Khan's effervescent style.

"You Got the Love" concerns power dynamics in sexual relationships; and to a significant degree, the song exposes men's contradictions when they manipulate women. If we situate the ideology of romantic love in the context of political economy, sex becomes an exchange value, a prize of infinite pleasure that men enjoy so long as they return women's love—hence the motive for pretense signified by the man's smile. However, the persona has superb critical skills. She reads his deceit and body-talk like an unreliable narrator. The man maintains his distance from the persona, but he also wants to maintain the relationship just to have sex. So he essentially engages in a scam—what she calls "running a game." But because the love song, as a form, is predicated on the theme of abiding love, the song has a traditional conclusion: the genuflecting woman dependent on a man's love. Khan sings, "You got the love / Gimme the strength."

Khan's role as a musical healer is especially evident in "Somebody's Watching You," which appeared on Rufus's third album *Rufusized* in 1974.

Co-written by Khan, guitarist Tony Maiden, and bassist Bobby Watson, the song showcases her ability as an artist to displace bourgeois values with the values of interiority reflected in many funk songs. While the lyrics demystify momentous aspects of the mundane, Khan alleviates distress with her singular sound. She simultaneously celebrates and generates resilience in the face of adversity. While the recording ranks among the funkiest in rhythm and blues, the lyrics illuminate Khan's musical and social philosophy. As in the blues, the song is a call to action. But rather than promoting an ideology or addressing a political issue, "Somebody's Watching You" shines the spotlight inwardly and encourages critical reflection. Using the cliché of darkness before the dawn, Khan conjures listeners to confront their contradictions in everyday life. Doing so, she also prefigures Parliament's premise in "Flash Light" by elucidating self-defeating notions of coolness that black men often internalize. The persona urges the male character to defy self-pity and resignation, so he can handle his business. Shortly after Maiden sets the tone with his guitar riff, Khan starts singing her story. The persona engages an anonymous every(wo)man whose frustrations typify those of others in the community. In the wake of the Civil Rights Movement, black youth were disproportionately affected by unemployment and other social problems, including police brutality and housing. But the lyrics are vague regarding the characters' ethnicity and gender, so while the song was especially resonant for African American listeners, Khan probably expanded her audience and listeners' thematic interpretations: loss of love, familial conflicts, economic anxieties, poor health, etc.

"Somebody's Watching You" demonstrates how Khan transposed black nationalist ideology into a distinctive manifestation of funk. Her notion of the singer as a healer or modern-day secular priest coincides with Iton's dream of a popular black art that promotes values, visions, and styles of life that comprise viable alternatives to those proposed by agents of monopoly capitalism regardless of their ethnicity, gender, sexuality, or social status. That "Somebody's Watching You" isn't a protest song is significant. Whereas protest art oftentimes, if not generally, addresses people in power (e.g., phrases such as "speaking truth to power"), more substantive art exemplifies or projects viable alternatives to the status quo. While Khan avoids political jargon, she underscores the notion that money and its derivatives (e.g., status and material objects) are specious measures of value. She sings, "There are fortunes here that can't be bought or sold / 'Cause your diamonds lie within your soul." The basic import here is compatible with values that most activists promoted during this period, including the Panthers. But Khan's emotive power lies in her talent as a singer. She sings all four verses initially, then skips the first verse and sings the last three in a higher register with increasing levels of intensity. Her treatment of the third verse is especially notable. Charting a universal vision in black vernacular lingo, Khan sings the entire verse in a sonic stratosphere of high notes that reach a crescendo with the word "lie" which punctuates the phrase like vocal percussion. We can observe a key aspect of her vocal style when she bends the long /i/ vowel so that it approximates a short /a/ sound that accentuates her punctuation. Khan's timbre recalls southern blues singers' tendency to pronounce "like" as "lak" or a facsimile thereof. Naturally, Khan speaks Standard English in normal parlance, but she strategically used aspects of black southern culture for artistic purposes like other funk singers. Funk scholar Scot Brown makes a similar observation in his discussion of Leroy "Sugarfoot" Bonner, lead singer and guitarist for the Ohio Players. Bonner used the diphthong "ow" to create his blues-flavored "signature growl" which influenced singers in "the Bar-Kays, Earth, Wind & Fire, Con Funk Shun, Cameo, the Commodores, and countless others."[67]

In "Once You Get Started," Khan shifts the focus from the funk ethos to recurring themes in funk songs: parties and pleasure. An outlier in Rufus's songbook, "Once You Get Started" memorializes the funk principle—which is to say, it describes the adrenalin that dancers experienced at house parties. As implied in the title-hook, the intense pleasure and energy of the atmosphere were such that people danced for hours at the pinnacles of their emotions virtually nonstop, retreating from the dance floor momentarily, only to return a few minutes later when they heard a captivating horn or bass line introducing another song. Though there are no images of blackness per se, key words and phrases such as "groove," "get down," and "party hearty" clearly reflect the lingo and ambience as Khan sings, "[D]ig the funky, funky music."

The band performed a lip-synched version of the song that was videotaped in the mid-1970s.[68] In the video, Khan performs her Wild Child persona in her leather-and-feathers outfit which consisted of black leather pants with bell bottoms, a black brassiere, matching platform shoes, and a braided silver headband with Indian feathers. The outfit was striking in its boldness and peculiarity—indeed, its eccentricity. When the clip begins, the band is already in a groove—then we hear Khan's signature wail. She dances fluidly as the rhythm of her steps and idiomatic body movement choreograph the music. When Khan kicks her feet out, swiveling her hips in perfect time with the beat, her dancing is a three-dimensional enactment of the song's description of house parties. Hosts generally welcomed anyone who showed up at their door. People were expected to wear stylish fashion and show off their latest dance moves. House parties were thus prototypical examples of black community theater.

One of Khan's favorite songwriters was singer Lalomie Washburn, who wrote two songs that appeared on *Rufusized*: "Your Smile" and "I'm a Woman (I'm a Backbone)." The latter is Khan's anthem,[69] which anticipated her 1978 hit single "I'm Every Woman." As such, "I'm a Woman" is Khan's earliest statement on gender politics. Barnett states that Khan's "work with Rufus [is an] embodiment of black pride, sexual liberation, and second-wave feminism."[70] When asked what determines her decisions to sing other songwriters' material, Khan replied, "I have to feel like I wrote the song before I sing it."[71] Typifying Rufus's style, the band initiates a lively vamp featuring Tony Maiden's guitar licks and Bobby Watson's soulful playing on bass, which creates an upbeat vibe and soundscape to accommodate Khan's singing. Considering the title, "I'm a Woman" is obviously a praise song for women; but here again, there's no mention of ethnicity. Instead, the song tells a story that encompasses women's experiences of various backgrounds, including nationality, ethnicity, ideology, and religion. But as a black woman herself, it's not surprising that Washburn's premise—that women's contributions are indispensable in human life—and imagery are especially pertinent to black women.

Washburn's use of poetic devices is also noteworthy. Her central metaphor (backbone) correlates with her use of concision. The first verse consists of four lines that encapsulate varied, and conflicting, social roles that—children notwithstanding—often overlap with labor roles: child, mother, lover, wife. There's also a suggestion that unhealthy social conditions compel women to become nurturers: "I'll bear your kids and be your mama." Naturally, internalizing such contradictory roles often produces dangerous psychological effects on women. Writing about the "strong black woman" stereotype, for instance, Tamara Winfrey Harris points out that "there is a dirty side to the perceived uncommon strength of black women." Her interviewee, Fatima Thomas, explains: "When you've been so strong for so long, even when you do break down and someone is there, you're on the floor saying, 'Somebody help me' and they'll be like, 'Oh, girl get up. You got this.'"[72] But reminiscent of blues singers, Khan focuses on everyday reality. The women didn't create their social conditions—they inherited them. So "I'm a Woman" celebrates the durability and toughness that women have demonstrated while grappling with social calamities.

That Khan embraced "I'm a Woman" suggests how thoroughly she renounced reductive aspects of black nationalism, particularly the tendency to conceptualize blackness in hyper-masculine terms. But where creative writers might measure cadences with syllables, Khan used vocal techniques to lend resonance to her arrangement. At the end of almost every line, she uses melisma, extending the vowel sound of the line's last syllable. She also modulates her tone to accentuate her meaning. When she sings the word "cry," for instance, she extends the long /i/ sound to suggest and simulate crying. Similarly, the last verse celebrates women's capacity to heal through loving and nurturing, and Khan accentuates the effect by singing softly in a lower, somewhat guttural note that complements the literal meaning. Thus she "plays her voice as an instrument."

CHAKA KHAN: WILD CHILD AS COMMERCIAL CONSTRUCT

Khan's electrifying performances launched her into the spotlight. ABC Records capitalized on her eroticism and promoted her as the Wild Child. The marketing strategy was a huge success, and increased record sales. But it demeaned Khan, and sowed dissension in Rufus. Having joined the band as a bright-eyed teenager, Khan found that her stardom created animosity among her male counterparts. The first rupture occurred in 1974. The album cover of *Rags to Rufus* was a hippie-style denim jacket ornamented with multicolored flowers, tiny images of the musicians' faces, and the title sewn in bright Vagabond font. But there were two pins next to the faces. One repeated the title; the other one read: "Featuring Chaka Khan." This effectively changed the name of the band to Rufus Featuring Chaka Khan. Khan states:

> I'd be lying if I said I didn't get some thrill from the attention. But also knew that what was thrilling me was killing the rest of Rufus. . . . I truly wanted us to be a group! . . . We had a good thing going, and I didn't understand why ABC would make a move that could very well create disharmony. Now I realize they singled out "the sexy woman"—it gave them a hook. It was market-driven, pure and simple.[73]

Musicians Al Kiner, Ron Stockert, and Dennis Belfield felt slighted, and decided to leave Rufus, and Tony Maiden and Bobby Watson, boyhood friends who had played with Billy Preston, replaced Kiner and Belfield on guitar and bass, respectively. And since Kiner was also a vocalist, his departure created more space for Khan and Maiden, which fine-tuned Rufus's sound.

Figure 4.2. "Chief Chaka," ca. 1975. Photo by Anwar Hussein/Hulton Archive via Getty Images.

Khan gave listeners goosebumps,[74] and her stage presence was irresistible. An early review of Rufus's performance in Los Angeles in 1973 serves as an excellent example. Writing for *Down Beat* magazine, Eric Gaer stated, "Chaka Khan, black, beautiful female vocalist, hides her true ability until about half-way into the set. But the minute she opens her mouth we know she can put us away—and does."[75] Maiden and Watson were similarly impressed when they saw her in Chicago before joining Rufus. "She was screaming her heart out," said Watson, who subsequently played with Michael Jackson and Stevie Wonder, "not screaming, but singing with conviction. . . . When she opened her mouth, you could feel her guts."[76] Watson's hyperbole notwithstanding, his characterization of Khan epitomizes classic funk.

Eroticism was also a critical and intentional part of Khan's aesthetic. Known for wearing outlandish outfits, she expressed her sexuality in ways that most women singers avoided during the period. She liked to "wear things the audience can't wear, but that they'd like to wear. You've got to stay one step ahead."[77] Notwithstanding the element of condescension in this statement, Khan's fashion indicates how untethered she was from social constraints. The most striking example of her theatrical approach was her leather-and-feathers outfit mentioned earlier (see fig. 4.2). A prototypical version consisted of red leather pants, a red fur bikini top, and a full headdress made with red feathers striped with yellow-and-white dapples. For Khan, the dress was a bold statement—what she calls "a conscious thing."[78] Having spotted an Indian headdress in a shop, she decided to wear it onstage: "[A]t the time I was really tapping into my Indian heritage . . . and I wanted to identify with that."[79] The peculiarity of the image was unquestionable, and her interpretation paralleled the meaning of "funk." She stated that "wearing leather and feathers was . . . a conscious thing . . . Be honest about who you are."[80] But apart from the significance of identity, Khan's explanation sounds somewhat curious. That is, her rationale seems analogous to a Native American artist discovering she has African American ancestry and wearing a dashiki afterward to affirm her cultural identity without appreciating its symbolic meaning. But no matter what Khan wore, her fashion transgressed codes of respectability regarding black women's apparel and public appearances. As her back-cover photo illustrates on *Rufusized*, Khan disregarded preexisting stigmas and flouted social conventions. From all indications, she conceptualized funk as "F-U-N with a special K."[81] In this sense, her stage apparel represented free expression that complemented the palette of her stratospheric wail, which evidenced "a funky vernacular truth that [didn't] answer to white-based or any other preconceptions of [her] reality."[82]

Record executives had other ideas. They interpreted Khan's sensuality through stereotypic lenses shaped by longstanding myths about race and gender. ABC Records promoted Khan as a sex symbol which she interpreted as "all body, no mind."[83] Of course, the mind-body split recalls our discussion in chapter 2. Whereas funk accentuates contrariety, stigmas related to the concept were based on racial attitudes based on the mind-body split. But the ramifications of the myth are especially demeaning to black women. The phrase "all body, no mind" invokes generations of exploitation and disfranchisement, including state violence, propaganda, and other forms of coercion used to pigeonhole black women into the excruciating role of reproducing cheap labor for American capitalism during slavery and Jim Crow. Not surprisingly, Khan felt insulted.

Part of Khan's anger was probably due to the striking difference between her actual appearance and ABC Records' representation of her. In a black-and-white photo taken at an outdoor Rufus concert (see fig. 4.3), she sings in her idiosyncratic style: eyes closed. Her full lips and straight white teeth are focal points of the image. She's wearing several necklaces. A tiny bikini top provides the clothing for her torso as two slight furrows on the left side of her nasal bridge suggest rapture and emotional intensity. And on the same side of her face, a faint line of perspiration forms a narrow streak that

Figure 4.3. Chaka Khan, ca. 1975. Photo by Michael Ochs/Michael Ochs Archives via Getty Images.

culminates in a single drop of sweat.[84] This photo is a visual transcription of Khan's sensuality. By contrast, ABC executives emblazoned an enormous, sexualized image of Khan's lips on the album cover of *Rufus Featuring Chaka Khan* (1975). Set in a pink background, the lips are noticeably exaggerated in size and shape, and protrude over white teeth and a hot-pink colored tongue. Drops of liquid—perhaps sweat or spit—comprise the coup de grâce. Marketers probably considered the image a harmless, cartoonish, and ultimately comedic depiction of Khan's all-out performance style, and it remains unclear how music fans interpreted it. But she read it as a caricature with racial overtones that reasserted the mind-body split. When asked about the cover, she replied, "Well, to be honest I'm not overkeen on it myself. . . . I guess what's happening is that the whole [sex] thing is being accentuated. Basically, I'm a wild natured type of person and on stage, I guess I really work hard and give over that image. The album sleeve is how people picture me I imagine."[85] Khan's statement provides added context for her headdress image and the consequent element of exoticism in her eroticism. For "wild natured," read eccentric. "[W]orking hard" meant immersing Khan's total being into the music: mind, body, spirit. She thus projected an assortment of idiomatic aesthetic expressions as a matter of course; and to the extent that viewers interpreted these through prisms of racial and/or sexual stereotypes (e.g., "all body, no mind"), they misread her sensuality as an affirmation of their own illusions. Hence the glaring contrast between Khan's actual expression and the way "[ABC] picture[d]" her as the "Wild Child."

Yet Khan's problems with ABC Records weren't the only ones she experienced with men at this time. On several occasions, there were conflicts with band members. The departure of Kiner, Stockert, and Belfield was only the beginning. Rufus was recording *Rags to Rufus* when Bobby Watson and Tony Maiden came onboard. Maiden became the group's de facto leader and eventually Khan's lover. She acknowledges him as an ingenious, talented musician, stating that "Tony and I made some wonderful music together."[86] But they couldn't get along. Khan found that Maiden could be simultaneously quixotic and inarticulate, and she soon discovered that his personality traits were toxic. She describes their relationship as "mastering the Ike-and-Tina tango." Khan states, "Tony and I were a disaster waiting to happen."[87] According to Khan, most of their fights erupted because of issues concerning the band. And just as ABC executives exploited her sexuality, her conflicts with band members were also related to gender politics. For instance, Khan believes that Maiden took out his frustrations on her partly because she was the only woman in the band, and their sexual relationship complicated matters. Maiden's difficulty verbally engaging with Khan compounded his frustrations, which prompted him to lash out.[88] There were additional conflicts. Her experience with Rufus was tumultuous. Khan has characterized her experience with the band as a familial one, but she also stated: "I've fought everyone in this group . . . I'm not kidding, we've had fist-fights."[89]

The most egregious acts of violence involved Andre Fischer, a six-foot-five, three-hundred-plus-pound giant of a man. On one occasion, Rufus performed at a Los Angeles nightclub called Whiskey A Go-Go during the period when the band was becoming a national attraction. Rufus was billed with singer and songwriter Iggy Pop, but he injured himself during his performance, and couldn't complete the gig. The club's manager asked Rufus to consider performing a double show, and a disagreement arose between Khan and Fischer. Both were willing to do an additional show. But where Khan insisted on receiving extra pay, Fischer argued that the band would benefit more from the extra exposure, and that they should do the extra show regardless of extra pay. Khan was pregnant at the time; and when it became clear to Fischer that she wouldn't budge, he resorted to violence: "Andre literally jumped all over me—pregnant with Milini. If the rest of the band hadn't been there to pull him off . . . I don't want to think about what might have happened."[90] Khan's recollection epitomizes the rank misogyny that she experienced and demonstrates how conflicts over financial interests intersected with gender politics during her career. From all indications, Fischer believed that his masculinity entitled him to decide what was most important for the band's future. And this mindset is analogous to male privilege in various societal institutions, including the family, church, business, and government. When Fischer's persuasive abilities were unproductive, he resorted to violence to enact his sense of entitlement. The second altercation with Fischer involved Khan's husband, Richard Holland. Before he met her, he had played guitar, and he wrote the song "Better Days," which was included on the album *Ask Rufus* (1977). Presumably, Holland went to the studio to check on the song's progress. When he got there, Fischer was working on it, and Holland complimented him on the way it sounded. But after a few moments, Fischer asked if he could speak to Holland privately, and the two men went to the restroom. Fischer then reprimanded Holland for issuing directives to him, and began beating him severely. At only five feet nine inches, the slightly built Holland was defenseless against Fischer, and began screaming loudly. Khan rushed to the restroom, and when she saw what was happening, she hit Fischer in the head with a Courvoisier bottle. He responded by pummeling her. Although the initial scenario between Fischer and Holland seems somewhat implausible, Fischer's penchant for violence and dislike of Holland, which may have been fueled by racial animus, suggest that he premeditated his attack. No charges were filed because of management's fear of controversy, but the incident effectively ended his career with Rufus.

CHAKA KHAN AS SONGBIRD

Perhaps the clearest indication of Khan's extraordinary talent is evidenced in one of her least favorite songs. Co-written with Richard Calhoun, "Stay" appeared on Rufus & Chaka Khan's album *Street Player* (1978). The song rose #3 on the R&B charts, and singer Erykah Badu, a self-proclaimed child of the funk,[91] covered it on her 1997 album *Live*. Essentially, "Stay" is a love song about a couple's troubled relationship in the midst of substantial economic and psychological challenges. Many of Khan's fans consider the song an "old school classic." But as the title suggests, the premise of the song is rather reductive: that women should subordinate themselves to the men they love. For her part, Khan denies having experienced similar situations, suggesting instead that her son inspired the song. "I used to call my son Stay," she said. "He would never leave home. . . . But truly I would never beg a guy to stay. I was having a moment I think. I don't recall. It has been a while."[92] Notwithstanding Khan's ambivalence, the more curious issue concerns the contrasting interpretations of the song. Why does "Stay" express such different meanings to Khan and her fans?

Similar reactions to another "old school classic" may provide a clue. Earth, Wind & Fire's popular song "Reasons" appears on the band's live album *Gratitude* (1975) and features singer Philip Bailey who delivers one of the most magnificent falsetto performances ever recorded. Co-written by Maurice White, Charles Stepney, and Bailey himself, "Reasons" is widely considered as the ultimate love song. Couples have often played it at their weddings to symbolize their commitment. But according to Bailey, the song has little do with love or commitment. Rather, it's a cautionary tale about casual sex, infidelity, and the lack of love and commitment. Bailey states, "'Reasons' was not meant to be a song that you play at your wedding. . . . It was far from that. In fact, it comes from a conversation me and Maurice were having about fidelity and being true to your mate. 'Reasons' was written from that conversation."[93] Clearly, Bailey and his fans have conflicting interpretations of "Reasons." However, the question is, why are their interpretations so different? As the singer and co-author, Bailey's understanding is based, quite understandably, on the literal meaning of the lyrics. By contrast, his listeners seem to be more concerned with the music itself, that is, Bailey's singing, the instrumentalists' musicianship, but perhaps most importantly, how the song makes them feel. Ironically, the disconnect is a testimony to Bailey's craft. He sings with such intense emotional force and ethereal beauty that his voice functions as "affective technology" that engenders an array of powerful sensations that listeners have apparently conflated with love and affection.

Khan engenders a similar effect on "Stay." Her invigorating sound stimulates a buoyant sensation that generates an effusive sense of agency. The
vernacular tone colors that distinguish her definitive funk sound are reflected
brilliantly in "Stay." Indeed, the song arguably exemplifies her notion of singing as medicinal expression, notwithstanding the considerable irony involved.
Khan's invocation of fortitude and resilience is palpable as she testifies to the
unvarnished truth: The world is filled with deceit, but the dialectics of life
are such that despite our setbacks and "hurt . . . the green grass grows from
the dirt," and "that's a fact of life alright." Here Khan functions as lyricist,
sage, and healer. And since hope is imbued within ecstasy, many listeners
seem to have interpreted the song as an inspirational statement about the
possibilities of reconciliation. After all, the premise of the story is that the
couple's commonalities outweigh its differences.

Khan's lyrics aren't always transparent, though. Her voice soars to such
incredibly high registers that only fragments of phrases are intelligible. For
instance, when she sings an internal rhyme ("that's life, al*right*"), the referent
to the rhyme is barely legible. Essentially, her lyrics liquefy into paralinguistic
sound—the words are virtually indecipherable. Khan "plays her voice as
an instrument," signifying nonverbally on a subcutaneous level like jazz
musicians. The ensuing enthrallment and obscurity of the lyrics arguably
render "Stay" more amenable to varied interpretations. From an ideological
standpoint, the persona's appeals normalize women's genuflection, but Khan
conveys such agency, resilience, and fortitude through her singing that the
cumulative impact may effectively offset the denotative meaning of the lyrics.
And her ability to rejuvenate listeners and generate agency demonstrates
why so many people envisioned Khan as a funk queen.

Khan eventually left Rufus, in 1983, and won five Grammy Awards thereafter. But like Jimi Hendrix, Sly Stone, Gil Scott-Heron, and others, she also
succumbed to drug abuse. Reflecting on her experience, Khan said, "Drugs
freed me of some shyness, believe it or not, that I did possess. It took the
place of a lot of stuff that I didn't have, like love of a man or a guy. . . . I was
very, very lonely."[94] Still, she remained productive. Writers of her generation
expressed conflicting views about her craft. For instance, the late Ntozake
Shange questioned whether Khan created an identifiable sound, a precondi-
tion for legendary status among black listeners. Shange writes: "i cd not say
to you: that's chaka khan singin 'empty bed blues,' not cuz chaka khan cant
sing empty bed blues / but cuz bessie smith sounds a certain way. her way."[95]
By contrast, Curtis Bagley, writing for *Essence* in 1986, characterized Khan
as "a new breed of singer: one who was self-taught, not manufactured; one
who ignored tradition and recorded exactly as—and what—she wanted to."[96]

Bagley might've pointed out that Bessie Smith was also self-taught. Nonetheless, his summarization of Khan's developmental process in black community theaters is a testament to his insight. Still, given Shange's immense knowledge of black women's artistry, it seems wise to consider the perspective of a contemporary artist to assess Khan's legacy. Bassist extraordinaire Divinity Roxx, former musical director for Beyoncé, shares the following statement:

> Anytime you can identify an artist simply by listening to them play or sing without seeing them, there's a clear indication to me that the artist has their own unique style and ability because they are clearly distinguishable from others. It's what every artist strives for. We know Miles when we hear him. We know Prince, Michael, Patty, Aretha, Anita, Erykah, Lauryn, Laylah, Marcus Miller, Victor Wooten, Larry Graham, Bootsy, etc etc just by hearing them play or sing. Can you imagine Bessie singing "Tell Me Something Good"?[97]

Chapter Five

Funky Bluesology

GIL SCOTT-HERON AS BLACK ORGANIC INTELLECTUAL

Gilbert "Gil" Scott-Heron was one of the most eclectic figures of his generation. A multitalented singer, poet, and musician, Scott-Heron wrote lyrics with insightful political analysis in a variety of musical styles, including soul-jazz, jazz-funk, and rhythm and blues. Known for his distinctive baritone voice, razor-sharp wit, street-corner rhymes, and hilarious political wisecracks, he was arguably the original prophet of black edutainment in the 1970s. He warned about the school-to-prison pipeline long before black activists and intellectuals made it a key concern in the twenty-first century. At the same time, Scott-Heron's performances with the Midnight Band, which he co-led with longtime collaborator Brian Jackson, impressed Don Cornelius so much that he invited him on his nationally syndicated television show *Soul Train*. It was a crowning achievement for an artist who studied political ideas. Indeed, Scott-Heron was a prime example of an organic intellectual. He functioned as a unique type of public intellectual in the 1970s and early 1980s. His biography, writings, recordings, and interviews form a composite narrative of his distinctive blend of resistive art and politics. During his career, he performed in such venues as Madison Square Garden and the Rose Bowl. He also appeared on lineups with leading artists of the period: Sly and the Family Stone, Chaka Khan, reggae star Peter Tosh, and the Crusaders, a popular jazz-funk band. In addition, Scott-Heron worked with Grammy Award–winning guitarist Nile Rodgers and toured with Herbie Hancock and Stevie Wonder, both Grammy Award winners themselves.

Versatility was an important attribute for Scott-Heron. He was equally adept at singing, songwriting, poetry, and political analysis. His proficiency at humor as a political raconteur rivaled that of professional comedians, and his artistry exemplified the radicalism implicit in funk's penchant for nonconformity and eccentricity. According to Bootsy Collins, "Brother Gil was in a class room [sic] by himself. He taught from his heart about true Funk, true Blues, with the coolness of Jazz but with the true Spiritual Soul of how we as people dealt with it."[1] Of course, contemporary images of black urban culture in the 1970s often evoke nostalgia: resplendent afros, blaxploitation films, *Soul Train* dancers, and so forth. However, the seemingly weekly or biweekly creation of new dances such as the Breakdown, the Robot, and the Freak camouflaged deep-seated sentiments of alienation. Scott-Heron's recordings responded to the resentment and skepticism the dance moves typically concealed. He cultivated a slow-jam vibe that typifies listening parties—what reggae singer Ziggy Marley later called a conscious party—as an alternative variant of blue funk. Whereas songs like Earth, Wind & Fire's "Mighty Mighty" (1974) and War's "Why Can't We Be Friends" (1975) captured the alienation that pervaded black youth culture, Scott-Heron's recordings presented political perspectives that were often implicit or understated in funk songs. He inverted this model by transfiguring the pleasure and nonconformity that characterized funk into a poetics of black resistance.

Scott-Heron's discography reflects a nuanced, Malcolm X–inspired, panoramic vision of blackness with motley textures of sound: a mosaic of funky (rhythm and) blues, soul-jazz music; pre-futuristic (rhythm and) blues-based spoken word; street-smart hipness expressed as comedic (blues) trickster signification; and hardcore social critique. His multimedia style coalesced several related principles of blue funk: 1) the core meaning of "funk" (e.g., honesty and integrity); 2) freedom expressed as nonconformity; 3) funk as intellectualism; 4) the relationship between funk and black power. Thus Kalamu ya Salaam argues retrospectively about the Black Arts Movement: "No single poet's influence is as extensive as Gil Scott-Heron [sic] who early in his career described himself as 'a bluesician' with a message."[2]

Born in Chicago in 1949, Scott-Heron spent his preadolescent years in Jackson, Tennessee. The region was a center of blues culture, producing John Lee "Sonny Boy" Williamson, Big Maybelle, and from nearby Brownsville and Nutbush, Sleepy John Estes, Yank Rachell, and Tina Turner, respectively. Scott-Heron would later interpret blues aesthetics in ways his forebears couldn't have imagined. His mother, Bobbie Scott, sang opera and became a socially conscious librarian. She was also a brown-skinned beauty. Scott married Gillie St. Elmo Heron, the first black professional soccer star who was known as "the black arrow." But Scott-Heron's parents split up shortly after he was born, and since his mother couldn't afford to take care of him, his maternal grandmother, Lillie Scott, raised him until her death in 1962. Scott raised him like a son and encouraged him to read voraciously.

Scott-Heron began writing stories at age ten, and later appeared on the front page of the *Jackson Sun* newspaper, in 1962, when he and two other black students witnessed bigotry firsthand when they integrated the all-white Tigrette Junior High School.[3] During the same period, Scott-Heron became active in music after Scott bought his first piano; but when she passed later that year, he began living with his mother. He moved to New York where he continued to nurture his dream of becoming a writer, which intensified after interviewing Langston Hughes as a teenager. By age twenty-two, Scott-Heron had two published novels, *The Vulture* (1970) and *The Nigger Factory* (1972). And though he never received a bachelor's degree at Lincoln University, he successfully applied to Johns Hopkins University's creative writing program on the strength of publishing his first novel *The Vulture* and releasing his first album *Small Talk at 125 Street and Lenox* (1970), which included songs and poetry. Two years later, in 1972, Scott-Heron was awarded his MA degree from Johns Hopkins University, and he later taught creative writing at Federal City College (now University of the District of Columbia).

Yet Scott-Heron remains a nebulous figure within intellectual discourse. He has received critical attention in recent years, but his political foresight is still largely overlooked by creative writers and scholars. He was known as the Godfather of Rap, but his cultural values and artistic vision were suffused with blues, so his artistic vision and sensibilities were probably closer to George Clinton's than, say, Ice Cube's despite the fact that few artists seem more dissimilar than Scott-Heron and Dr. Funkenstein. Depending on his mood, which was occasionally "influenced" by LSD, Clinton performed in parodic pimp suits, diapers, or his birthday suit. Scott-Heron struck a more sedate figure, performing in slacks and dashikis. Even so, he and Clinton are estranged cultural kinfolk in blue funk—artistic counterparts who developed contrasting interpretations of what Amiri Baraka called the "blues impulse transferred." As Scott-Heron himself stated, "George Clinton and them didn't invent funk, and they aren't the only ones who can hit on the one. . . . But I do feel as though there are things that can be provided as food for thought, things that can be used as inspirational tools, things that can help people feel better about themselves and their potential."[4] Scott-Heron's blue funk was counter-ideological in form and content. Although he studied academic literary conventions, he used variations of black vernacular forms and expressions to illuminate his ideas. He recalls, "I got into recording as part of the consideration that . . . a lot of our school children and a lot of our adults . . . do not read comprehensively enough or often enough to really enjoy dealing with novels."[5] Scott-Heron's artistic objectives, then, were coextensive with the black fantastic. His work engaged and highlighted stylistic idioms and social perspectives of black working-class "constituencies," which included "experiences of the underground [and] the vagabond."[6]

BLUE FUNK AS ARTISTIC MODEL

Scott-Heron's blues model recalls Langston Hughes's quote that blues-oriented expression is rooted in contemporaneous experiences: "[T]he Blues are *today* songs, here and now, broke and broken-hearted, when you're troubled in mind and don't know what to do and nobody cares."[7] Scott-Heron blended music making with internationalist analyses of racial and class issues, which he imbued with humor and satire. And though his music was dance-beat-oriented, he didn't conceptualize dancing as his primary objective. Instead, he tended to think of pleasure as a way to inculcate ideas. In a 1980 article published in the *New York Times*, Robert Palmer noted:

> [Scott-Heron's] present unit purveys a kind of mellow, lilting funk. The group rarely builds a powerful rhythmic momentum, but perhaps that isn't what Mr. Scott-Heron has in mind. Bob Marley and the Wailers communicate an equally politicized vision using sensual, hypnotic music that flows rather than bludgeons, and Mr. Scott-Heron and his band accomplish something similar in a more North American idiom.[8]

Palmer's reading is perceptive. What stands out about Scott-Heron's recordings is that he consistently commingled performance and intellectualism in his aesthetics. Neither element is independent of the other. As with funk artists generally, Scott-Heron routinely affixed matters of the mind with the body, but he formulated a unique approach similar to reggae legend Bob Marley's use of sensuality to engage controversial political topics. This chapter examines Scott-Heron's political vision and blues-tinged aesthetic in conjunction with two critical frameworks: Richard Iton's notion of the black fantastic and philosopher Charles Mills's critique of race in *The Racial Contract*, which elaborates on Fanon's classic study of imperialism in *The Wretched of the Earth*. To the extent that Scott-Heron's political perspectives and analyses parallel Mills's study, he personified Iton's vision of the black fantastic. Indeed, Iton's definition summarizes Scott-Heron's cultural politics. Throughout his career he created art that "transcend[ed] prevailing notions of the aesthetic and the predominance of the state as the sole frame of subject formation and progressive and transformative discourse and mobilization."[9]

Perhaps the most crucial component of Scott-Heron's philosophy is his notion of bluesology. Growing up in Tennessee, he listened assiduously to a wide range of blues singers, including Big Mama Thornton and Jimmy Reed. And while such songs were full of good humor and fun, he began to recognize the critical acumen inscribed in blues shortly after he arrived in New York. For instance, Reed's recording "Down in Mississippi" (1964) is a scathing critique of Jim Crow just as Thornton's "Hound Dog" (1953) is a critical reading of (black) men's philandering in male-female relationships. Scott-Heron's new geographical setting also motivated to contemplate blues. Unlike people he had known in Tennessee, it seemed that "Blacks in New York didn't have the blues tradition—or they'd lost it . . . I began to work on urban blues poems . . . I've found that humorous [analogy] . . . doesn't put down or look down. It suggests suggestive criticism."[10] At the same time, Scott-Heron adopted leftist artist-intellectuals such as Paul Robeson, Langton Hughes, and Amiri Baraka as models. The insights from their writings and the musicians he studied prompted the young artist to disregard arbitrary barriers between creativity and criticism. Scott-Heron writes:

Different ideas call for different vehicles and the artist who limits himself to one medium has lost a valuable opportunity for further growth. I generally use as my . . . reference point . . . the examples of Paul Robeson and Langston Hughes, men who used a range of artistic media—song, poetry, acting and oration to convey . . . contemporary social ideas and political circumstance.[11]

Scott-Heron's commentary epitomizes his multimedia interpretation of blues aesthetics. As I've written elsewhere, "to be privy to a performance of the blues network is to claim witness to a dialogue of creative recipes that culminates in a veritable gumbo of art."[12] For Scott-Heron, blues modalities functioned as epistemological indices, coded styles of sense making in creativity and critical analysis. Hence the satirical subtitle of his 1975 poem: "We Beg Your Pardon (Pardon Our Analysis)."

Scott-Heron's blend of propulsive music and social commentaries appealed to different, and sometimes conflicting, demographics in African American culture. While many black youth admired the Black Panthers' opposition to state violence, not to mention their advocacy of self-determination in politics, education, and community development (e.g., breakfast programs for children), the Panthers' dogmatism toward parties and pleasure could get tiresome. Figuratively speaking, party people lived on the west side; activists lived on the east side. Of course, these groups weren't mutually exclusive, but the chasm was quite evident. Rickey Vincent notes that "one ex-Panther described the downfall of her organization . . . along 'party' lines— too much partying: 'The bloods were comin' in late talkin' 'bout *colored-people-time*, while the revolutionaries were synchronizing their watches.'"[13] Interestingly enough, Scott-Heron was similarly prone to parochialism early in his career. He once said, "We spend our money on foolishness that fades away in weeks; solid black things live on and on—these are the things we need to invest in—not 45s or learning 'the latest dance craze.'"[14]

Nonetheless, Scott-Heron was a rare talent. In addition to progressive white writers and music fans, he appealed to conflicting sectors of black youth. And though his music wasn't usually considered dance music, his aesthetic was distinctly groove oriented. In a 1976 interview with Don Snowden, Scott-Heron outlined a dance-oriented approach that bears similarity to Olly Wilson's ideas about the interrelationship between body movement and music making:

> You see I play with African drummers, you know, master drummers. They're not African but they play African drums and African rhythms. They come from African dance troupes and ensembles so all the rhythms are dance rhythms. . . . We, as members of the band, can dance to all of them because we know the dance that goes along with that rhythm. We consider all of it dance music in terms of the fact that dance is the natural extension of music and rhythm.[15]

Although Scott-Heron uses the word "play," he didn't make sharp distinctions between poetry and songs. Rather, he conceptualizes the words "song" and "poem" synonymously. He uses them interchangeably when he describes his breakthrough recording "H2O Gate Blues."[16] Much of Scott-Heron's inspiration came from watching Baraka and other Black Arts writers project poetic cadences over conga beats while dancers visualized the rhythms.[17] But the poets weren't musicians. Attuned to the music of language (e.g., alliteration, assonance, morphemes, phonemes), Black Arts poets simulated, with varying degrees of success, musicians' affective power. Scott-Heron, however, was a professional singer who merged political analysis with musical composition. "The objective," he said, "is to be more like an instrument in an attempt to blend in with the music, rather than have one over the other."[18] Scott-Heron infused the funk/spirit into political critiques so that his "food for thought" resonated more thoroughly.

Although Scott-Heron's vocal range paled in comparison to Al Green, Marvin Gaye, and other singers of his generation, he developed an endearing sound quality that enhanced his appeal. Joyce Ann Joyce describes Scott-Heron's voice as vaguely reminiscent of Lou Rawls, the Grammy Award–winning soul singer from Chicago who was immensely popular during the 1960s and 1970s.[19] Bassist Ron Carter, a member of Miles Davis's famous second quintet, played on Scott-Heron's second album *Pieces of a Man* (1971). He recalls, "He wasn't a great singer, but with that voice, even if he whispered, it would have been dynamic."[20] And poet Harmony Holiday tweeted: "His timbre is the forth side of the three sided dream in audio color . . ."[21]

But unlike most singers, Scott-Heron wrote lyrics with the precision of poetry. As Roger St. Pierre observed, "Scott-Heron's writing has a hauntingly poetic quality. So his songs look as good in cold print as they sound when performed."[22] Scott-Heron's ability to combine singing, killer rhymes, and variations of black street lingo enabled him to entertain audiences even when his lyrics were overtly rhetorical and didactic. The unique instrumentation of the Midnight Band, which he assembled with pianist and flutist Brian Jackson, his longtime collaborator he met as a student at Lincoln University, was also an important factor. The band included other college mates who previously performed as members of Black and Blues at Lincoln: singer Victor Brown, who formed the band, and percussionist Eddie "Ade" Knowles. Eventually, the band would add Bilal Sunni-Ali, who played tenor saxophone, flute, and harmonica; electric bassist Danny Bowens; drummer Bob Adams; and two more traditional percussionists: Charlie Saunders and Barnett Williams. In the mid-1970s, Adams left the band, and was replaced by several other drummers. But regardless of who played drums, the result was a highly percussive mosaic of sound that could be described as jazz-influenced rhythm and blues or perhaps funky soul jazz.

Scott-Heron's approach to poetry was equally unique. Even when he performed poetry solo, which he did quite often,[23] his political insight and satire were unparalleled in popular culture. Where Clinton transmuted black cultural nationalist iconography into popular music, Scott-Heron transmuted black power principles into blue funk. Baraka was of the few black writers who respected Scott-Heron's artistry. Recollecting the impact of Scott-Heron's debut album *Small Talk at 125th and Lenox* (1970), which included his famous recording "The Revolution Will Not Be Televised," Baraka states: "When it first came out, I heard it and people were talking about it in the streets and quoting it. It became part of the language. Gil was more popular than The Last Poets because he was taking a pop form and using it to the extent that it could be used as a message."[24] Singer Kathy Sledge, the youngest member of Sister Sledge, corroborated Baraka's statement when she said, "[A] lot of my friends from school are into political music—such as Gil Scott-Heron, for example."[25]

Scott-Heron expressed his critiques in baritone vocals, witty rhymes, and razor-sharp irony of blues signification. The effect was electrifying. Baraka's comment on Scott-Heron's poem "Whitey on the Moon" is characteristic of his blues-based approach: "It had that kind of ironic twist to make people understand how bad things were in the ghetto. It was very funny but sobering to think about what that really meant."[26] Baraka's statement exemplifies the "affective power" of blues signification. Obviously, Scott-Heron's recordings were structurally dissimilar from twelve-bar blues, but his conceptual approach to songwriting was comparable to blues singers' penchant for confession. Consider his following statement: "A lot of times, people can say things in poems they can't say to you personally, but they need to get that information across."[27] Now compare Scott-Heron's approach with blues singer Henry Townsend's statement:

> It's a sort of thing that you like to hold to yourself, yet you want somebody to know it. I don't know how you say that two ways: you like somebody to know it, yet you hold it to yourself. Now I've had the feelin' which I have disposed it in a song, but there's some things that have happened to me that I wouldn't dare tell, not to tell—but I would sing about them. Because people in general they takes the song as an explanation for themselves—they believe this song is expressing their feelin's instead of the one that singin' it.[28]

This passage helps explain Scott-Heron's widespread appeal. He tapped into people's personal pain and anguish and transfigured these sentiments into public discourse shaped by historicity and conveyed with resonant styles. He told spoken word artist Michael Franti that "rap is poetry put to music and the role of the poet in our society is to make difficult things easy to understand."[29] Scott-Heron's ability "to make difficult things easy to understand" points up his role as a poet-singer-cum-political-philosopher at the height of his career.

BLUE FUNK AS CULTURAL PHILOSOPHY

Scott-Heron's recordings illuminate two distinct aspects of blue funk aesthetics. His commingling of creative expression and critical analysis reflected contrariety, and his political ideas reflected the radicalism inscribed within blues-suffused ontologies. Joyce has pointed out that Scott-Heron personified Larry Neal's ideal of a Black Arts poet. Quoting Neal, Joyce describes Scott-Heron as "the 'priest' or Black magician who makes 'juju with the word on the *world*.'"[30] Thus we can reasonably say that Scott-Heron's songs and poems offer a semblance of a response to Neal's question: "What if James Brown read Fanon?"[31] Of course, nobody rivaled the Godfather's emotive power, and there's no evidence to suggest that Neal paid much attention to Scott-Heron. It's also unclear whether Scott-Heron read Fanon. Nonetheless, his combination of performative talent and progressive intellectualism exemplified Barbara Christian's reminder that African Americans and other marginalized "people have always theorized, though often in forms quite different from the Western form of abstract logic . . . in narrative . . . in riddles and proverbs, in the play with language."[32]

Scott-Heron echoed one of Fanon's most important ideas in an explanation of his poem "The Revolution Will Not Be Televised." When asked about the title, Scott-Heron replied, "The catch phrase, what that was all about— 'The Revolution Will Not Be Televised'—that was about the fact that the first change that takes place is in your mind. You have to change your mind before you change the way you live and the way you move."[33] Of course, Scott-Heron's statement doesn't preclude alternative interpretations of the poem, including the critique of capitalist media conglomerates and their age-old misrepresentations of African American culture. But his explanation is directly related to Fanon's analysis of black subjectivity in colonial situations. Observe the following commentary on fellow Martinican writer Aimé Césaire: "Then, once [Césaire] had laid bare the white man in himself, he killed him. . . ."[34] Apart from the semantics, Fanon's characterization of psychic assassination is quite similar to Scott-Heron's statement that the foundational revolt against systemic disfranchisement is a psychological "change that takes place . . . in your mind."

Scott-Heron's singularity, then, wasn't that he registered social critiques but that he did so with such depth and insight. His political ideas were dialogic with major writers throughout the African diaspora who were highly regarded among intellectuals for their internationalist visions of resistance. Such writers included Amiri Baraka and Jayne Cortez in America and Ayi

Kwei Armah and Ngugi wa Thiong'o in Ghana and Kenya, respectively. In this way, Scott-Heron's perspective was unique among fellow performing artists, and his artistic talents distinguished him from other intellectuals. In his prime, Scott-Heron was a rare artist-intellectual who captivated audiences as a singer while simultaneously posing thought-provoking questions and providing clear-sighted explanations for complex political issues. He was an autodidact who read the Bible, the writings of Karl Marx, and became knowledgeable of such Third World socialists as Mao Tse-tung.[35] He also read conservative writer Ayn Rand, who influenced neoliberal economists and politicians.[36]

According to biographer Marcus Baram, Scott-Heron "believed in socialism."[37] However, his recordings seem to refute the idea that he supported dictatorships of any sort, including those purportedly controlled by labor. He was, on the contrary, a fervent believer in democracy; and though his democratic vision may have been shaped, in varying degrees, by socialist writings, Scott-Heron was deeply invested in the philosophy of blue funk. He situated much of his thinking within his notion of bluesology which referenced precepts and cultural values inscribed in blues-oriented music and writings. For Scott-Heron, blues aesthetics functioned coextensively as sites of ideological contestation and creative expression. Indeed, his framing of bluesology is dialogical with Mills's twin concepts of the racial contract and white supremacy. Throughout Scott-Heron's work we find a recurring theme: the contradiction between America's public commitment to democracy in the abstract and her denial of the social contract, that is, democratic rights to African Americans in everyday reality. His song-poems foreground the following questions: Why are black people so blest? How do we explain the super-exploitation of dark-skinned peoples of the world? And why do people who promote democracy and envision themselves as fair-minded, rational, and ethical, tolerate and/or participate in the systemic exploitation and disfranchisement of black and brown peoples?

Scott-Heron's various responses to these questions anticipated Mills's analysis of racial capitalism in *The Racial Contract* (1997). According to Mills, "White supremacy is the unnamed political system that has made the modern world what it is today."[38] Reprising the principles of social contract theory established by Western philosophers such as Jean-Jacques Rousseau, Immanuel Kant, and John Locke, Mills argues that the process in which white privilege is normalized and reproduced—what he calls white supremacy—is underwritten by a racial contract that operates as a proxy for the social contract that theoretically extends democratic rights to all citizens, but in actuality reserves such rights for persons classified as white. Mills states, "The Racial Contract is that set of formal and informal agreements" that designate some people as white and nonwhite.[39] "The general purpose is always the differential privileging of whites as a group with respect to nonwhites as a group. . . ."[40] The "informal agreements" herein stipulate a "color coded morality"[41] "enforced through violence and ideological conditioning."[42] And because the system requires that white privilege is reproduced, the racial contract must be continually renewed. Consequently, there are multiple versions and/or phases of the contract, including pre– and post–Civil Rights versions that stipulated different racial norms and codes. The Civil Rights Movement represented an attempt to dismantle the racial contract. And though activists were unable to extend the full measures of the social contract to African Americans and other nonwhite peoples, the cumulative moral and ideological impact on American society compelled the implementation of key clauses of the social contract in vital areas such as voting and education that had been crucial impediments for African Americans during Jim Crow. Scott-Heron's recordings address the reinstatement of the racial contract, that is, the denial of democratic rights and privileges to African Americans in the aftermath of the 1960s.

Significantly, both Mills and Scott-Heron represent racism in empirical terms. Scott-Heron understood race as a construct—which is to say, tool—of racial capitalism; he didn't assign intrinsic qualities to social groups based on phenotypes. Instead, he read black disfranchisement as a by-product of what Mills describes as "a set of power relations."[43] In other words, Scott-Heron put onus on people's actions—that which they *can* control—rather than physical features. Mills writes, "Even liberal whites of good will are sometimes made uneasy by racial politics, because an unsophisticatedly undifferentiated de-nunciatory vocabulary ('white') does not allow for standard political/moral distinctions between a politics of choice—absolutist and democrat, fascist and liberal—for which it is rational that we should be held accountable, and a skin color and phenotype that, after all, we cannot help."[44] Like Mills, then, Scott-Heron harbored "no essentialist illusions about anyone's intrinsic 'racial' virtues. All peoples" are susceptible to disfranchising social groups on the basis of a racial contract "as shown by the . . . black Hutus' 1994 massacre of inferior [800,000] black Tutsis in a few bloody weeks in Rwanda."[45]

We can observe how Scott-Heron navigated interracial complexities within the racial contract in his reprisal of Jean Toomer's story "Becky" in his experimental book *Cane* (1923). As with Toomer, Scott-Heron's "Cane" (1978) is a story about Becky, a white mother of two black sons who are all treated as outcasts in both black and white communities. In both narratives, Becky's refusal to adhere to the sexual stipulations of the racial contract stigmatize her as what Mills calls a "white renegade."[46] As punishment, she and her sons are banished to the outskirts of town, where they live in a one-room shack, in virtual exile on a tiny strip of land. Not surprisingly, her sons grow up resenting their vagabond status. They become violent, and shoot two men before leaving town, cursing black and white townspeople alike. That Scott-Heron reads Becky as a renegade is evident in his retelling of the story. He represents her sympathetically, singing plaintively about her predicament, worrying his lines like a blues singer as his persona invokes her prayers. Whereas Toomer emphasizes the psychological process of stigmatization, Scott-Heron exposes an ugly stipulation of the racial contract within the black community: marked intolerance toward sexuality that deviates from socially approved norms. So when Becky appeals for help, Scott-Heron sings, both black and white communities "turned away." Scott-Heron's reading of race contrasts sharply from prototypical black cultural nationalists who tended to conceptualize racial issues in Manichean terms—which is to say, they inverted blackness into goodness and virtue, and whiteness into evil and devilment. Given Becky's status as a white outcast, Scott-Heron's retelling of Toomer's story demonstrates that his perspective was equally compatible with Mills's racial contract and Iton's representation of social deviants as cultural rebels.[47]

Scott-Heron focused much of his attention on the post–Civil Rights era, particularly the onset of neoliberalism and the beginnings of a new Jim Crow.[48] His recordings chronicle the changing climate of American politics and foretell an ominous future for many African Americans: economic disintegration, deindustrialization, unemployment, imprisonment, and alienation. To the extent that the Civil Rights Movement attempted to replace the racial contract with the social contract, it was an appeal to redistribute wealth and power in American society even if activists didn't express their demands in those terms. However, President Richard Nixon steadfastly opposed economic populism. His social policies were reactionary responses to the movement's progress, which demonstrated the resiliency of the racial contract. African Americans received fewer provisions of the social contract during Nixon's administration. Then Vice President Spiro Agnew signaled Nixon's position in his rhetoric. He reportedly said, "If you've seen one slum, you've seen them all."[49] For Nixon, black resistance was public enemy number one, and he devised a "southern strategy" to thwart it. According to his adviser H. R. Haldeman, "[Nixon] emphasized that you have to face the fact that the whole problem is really the blacks. The key is to devise a system that recognizes this while not appearing to."[50]

Nixon's calls for law and order were dog whistles that resonated deeply among white voters who resented the Civil Rights Movement and the fury of black urban uprisings. Union membership declined during Nixon's administration. The jobless rate for married white men rose nearly 400 percent.[51] Yet Nixon used "dog whistles" to foment white resentment against policies that impacted black people disproportionately but also created opportunities for white people. The bellicose atmosphere emboldened police and right-wing groups. The same year Nixon was elected to the presidency, in 1968, off-duty police officers joined a mob that attacked Black Panthers outside a courthouse in Brooklyn.[52] By the mid-1970s, police had escalated violence against black people and other nonwhite social groups.[53] For Scott-Heron, the chilling new political climate was typified by the Houston police department's killing of Latino Vietnam War veteran José Campos Torres in 1977. Scott-Heron interpreted the killing as an indication of the brutal repression that would characterize the new era. In his eulogy "Jose Campos Torres" (1980), Scott-Heron says, " . . . the dogs are in the street."

GHETTO CODES AS BLUE FUNK AESTHETICS

Scott-Heron burst into prominence with his recording "The Revolution Will Not Be Televised," which reflects the rhetorical tone and pyrotechnics of the Black Arts Movement. But even during this early period, he foreshadowed the humor and satire of his later recordings. Scott-Heron's explanation of the title phrase notwithstanding, the poem examines the media's reinforcement of the racial contract in portrayals of black activism. Although the recording and the visibility it afforded him were by-products of capitalism, the young artist was deeply skeptical as to whether corporate-controlled news outlets could represent black politics in accordance with the social contract. Scott-Heron scrutinizes the media's role in decelerating the movement's progress by transfiguring its symbolism and iconography (afros, raised fists, dashikis, etc.) into commodities that neutralize their meanings and tend to (re)frame blackness in terms more amenable to the racial contract. The poet therefore suggests that a televised revolution is a contradiction in terms. "The Revolution Will Not Be Televised" urges listeners to think more critically about their sources of information about the movement; and doing so, the poem implicitly invokes a more autonomous and populist-oriented infrastructure that might represent human experiences in ways that coincided with art-ists' and activists' points of view. Initially recorded live on his album *Small Talk at 125th and Lenox* in 1970 on Flying Dutchman Records, Scott-Heron is accompanied by Eddie "Ade" Knowles and Charles Saunders on congas and David Barnes on percussion. In this version of the poem, there's little interplay between Scott-Heron and the musicians; he reads straight through the piece with few pauses that allow the music to fully complement his voice.

Scott-Heron recorded "The Revolution Will Not Be Televised" again a year later with a stellar group of musicians that included Jackson on piano, Carter on acoustic bass, Hubert Laws on flute, and the funky drummer Bernard "Pretty" Purdie, who had played with James Brown and a long list of notable jazz and rhythm and blues artists, including Herbie Hancock, Shirley Scott, Albert Ayler, Nina Simone, Jimmy McGriff, and Jack McDuff, to name a few. Unlike his first recording, the 1971 version blurs the boundary between poetry and song. Scott-Heron's phrasing is more complex. He varies rhyth-mic cadence and intonation, and his interactions with the musicians create a sense of cohesion. Meanwhile, Laws adds color on flute with improvised embellishments of Scott-Heron's solo on vocals. The young artist opens with a distinctive proclamation:

> You will not be able to stay home, brother
> You will not be able to plug in, turn on and cop out
> You will not be able to lose yourself on skag and skip.[54]

The rhetorical lines are unabashedly prosaic, but the poet's voice is fluid inside the pocket of the music. He even pauses after the first line to create a lingering effect.

Scott-Heron promotes critical thinking in the passage, comparing televi-sion consumption with using "skag" (heroin). When viewers "plug in," they enjoy a soporific effect that makes them more susceptible to subtleties of bourgeois ideology that obscure and/or distort contradictions between la-bor and capital so that people "see" privilege and poverty as natural and/or inevitable interconnections that are virtually impossible to oppose. For Scott-Heron, ideological conditioning is a discursive mode that produces what Mills calls "an epistemology of ignorance,"[55] that is, a mindset that complicates an ordinary critical process in which people distinguish fact from fiction, and thereby discern truth and historicity. In this regard, "The Revolution Will Not Be Televised" prefigures Scott-Heron's statement on ide-ology ("right looked wrong" and "up looked down") in "Jose Campos Torres" and recalls the camera obscura metaphor in Karl Marx and Friedrich Engels's *The German Ideology* (1846): "[I]n all ideology men and their circumstances appear upside-down as in a *camera obscura.* . . ."[56]

In addition to prefiguring later themes, Scott-Heron's early recordings illustrate his expertise as a songwriter. "Home Is Where the Hatred Is," a song about drug addiction, presages his theme of alcoholism in "The Bottle" (1974) and demonstrates his ability to entertain listeners while grappling with difficult topics. Originally released on *Pieces of a Man* (1971), "Home Is Where the Hatred Is" was covered, in 1972, by noted rhythm and blues singer Esther Phillips, who had suffered from heroin addiction herself. Stylistically, Scott-Heron's songwriting was often somewhat ambiguous. The title track of *Pieces of a Man* is a prime example. The song tells the story of drummer Eddie Knowles's father, who became mentally ill after he lost his job as a bricklayer. Because "the union was all-white . . . [h]e wound up working as a bellman at the Times Square Hotel . . . [and] the fact that he couldn't manifest what his real talents were" ate away at him, and he deteriorated mentally.[57] However, Scott-Heron's lyrics include imagery found in modernist poetry, and the track could almost be experienced as a visual artifact without music. His depiction of the layoff letter includes imagery often found in modern poetry. He sings, "jagged jigsaw pieces / tossed about the room."

Similarly, "The Vulture," recorded live on *Small Talk at 125th and Lenox*, elaborates on a central image in Scott-Heron's novel *The Vulture*. The ambiguity of his prefatory remarks regarding the recording's exact medium is exemplary. He states: "This is called 'The Vulture,' and a lot of people think it's a poem; and after they hear me sing it, they're sure it's a poem." However, immediately after implying "The Vulture" isn't a song, Scott-Heron foregrounds the funk principle in his remarks about the song: "Remember this is a feel-like thing. Do whatever you feel like. If you feel like clapping your hands, you can do that."[58] His self-deprecating humor aside, the song is a political allegory about the systemic disfranchisement of black working-class people. While Knowles, Saunders, and David Barnes establish the rhythm on conga drums, Scott-Heron plays a bluesy antiphonal riff on piano. He uses his stirring baritone and the cryptic imagery of his lyrics to depict American capitalism as a system that is predatory toward working-class black people: "the ghetto was a haven for the meanest creature ever known."[59] Although it never became popular, "The Vulture" is emblematic of Scott-Heron's songwriting and cultural politics. His use of imagery reflected his poetic talents and social awareness, and his singing was a musical transcription of the racial contract.[60]

Scott-Heron realized his artistic potential on the critically acclaimed 1974 album *Winter in America*. The project included his signature song-poem "H2O Gate Blues," a fan favorite in the mid-1970s. Unlike the strident tonality and black power rhetoric that characterized "The Revolution Will Not Be Televised," "H2O Gate Blues" eschews polemics, and relies instead on satire and humor. The track is a basic blues tune, featuring Scott-Heron on vocals accompanied by a trio of bass, piano, and drums. But what's especially notable about the recording is Scott-Heron's strategic use of technology to give listeners the impression that the band performed before a live audience. In his memoir *Last Holiday*, Scott-Heron says the Midnight Band "set up to do one take, 'a live ad-lib' to a blues backing."[61] As it happened, he made a mistake while reading the poem, and his decision to retain this version rather than recording another one contributed to the "ad-lib" impression and overall freshness of the performance. But Scott-Heron's most ingenuous maneuver was to play the tape back and have the band respond as though the music were live. The size of the studio was also decisive. Since it was small, the dynamics magnified band members' wisecracks and other vocal responses. Consequently, the track creates the impression of an intimate performance in a small nightclub where the laughter and signifying on the track would've ideally occurred.[62] He explained his approach in a 1976 interview with Davitt Sigerson of *Black Music* magazine:

"H_2O Gate Blues" was simulated live to give the same type of night-club-with-blues atmosphere. We're mostly not pointing out the mainstream errors or positive things that have been done by government, or a specific group of people or individual. It's the oversize things, the things that are the meat of satire, because that's what the public enjoys, what they know about. And you use them as examples of the smaller, more specific wrongs that you want corrected, or the things that have been done correctly that you want to say something positive about.[63]

While Scott-Heron's explanation specifically concerns "H2O Gate Blues," his commentary also sheds light on his use of blues humor in subsequent recordings.

Naturally, the primary focus of "H2O Gate Blues" is President Nixon's attempt to sabotage the presidential election in 1972. Scott-Heron reads and represents the break-in at the Watergate Hotel and subsequent cover-up as metonyms of neo-fascist criminality run amok. Recorded in November

1973, "H2O Gate Blues" is a prime example of the artist's foresight. Beltway pundits and journalists had yet to determine Nixon's role in the break-in, and the president did not resign until the following year. So Scott-Heron's suggestion in "H2O Gate Blues" that Nixon orchestrated the break-in defied conventional wisdom at the time. In a 1975 interview with Sheila Weller for *Rolling Stone*, he gloated: "Right after the burglary, Brian and I figured out that Nixon did it."[64] As with the Honey Drippers' recording "Impeach the President" (1973), "H2O Gate Blues" exemplifies the street-smart politics that shaped Scott-Heron's blues-inflected satire: "I'm sorry, the government you have elected is inoperative / Click! Inoperative."[65] Scott-Heron blends onomatopoeia ("click," i.e., the sound of telephones in 1970s) with parody to direct listeners' attention to structural problems in American political economy. But unlike many black intellectuals of his generation, not to mention entertainers, his internationalist perspective enabled him to highlight various ways in which racial capitalism not only impacted African Americans but other nonwhite peoples abroad in countries such as Vietnam and Chile. He muses, "[S]ometimes one idea provides the opportunity to speak about other things."[66]

In "H2O Gate Blues," Scott-Heron intersects two motifs: 1) the relationship between systemic racial violence in the United States and violence against nonwhite people abroad; 2) the role of ideological conditioning in both contexts. Scott-Heron represents capitalist ideology as a discursive method that fostered political attitudes that facilitated corruption, which compounded and normalized preexisting inequalities. As Mills puts it, "[I]n a racially structured polity, the only people who find it psychologically possible to deny the centrality of race are those who are racially privileged, for whom race is invisible precisely because the world is structured around them. . . . The fish does not see the water, and whites do not see the racial nature of a white polity because it is natural to them, the element in which they move."[67] To underscore the political stakes at hand, Scott-Heron suggests that Nixon's autocratic proclivities included strains of fascism: "How long will the citizens wait / It's looking like Europe in '38."[68]

At the same time, Scott-Heron suggests that notions of American exceptionalism complicate citizens' ability to grasp the horror of international violence that's been perpetrated in their name under the guise of maintaining democracy. The political upshot is the reification of racial capitalism and its fetishizing of the almighty dollar. Note his commentary on the Vietnam War: "[A]sk them what they're fighting for and they never mention the economics of war."[69] The line points up Scott-Heron's role as an organic intellectual in the 1970s. He raises a simple, and apparently obvious, question that was often ignored in American educational, religious, and cultural institutions that shaped black people's perspectives: Why were "the economics of war" so seldom discussed? Scott-Heron's response correlates profits and propaganda. He suggests that corporate media outlets often downplay "the economics of war," because public awareness of such economics would dissipate popular support and undercut the moral basis of war, particularly insofar as democracy is cited as an objective for fighting. From Scott-Heron's perspective, corporate media outlets misrepresent pertinent issues in geopolitical conflicts and simultaneously invoke the word "democracy" as a default explanation for military actions, especially in locations where nonwhite people and/or non-Christians comprise majorities of the populace. As such, Scott-Heron suggests that when politicians and pundits invoke "democracy," it has a beguiling effect of concealing the economic interests and contradictions that provoke political conflicts and ultimately military action.

An important premise of "H2O Gate Blues" is that racial conditioning engenders specious acts of altruism that morph into self-righteousness and jingoistic entitlement. Naturally, debates over race and representation are as old as America itself. But where many black artists and intellectuals often interpreted racial politics in isolation from class issues, Scott-Heron developed an internationalist cultural politics. He routinely intersected race and class, while situating his commentaries in relation to international politics and perspectives. So when Scott-Heron rhymes about "The CIA in Chile / knowing nothing about [President Salvador] Allende,"[70] he demonstrates that the American government, which supported the 1973 Chilean coup d'état resulting in Allende's death, the torture and killings of thousands of artists and intellectuals, and the dictatorship of Augusto Pinochet, also authorized "[t]he chaining and gagging of [Black Panther co-founder] Bobby Seale."[71] The passage specifically refers to a court hearing in which Seale was ordered by a judge to be gagged and chained. However, the gag image also symbolizes America's general reaction to black militancy. Scott-Heron represents Gestapo-like tactics as by-products of white supremacy and its epistemology of ignorance.

The late political scientist Manning Marable pointed out that as early as 1965 the FBI received approval to wiretap SNCC leaders' telephones, and proceeded, under the leadership of J. Edgar Hoover, to liquidate the Panthers through the aegis of COINTELPRO. But instead of interpreting the government's repression of the movement as an assault against working-class Americans, white union leaders responded favorably to Nixon and President

Spiro Agnew's bigotry even though the jobless rate for married white males rose nearly 400 percent during the Nixon and Ford administrations, and union membership declined significantly.[72] So in the climatic section of the poem, Scott-Heron uses black vernacular lingo and tonal semantics to poke fun at the situation:

> McCord has blown, Mitchell has blown
> No tap on my telephone
> Haldeman, Erlichman, Mitchell and Dean
> It follows a pattern if you dig what I mean.[73]

Note the sly signification in the line: "No tap on my telephone." Although the passage contains little of the subtlety that typifies academic poetry, Scott-Heron commands attention with tonal semantics. Speech and music merge as his voice becomes an instrument. In other words, the sound and cadence are intrinsic to the "affective power" the track generates. Scott-Heron's use of black vernacular lingo is also notable. The term "blown" is a variant of a colloquial expression that reflects black speakers' propensity for elision. Instead of using the entire phrase (McCord has blown his cover), Scott-Heron shortens it to enhance the melodic effect. Short verbal riffs, alliterative repetition, and virtuoso rhyming establish a rhythmic cadence that culminates with a black street phrase that implicates Nixon with blues-inflected satire. Except for John McCord, an ex-CIA operative who was caught in the break-in, all the men were members of his administration. And with the threat of impeachment looming, Nixon resigned. Gerald Ford became president, and he pardoned Nixon shortly thereafter.

For Scott-Heron, Nixon's presidency signaled a new phase of American politics marked by hyper-conservatism, a reactionary political movement initiated by the assassination of John F. Kennedy. Given Kennedy's progressive image and posturing, Scott-Heron interpreted his assassination as an attempt to enforce the racial contract. Coining the metaphorical phrase winter in America, he said: ". . . that started the Winter in America. The deaths of Robert Kennedy, Malcolm X and Martin Luther King were all part of that."[74] The cold political climate ushered in social policies that disproportionately impacted working-class black people, especially rising unemployment, which was coextensive with an escalating sense of desolation that often led to alcoholism. Scott-Heron addressed these problems in "The Bottle." Arguably his finest song, "The Bottle" was inspired by a group of alcoholics Scott-Heron met while living in Washington, D.C. He watched them return to the local liquor store every morning and became fascinated. "And I got so curious," he said," that I had to go out there and sit down and talk to them."[75]

Scott-Heron found that the complexities of alcoholics' lives belied their appearances, and that their stories conflicted with stereotypical narratives about black alcoholics. One black woman was a former teacher who had presumably been fired because she "had somehow juggled her grades to get somebody else promoted that shouldn't have been."[76] In his memoir *The Last Holiday*, Scott-Heron recollects:

> I found out that none of them had hoped to be become alcoholics when they grew up. Things had arrived along the way and turned them in that direction. I discovered one of them was an ex-physician who'd been busted for performing abortions on young girls. There was a military air-traffic controller who'd sent two jets crashing into a mountain one day. He left work that day and never went back. In the song, I was saying, Look, here's a drunk and this is why he is an alcoholic, instead of just glossing over the problem.[77]

Included on *Winter in America* and released as a single in 1974, "The Bottle" reached #15 on the R&B chart, which was impressive for a rhythm and blues song recorded on a small jazz label. At the time, Scott-Heron taught creative writing at Federal City College (now University of the District of Columbia), and "The Bottle" demonstrates how he incorporated elements of creative writing into songwriting.

For Scott-Heron, the bottle symbolized systemic structural problems that create and/or exacerbate preexisting complications in people's everyday lives. The problems are played out in symptomatic behaviors such as alcoholism and drug abuse. Scott-Heron's statement on his songwriting is especially applicable to "The Bottle." Reminiscent of his approach to writing "H2O Gate Blues," he states, "I generally used an individual or individual circumstance as an example of a larger thing."[78] He also foregrounded history to create more compelling counternarratives to offset stereotypic images. In contradistinction to the normative trend of representing his characters as inherently or unexplainably irresponsible, Scott-Heron strived to depict them as victims of circumstance who offered gut-wrenching testimonies to the nightmare of history.

Yet from a musical standpoint, "The Bottle" is distinctly groove oriented. The song is a soulful sketch of inner-city blues. Joined by Danny Bowens on bass, Bob Adams on drums, and Brian Jackson, who performs masterfully on flute, Scott-Heron creates a soothing groove on vocals and keyboards. The first verse showcases Scott-Heron's synecdoche-centered approach to song-writing. He focuses on a little black boy whose father's alcohol addiction is so acute that drinking has become his sole preoccupation in life. He contemplates his entire existence around the ephemeral rush of alcohol, which sets off a chain of events. He quits his job and resorts to pawning family valuables, such as his wife's wedding ring, for money. The instability creates havoc in the household, and Scott-Heron illustrates the psychological devastation by using an image of the most vulnerable member of the family—a confused and frightened little boy whose living nightmare threatens the emotional sustenance he needs to avoid replicating the disfigurement of his father.

After describing cyclical problems that disproportionately affect black men, Scott-Heron narrows his focus to the former doctor. He lost his medical license after performing the abortion and lost his family afterward. His story was a modern-day blues. And just as blues music dissipated the blues as such, the Midnight Band's "affective power" accentuated Scott-Heron's critique. The music swings as the poet sings baritone. His lyrics lilt and flow with the rhythm, creating a sense of buoyancy. There's even a splash of humor to lighten the mood. When a local preacher realizes that a young woman he knows has turned to prostitution for sustenance, he attempts to show her the error of her ways—only to be cursed and clobbered in outright defiance. Thus listeners literally *feel* the message and thereby gain an added sense of understanding through memory. Theorizing the cognitive process inherent in such performances, Gerald Davis writes, "The power of the performance moves beyond the walls of the auditorium. . . . As in church, the spiritual *essence . . .* of the performance may well be carried into the days and weeks following the actual performance as those who experienced [it], or those who have reports of [it], discuss it, evaluate it, and relive it."[79] Scott-Heron's use of tonal semantics is especially notable when he accentuates his sly ideological subversion by softening the /ɪ/ sound in the word "bottle," so that "bottle" is sometimes blurred with "bottom," suggesting a correlation between drug abuse and socioeconomics.

However, the tragicomedy also illuminates Scott-Heron's blind spot regarding gender politics. Like countless men in American society, he internalized the notion of male privilege. And though Scott-Heron was too sensitive a thinker to promote overt misogyny, his vision of an oppressed black collectivity within the United States encompassed a corollary vision that normalized women's subordination. Scott-Heron's ability to create such a beautiful song based on his interaction with black alcoholics was a commendable achievement as a funky bluesologist. He exemplified Black Arts theorist Larry Neal's belief that artists should be "integral parts of the community's life-style,"[80] but unfortunately, Scott-Heron's liberationist vision didn't include women in leadership roles. It is revealing that the men in "The Bottle" are fallen heroes, and the lone woman character has no agency outside of her man. Herein Scott-Heron evidenced negligible imagination and intellectual labor. The woman is down and out because her man is imprisoned, and she becomes violent after losing him and his financial security. So she becomes the butt of a joke in a song that posits compassion as its subtext—this despite the fact that most black women in urban areas worked outside their homes in the 1970s regardless of their marital status. "The Bottle" is so groove oriented, though, that few listeners probably recognized Scott-Heron's contradiction. Nonetheless, his stereotypical depiction of the woman typifies what Iton called "hidden imperialisms"[81] that undercut male funk artists' efforts to fully manifest the black fantastic.

Scott-Heron's social critique of American political economy becomes more pointed as "The Bottle" nears conclusion. Whereas Hollywood films and media outlets tend to represent black alcoholics and drug addicts as criminals, Scott-Heron suggests that the real crimes are the social policies that create nightmarish conditions that lead to despair and therefore alcoholism, drug addiction, and sometimes criminal behavior (e.g., the woman hitting the preacher). He sings, "Don't you think it's a crime / when time after time people in the bottle."[82] That Scott-Heron's hit song anticipated critical discussions that correlate deindustrialization and the war on drugs with the underground economy, crack addition, gang violence, and the prison-industrial complex demonstrates his political foresight. Unfortunately, though, it also presaged a tragic irony. Scott-Heron was singing about his own future. At the conclusion of "The Bottle," the persona says that he, too, will wind up living in the bottle. Scott-Heron probably ad-libbed "it's gonna be me" to accentuate an important supposition in the song: that everyone in the community was subject to catastrophe and therefore vulnerable to some form of drug addiction. Scott-Heron's addiction to crack cocaine compromised his character, health, talent, and eventually led to imprisonment.

Still, 1975 marked a new beginning for the funky bluesologist. Scott-Heron became the first artist signed to Arista Records. The legendary mogul Clive Davis had been impressed by "The Bottle," and went with Stevie Wonder to see him and the Midnight Band shortly after starting his new label. Davis recollected, "I remember it vividly and I remember being floored. . . . He was such a charismatic, compelling young artist, very much in his moment in time. I was very taken by him."[83] In collaboration with Brian Jackson, Scott-Heron aptly titled the new album *The First Minute of a New Day* and extended his political metaphor in the liner notes: "Winter is a metaphor; a term not only used to describe the season of ice, but the period of our lives through which we are traveling. . . . We approach winter, the most depressing period in the history of this industrial empire, with threats of oil shortages, and energy crises."[84] Jackson's recollection of the album is also pertinent. "People were still trying to effect change en masse," he said, "and we were just hoping if we put it out there, people would say, 'Oh yeah, the window is closing rapidly.'"[85] Jackson's political assessment illuminates the song's ominous tone. Whereas *Winter in America* counterbalanced doom with dance rhythms, the title track of the album is haunting. Scott-Heron's baritone is drenched in blues, his lyrics pitch-dark and stripped of humor. His voice is a sonic illustration of pain, a paralinguistic narrative highlighting deteriorating conditions in America's cities. "Winter in America" is thus among his most prescient songs.

Scott-Heron's multiethnic reading of the racial contract is evident from the outset. Although black disfranchisement is the focal point of "Winter in America," he foregrounds Native American historicity. Highlighting the exploitation and ruthless decimation of Native peoples, Scott-Heron interprets their history as a foundational component of the racial contract. He sings, "From the Indians who welcomed the pilgrims / And to the buffaloes who once ruled the plains."[86] The passage illustrates the hypocrisy and violence encoded in the racial contract. White Americans waged war against Native peoples, killing large numbers of buffaloes that provided indispensable sources of meat and clothing for Native Americans. Even though Native peoples treated early white settlers with considerable degrees of compassion, the ideological stipulations of manifest destiny dictated that Indians be misrepresented as intellectually inferior and morally deficient beings—in brief, people who had no legal or moral rights to their land.

This gruesome chapter of American history, which has been erased from school textbooks and caricatured in popular films, cartoons, and television shows, serves as a backdrop for Scott-Heron's narrative in "Winter in America." Using bleak, barren images, Scott-Heron depicts post–Civil Rights America as a political wasteland where vultures circle the sky, hovering over cities that are decaying like hollow trees along the eastern shore. The landscape is a parched, expansive surface devoid of greenery and life. Scott-Heron uses ecological motifs in the song to illustrate the economic effects of right-wing political programs such as COINTELPRO and other measures designed to neutralize black political organizations, impede the momentum of progressive politics generally, and thereby stabilize the status quo. Not surprisingly, in "South Carolina (Barnwell)" (1975), he wonders, "Whatever happened to the protests and the rage?"

"South Carolina" appeared on Scott-Heron and Jackson's album *From South Africa to South Carolina*, which also includes Scott-Heron's song "Johannesburg." Herein Scott-Heron engaged thorny political issues in South Africa a decade before American activists called for Nelson Mandela's freedom from prison while demonstrating against apartheid in the 1980s. As the pan-African album title suggests, "Johannesburg" intersects national and international conditions of the racial contract. At the time, the African National Congress was waging battle against the Afrikaner government apartheid policies. Led by B. J. Vorster, South Africa's National Party, which had risen to power in the 1948 election, was determined to maintain apartheid. And though Scott-Heron had never traveled to South Africa, he conceptualized white supremacy as a political system that prompted him to write "Johannesburg," one of his most popular political songs, which reached #29 on the R&B charts. In the recording, Scott-Heron posits the city of Johannesburg as a symbol of black South Africans' growing resistance. However, the initial events that precipitated strikes throughout the country occurred in Durban in 1973, when black workers engaged in wildcat strikes. Black South Africans' rights to vote, assemble, and form trade unions had been outlawed by the government. "The typical protests of the period focused primarily on the issue of wages, working conditions, and grievances procedures. . . ."[87] The Durban strikes marked a crucial point in the struggle against apartheid.

For Scott-Heron, the struggle against apartheid seemed all too familiar. His pan-Africanist leanings prompted him to envision "Johannesburg" as a song that offered an internationalist reading of the racial contract. He parallels apartheid with African Americans' disfranchisement in the United States, cataloging several cities with large black populations: New York, Washington, D.C., Los Angeles, Detroit, London. Scott-Heron's liner notes to the 1977 album *Bridges* is equally pertinent to his political perspective in "Johannesburg":

> There is a revolution going on in the world. We are very much a part of it and have a great deal to contribute to the force and direction of this revolution. There are many fronts within this struggle, many far flung outposts geographically isolated and distant from our mainstreams of communication. But everyone who struggles for a better

life for oppressed people is an ally who can use any symbol of our concern and solidarity.[88]

Scott-Heron uses rhyme and vernacular lingo in his role as bluesologist. Rather than condemning the events in South Africa or stating his views outright, he uses a more subtle, interrogative approach. Scott-Heron asks whether listeners are aware of recent goings-on in Johannesburg. Then, without stating what is happening, he implies that black South Africans might be revolting but holds back from stating it outright. This is an age-old method to excite interest or arouse curiosity.

The musical energy of "Johannesburg" reaches a crescendo with Scott-Heron's repetition of the title. Using black vernacular phrases, he engages in call and response with band members: "What's the word? Johannesburg!" As with "H2O Gate Blues," multiple voices in the recording respond, shout "Johannesburg!" in unison. But what's notable about Scott-Heron's political phrase is his blues-oriented parody of a jingle: "What's the word? Thunderbird!" Thunderbird is a cheap wine sold by Gallo Brothers that was once popular among poor black city dwellers. The poet-scholar Aldon Lynn Nielsen, who took classes from Scott-Heron at Federal City College, remarks: "It was genius. People would walk around humming that jingle. . . . Gil was always finding something that could be reread as commentary."[89] In "Johannesburg," the parodic exchange is repeated several times before Scott-Heron invokes percussive incantation ("Say get it from the drums!"), indicating that the band has constructed pure funk. But where James Brown might've taken it to the bridge, or Clinton might've invoked the mothership, Scott-Heron interjects blue funk phraseology ("You gotta get one") into pan-Africanist ideology. He accentuates the effect with a verbal riff wherein he prefaces a repeated line ("is like Johannesburg") with names of American cities. And when the music reaches a feverish pitch, he uses an ironic rhetorical device—a mock-personal request delivered in a half-sung pitch: "Somebody tell me what's happening in Johannesburg." The point, of course, is to rally people's interest in South Africa's struggle without being preachy. With his voice a near-cry, Scott-Heron magnifies the emotional effect by using enjambment which makes "some" and "body" sound like separate words.

Scott-Heron shifts the focus of geopolitics back to the American landscape on the album *Bridges* (1977). The narrator in "Delta Man" maps a black diasporic trajectory inside the United States after the Civil War. But while the song engages the specific historicity of black (male) agency and resistance, it projects African Americans' dreams of freedom in relation to liberation movements in Africa, Asia, and the Caribbean. In the liner notes, Scott-Heron theorizes change as a constant in human life: "All things change. From the wheel to the automobile. . . . And the social dynamics and perimeters during your lifetime have exploded into a thousand fragments of liberation movements and human rights demands."[90] Scott-Heron prefaces his singing with a spoken-word prelude to a political performance that was analogous to a position paper ("where I'm comin' from"). He dedicates the song to "brothers" fighting elsewhere in the African diaspora. As the story begins, Delta Man is awakened by a crow that symbolizes black historical consciousness. Just as the Sankofa bird in Haile Gerima's film *Sankofa* (1993) leads the protagonist Mona on a flight to her ancestral past in Ghana, the crow in "Delta Man" escorts him on a similar flight of historical consciousness that aptly begins in the Mississippi Delta—the primal site of the blues.

As the funky bluesician sings about black men's migration patterns after the Civil War, Jackson simulates blues cries on synthesizer while the singer himself tickles the keys with sporadic splashes of blue notes, using tonal semantics for added effect. Scott-Heron's use of heavy-breath vocables ("hunh") evoke the grunt work plantation bosses shunted onto black agricultural laborers. From Mississippi the crow flies to Nebraska, where black men were cowboys in the Wild West. Scott-Heron sings about "rootin'-tootin'" six-shooters, and Jackson simulates the sound of gunfire to accentuate the effect. The narrative culminates in the hood, where "brother-man" lives on welfare in a neighborhood rife with disrepair and drug addiction. As with "Johannesburg," the artistic objective wasn't to board the mothership but rather to effectuate forms of pleasure and kinesthesia that facilitate politico-historical analyses of black cultural history. So while the melody engenders buoyancy, the rhythm is a medium-tempo two-step dance instead of a full-fledged, party vibe. The accompaniments of percussionist Barnett Williams and Brian Jackson, who introduced a synthesizer bass to the music, are especially noteworthy. The new instrument opened up entirely new textures of sound and noticeably accentuated his resonance as an accompanist. Commenting on the instrument, Jackson said, "A bass is a bass. There's only so much you can do with it. But with a synthesizer, you can create all kinds of sounds and tunes."[91] Like many funk instrumentalists, Jackson is a jazz musician at heart, and he adds significant flavor to the song with his improvisatory treatments of Scott-Heron's phrases. At times, he embellishes the line in between Scott-Heron's phrases; sometimes he plays contrapuntal phrases; and sometimes he plays complementary phrases while Scott-Heron sings and Williams comps on percussion.

"Delta Man" exemplifies the complicated nature of Scott-Heron's blue funk. On the one hand, the song demonstrates how he translated funk's contrarian impulses as counter-ideological discourse. The song's story reflects Scott-Heron's belief that meaningful social change could only be attained by a popular movement—what he termed "revolution," which meant non-violent demonstrations, not "pitched battles in the street."[92] On the other hand, "Delta Man," like "Johannesburg," reveals the gendered limitations of Scott-Heron's vision. When he telescopes blackness into a male bailiwick, he deemphasizes gender and sexual issues and undermines his political objectives. That Scott-Heron envisioned a black liberated future in primarily masculine terms exemplifies a salient contradiction in funk aesthetics. It also partly explains why so many post–Civil Rights Era activists and artists have found it exceedingly difficult to mobilize the sort of popular social movement that Scott-Heron advocated. Such efforts would require the respect, trust, and cooperation of disparate, and sometimes conflicting, sectors of African American culture, not to mention various other social groups in the United States. To the extent that political approaches exclude or alienate potential collaborators or supporters, they are counterproductive.

Nonetheless, Scott-Heron displayed remarkable foresight in his songwriting. "We Almost Lost Detroit," also on *Bridges*, is an excellent example of his distinctive blend of resistive art and intellect. At the time, the song marked a rare instance in which a black public figure addressed the dangers of environmental pollution. Scott-Heron was inspired by John G. Fuller's book *We Almost Lost Detroit* (1975). He explains: "I found myself in opposition to the expansion of nuclear powerplants [*sic*] and did some research about them. One of the sources was Fuller's book which explains how incalculably unsafe these things are."[93] The book examines the partial meltdown at Detroit Edison's Fermi-1 nuclear plant in 1966; and since Scott-Heron's father, stepmother, two brothers, and a sister all lived in Detroit, the implications of Fuller's narrative were personal. He decided to write a song about the incident.[94] But from a musical standpoint, what's most striking about "We Almost Lost Detroit" is the stark contrast between its idyllic tone, especially at the outset, and the dystopic theme of nuclear disaster. The band's mosaic of sound is wistful and serene—so much so that the mood and sound quality are vaguely reminiscent of late-night slow jams on "Quiet Storm" radio programs. Jackson, who was largely responsible for the tranquil ambience, plays the synthesizer fluently and effusively, and Fred Payne's soft strumming on guitar also enhances the tranquility. When Scott-Heron begins to sing, his voice is somber, the lyrics mundane. Without mentioning the reactor specifically, he sings about it as an apparently innocuous oddity—something like a strange building or monument that might pique a young child's curiosity. His voice has the poignancy reminiscent of lost love or another heartfelt experience—indeed, anything but a near nuclear disaster—until he sings the hook: "We almost lost Detroit."

The premise of the song is that the interests of capitalism and the commonweal are altogether contradictory. Scott-Heron sings, "When it comes to people's safety money wins out every time." He substantiates his statement by invoking the memory of Karen Silkwood, a young laboratory analyst who became a union activist at Kerr-McGee Corporation's plutonium production plant in Crescent in Oklahoma. Her case was publicized by the Hollywood film *Silkwood* (1983), starring Meryl Streep as Silkwood. Although Silkwood initially believed that nuclear energy could be safe, she eventually concluded that plutonium is hazardous, and became critical of management's policies. She decided to gather company documents clandestinely to substantiate her criticisms; and once she had possession, she agreed to meet *New York Times* reporter David Burnham. But Silkwood was killed on her way to the meeting when her car collided with a concrete culvert under dubious circumstances. *Rolling Stone* magazine reported that the highway patrolman on the scene said that he put the muddy papers he found back into her car, but when Burnham and Silkwood's boyfriend, Drew Stephens, searched the car the next day they were gone.[95] Fittingly, in the latter portion of "We Almost Lost Detroit," Scott-Heron sings variations of the hook and ponders the psychological devastation of nuclear disaster. As he repeats the chorus, the band gains momentum. The song closes with an exhilarating horn line played by Sunni-Ali and Delbert Taylor on tenor sax and trumpet, respectively.[96]

Scott-Heron seemed on top of his game at the end of the decade. He released the hit single "Angel Dust," one of the best songs he ever recorded, in 1978. The song reached #15 on the R&B charts and was included his album *Secrets* (1978), which introduced a completely new sound. To increase Scott-Heron's visibility, Davis recruited producer Malcolm Cecil to work on *Secrets*. Cecil had worked previously with Stevie Wonder and was known for his innovative use of electronic instruments, which excited Jackson even though Cecil's arrival displaced his role in the band as a co-producer. Jackson said, "I had been waiting to do something like this."[97] Backup singers Maxine Waters Waddell, Julia Waters, and Marti McCall, were also recruited for the album. Their soulful voices were significant contributions to the band's new sound. In fact, the women set the tone for "Angel Dust," singing the title ensemble as a mid-tempo hook, while drummer Alvin Taylor plays catchy rhythms on the hi hat, and Jackson plays a pulsating bottom riff on bass synthesizer. When Scott-Heron adds his baritone, the vibe is infectious. While Waddell, Waters, and McCall sing the refrain, Scott-Heron assumes the role of the wise elder advising youth about the grave dangers of using PCP: "I ain't tryin' to run your life." Aside from the sheer pleasure of the music, the stark realism of Scott-Heron's lyrics was also part of the appeal. He sings a detailed narrative about an individual under the influence: "The room was exploding but that was all part of the high." Revelations of unpalatable truths were part and parcel of funk aesthetics, especially Scott-Heron's version, and the song stirred controversy. Radio stations in Buffalo and Miami refused to play "Angel Dust."[98]

For some people, though, especially older adults, Scott-Heron's meticulous portrayal of the PCP experience sounded all too wise, not to mention counterproductive. Of course, it goes without saying that Scott-Heron was hypocritical for assuming the mantle of abstention. But it should be noted that, given his dedication to providing social criticism, the contradiction may not have appeared especially stark back then. In the political economy of black street culture, drugs were assigned different reputations with corresponding degrees of cultural value. Generally, heroin and PCP were stigmatized while marijuana was considered innocuous, and cocaine was regarded as chic and cosmopolitan. This view of cocaine was shared widely by many black urban youth after Gordon Parks's blockbuster film *Superfly* (1972) in which the protagonist Priest is a cocaine dealer and recreational user whose Cadillac, fashion, and personality symbolized coolness and cosmopolitanism. But "Angel Dust" reflected contradictory impulses in Scott-Heron's personality that he couldn't resolve. He was addicted to cocaine but maintained his sense of social responsibility as an artist-intellectual. He even issued a formal warning about angel dust, and was given a public service award at an annual Communications to Black Audiences ceremony.[99] Many youth reacted positively to the song. Scott-Heron's frankness was probably a contributing factor,[100] and the latent rebellion of flouting social conventions may have also added to the appeal. Besides, the song was aesthetically appealing.

But Scott-Heron faced trouble ahead. The album title *Secrets* contained a hidden layer of meaning—his cocaine habit was worsening, though from all appearances everything seemed fine. Later in 1978, Arista released the compilation *The Mind of Gil Scott-Heron*, which included the spoken word piece "The Ghetto Code (Dot Dot Dit Dit Dot Dot Dash)," one of Scott-Heron's finest works. As suggested in the title, the poem showcases the ingenuity of black folk practices. Using Pig Latin and Tut-language, Scott-Heron highlights the dialectics of racial politics. The term "ghetto" denotes what Mills calls the racialization of space,[101] and "code" refers to black speakers' discursive procedures which Scott-Heron represents tongue-in-cheek as covert communication. Assuming the role of blues trickster, he lampoons the racist notion that black vernacular expression only transmits idiocy, pointing the finger of ignorance back toward the outside world.

"The Ghetto Code" showcases a form of Pig Latin that was popular in black vernacular expression in the mid-1970s. Generally, speakers interpolated the sound "iz" immediately after a syllable—or after the initial consonant and/or vowel sound in words with one syllable. Thus "feel" becomes *fizeel*. According to Scott-Heron, the lesser known phrase "Dot dot dit dit dot dot dash," a parody of the Morse code, referenced political and economic absurdity, and literally meant "Damned if I know."[102] Scott-Heron approached these phraseologies as primary resources that served two distinct purposes. First, they documented how working-class black folk often viewed their economic predicament in postindustrial America. Second, the vocables provided Scott-Heron with fresh experimental material to effectuate his analyses of the racial contract.

Although it's unclear whether Scott-Heron recorded "The Ghetto Code" live or simulated a live performance, his interaction with an audience is audible throughout its duration. He weaves a comedic narrative in which CIA and FBI agents attempt to monitor black folks' conversations, but invariably become perplexed in their efforts to decode the ghetto code: "[H]ey bree-is-other me-is-an? You goin' to the pe-is-arty to ne-is-ite?" / "Oh yeah! Well, why not bring me a ne-is-ickel be-is-ag? You dig?"[103] Scott-Heron represents the passage as linguistic subterfuge that he describes as "old fashioned ghetto codes."[104] The translation into Standard American English would read: Hey brother man? Are you going to the party tonight? Really? Well, would you bring me a nickel bag? Of course, most English speakers could probably denote the passage in print-form, but on the recording Scott-Heron accelerates the flow so that the language morphs into a "code" that renders the correspondence virtually unintelligible.[105]

"The Ghetto Code," then, epitomizes Scott-Heron vernacular intellectualism. Many hip hop fans will recognize similarities between his syllabic experiments and stock phrases that Snoop and other MCs used many years later. But Scott-Heron's use of the technique wasn't merely stylistic. On the contrary, he used pig Latin to challenge conventional epistemology. The title itself is an ironic commentary on lingering presumptions in American society about poor African Americans' supposedly limited critical faculties.

The recording is thus an artifact of political philosophy expressed as spoken word. Scott-Heron uses black vernacular phrases as critical tools to expose the faulty foundations of imperialist logic that's been normalized by the ascendancy of racial capitalism. For instance, he uses the ghetto code to reexamine Western historiography, and his resultant critique illuminated the sorts of myths that Martin Bernal examined in his groundbreaking 1987 study *Black Athena: The Afroasiatic Roots of Classical Civilization: Volume I: The Fabrication of Ancient Greece 1785–1985*. Obviously, Scott-Heron's spoken word is a popular recording whose breadth isn't the least bit comparable to Martin Bernal's painstaking investigation. But there are conceptual parallels between the two artifacts. Scott-Heron's rereading of the Western calendar in "The Ghetto Code" is analogous to Bernal's method of reexamining Western historiography. The funky bluesologist reads mundane materials that articulate and normalize dominant ideologies, and he and Bernal both examine myths related to prevailing epistemological models while raising the following questions: How do we know what we know? How is cultural knowledge authenticated in Western societies? How is history constructed? And how do we question normalized discourse when we already presume it is true? In his work, Bernal demonstrates that Western historiography was reconstructed by displacing Egypt with Greece as the cradle of human civilization in the mid-nineteenth century to lend theoretical support for colonization and slavery. For his part, during roughly the same period, the funky bluesologist "reinvestigate[d] astrology," and his study revealed that someone had "been messing with the calendar"—namely, that Julius Caesar and Augustus Caesar commanded that July and August were respectively instituted in their honor.[106] The Romans' apotheosis of the two emperors produced numerical and chronological asymmetries. Scott-Heron observes that September is the "ninth month on our calendar" despite the fact that the term signifies "'seventh' in Latin"; and that October (*octo*), November (*nove*), and December (*deci*) are all derived from Romance prefixes that mean eight, nine, and ten, respectively. Facing the challenge of explaining the disjunctions, he points up the absurdity and says: "Dot dot dit dit dot dot dash / I'm damned if I know."[107]

After probing the epistemological implications in the calendar's asymmetry, Scott-Heron concludes with mock seriousness that the contradiction is conspicuous in February because of the leap years. He half-jokingly cites February 28 as incontrovertible evidence that our sense of time has been arbitrarily constructed. Why, he asks, wouldn't January 32 have been equally appropriate? The playful implication here is that ideologies and policies that recreate black disfranchisement are characterized by similar arbitrary inconsistencies. After priming the audience for skepticism, Scott-Heron reimagines February as an allegory of the racial contract. Using ribald humor, he narrates a hypothetical scenario in which everyone receives a package that contains four weeks of time; but when people go home and unwrap them, they discover one week only has five days. Whereas people living under the social contract might experience a shorter work week, Scott-Heron suggests that people living under the racial contract would have a very different experience: "[Y]ou know white folks; ain't gon be no weekend. You gonna go home Friday night. Get up, the next day is Monday. You have to go right back to work."

Scott-Heron's creative talents were at their peak, but cracks were beginning to show behind the scenes. He formed a new band called Amnesia Express with saxophonist and pianist Carl Cornwell, another college mate from Lincoln University. Amnesia Express played an arguably funkier style on the album *Reflections* (1981). The central track is Scott-Heron's song-poem "'B' Movie," which reflects the full range of his multifaceted artistry—poet, singer, songwriter, co-producer. The twelve-minute magnum opus consists of three parts: an introductory monologue, a poem, and a song. Scott-Heron layers vocals over a toe-tapping groove created by a rhythm section that included drummer Kenny Powell and bass player Robert Gordon. Roughly three minutes into the track, keyboardist Glen "Astro" Turner plays the chorus, which is embellished by the horn line played by tenor saxophonist Carl Cornwell, alto saxophonist Vernon James, and trumpeter Kenny Sheffield. Meanwhile, Scott-Heron adds spice to the mix with prerecorded vocal effects. As a brilliant example of creative criticism, "'B' Movie" thematizes the racial contract in Ronald Reagan's political strategies.

For Scott-Heron, Reagan's presidency was a dialectical response to progressive social movements on behalf of marginalized groups, including African Americans, women, and queer people. That is, he interpreted the election as a reinstatement of earlier features of the racial contract—a kneejerk reaction to the impulse for freedom manifested not only in the Civil Rights Movement but the Feminist Movement and the movement for LGBT people's rights as well. Parodying Reagan, Scott-Heron says mockingly:

> Civil rights. Women's rights. Gay rights. They're all wrong. Call in the cavalry to disrupt this perception of freedom gone wrong. First one of them wants freedom and then the whole damn world wants freedom.

Nostalgia. That's what America wants. The good old days. When "we gave them hell!" When the buck stopped somewhere and you could still buy something with it! To a time when movies were in black and white and so was everything else.[108]

Note the cavalry image juxtaposed against the freedom dreams of racialized, gendered, and sexualized Others. In a 1976 interview, Scott-Heron made a statement about his song "The Summer of '42" that also informs his thinking in "'B' Movie."

[W]hite America wants to go back . . . before Montgomery. And there's a mania related to happy times before people started to challenge the status quo, when women cooked dinner and sewed socks, and black people swept floors and smiled. And I'm saying that we can't afford to go back there, we can't afford to allow that type of imagery, which is fascist when it's done to the max. . . .[109]

Once again, Scott-Heron demonstrates profound foresight on racial politics. Indeed, we could argue persuasively that his commentary anticipates Trump's campaign slogan: "Make America Great Again." According to historian Robin D. G. Kelley, Trump's core constituency, like Ronald Reagan's, "look[ed] in terror at the erosion of the American Dream, but they were looking at it through the prism of race."[110] In other words, the extent to which capitalism exploited white workers was commensurate with their willingness to scapegoat African Americans, feminists, LGBT people, and others associated with so-called liberal America. Such is the impact of ideological conditioning.

Another recurring theme in "'B' Movie" is Scott-Heron's reading of Reagan's imaginative use of pop culture to construct American machismo which the poet-singer posits as a foundational ideological tool that proved invaluable to Reagan's campaign. The melodrama and seduction of the B-movie tend to impede critical analysis and titillate viewers into cinematic cells of capitalist desire. As with Scott-Heron's earlier western imagery ("Circle up the wagons / To defend / Yourself from nuclear attack"), in "We Beg Your Pardon" (1975), he uses knee-slapping humor to illuminate the epistemic shortcomings inherent in western films. Of course, the hero of American machismo in B-movies was actor John Wayne, whose characters rescued imperiled white citizens against so-called red-skins (i.e., Native peoples) and other amoral antagonists. In Scott-Heron's work, the western and its genocidal subtext function as paradigmatic narratives in the white popular imaginary. To put it differently, the western encoded the ever-ready (pre) texts of white nationalist expression, and Scott-Heron captured the hubris therein: "Get off my planet before sundown."[111] The strategic use of rhetoric and iconography in the western facilitated the process whereby political novices like Reagan could be transformed into an effective, ultra-conservative politician. In "'B' Movie," Scott-Heron represents Reagan's campaign as a product of multinational corporations whose ads and symbolism invoked the most reactionary aspects of American mythology to create "[t]he ultimate in synthetic selling: [a] Madison Avenue masterpiece. A miracle, a cotton candy politician: 'Presto! Macho!'"[112]

Of course, the ultimate manifestation of machismo is violence and the power associated with it. In "'B' Movie," Scott-Heron intensifies his satire to correlate machismo with American militarism and political economy: "Company!!! . . . Two-three-four." Similarly, he parodies the Dow Jones report to highlight the political ramifications of Reagan's presidency: "Racism's up. Human rights are down. Peace is shaky. War items are hot . . . Jobs are down, money is scarce—and Common Sense is at an all time low with heavy trading."[113] Scott-Heron's allusion to the lack of "Common Sense" is dialogic with Mills's argument that the racial contract is underwritten by "the epistemology of ignorance." As James Baldwin said, "It is certain, in any case, that ignorance, allied with power, is the most ferocious enemy justice can have."[114] Thus Scott-Heron represents reductive thinking as a by-product of right-wing ideologies—which is to say, ignorance is a discursive adhesive connecting disparate political positions. Accordingly, the band closes the tune with Scott-Heron singing the refrain, "This ain't really your life . . . ain't really ain't nothing but a movie."

"'B' Movie" was Scott-Heron's last momentous political recording. His later songs about politics lacked the magic they once had, but his personal songs became more resonant. His poignant remake of "Your Daddy Loves You" is dedicated to his daughter Gia Scott-Heron, who is photographed on the album cover as an infant with Scott-Heron touching her affectionately with his forehead. Like many men, the contradictions of male privilege and misogyny become abundantly clear when they consider their impact on women in their families, especially daughters. Indeed, fatherhood may have prompted him to reexamine his actions in relationships, particularly his complicity in reproducing cycles of fatherless black children. In "A Legend in His Own Mind" (1980), Scott-Heron pokes fun at himself, and redirects the critical lens toward his contradictory behavior in his relationships with women. Sampled by Mos Def (now Yasiin Bey) on "Mr. Nigga," and Phife Dawg on

"Beats, Rhymes and Phife," the song's musical texture is characteristic of Scott-Heron's distinctive hybrid sound. The drummer's jazzy, mid-tempo drum rhythm is complemented by jazz licks on acoustic piano, and a bass line interspersed with stank-encrusted plucking sounds that create a melodic, head-nodding groove for Scott-Heron's signature baritone. Although he often wrote in first-person to engage social issues, "A Legend in His Own Mind" was written in third-person, a strategy in life-writing that memoirists sometimes use to create distance from the protagonist. Scott-Heron uses third-person for ironic purposes. Using hyperbolic blues humor, Scott-Heron holds a critical mirror up to himself, and reads his own contradictions as a case study of black masculinity, particularly insofar as black men envisage and/or equate (black) manhood largely in terms of promiscuity.

Ultimately, though, Scott-Heron's drug addiction affected his relationships with musicians and other close friends, which ruined his career as a performing artist. After releasing his 1984 single "Re-Ron," another critique of Ronald Reagan, he spent the rest of the decade without recording. In fact, it would take another decade before he released his album *Spirits* (1994). Strung out on crack, Scott-Heron eventually went to rehab in the 1990s—and got booted out of the program for smoking crack.[115] He tried to revive his career, and recruited his old friend Jackson to travel to South Africa to perform "Johannesburg" and other popular songs. But it was a sobering experience for Jackson. Drugs had changed Scott-Heron's personality. Jackson states that "he was a completely different cat. . . . He would take half the deposit for a gig and spend it on drugs, skip the flight to the show, and leave the rest of the band hanging."[116] Scott-Heron was arrested several times, and in 2006 he received a sentence of two to four years in prison. He died five years later.

Nevertheless, Scott-Heron's recordings highlighted the intellectualism implicit in blue funk. His art demonstrates that it's erroneous to separate thinking from feeling, art from analysis, and creativity from criticism. But like many of the blues singers he listened to, not to mention the black nationalists, the very experiences and critical talents that enabled him to elucidate the dynamics of white supremacy also limited the scope of his analyses regarding women's experiences. This impairment, coupled with his drug addiction, impeded his progress toward realizing a more transformational aesthetic framework. Even so, Scott-Heron's discography represents a distinctive version of blue funk. In a manner previously inconceivable, he channeled remarkable political insights through blue funk aesthetics, which was a significant gesture toward the black fantastic.

Chapter Six

The Kinkiness of Turquoise

BETTY DAVIS'S LIBERATED FUNK-ROCK

Betty Davis personified funk in the 1970s. Her inimitable performance style, stunning beauty, and quintessential afro emblematized funk aesthetics. Davis led her own band, produced her own music, and arranged her own songs during a period when this level of independence was unattainable for most women in the music industry. No other black woman singer achieved a comparable degree of autonomy at the time. According to funk singer Rick James, Davis "was totally cutting edge. I mean, she was what funk was. . . . She was funking. Rock and rolling. Doing it all."[1] It seems fitting, then, that Davis's band dubbed itself Funk House. During her career, she created and conveyed recurring themes and images in funk performances, including Egyptian iconography and Afrofuturism. These concepts generally were associated with more popular performers such as Earth, Wind & Fire, Parliament-Funkadelic, and Labelle. But Davis prefigured the trend. P-Funk's visual artist Ronald "Stozo" Edwards recalls, "Betty would walk out on stage with the most amazing, designed outfits to look like an Egyptian queen. That shit was outrageous!"[2] A photo of Davis wearing such an outfit appears inside the cover of her album *They Say I'm Different* (1974). Scholars have acknowledged that bands such as Labelle, P-Funk, and Earth, Wind & Fire experimented with Afrofuturism a generation before Mark Dery coined the term in 1993. But it's important to note that Davis prefigured funk artists' engagements with Afrofuturism.[3] Davis mused wistfully, "The one thing that I wish was an advantage, but isn't, is being the first to do something. I made it easier for people like Labelle and Chaka Kahn. Hell, I even had a silver space suit two and a half years ago when Labelle were still in jeans."[4]

Yet film footage of Davis's performances remains limited. And since theater was such a central element of her live performances, the lack of footage presents a critical challenge. How do we examine Davis's aesthetics without live footage? As we'll see, photos comprise one alternative. But for the moment, I'd like to propose an excerpt from jessica Care moore's long commemorative poem "They Say She's Different" as our point of departure. Using a montage of word pictures, moore illustrates Davis's style in a painstaking manner, while framing her painful struggles against misogyny and male normativity within a black feminist critical perspective. A veteran poet and electrifying performer, moore has recorded with hip hop artists Nas and Talib Kweli as well as jazz artists like Roy Ayers and Jose James. In 2004 she founded Black Women Rock to celebrate Davis as a forerunner of contemporary black women rockers. The organization sponsors annual Black Women Rock performances that feature black women musicians such as Nik West and Kat Dyson, who played with Prince, and Divinity Roxx, who played with Beyoncé. Riffing on Davis's title "They Say I'm Different," moore's tribute is a poetic biography that encapsulates Davis's aesthetics, sexual politics, and performance idioms as well as the misogynous responses to her music and liberated spirit that drove her out of the industry.[5]

They Say She's Different
Betty Davis
. . . Betty found herself inside a movement
that did not include self defined, self empowered
sexually confident women, especially beautiful
brown ones.

How high was that Egyptian leg kick, that pushed you into
american music non history?

How do you measure the time it takes to suspend your leg
minus the minds you blow when you finally decide to place
it back on the ground and howl inside the mic.

why do women, ordained as goddess, legend,
get swallowed whole by the fear of industry.

we just the blues, sped up . . .[6]

moore's representation of Davis coincides with the singer's characterizations of her aesthetic and experiences. Indeed, Davis's song "70's Blues" (1974) is a self-reflexive commentary on her approach to music making. Its basic premise—that blues is an aesthetic framework, not merely a musical genre—reiterates Amiri Baraka's notion of "the blues impulse transferred,"[7] and prefigures George Clinton's 1996 statement: "Funk is just speeded-up blues."[8] During her career, Davis transposed blues principles into songs and performances that parodied, lampooned, and/or otherwise flouted conventional codes of sexual decorum. Doing so, she developed a contrarian funk-rock aesthetics that was utterly irreverent and fundamentally unruly.

DAVIS AS ILLEGIBLE FUNK-ROCKER

Davis reinterpreted blues aesthetics and developed a remarkably unique style that reprised the eroticism of women blues singers in the 1920s. As a free-spirited black woman funk-rocker in the music industry, she was a cultural rebel and organic intellectual. Yet her artistry and ideas, which she conveyed via songwriting and performance, were often illegible to music fans. A walking embodiment of the black fantastic, Davis once attracted 7,000 fans to a concert at Loyola University, whose auditorium near Baltimore could only seat 5,000, and a riot almost ensued.[9] Such was her emotive power. If Funkadelic was P-Funk's "voice and body of the critique of capitalism," as funk scholar Francesca Royster argues, then Davis's sexual politics was equally resistant to the logic of late capitalism. Just as blues women's songs were dialogic with Zora Neale Hurston's writings, her recordings and performances were coterminous with writings of Toni Morrison, Gayl Jones, Ntozake Shange, and many others. According to Maureen Mahon, "Davis responded to the same set of social and political conditions that led black feminist activists and critics . . . to identify and problematize patterns of belief and behavior that marginalized, demonized, and diminished black women. They countered these tendencies by placing black women and the fight for black women's equality at the center of their work."[10] Implicit in Mahon's analysis is the notion that Davis is an organic intellectual. While examining her biography, songwriting, artistic methods, and social views, we'll examine her sexual politics in relation to black women's writings in the 1970s. In retrospect, Davis's songs were counterparts to these women's writings, but her brazen representations of contemporaneous women's erotica in black street culture, particularly BDSM, contrasted with writers' concerns and sensibilities.

There's little disagreement over the peculiarity of Davis's style, but her music and performance style evoked vastly different reactions. She mesmerized many people and provoked consternation from others. Much has been written about her sexuality, which obviously contributed to controversy surrounding her recordings and performances. But sexual themes were common in funk songs.[11] Indeed, unadulterated sensuality was one of the characteristics that distinguished funk from soul. Consider, for instance, Sly and the Family Stone's "Sex Machine" (1969), James Brown's "Get Up (I Feel Like Being a) Sex Machine" (1970), and the Commodores' "Brick House" (1977). Women artists also sang risqué songs. Funk singer Lalomie Washburn, who wore a platinum afro, co-wrote "Freaky Strangeness" which appears on her album *My Music Is Hot* (1977). Likewise, Rickey Vincent points out that Millie Jackson "generated a career of low-down language and high struttin' sass [with] her aggressive sex appeal and snappy one-liners . . ."[12] However, Jackson and Washburn sang songs that tended to fit more comfortably within the masculinist conventions of black popular culture. What made Davis so controversial was the unparalleled degree of her nonconformity. She scandalized the music world by representing freaky erotic pleasures from women's points of view, and by singing in a style that derided established notions of the art form.

In a 1974 *New York Times* article, journalist Led Leibeiter corroborates this point when he compares her to Bessie Smith: "Her recognition by most of the pop world will be a long time coming. For, like Bessie Smith and all those other dirty-blues singers of forty years ago, Miss Davis is trying to tell us something real and basic about our irrational needs; and Western civilization puts its highest premiums on conformity and rationality and rarely recognizes the Bessies or the Bettys until they're gone."[13] Leibeiter's observation was astute. However, Davis's interpretations of blues stretched the boundaries of blackness. During a period when African American culture had shifted to large cities, she elaborated on black southern styles and sensibilities. And like many young musicians, including Clinton and her close friend Jimi Hendrix, Davis recognized that rock was where the most daring blues experiments occurred. In addition, her marriage to Miles Davis enabled her to become more familiar with various concepts of music. Thus she created a unique variation of funk. Her sound was indelibly rock-inflected, and her outrageous performance style was theatrical and quasi-burlesque. Still, the most notable aspect of Davis's aesthetic was her vocal style. She rarely sang in the usual sense of the term, and her bad-girl persona was closely related to her sound.[14] Davis's phraseology included relatively few features that people usually imagine as singing. Rather, she used the term "projector" to describe her approach which often featured onomatopoeic sounds and various forms of intonation. Her drummer Nicky Neal has suggested she was "the first innovator of rap." Davis's phraseology was characterized by a sort of half-singing. The levels of her pitch tended to reverberate within the miniscule space between normal speech and conventional singing. Davis thus envisioned an avant-garde popular art form with progressive sexual politics.

Considering the immense popularity of Beyoncé, Rihanna, Cardi B, and other recording artists today, it may seem odd that Davis's music didn't garner wider acceptance. But several factors rendered her artistry illegible[15] to various audiences. Though her sound played a significant role, the intractable contradictions of gender and sexual politics often shaped the parameters in which audiences interpreted her artistry onstage. The persistence of misogyny and its impact on black expressive culture proved to be far more difficult for African Americans to engage than issues solely related to race. The black consciousness movement of the late 1960s provided the conceptual foundations for funk in the 1970s. As we've observed in previous chapters, the movement to create genuine democracy and white authorities' violent attempts to suppress it created an indelible impression for African Americans.

Nationalistic iconography and ideologies permeated black expressive culture in the late 1960s. The images and ideas effectively primed listeners for James Brown's 1968 recording "Say It Loud (I'm Black and I'm Proud)," which resonated among black folks young and old. Less than a decade earlier, even African Americans had used the word "black" as an intra-racial insult. And since cast and class have always been related to skin color in the United States, Brown's appeal was particularly evident in black street culture. For many people who danced at house parties and thronged nightclubs in black communities, the Godfather of Soul and Black Panthers Huey P. Newton and Bobby Seale were popular heroes.

The feminist movement, by contrast, consisted largely of intellectuals, especially scholars, essayists, and fiction writers whose names were barely recognizable to many working-class black women. Notwithstanding Aretha Franklin's 1967 hit single "Respect," there hadn't been substantive opposition to misogyny and male normativity in black music since the classic blues era of the 1920s when Ma Rainey, Bessie Smith, Ida Cox, and a host of other women artists highlighted men's contradictions in their songs. And since most black women worked long hours as homemakers and wage laborers, they naturally prioritized pleasure in their limited time of leisure—and fun generally meant movies, music, dancing, or casual conversations. To compound matters, most of the institutions that shaped black people's worldviews promoted traditional notions of gender and sexuality. According to Denise Oliver-Velez, Davis's former roommate, "She was actually the antithesis of what Black femininity was supposed to be about. She'd wear things that were see-through, and, to your average Black go-to-church-on-Sunday Baptists, that was a no-no." Thus Oliver-Velez states, "People like Betty and Hendrix [were] anomalies."[16] One reason for people's reactions to Davis is that few women owned or controlled churches, schools, newspapers, or radio stations, so the normalization of male privilege continued largely unimpeded. Discussions of blackness were often framed in patriarchal terms that minimized inequities that accrued from gender politics, which in turn complicated feminists' efforts to build mass support among working-class black women.

The entrenchment of traditional views toward gender politics and sexuality created ideological chasms between the movement and many working-class black folks. Ruth Pointer, who sang in the acclaimed Oakland-based funk group the Pointer Sisters, drives this point home in her memoir *Still So Excited: My Life as a Pointer Sister*: "It was the early '70s and the women's lib movement was chugging right along—if you were a white chick, anyway. That 'I am woman, hear me roar' stuff didn't go over so big in the hood. The dude was the breadwinner and the boss. . . ."[17] It goes without saying that Pointer's vulgar tone and representation of feminism highlight the urgency of feminists' interventions. Nonetheless, her statement reflects a view shared by other black women from working-class backgrounds. For instance, in her book *I, Tina: My Life Story*, Tina Turner remarks: "I couldn't really relate to that 'movement' kind of thing. They were talking about 'liberation'—but liberation from, like, housework. That was the least of my problems. My problem was simply survival."[18] The prevalence of misogyny and traditional attitudes toward gender in African American culture provide a context for understanding some listeners' visceral reactions to Davis. Though her music was circulated on radio stations and other venues in her hometown of Pittsburgh, she received meager support from black listeners in other areas of the country, especially black men who wielded significant influence as deejays and club owners. And without the insight of feminists' critical vision, the liberationist impulse in Davis's artistry was often illegible. Contradictory attitudes about black respectability, gender politics, and modest support for black women's liberation had dire effects on Davis's career.

Music critics represented black male artists' eroticism as "natural" and non-threatening but criticized Davis for hers. When Portia K. Maultsby argues that "[James] Brown and [Sly] Stone symbolized change; their music captured the spirit of defiance and their lyric themes of social and political change challenged the status quo,"[19] she outlines the analogous terms in which Davis challenged the "status quo" in sexual politics. She also "symbolized change," but she conceptualized the black fantastic in terms of women's eroticism. Her songs and performances comprised the obverse to Brown's and Stone's liberationist impulses, but she was rarely credited for her contributions at the time. Clinton boasted that P-Funk was "gonna be dirty,"[20] Hendrix simulated oral sex with his guitar, and Brown danced the Funky Four Corners in visceral displays of sensuality and sexuality. But as the "bad girl" of funk, Davis was stigmatized and faced censorship[21] when her brazen lyrics and unfiltered performances ran afoul of prevailing codes of propriety. Music fans' contrasting reactions to Davis and P-Funk guitarist and singer Garry Shider highlight the double standards that operated during the funk era. Shider typically appeared on stage virtually naked except for his diapers, which was his signature stage prop as the "baby" of the collective. Audiences overwhelmingly greeted Shider with warm affection, but people picketed the radio station in Kansas City when the disc jockey played Davis's song "If I'm in Luck I Might Get Picked Up" inadvertently on the air, and listeners complained when it was played at a popular radio station in Detroit. The NAACP even suggested that she was promoting prostitution.[22]

Aside from Davis's X-rated lyrics and kinetic expressions, her guttural black rock tonality further complicated her legibility. Her vocals were self-conscious manifestations of alterity. Reminiscent of blues singers' use of satire, her peculiar sound quality and onomatopoeic phrasings were divergent artistic methods she used to lampoon preferred images of black women, especially rhythm and blues singers in the music industry: black, demure, and doll-babyish—objectified. "Yes, she admits, "I guess you could call my show . . . filthy!" The conflicting reactions that Davis elicited not only reveal the fault lines of gender and sexuality; they also point up class divisions and ideological differences among African Americans. Such is the history of blue funk. Davis's songs reflect desires and predilections of black working-class women in street culture, a segment of society that scholars and creative writers generally ignored. Depending on the listener's mindset, her bold decentering of men's sexual pleasure was exhilarating or gauche or perhaps even both. Music critic Vernon Gibbs's remarks on Davis's debut performance in New York at the Bottom Line illustrate her emotional impact on audiences and, in this case, her illegibility. Gibbs writes, "The horror was universal. The women were all jealous and the men felt emasculated. Davis's group, one of the best post-Sly curdling bands, was fingered as incompetent;

her act was called 'disgusting,' and critics whose job it is to recognize novelty where it exists could only come up lame lines like, 'Well, at least we know Miles Davis is a leg man.'"[23]

Gibbs's commentary calls attention to Davis's innovation and the illegibility of her aesthetic. Both of which invoke an effective critical framework to illuminate and contextualize the political implications of her art. Davis's blues-based funk-rock interfaces with two critical models that include musicologists Lori Burns and Melisse Lafrance's book *Disruptive Divas: Feminism, Identity, and Popular Music* (2001) and cultural philosopher L. H. Stallings's groundbreaking study *Funk the Erotic: Transaesthetics and Black Sexual Cultures* (2015). Let's briefly discuss *Disruptive Divas*, then turn our attention to *Funk the Erotic*. In *Disruptive Divas*, Burns and Lafrance coin the phrase "disruptive diva" to commemorate four women artists of the 1990s: PJ Harvey, Meshell Ndegeocello, Courtney Love, and Tori Amos. Given Ndegeocello's relationship to funk because of her background playing bass in go-go bands in Washington, D.C., the authors' foregrounding of "disruptive musical expression" as a defining characteristic is especially pertinent to Davis. Additional criteria include: 1) "creative interrogation of dominant normative systems . . . through a range of musical techniques (that is, lyrical and sonic). . . . they adopt marginal, countercultural positions in and through their creative work"; 2) "the artist's music disquiet[s] and unsettle[s] the listener . . . and make[s] their audiences uncomfortable"; 3) "manipulations of conventions and styles, which play on listener's expectations and understanding of established codes"; 4) "seizure of both the creative and productive reins" of "the technical and creative operations of music making."[24] A cursory view of Davis's career reveals that she epitomized Burns and Lafrance's critical metaphor a generation before Ndegeocello's recordings, which demonstrates the magnitude of her alterity. After all, the stakes were considerably higher for Davis in the 1970s, and her exemplification of such a critical model suggests how forcefully she challenged prudish attitudes and repressive social norms. Burns and Lafrance's emphasis on artistic disruption provides a conceptual introduction to Davis's cultural politics. We can examine her legacy more fully by contextualizing our discussion within Stallings's critical framework of funky erotixxx.

In *Funk the Erotic*, Stallings applies her metaphor primarily to films and fictional narratives that deploy forms of symbolic inversion—what she describes as "sacredly profane sexuality."[25] According to Stallings, such expression "ritualizes and makes sacred what is libidinous and blasphemous in Western humanism so as to unseat and criticize the inherent imperialistic aims within its social mores and sexual morality."[26] Thus she argues that "funk produces fictions of sex to counter the truth of sex."[27] However, Stallings's notion of funky erotixxx is equally pertinent to Davis's artistry and sensibility. If I read Stallings correctly, her reference to "truth" is actually tongue-in-cheek. She's criticizing *constructed* notions of truth and normality—what she calls "the coloniality of being."[28] Davis was similarly opposed to (neo)colonial mindsets. As with the writers and sex workers that Stallings examines in her work, Davis wrote, recorded, and performed songs such as "Whorey Angel" to express "sacred profane sexuality" (read: funky erotixxx) to subvert "the moral and ethical claims of Western imperialism and capitalism that make sexual terrorism, sexual colonization, and human trafficking possible."[29] Of course, Davis didn't use Stallings's language, and there are no references to imperialism in her songs. But her songbook is filled with characters that resist and/or represent imperialist logic in the form of patriarchy. So Davis sought to empower women sexually through her music.

WALKING UP THE ROAD

Davis was born Betty Mabry in 1945 in Durham, North Carolina. She spent much of her early childhood doing farmhand chores and listening to her grandmother's vintage collection of blues singers, including John Lee Hooker, Jimmy Reed, Big Mama Thornton, and many others. Neither of her parents were musicians, but her father danced the blues; and on a few occasions, she watched him bust a move. He was so amazing that he inspired her to dance, too. She recalls, "He used to dance like Elvis Presley before Elvis. He only did it for me a couple of times, but he blew my mind. I said, 'I want to dance like that someday.'"[30] Thus Davis developed her own talents as a dancer. Her recollection of her father suggests that her learning process was participatory, which required endless hours of practicing and thus autodidactic training. Whether she danced in her living room, house parties, or some other form of black community theater, she was studying principles of extemporized blues-oriented choreography. Such dancers accumulate and revise backlogs of gestures, including fragments and sometimes entire vocabularies of dances and dance styles in the process of creating their own idiosyncratic expressions. Davis's expertise as a dancer became the centerpiece of her performance style, which in turn helped her develop her controversial sound.

Davis's father found work in the steel mills in Pittsburgh, and the family moved to Pennsylvania when she was twelve. The move proved to be a life-changing event. Davis blossomed in her new home. Living in closer proximity with her neighbors enabled her to interact more with other teenagers. The community center held dances where Davis discovered the music of Motown, the Isley Brothers, and James Brown. New experiences sparked new interests that inspired her to pursue new opportunities. At age sixteen, Davis moved to New York to study fashion and design at the Fashion Institute of Technology. She also studied texture in her voice, speech, and acting at the American Musical Dramatic Academy, and later found success as a Wilhelmina model. That she was offered a part in the Broadway musical *Hair* suggests that her studies of performance arts enhanced an impressive array of talents that she eventually deployed during her career as a performance artist. Exemplifying the daring spirit that has endeared her to many fans today, Davis introduced herself to the music world as a showstopper at the Cellar in New York, a hotspot nightclub that she opened and transformed into a locus of the music scene.

At the time, Davis was a member of a collective of stunning young women alternately referred to as the Electric or Cosmic Ladies. As exemplars of style, taste, and hipness, the women lit up the atmosphere. Their vivifying presence formed the nucleus of the proverbial in-crowd. Miles recalls, "Being around her and the other girls made us feel that we were at the cutting edge of music, especially that New York scene."[31] With their beauty and splendor of fashion, the Cosmic Ladies must have been delightful to see when they sauntered onto the dance floor, jamming gracefully to Jimi Hendrix's live music.[32] As the renowned South African jazz trumpeter Hugh Masekela remembers, "[S]he could really dance."[33] Regular visitors also included Miles Davis and Sly Stone. According to Oliver-Velez, "It was a mecca for young people on the cutting edge of dance and music. Betty not only ran the place, she was the trendsetter and maestro of the scene."[34] Oliver-Velez's remembrance is notable for two reasons. First, she emphasizes Davis's uncanny ability to detect obscure stylistic concepts imprinted in the social currents of the historical moment: such foresight would become an invaluable attribute in Davis's maverick approach to songwriting when she embarked on her recording career. Second, Oliver-Velez's casual allusion to the "cutting edge" dancing at the Cellar belies the emphasis that Davis attached to it. The club's reputation as a trendsetter almost certainly didn't occur through happenstance. In all likelihood, Davis made strategic decisions in her role as "maestro" that created the "chill" environment that appealed to stylish cosmopolitan dancers. Moreover, her keen understanding of black dance vocabularies informed the melodic frequencies that later shaped her blues revisions into funk.

The period that immediately preceded Davis's marriage to Miles was also productive for her as a songwriter. Unlike many funk artists who evidenced early musical talent by performing as toddlers and preadolescents, Davis began writing songs at ten years old. Her first big break came when she collaborated with the Chambers Brothers, the house band at the Electric Circus, where Sly and the Family Stone and other standout artists performed. After writing their 1967 hit "Uptown (to Harlem)," she proceeded to write the songs the Commodores submitted to Motown when the group signed its contract. That the Commodores became one of the top singing groups in America, and eventually won a Grammy Award, is a testimony to Davis's songwriting. At the same time, her failed collaboration with the Commodores turned out to be fortuitous. When Motown balked at Davis's insistence on maintaining her rights to her songs, she pitched them to Just Sunshine Records. And since she didn't have a singer, Davis sang the material herself. Executive Mike Carabello was so impressed that Just Sunshine signed her as a recording artist, and the songs were released on her 1973 debut album *Betty Davis*. She went on to record four more albums: *They Say I'm Different* (1974), *Nasty Gal* (1975), *Is It Love or Desire* (1976), and *Crashin' from Passion* (1979).

Davis's first recording was "Get Ready for Betty" in 1964. Shortly afterward, she and Roy Arlington recorded a duet of the doowop song "I'll Be There." In early1968, Davis recorded the songs "Live, Love, Learn" and "It's My Life." Both were written by Davis and arranged by Masekela for Columbia records. At the time, she was in a relationship with Masekela; and shortly after their breakup, she began a tumultuous relationship with Miles. The two were married later that year. As several people have noted, including Miles himself, Betty introduced him to the music of Sly Stone and Jimi Hendrix. And since the two younger artists inspired Miles to begin experimenting with rock and funk, Davis was partly responsible for Miles's groundbreaking album *Bitches Brew* (1969). However, the marriage was short-lived. The relationship soured because of Miles's physical abuse, and Betty left the marriage the next year.

Nonetheless, Miles admired Davis's talent. He spearheaded a recording session of all-star musicians who collaborated with Betty on an album that was recently released with the title *Betty Davis: The Columbia Years: 1968–1969*. Personnel included jazz musicians such as pianist Herbie Hancock and saxophonist Wayne Shorter, who had both starred in the second famous Miles Davis Quintet a few years earlier. Still, the presence of Hendrix collaborators Billy Cox and Mitch Mitchell reflects Davis's admiration for the guitarist and prefigures her unique brand of funk. Though she hadn't developed her rock-sounding vocals, her predilection for codeswitching and intoning in pitches between usual singing and spoken word was already evident. Like Hendrix, who fashioned his cadence after listening to Bob Dylan, Davis understood the limitations of her voice. But her keen understanding of blues precepts enabled her to envision herself as a "projector" of sound, and thereby extend the voice-instrument dynamic we examined in chapter 2.

So while the Columbia sessions amount to little more than a demo tape, they bear historical significance. In the opening track of the album "Hanging Out," for instance, Davis invokes the funk principle ("get funky") which demonstrates that she was among the earliest artists to experiment with the concept. She engaged the topic several years before George Clinton and Bootsy Collins promulgated the term during interviews. And since the music differs significantly from the genre that became known as funk, these early recordings suggest that other models could have developed under different circumstances. Also notable, the Columbia recordings unveil glimpses of what made Davis so controversial. Her eroticism is unmistakable in her rendition of Eric Clapton's "Politician," especially when she tells Miles to get in the back seat of the car. Equally important, Davis's predilection for experimentation is readily apparent, which demonstrates that the sui generis funk she recorded as a band leader didn't occur willy-nilly. There's a clear trajectory between her sound on the Columbia sessions and her recordings as a mature performing artist. Fred Moten's comments on the fallacy of equating experimentation with so-called "high art" are pertinent here: "stuff that gets placed under the rubric of black vernacular is as much an experiment as that which is coded as avant-garde."[35] Davis's gnarly sound disrupted the silence surrounding black women's sexuality in street culture. Her songs and performances about these women recall June Jordan's famous statement: "Freedom is indivisible or it is nothing at all. . . ."[36] Davis was both a fearless artist and a bona fide organic intellectual whose recordings paralleled black feminist writings during the period.

DAVIS AS LYRICIST AND ORGANIC INTELLECTUAL

In some ways, Davis's themes exemplified funk aesthetics. Her songs reflected experiences, sensibilities, and styles of life in black working-class culture.[37] She also wrote songs that coincided with common themes in funk, including the following: the uplifting effects of partying and dancing on the funk; black urban life; economic conditions; black cultural liberation; self-awareness; black feminine beauty; and heterosexual relationships.[38] But her background in blues was probably the biggest influence on her songwriting. The independent spirit that was part and parcel of blues music is evident in the shapes and forms of cultural deviance that Davis infused into funk. While she engaged common themes in funk (self-awareness, liberation, black urban life, etc.), she interpreted the concept in relation to black women's street sensibilities. Her primary themes included sexuality, party festivities, funk, and dancing. At times, Davis correlated some of these topics, and her recurring theme of sexual freedom reflected her determination to disrupt the normalization of male privilege in American society.

Ironically, one of the most noticeable aspects of Davis's songwriting is her understatement of the funk principle. Whereas Sly Stone, George Clinton, and other male artists assigned metaphysical properties to the funk, Davis virtually ignored the themes of healing, spirituality, and psychic elevation that male songwriters celebrated in their representations of funk. Recordings such as Sly and the Family Stone's "I Want to Take You Higher" (1969), Parliament's "Mothership Connection" (1975), and Lakeside's "Fantastic Voyage" (1980) exhorted listeners to "ride on the funk." However, Davis posited women's experiences as her main concern, and since the contradictions that directly affected women typically occurred in relationships with men, she held no illusions that ascensions on the mothership would dismantle male normativity. In fact, although Dr. Funkenstein's pimp-image was parodic to some degree, it nonetheless suggested that entourages on the proverbial mothership reconstituted the gendered objectification that Davis's songs resisted.[39] Consequently, the songs she wrote that were especially dance-oriented tended to represent funkiness and pleasure as normal aspects of a healthy lifestyle rather than psychological elixirs. For instance, Davis's song "Ooh Yeah" highlights the pleasure of the funk. In a series of interactions with the Pointer Sisters, who served as background singers, Davis poses a question that is meant to be rhetorical: "Can you feel it?" Yet there's no hint of a medicinal, nirvana-like sensation that might transform black women's lives, especially the power dynamics that shaped their experiences with men.

On some occasions Davis merged blues and funk themes. In "Walkin' up the Road" (1973), for instance, she pays homage to the blues for promoting funkiness as a defining characteristic of black music during Jim Crow. After promising to infuse "funky" feeling into the atmosphere, she warns that it will eventually penetrate the soles of listeners' feet. At which point, "You gon *feel* good!" Thus Davis riffs on the phrase "walk on." Her best dance song is arguably "Git In There." In fact, music critic Vernon Gibbs said that "Git In There" was "the greatest dance record of 1974."[40] In the brief overture,

Davis creates a festive mood through laughter, and amidst the sounds of drums and guitar, she calls on listeners to "get funky like a skunk." Although Davis avoids the sort of metaphysical tropes that Clinton, Stone, and others associated with funk, she still represents it as a sensual and psychological sphere of pleasure. This notion is encapsulated in the title-hook, which is performed by background singers Debbie Burrell, Elaine Clark, and Trudy Perkins, who assist the band in its construction of funk with short, percussive lines (e.g., "dance, dance, dance"). Meanwhile, Davis's lyrics consist largely of spoken word, although sporadically she exhorts listeners to "move your feet." At times, she intones the song's title, but a significant portion of her vocals highlight her role as a bandleader in her effort to showcase her band Funk House. She invokes band members' names and instruments, while extolling their virtuosity. Davis sings, "[P]lay that bass funky Larry!"

Davis also correlates dancing with funk in "Bottom of the Barrel." In the song, she uses dialogue, onomatopoeia, and figurative language to signify the funk. Davis's method elaborates on James Brown's technique in "Make It Funky" wherein he catalogs black vernacular images (e.g., cracklin' bread and candied yams) to symbolize funk. In Davis's song, though, unidentified members of Funk House invoke the funk by repeating the title and common terms such as "lowdown," while interjecting high-pitched onomatopoeia to represent the infinite pleasure of the Funk: "Oo!" However, Davis's definitive statement on funk is her 1975 recording "F.U.N.K." In the song, Davis commemorates a litany of outstanding singers and instrumentalists. Many of them achieved iconic status as funk musicians; others were associated with soul or rock: Aretha Franklin, Sly Stone, Jimi Hendrix, Tina Turner, O'Jays, Ohio Players, Chaka Khan, Larry Graham, Ann Peebles, Al Green, Stevie Wonder, Isaac Hayes, and others. As the allusions indicate, Davis did not interpret funk solely as a musical genre. For her, the genesis of funk was unknowable: an inimitable, subcutaneous quality that only a few artists could manifest in virtuoso performances. Franklin, Peebles, Green, Hayes, White, and the O'Jays epitomized soul music; and according to conventional wisdom, Hendrix wasn't associated with funk. He was typically marketed as a rock artist, and he's still mostly remembered that way today. Yet Davis posits these very same musicians as exemplars of funk, which she describes as a characteristic that she and her musical counterparts carry in their blood. In the space of a single verse, she tries to pinpoint the essence of grandeur which is ultimately unknowable. James Baldwin's characterization of love is equally true of great art: "the force and mystery that so many have extolled and so many have cursed, but which no one has ever understood or ever really been able to control."[41] Of course, Davis's notion of "born" talent is dangerously close to the premise of racial ideology—that all black people have rhythm. But her main suggestion is that virtuoso artists emanate unique auras, and that their music reflects their distinctive personalities.

"F.U.N.K." is also notable because of its self-reflexive representation of Hendrix. Davis's approach as a lyricist in "F.U.N.K." is somewhat reminiscent of black poets' methods in the twentieth century. For instance, Robert Hayden incorporated "a wide range of forms, images, titles, lyrics, quotations, and names to create a poetic collage."[42] Similarly, Davis alludes to Wonder's 1973 groundbreaking album *Innervisions* as well as other titles by Stone, including "Dance to the Music," "Sing a Simple Song," and "I Want to Take You Higher." But the most notable aspect of Davis's allusions in "F.U.N.K." is that she devotes far more attention to Hendrix than anyone else. Along with her reference to his early single "Foxy Lady," Davis's section on Hendrix encompasses nine lines. That Stone is the only other musician who receives more than a single line is indicative of her admiration for Hendrix. She has cited both musicians as influences, and Hendrix was her dear friend. But what's important here is that Davis pays special attention to Hendrix's voice/ instrument technique—his ability to create onomatopoeic effects with his guitar. Davis extols his ability to approach his guitar as an extension of his body, and she uses hyperbole to pay homage to his virtuosity, noting that he could anthropomorphize his guitar: make it walk, talk, and sing just like a human being. As we'll observe shortly, Davis created an analogous approach by way of inversion. She used her voice as a rock instrument in her approach to singing.

Oftentimes, Davis melded party themes with sexual freedom. Her song "If I'm in Luck I Might Get Picked Up" (1973) is a prime example. The song is a story about a free-spirited young woman who deviates from her weekly workaday schedule, adorning her beauty with sexy outfits to spend a night out on the town, and Davis uses a polyphonic method when she sings the line "Take me home" as a triplicate refrain. That Davis's personal experience inspired her to write the song exemplifies Portia K. Maultsby's observation that funk musicians "drew from their experiences in [black] communities for lyric content...."[43] Davis said, "I went to a party in California and there were a group of girls there. They inspired the song."[44] Here, too, the title serves as the hook, while introducing two interrelated themes: unabashed feminine sexual desire and conflicting, sexualized definitions of "funk."

The persona is a femme fatale figure who envisions house parties and nightclubs as ritualized sites of sexual empowerment. A photo of a *Soul Train*

Figure 6.1. Soul Train dancer, ca. early 1970s. Photo by Michael Ochs/
Michael Ochs Archives via Getty Images.

dancer (see fig. 6.1) provides a touchstone for our discussion. The woman's majestic posture typifies the beauty and elegance that characterized black women's dance styles during the funk era. Davis's character in "If I'm in Luck" also gets attention on the dance floor; but unlike the *Soul Train* dancer, she's wearing a steamy outfit that accentuates her curves. Adept in the agency of freakdom, she dances seductively, perhaps with one arm raised or her face nonchalant. And as her body flows in perfect time with the beat, the titillation is electrifying. One man screams ("Oo!"), then shouts, "Get down!" Her mission is to mesmerize a "catch," a man who has the qualities to seduce her in kind. She's particularly attuned to coolness. He must be fluent and fluid in sensual lingos of dance. She says, "I want you dancing, I'm a movin' it, movin' it," and he responds, "Man, I'm a take her home man." But reminiscent of women's blues, Davis's persona isn't searching for romantic love. She relishes the spotlight because she enjoys the attention; plus, it helps her captivate men and whip them into a frenzy: "try not to pass out."

However, men are mere props to Davis's concerns. Her song chips away at stigmas and stereotypes that hinder black women's sexual freedom. Throughout Davis's songwriting, female personae act as destabilizing figures in male-dominated spaces. The woman in "If I'm in Luck" is no exception. She says, "I'm vampin' trampin'." The word "vamp" references "a woman who uses her charms or wiles to seduce and exploit men."[45] Davis converts "vamp" and "tramp" into verbs. The rhyme accentuates both the music of the lyrics and the persona's agenda. That "vamp" is short for vampire[46] suggests the negative connotations associated with women's sexual agency. Yet the persona is fully aware of unwritten sexual codes. Like earlier blues artists, Davis uses symbolic inversion to signify unruliness. The woman is "rituraliz[ing] and mak[ing] sacred what is libidinous and blasphemous" in African American culture. She thus describes herself as "wild," "crazy," "nasty" with total disregard for social conventions: "you can call it what you wanna." As such, Davis prefigures Janelle Monáe's theme in her song "Q.U.E.E.N." from her 2013 album *The Electric Lady*. In a recent interview, Monáe stated, "I want to redefine what it means to be young, black, wild, and free in America."[47] Like Monáe, Davis's song exemplifies what Stallings, in her reading of Monáe, describes as "the moral split between dance as sacred movement, dance as sexual expression, and dance as art."[48] In "Q.U.E.E.N.," Monáe sings, "Am I a freak for dancing around? / Am I a freak for getting down?" Monáe explains that her acronym represents outcasts of society: "'Q' represents the queer community, the 'U' for the untouchables, the 'E' for emigrants, the second 'E' for the excommunicated and the 'N' for those labeled as negroid." Davis's character exemplifies at least three and possibly all the components of Monáe's acronym.

But while Davis anticipated contemporary recording artists, her songwriting paralleled Ntozake Shange's representation of black working-class women in *For Colored Girls Who Have Considered Suicide / When the Rainbow Is Enuf* (1975). Indeed, both artists received similar reactions from men. In the interview with Weinstein and Richards, Davis said, "I've had guys get up and walk out while I'm performing. I get more hostility from white males than I do from black males. . . . You put me in New York with a predominantly white male audience and I get a weird reaction."[49] Likewise, thirty-five years after *For Colored Girls* appeared on Broadway, Shange stated:

The reaction to for colored girls was in a way very much like the white reaction to black power. . . . For men to walk out feeling that the work was about them spoke to their own patriarchal delusions more than . . . the work itself. It was as if placing the work outside themselves was an attack. colored girls was and is for colored girls.[50]

As it happened, Shange and Davis both lived in the Bay Area around the same time. Davis recorded *Betty Davis* in San Francisco in 1973, and Shange began performing *For Colored Girls* in bars across the Bay at the Bacchanal, a women's bar located in Berkeley in 1974. But their subsequent experiences in their respective fields point to the differences between the music industry and literary culture. Several factors, including music moguls' anti-intellectualism, traditional attitudes about gender and sexuality in black popular culture, and aversion to rock, led leading black radio stations to exclude Davis's recordings from their playlists. By contrast, literary culture provided substantial support for Shange and other black feminist writers who were among the movement's vanguard thinkers. There were notable tensions between black and white feminists, but the Bacchanal's sponsorship of Shange's performance typified the institutional support that facilitated the broad distribution of black women's writings. The bar was located near Albany, a small town of predominantly upper middle-class white people. The music industry never afforded Davis a comparable form of support. Executives had little interest in her creative vision and felt little compulsion to market it. Consequently, she found it difficult to make inroads into black popular culture; and since rock was racialized as "white" music, she was excluded from white radio playlists as well.

Yet Davis's effort to eliminate the moral impediments to women's sexual freedom is fully displayed on "Getting Kicked Off, Havin Fun" (1975). Here, too, she conflates partying with sexuality; but in this X-rated musical space, she represents fetish as an intense dimension of pleasure. For Davis, fetish is a universal aspect of human life. Her premise, which prefigures Parliament's "Flash Light" (1977), is that orgasmic pleasure is universal. But as is often the case in her aesthetic, we find a tension between social etiquette and risqué sexuality. Thus far, we've seen how Davis's sexual politics often parallels with black women writers of her generation. But her interpretation of fetish and freakiness stood out in sharp relief against writings of feminist legends such as Audre Lorde and Alice Walker. For Davis sadomasochism epitomized sexual freedom, whereas Lorde and Walker believed that pornography and BDSM reenacted dominance and the slave master's logic. Walker described porn as "Poor: Ignorant: Sleazy: Depressing."[51] And Lorde writes, "*Even in play* . . . [s]adomasochism is an institutionalized celebration of dominant/subordinate relationships."[52] It's a testimony to Davis's vision, then, that her racy themes anticipated black feminist scholar Ariane Cruz's research on BDSM.

Writing forty years after Davis's heyday, Cruz observes that BDSM can be "pleasurable and empowering"[53] because "[i]nside the realm of fetish, what would be outside the boundaries of conventional social mores and political correctness is not merely sanctioned but eroticized."[54] Cruz might as well have been writing about Davis's concept of funk. While men funk artists "captured the spirit of defiance and . . . challenged the status quo,"[55] Davis challenged conventions of sexuality. In "Getting Kicked Off," she uses parody as a rhetorical strategy. Doing so, she destigmatizes eroticism, and illuminates the arbitrary terms wherein freakdom is consistently sullied. But what's interesting about the song is Davis's working-class point of reference. Prefiguring Parliament's premise in "Flash Light" ("Everybody's got a little light under the sun"), she states that whether people are rockers, (be)boppers, hustlers, or workers who toil on nine-to-five jobs, everyone wants to "get kicked off." The problem, of course, is that "squares"—what Ishmael Reed calls "haters of dance"—normalized the notion that the mind and body are opposites. And despite its arbitrary basis, this social construction established a moral justification for "haters" to proscribe and anathematize sexual deviance in accordance with political inclinations and whims.

While it was impossible to decree the denial of freaky-deke pleasure, stigmas associated with certain sexual activities led to various forms of denial. Fetishes became off-color, prompting people to suppress, repress, or simply conceal certain preferences to avoid being shamed. But the implicit idea in "Getting Kicked Off" is that such concealment exacerbates the defamation people seek to avoid by reaffirming the specious reasonings and rationales that normalize the ostracism. Thus Davis lampoons the stigmatization of sexual kinkiness to forestall the process. Her pianist-vocalist Fred Mills confides, "I eat 'em with my funky fingers."

Perhaps Davis's most powerful statement on sexual liberation is "Anti Love Song" (1973). Reminiscent of women's blues, the song is ostensibly about two people who share a mutual attraction for each other. However, "Anti Love Song" can be interpreted as an allegorical narrative of resistance to male domination. The persona decides not to pursue a relationship in spite of her feelings: "'Cause I know you like to be in charge." To the extent that Davis examines power dynamics in the mind games that men play, "Anti Love Song" recalls Ida Cox's defiant 1924 recording "Wild Women Don't

Have the Blues." Cox sings, "I never was known to treat no one man right." As with blues women generally, Cox represents sexual relationships as sites of contestation as well as competition. But while Davis's persona is confident that she could turn the tables and "possess [his] body," her persona avoids competition altogether. That Davis imagined sexual freedom as experiences in which no party is exploited demonstrated immense perspicacity and theoretical imagination.[56] And since competition is endemic to hierarchy, which is essential to imperialism, "Anti Love Song" casts a critical light on mythic notions of romantic love. The song allegorizes the logic of imperialism as its drama is played out in male-female relationships.

Davis's treatment of love transforms actionality into a rhetoric of resistance, and she occasionally creates stories in which traditional sex roles are parodied and reversed. For instance, the woman persona in "Turn Out the Light" initiates sex and issues commands to her partner—ignore the phone and anyone knocking at the door. According to Davis, "'Turn Out the Light' is more of a thought than anything. The funny thing is, if your average guy said 'turn out the light,' no one would think twice, but if a girl says it all of a sudden it puts him off. It's a funny thing about men; they do what they want and never feel they have to ask you how you're doing."[57] Writing in the pre–hip hop era, Davis uses musical euphemisms (e.g., "boogie" and "get down") to reference coitus. And though her rhetorical strategy may not have been a deliberate criticism of the music industry, her language demonstrates the restrictions that record companies and corporate media outlets placed on women's sexuality. Thus the subtext in "Turn Out the Light" is that power is usually an aphrodisiac for men, so the song is arguably a discursive experiment. Davis creates a context wherein men are denied sexual power in order to demonstrate what happens. The persona says, "You say you want it and you got it now." The man's hesitance typifies the cognitive dissonance that often occurs when normalized power relations are destabilized.

Davis's representation of role reversal becomes full-blown sadomasochism in "He Was a Big Freak" (1974).[58] She creates a dominatrix character who not only delights in freakiness herself, she whips him to the point of ecstasy, too. In this way, Davis demonstrates how "rituals of domination and subordination in BDSM reveal such positions as . . . unnatural [and] socially constructed. . . ."[59] Such recognition is critical because it can inspire people to change their attitudes and lifestyles. "He Was a Big Freak" should therefore be understood as a song of erotic provocation. By depicting a scenario in which both people receive ultimate satisfaction, Davis hoped to stimulate audiences to reevaluate staid notions of sexual pleasure, and to reimagine possibilities they may have refused to consider previously. Yet there is confusion about Davis's inspiration for "Big Freak." Many people presumed the song was autobiographical. Some listeners associated it with Miles Davis; others interpreted it as Betty's tacit admission of widespread rumors that she had an affair with Jimi Hendrix. To complicate matters further, she gave conflicting explanations of the song herself. At no point has Davis ever implied that she had any sexual attraction to or involvement with Hendrix, but she has intimated that "Big Freak" was about Miles. When Robin Katz nudged her about "Big Freak" in a 1975 interview, Davis replied, "Miles just said, 'Betty, how could you write that song?' Because I figured I had better sing it to him before he heard it on the radio. But he loves it, you know I told him 'Miles, everyone knows about you. What can I say?' And he just laughed."

Eventually, though, Davis set the record straight, explaining that she didn't write the song about any specific individual: "Well, to be quite honest with you, Jimi didn't inspire the song. . . . But the 'turquoise chain' [*I used to beat him with a turquoise chain*] did because Jimi liked turquoise. Seattle, where he's from. You know Seattle the Indian chief? That's their stone. . . . It wasn't about anybody, I just wrote the song." Davis's explanation is notable for two reasons. First, it's similar to the creative process that poets used during her era. Second, her comments reveal how deeply she thought about Hendrix's aesthetics and, therefore, how vital he was to her music. Davis used her creative faculties to conflate Hendrix's affinity for turquoise with Seattle's history, myths, and imagery, particularly the Native American myth of turquoise, "the fallen sky stone," which symbolized the gods' blessings with rainwater, and Chief Seattle, who inspired the name of the city. Davis's crowning act of creativity, though, was her ability to reimagine Hendrix's chain and Native American mythology as funky erotixxx.

As with "Turn Out the Light," "He Was a Big Freak" is a satirical exultation of funky erotixxx. The song mocks and parodies "social mores and sexual morality" that bolster "hidden imperialisms" embedded in arbitrary stratums of human value.[60] "Big Freak" illustrates the tension between capitalism and black women's sexual freedom, particularly inasmuch as the former hinges historically on the occlusion of the latter. Thus Stallings contends that black freaks are situated at "the crossroads of resistance, spiritual transcendence, freedom, and art and entertainment."[61] The range of the persona's sexual options in "Big Freak" exemplify Davis's liberationist vision. She engages in various types of role-playing in this anthem[62] of freakdom: wife, mother, woman, mistress, lover, princess, geisha, flower, daydream. Observe the following: she tickles his fancy as his side-woman; she provides cheap thrills as his mistress; she wears satin and lace as his princess; she scrubs him down, loves him hard, and cooks his meals as his wife; she fondles his testicles as his geisha; she pretends that she's Rosie May as his flower; she rocks him like a baby as his mother; and she drives him wild as his lover. They delight together in his fetishes and fantasies of pain.[63] She whips him, beats him, and ties him up, too, proudly proclaiming, "I'd get him off with my turquoise chain." Naturally, incest, polyamory, and freakiness are blasphemous according to patriarchal dictates; but like older blues artists, Davis points the blasphemous finger back at capitalism's bogus moral standards that regulate sexual preferences and identities. "Big Freak" discursively dismantles the cornerstones of patriarchal privilege.

Davis's bohemian songs brought scandalous truths to the fore. In "Don't Call Her No Tramp" (1974), she criticizes stigmas of sex workers. Today there is a growing trend to regard the women's labor in economic rather than primarily moral contexts, but this perspective was rare among artists and intellectuals in Davis's heyday. For instance, Donna Summer, the Queen of Disco, also addressed this topic. In her song "Bad Girls" (1979), which was nominated for a Grammy Award, Summer represents sex workers in a manner that arguably reflects her belief in Christian fundamentalism. Where she had previously offered a sympathetic depiction in "Lady Of The Night" (1974), "Bad Girls" seems to play on literal meanings of "bad" and "sad," condemning the women somewhat subtly for their purported immorality: "Sad girls / Talking about bad girls . . ." But Davis demonstrates little vacillation. Her song interrogates the piety and hypocrisy that underwrite such stigmatization. "Don't Call Her No Tramp" defied conventional thinking by representing sex labor as one of various types of labor and exchange value in American political economy. From this vantage point, Davis undercut the specious moral high ground that prudish social critics used to demonize sex workers and Davis herself. She was harshly criticized, and her response was remarkably astute. Underscoring the seldom discussed issue of class privilege in African American culture, Davis said:

> What people need to realize is that there are all levels of blacks. We are not all doctors, lawyers, nurses, and social workers. That man standing on 116th in Harlem selling cocaine is a real man, a pusher, and you can't put that under a rug. Those girls standing in the doorways on Broadway and 46th Street are valid; they are out there existing—they are also black. Regardless of what they stand for or what they are doing, they are valid.[64]

Davis's commentary exemplifies her organic intellectualism. Although black women writers such as Morrison, Jones, and Shange examined similar contradictions related to sexual politics in their works (Morrison actually depicts sex workers in her novel *The Bluest Eye*), their stories are generally set in earlier periods.[65] Davis represented black women in street-life in the underbelly of contemporaneous America.[66]

This distinction is important on two accounts. First, capitalist inequities are reproduced by contradictory policies related to race, gender, and class politics, so critiques of ongoing double-standards tend to be more controversial and thornier than those that focus on earlier periods because they expose contemporaneous problems and inequities that accrue from them. Second, Davis's song highlights the thematic singularity of her songwriting. For instance, Funkadelic's "(not just) Knee Deep" (1979) is a self-reflexive song that defines pure funk in terms of spontaneity and contemporaneity. In other words, pure funk is constantly in flux. Dancers reconstruct the funk when they (re)create new dances that choreograph their emotional fervor and the music itself. However, Davis's notion of funk as emotional honesty compelled her to confront the stank-ugly politics that impacted black sex workers' lives.

In a brilliant example of counter-ideology, Davis represents the women as complex agents who are far more cerebral than the caricatures created by the male gaze of Hollywood films and other dominant narratives. Her central strategy is typical blues irony. To the extent that men in "Don't Call Her No Tramp" internalize myths of their purported superiority and entitlement, they're prone to making erroneous presumptions about sex workers— namely, that they lack sound judgment. And this faulty premise leads to other miscalculations: that the women are easily feted by pocket money, expensive restaurants, and the like. Davis points up the dialectics in this reasoning by demonstrating that hubris is self-defeating. Women read men's conceit and use it to flip the script: "you find out she's just using you." As the hip hop feminist Joan Morgan would observe a generation later, "trickin'" becomes a means of leveling the playing field" when "protection, material wealth, and the vicarious benefits of power" are otherwise inaccessible.[67]

WOMEN'S BLUES TRANSFIGURED AS FUNKY EROTIXXX

Davis's funk aesthetic extended a tradition of eroticism in women's blues. In Phil Cox's film *Betty: They Say I'm Different* (2017), she recollects her childhood. "I asked my grandmother," said Davis, "if I had to just fit in and be like I was told: 'be sweet and pretty for the boys.' Grandma, she didn't say nothin. She sat down and played me the women of the blues."[68] In addition to Bessie Smith, Ma Rainey, Sippie Wallace, Alberta Hunter, and Ida Cox, there was also Blanche Calloway, a slightly younger artist influenced by Cox. An accomplished composer, singer, dancer, and the older sister of Cab Calloway, Calloway prefigured Davis in several notable respects. Based in Chicago in the mid-1920s, Calloway is credited as the first woman to lead an all-male orchestra. Billed as Blanche Calloway and Her Joy Boys, the band featured such musicians as Louis Armstrong and Ben Webster at early stages of their careers. They later became renowned as innovators in jazz. In addition to her popularity in Chicago, Calloway and her orchestra played at top venues in New York and packed the house in Boston, Atlantic City, Pittsburgh, St. Louis, and Kansas City.[69] Yet reviews of her performances often sound like Davis facsimiles. For instance, a 1936 review published in *Variety* characterized her as "a thigh-grinding shouter type that shortly begins to wear," and stated that "Miss Calloway's attempted clowning . . . detracts instead of helping."[70] Needless to say, there are striking parallels between Calloway and Davis.

Such blatant disregard for propriety in blues culture wasn't restricted to artists, though. Working-class women, especially lesbians, who lived on the edges of black social life, consistently defied sexual conformity. Harlem, for instance, was an enclave for the black queer community in the 1920s, and buffet flats were main attractions.[71] Often owned or operated by women, they existed primarily "on the low" and stayed open after cabarets closed,[72] in "elaborately appointed dwellings and apartment houses."[73] According to Ruby Walker, Bessie Smith's niece and confidante, these undercover venues were among Smith's favorite pastimes. In fact, Smith sings about a buffet flat in her song "Soft Pedal Blues" (1925). Buffet flats specialized in sexual enter-tainment, including erotic shows and sexual activities. Walker described one in the following manner: "Everything went on in that house—tongue baths, you name it."[74] According to Smith's biographer Chris Albertson, "Bessie was most intrigued by an obese lady who performed an amazing trick with a lighted cigarette, then repeated it the old-fashioned way with a Coca Cola bottle."[75] Walker stated that "she could do all them things with her pussy—an educated pussy, you know."[76]

Davis's erotic gestures were also prefigured by the classically trained danc-er Lottie "The Body" Graves—or as she put it, "'Lottie 'De Body' because 'she had a body like a Lottie.'"[77] At the height of her career, Graves, who refers to her art as exotic dancing, performed with illustrious blues artists, including

T-Bone Walker, Billie Holiday, and B.B. King, to name a few. Graves also made an important contribution to funk. She appears in the documentary film *Standing in the Shadows of Motown*,[78] which pays tribute to Motown's mostly uncredited and theretofore unheralded session musicians who dubbed themselves the Funk Brothers. In the film, several Funk Brothers state that collaborating with Graves in Detroit's nightclubs enhanced their musicianship.[79] Generally, she "wore little more than heels [and] a few strategically placed rhinestones," and performed a high kick like Davis's signature move.

Clearly, Davis transfigured women's blues into liberated funk-rock. She remarked, "The music is physical and it's about sex. . . . It's hip to eat pussy these days."[80] Davis also highlighted blues as the foundation of her aesthetic: "I was brought up in the blues," she said, "and the blues is a very pure art form. . . . So what happened was, being brought up on the blues and integrating that with people I was into in the 1970s—that's how I came into myself."[81] Hendrix was one of the "people [she] was into." The two were kindred spirits. "I met Jimi in the Village," she recalls. "Jimi Hendrix—he understood crow."[82] The bird image references her indomitable personality and her insistence on maintaining her independence as a black woman; but more to the point, Hendrix's blues-based experiments with sound, his bohemian sensibility, and his kinetic eroticism onstage—pelvis movements, tongue-flicking, and so forth—provided a model for Davis's transpositions of women's blues into funk-rock. She stated, "Hendrix was real, Dylan was real, but I'm a woman."[83] Whereas Hendrix foregrounded dancing as a basis of his persona, Davis envisioned dancing as a foundation of her performance style. Explaining her transition from songwriter to singer, she said that "[performing] came natural with the music because I could dance. So movement was a part of my stage performance."[84] Similarly, Davis stated in a 1975 interview: "I like to move about a lot on stage, dance around, you know. I guess that my country roots come out in me!"[85] For "country roots," read blues. Thus Davis flouted bourgeois moral codes just as earlier blues women had. As Stallings puts it, although in relation to strip-dancers, "Black dance becomes [an] alternate cartography. . . ."[86]

Like Graves, Davis was fluent in various forms of kinesthesia, especially blues-based dance vocabularies. Her signature kick was captured in a powerful photograph (see fig. 6.2) taken during one of her performances. The photo is a black-and-white close-up that reveals an enraptured Davis singing and wearing her iconic afro. She rocks the mic with a closed right fist, fingernails immaculate with fresh manicure and dark polish that matches her lipstick. Her left hand is raised high in the air right beside her afro; her

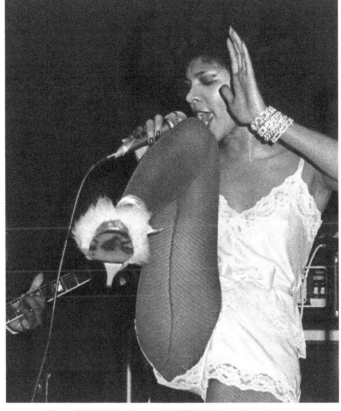

Figure 6.2. Betty Davis, ca. mid-1970s. Photographer unknown.

fingers are straight, palm open and wrist bedazzled by bracelets. However, the foregoing imagery is mere embroidery in the narrative of the photo. The central image is Davis's lithe brown body adorned in white lingerie. Suitably poised and fashionably arrayed, she gracefully funks the erotic. Her right leg is lifted high, knee bent at a forty-five degree angle, covering a portion of her chin. This movement reveals the underside of her thigh and a faint hint of her butt, which enabled Davis to enthrall audiences in fleeting moments. In another photo, her legs are spread slightly akimbo, her feet firmly planted in long shiny boots that cover her knees. Here Davis rests both hands together just above her vagina, placing her elbows akimbo so that her Afro forms the tip of a triangle as she transforms the mic into a phallus. Her lips are somewhat pursed and protruding, and the intense, semi-frown on her face could simultaneously suggest a dominatrix's fury, groans of ecstasy, and/or orgasmic pleasure.[87]

Figure 6.3. Betty Davis, ca. mid-1970s. Photographer unknown.

Yet another photo captures Davis's substantial emotive power (see fig. 6.3). This photo is unquestionably one of the most evocative images of the funk era. Here again, Davis is scantily clad. The camera shot, taken in the audience near stage right, projects a profile of her body. Reflecting the very best of 1970s fashion, Davis personifies panache in her high-heeled platform shoes while leading her band Funk House. On the left side of the photo, Carlos Morales, her lead guitarist, plays behind her. Nicky Neal, her cousin, appears in the background playing drums, facing the camera and audience, while another cousin, bassist Larry Johnson, is pictured on the right side of the photo accompanying the band. Two black women—known as "The Ladies"—are singing background vocals.[88] Their hands are frozen in midair, torsos curved in the midst of a dance gesture. But Davis is the main attraction. She sings at center stage, facing her singers, not the audience, and positions herself in front of the band. A slight bulge of skin underneath her chin indicates the intensity of her emotion as one of the background singers smiles back at her. Davis holds the mic just below her chin; and as she tilts her head and shoulders backward, her body becomes an arc. This is no small feat—it rivals a gymnast's agility and dexterity. Characteristic of her stage persona, Davis wears a short outfit that highlights her long legs. Her left leg is jutted outward several feet in front of her torso; her right leg is positioned even further behind. And since Davis is leaning backward, most of her weight is balanced on her right foot. Her mouth is wide open, and she appears to be roaring in raucous splendor. The nature of Davis's raw unfiltered funk is unmistakable in this image, and her use of kinesthesia is especially notable in this regard. The way she flexes her torso suggests that this gesture may have helped her maximize the volume of her voice, accentuate her tone color, and project her rough, gruff, gnarly sounds just as rock and funk guitarists used amplifiers for added volume and creating specific sounds.

At the same time, Davis created a hybrid form of vernacular theater which became a funk trademark. She shook her butt, licked out her tongue, and transformed the microphone into a penis-prop while portraying female characters that preceded Clinton's comic-strip-inspired characters Dr. Funkenstein and Sir Nose and Collins's Casper the Holy Ghost. But where Clinton and Collins created allegories and soundscapes that black audiences found legible, Davis's parodies and comedic expressions related more to rock bands like the Mothers of Invention or perhaps the Velvet Underground, which was known for playing songs with bizarre sexual kinkiness. So Davis created "a kind of comic-book heroine, a bad-assed, X-rated Superwoman capable of spinning hopelessly sex-addicted men around the tip of her bejewelled finger."[89] Her performances combined music, singing, storytelling, ribald humor, erotica, and acting.

Davis was sizzling hot on stage. Many of her lyrics were unmistakably risqué; but even when they weren't, her kinetic approach to stagecraft was ineluctably sensual and seductive. At times, the funk was so palpable that audiences began "throwing money, throwing panties, drugs, everything on stage."[90] Chuck Mabry, her brother and manager, recollects: "Audiences had never seen anything like Betty. She was the first woman ever to go on stage, wearing a night gown, and not be stripping. The guys you wouldn't think would get excited, would get excited. I thought it would be young boys, it was the men, grown men with good jobs—lawyers, doctors—they got turned on." Men weren't the only ones who got excited, though. Women were turned on, too: "One of them got on stage and grabbed me," Davis recalled. "She was on the floor and she grabbed me around my ankles and I couldn't move. They had to pull her off."[91]

The funk was in full effect. The emotive power that Mabry and Davis describe is extraordinary. She induced spasmodic pleasure via funky erotixxx. Stallings's writing on dancers in strip clubs contextualizes Davis's power. The responses she elicited from women are analogous to the effect that dancers have on women in strip clubs. Stallings explains: "The collaboration between female audience and dancers as well as certain aesthetics of dance provoke the will to remember, and it is why some black women find themselves patrons in strip clubs marketed to male consumers."[92] Though neither Davis nor Mabry suggest there was any collaboration with her audiences, Stallings's reference to the provocative nature of "certain aesthetics of dance" is nonetheless applicable to Davis. The siblings' recollections demonstrate her emotive power, particularly her ability to compel "viewer[s] to examine their own sexuality. . . ." That both Davis and Mabry seemed surprised by the women's reactions suggest the extent of her impact. Funk House's grooves and Davis's dance moves and vocals resonated with the women on a psychosomatic level, and may well have evoked latent desires and/or memories.

Edwards and Mabry take special care to distinguish Davis's performances from stripping, and understandably so. Not only was Davis's use of kinesthesia different from stripping as such; it's quite probable that black men and women of their age group associated stripping with immorality. And since Davis suffered untold amounts of pain because she was demonized like strippers, it's even more understandable why Mabry couched his description the way he did. Historically, Davis's body-talk was a bridge between Lottie "The Body" Graves and contemporary black dancers in strip clubs. The novelty of her stagecraft, like her vocal style, couldn't be adequately described by extant terminology—at least from Davis's and Mabry's viewpoints. And since she preceded hip hop's mainstreaming of strip club dancing in black popular culture, she and Mabry would probably be offended by associating her artistry with strippers. But even so, Stallings's central argument about the political implications of strip dancers' aesthetics illuminates Davis's significance. When Stallings characterizes strippers' dance moves as "the practice and aesthetics of black dance and its resistance to being colonized into 'appropriate' social spaces, venues, functions, and moral purposes,"[93] she delineates Davis's artistic objectives as a cultural rebel—a sexual anarchist who challenged the moral edits that determine what is and isn't appropriate regarding black women's eroticism and sexual pleasure.

BLACK FEMALE BODY AS FUNK-ROCK TECHNOLOGY

Davis's rebellious spirit was reflected most notably in the textures of her sound.[94] Like many funk artists, she developed a psychosomatic approach to music making. The ethnomusicologist Cheryl L. Keyes emphasizes this point in her analysis of Davis. According to Keyes, Davis "incorporated a corporeal approach to creating musical arrangement via kinetic orality."[95] Keyes develops her idea more fully by quoting bassist Larry Graham, founder and lead singer of Graham Central Station. And though we discussed Graham's statement in chapter 2, it bears repeating:

> [Betty] didn't play, but her mind, her body, her spirit would become an instrument that she used to get across what she was feeling, how she was flowing, and we'd catch that and roll with that. And then we'd tell from her reaction if we were on the right track or not. If something hit her and she was feeling it, you would immediately see it. So our job was to try to move her. We were feeding off each other in that sense.[96]

Graham's comment is remarkably similar to Bootsy Collins's description of translating James Brown's dance moves into rhythm, which we discussed in chapter 4. Considering the pivotal role of bass players in funk, Graham's emphasis on Davis's kinesthesia underscores the pivotal role of the body in funk. Still, Davis's blues-inflected rock sound set her apart from other singers. Few artists have provoked such conflicting reactions from critics and fellow artists. Depending on listeners' tastes and sensibilities, her singing could be avant-garde or amateurish. But if we consider the fact that Davis "thought of herself as a musician who used her voice to convey her musical ideas,"[97] we can examine her style more effectively. Actually, her musical philosophy wasn't dissimilar from Chaka Khan's. The vast differences in their sounds and objectives notwithstanding, both women emphasized honesty and envisioned their voices as instruments. But where Khan avoided controversial issues and preferred to sooth listeners' pains, Davis highlighted issues that bedeviled women's lives to invoke political interventions.

Eyewitnesses of Davis's performances, including those who lauded her, typically used quotation marks when they described her singing. Critics attacked her singing because it defied their tastes and expectations of the art form. Charles Shaar Murray, for instance, writing for the British magazine *New Musical Express*, denounced her singing in racist overtones. He said, "It would be less than charitable to suggest that Betty Davis cannot sing, and I wouldn't for one moment dream of making such an improper allegation, but she sho' can't sing too good."[98] Undoubtedly, Murray's statement bears all the marks of racial caricature, but there were also accomplished funk artists who found Davis's singing less than appealing. Patryce "Choc'Let" Banks, lead woman singer of Graham Central Station, sang background vocals on Sly & the Family Stone's album *There's a Riot Goin' On* (1971) and Davis's debut album *Betty*. So Banks made significant contributions to funk, and her perspective is based on extensive experience as an artist. She candidly admits her distaste for Davis's singing: "When I first heard Betty's voice I thought her delivery was a joke. I kept waiting for her to stop. I discovered this *was* who she was, so I chalked it up to 'different strokes for different folks.'"[99] As Banks demonstrates, Davis's raspy sound offered a stark, and sometimes unsettling, contrast to such virtuoso funk singers as Chaka Khan, Joyce "Baby Jean" Kennedy, Patti LaBelle, and naturally Banks herself.

Given the prevailing sensibilities of black popular culture during the period, Banks's criticism isn't surprising. Many black women of her generation had set ideas about singing. As mentioned earlier, partying was a preferred form of leisure for most working-class black women, and successful parties hinged largely on rhythm and blues recordings to enthrall listeners and set the mood. Gospel-trained singers reigned supreme because their training emphasized the inducement of eargasms. Funkadelic "promise[d] to be good to your earhole," and the ultimate manifestations of such pleasure was often symbolized in terms of travel. The Staples Singers' popular song "I'll Take You There" (1972) is a great example. Even though they were a gospel group, the metaphysical "place" they "took" people to was right beside the destinations of P-Funk's "Mothership Connection" (1975) and Lakeside's "Fantastic Voyage" (1980). In this context, the singer's ultimate achievement is creating such exhilarating beams of musical pleasure that listeners are affected beneath their skins. This experience stimulates irresistible urges to participate in the performance by singing along and/or dancing to the music. This is why rhythm and blues was favored at house parties, and rock was generally excluded from the soundscapes. Davis probably encountered the same problem with black listeners that Hendrix did. Despite his astounding musicianship, it would have been unthinkable to play his song "Foxy Lady" in most house parties or clubs. And in all likelihood, the same principle would have applied to Davis. Relatively few black music fans had sufficient appreciation for rock to adequately process the peculiarities of her sound. The illegibility of Davis's style among black listeners probably affected their ability to appreciate the scope of her artistic experiment, not to mention the political implications therein. But she was fully aware of her alterity. Davis said, "I look one way and people think I should be sounding another way."[100]

The question, then, is, what constitutes an effective method to analyze Davis's style? Mahon has noted that much of Davis's criticism was based on parochial notions about black women singers—namely that her sound of blackness couldn't have resembled gospel-trained singing because she didn't grow up singing in church. And, of course, misogynous attitudes toward free-spirited black women were also factors. But as we observed in our discussion of Khan, churches weren't the only sites of musical development for black youth. That Davis didn't sing in church is only a partial explanation. Recordings such as "Hangin' Out in Hollywood" (1979) and "All I Do Is Think of You" (1979), which reflect a rather conventional pop style after Island Records cancelled her contract, suggest that she may have become a pop star if she sang according to conventions. But she was a firm believer in the philosophy of blue funk—she valued unvarnished truth as an essential characteristic of artistic innovation.

That Davis preferred the term "projector" as a description of her style is an important clue to her aesthetic. "Aretha Franklin is a singer," she said. "I consider myself more of a projector. I'm into sound. Like I'll work my voice a thousand different ways. I'm into making my voice work with the rhythm track. Whatever I feel I'm getting from the rhythm track I'll do it with my voice."[101] Davis's notion of "work[ing her] voice" revisits a recurrent theme throughout our discussions. Her projector metaphor is a variation of blues aesthetics; but since she didn't play instruments, a critical approach to her artistry should account for modulations of the human voice. Davis's pitch typically fluctuated between conventional singing and spoken word, and she often intoned or half-sang instead of singing in the usual sense of the term. Thus one possible method involves the concept of paralinguistic expression, which has been effective in analyses of African American poets, such as Jayne Cortez, Amiri Baraka, Sonia Sanchez, and Kalamu ya Salaam, who crafted styles based largely on sound, including blues-oriented music.

According to performance scholar Richard Bauman, "Paralinguistic features, by their very nature, tend not to be captured in the transcribed or published versions of texts."[102] Several of Salaam's erotic poems include wordless simulations of oral sex that have excited diverse audiences. Likewise, the beginning of Baraka's poem "Dope" expresses meaning through sound. In the printed version of the poem, readers encounter the following three lines in which the letter /u/ is repeated ten times:

uuuuuuuuuu
uuuuuuuuuu
uuuuuuuuuu[103]

These three lines actually represent the sound of a heroin junkie nodding out ("oo," "oo," etc.). But few readers recognize this at the outset. Only after listening to the audio version wherein Baraka parodies a junkie do most readers begin to correlate his sound with the printed letters on the page. This is the point when the passage signifies meaning.[104] Thus wordless sound, not print, conveys meaning in the passage—and Baraka's sound exemplifies paralinguistic expression.

The contemporary sound poet Tracie Morris is also pertinent here. Having won the Nuyorican Grand Slam and the National Haiku Slam in the 1990s, Morris began experimenting with a new style, and her comments about her transition are analogous to Davis's technique. For instance, she emphasized kinesthesia. "Eventually," recalls Morris, "I began to work more . . . with the sound itself (trying to tease it away from literal meaning) and started to feel it in the body and adjust it within the body. This led me to make physical not just conceptual segues, uttered and nonuttered choices. (At a certain point it becomes impossible to distinguish between the two.)"[105] Of course, Davis didn't write poetry, but there's a clear correlation between her notion of a projector and black poets' paralinguistic techniques, especially Morris's indistinction between "uttered and nonuttered" sounds, not to mention her attempt to "tease [sound] away from literal meaning." Implicit in both Davis's projector-trope and Morris's paralinguistic (non)utterances are variations of blues musicians' notions of voice-instrument dynamics. But whereas Morris melds words and vocables into "projections" of multi-syllabic and diphthong-oriented signification or representation, Davis projected her voice as an instrumental sound of hard rock. And, of course, many of the sounds she uttered were paralinguistic expressions. The groundbreaking linguist Geneva Smitherman examined such expressions in African American culture at the height of the funk era. Writing in 1977, Smitherman coins the term tonal semantics in her analysis:

> In using the semantics of tone, the voice is employed as a musical instrument with improvisation, riffs, and all kinds of playing between the notes. This rhythmic pattern becomes a kind of acoustical phonetic alphabet and gives black speech its songified or musical quality. Black rappers use word sounds to tap their listeners' souls and inner beings in the same way that the musician uses the symbolic language of music to strike inward responsive chords to his listeners' hearts.[106]

Smitherman is primarily concerned with black speech as such, but she might as well have been writing about Davis. For instance, Keyes found the following sounds in Davis's style: growling, a purr-like sound,[107] and "a semibreathy vocal quality."[108] Likewise, the funk scholar Rickey Vincent states, "Her album was so noisy. It's gnarly raw grooves with thunderous rock chords and her chainsaw voice on top of it."[109]

Davis used tonal semantics to transmute blues into black feminine rock. Her rough-hewn vocals approximate and reverberate the sounds of rock, especially musicians' distortion. That she envisioned her music as avant-garde seems fairly clear from her public comments. Observe her skepticism toward commerce as a measure of artistry: "What I'm doing is really me and it's *honest*. If I wanted to be commercial and get a top 40 hit, I could. But I think there are enough people out there already. I want to do something different and being creative is a bit challenging whereas being commercial isn't."[110] Davis's emphasis on honesty exemplifies the core meaning of "funk," and her belief that art should involve "do[ing] something different" is nearly identical to Clinton's advocacy of eccentric expression—all of which exemplify Iton's notion of the black fantastic.

Davis's popularity in the Pittsburgh metropolitan area provides an inkling of her impact on listeners who understood her. Renée Stout, a black avant-garde visual artist, has cited Davis as one of her earliest influences. Stout recollects her teenage years when she listened to Davis on a local radio station that incorporated rock into its playlist:

> In Pittsburgh some rock was crossing over to the soul stations and we were listening and skating to some Black Sabbath, Edgar Winter and stuff like that. Jimi was right in there too. I think the fact that I already knew Blues, Rock and Funk, every thing [sic] Jimi did made sense to me. . . . The Betty Davis song that they used to play on the radio all the time was "[Turn] Off the Light." I heard that and I was hooked.[111]

Stout's recollection elucidates the conceptual stumbling blocks that hindered many people's understanding of Davis's style. Note Stout's allusions to rock (Black Sabbath and Edgar Winter), then observe her mention of blues. Like Davis, Stout's family members enjoyed dancing the blues,[112] and Stout also listened to funk. Thus she says, "every thing Jimi did made sense to me" before immediately shifting her focus to Davis's "Turn Off the Light," which "hooked" her. Davis fashioned a sophisticated, iconoclastic brand of funk that reflected the richness, beauty, and political acumen that was both explicit and implicit in black working-class women's experiences. However, the ability to grasp the complexities of her experiment required familiarity with diverse musical soundscapes. This helps explain why accomplished instrumentalists demonstrated respect for Davis's artistry. Her songs and performances reflected a kaleidoscope of black women's delights, desires, and dilemmas seldom registered in American society. But since most radio stations racialized rock as white and rhythm and blues as black, relatively few listeners had the wherewithal to appreciate her artistic accomplishment.

For Davis, representing women's sexual experiences via funk required an unsettling or disruptive timbre. She wanted to assail doll-babyish images of black women singers, which she interpreted as symbols of subservience. It seems fitting, then, that Davis formulated her funk as disruptive signification: the gnarled, sonic discomfort of ugly beauty amidst the hard-rock turbulence of anti-love songs. And though she didn't sound like women blues singers, her approach was invariably blues-inflected—reminiscent of artists who developed aural techniques of illustrating moods and feelings with tonal coloration, onomatopoeia, and other voice/instrument devices. To cite but one of many examples, the jazz legend Eric Dolphy once said: "The human thing in instrumental playing has to do with trying to get as much human warmth and feeling into my work as I can. I want say more on my horn than I ever could in human speech." In chapter 2, we discussed the ways that horn players approximated slurs, screams, laughter and the like on a routine basis. In rock, Hendrix exemplified this approach in songs such as "3rd Stone from the Sun" and "Machine Gun." Davis's use of tonal semantics is analogous to these trailblazing instrumentalists.

Davis signified cultural politics in the frequencies of her pitch. For this reason, Fred Moten's perspective may be helpful. In an interview with editor Charles Rowell, Moten, a black avant-garde poet and influential theorist, shares his insight on the limits and complexities of language. Doing so, he provides a conceptual framework for Davis's idiomatic expression. Moten states:

> I think poetry is what happens on the outskirts of sense, on the outskirts of normative meaning. I'm trying precisely to work on that edge, and I assume that the content that is conveyed on that edge, on that fault line, is richer, deeper, and fuller than those things that are given in writing that passes for direct. . . . The art that always threatens the boundaries of sense has been the art that has been the most beautiful for me.[113]

As a poet-theorist, Moten is concerned with matters of epistemology, signification, and inherent limitations of language. However, his statement that "richer" and "fuller" art "threatens the boundaries of sense" is equally applicable to Davis's growls, gnarls, purrs, and other sounds outside the "boundaries" of normative speech and singing.

Davis projected sounds that represented her characters' various moods. She enlivened her lyrics with multifaceted arrangements, a hybrid vocal style that encompassed vocables, chants, and singing. Oftentimes, though, her voice reverberated near the indeterminate spaces that separate conventional singing and spoken word. Davis was so adept at tonal semantics that, according to Keyes, she could use her "semibreathy vocal quality" to "gently caress each word in [a] song. . . ."[114] Her use of tonal semantics is especially noticeable in the autobiographical title track of *They Say I'm Different*. The song is both a tribute to blues culture and a self-reflexive commentary on her aesthetic. Davis begins the song by highlighting her grandmother's distaste for the foxtrot, which is juxtaposed against her passion for Delta blues. She cites a litany of artists who effectively functioned as her mentors: Robert Johnson, Jimmy Reed, Big Mama Thornton, John Lee Hooker, Elmore James, and Chuck Berry. Of course, the foxtrot symbolized staid notions of style that blues people mocked as representative of the supposed superiority of the dominant culture. Davis's mocking gesture harkens back to Smith's use of satire in "Trombone Cholly" and "Jazzbo Brown from Memphis Town." Both songs memorialize formally untrained black musicians who created musical innovations that were inconceivable to most white musicians,[115] and there is evidence suggesting that W. C. Handy's "Memphis Blues" influenced the foxtrot.[116] For Davis, funk was a by-product of black southern culture. Hence her valorization of staples such as dipping snuff and chitlins just as James Brown used southern cuisine to symbolize funk in "Make It Funky" (1971).

Tonal semantics become more pronounced when Davis sings about Berry. She improvises a hyperbolic variant of a twang, a common paralinguistic feature of southern-derived black phonetics that has long been a subject of ridicule in American society. However, Davis uses her elaboration of the twang to commemorate blues culture. Her intoned pronunciation of Berry's name is an exaggerated diphthong that celebrates black southern phraseology. Similarly, in "Shoo B Doop and Cop Him," she creates a young black woman persona who expresses her intense sexual attraction to a handsome young man. The first line waxes on his fineness: "Gals, He's a fine fine thang." Naturally, Davis's emission of a long /a/ vowel sound in her pronunciation of "thing" is a dead giveaway, but her entire line is twanged. In other words, it's precisely when Davis wants to convey her persona's innermost desires that she resorts to the twang. Likewise, her pronunciation of "Chuck Berry" is an exaggerated twang reminiscent of sounds in festive gatherings and trash-talking sessions. Yet the most intriguing aspect of Davis's phrasing is that her twang isn't immediately recognizable as such. In fact, it's questionable whether people who aren't familiar with the sounds and nuances of black southern speech would be able to recognize what Davis is improvising. Only after conducting repeated listening sessions does the relationship between her referent and her improvisation become legible. And this is important, because many black southern migrants to larger American cities associated blues—and black southern culture generally—with backwardness. Southern accents and countrified manners were constant targets of derision in America's cities. But Davis riffed on the sound in much the same manner that jazz musicians improvised on blues licks, reworking them until only echoes of the referent remained.

Davis sculpted her voice into a kinesthetic instrument to lend resonance to her lyrics and tone color to her band. Whenever the mood shifted, she altered her sound to signify an appropriate sensation. For instance, in "Shoo B Doop and Cop Him," Davis sings the line "I'm gonna do my best" in a high note to add a lighter touch to the song. She used a variety of pyrotechnics: growls, purrs, snarls, gnarls, and the like. Think of Koko Taylor or Big Mama Thornton's gravelly slurred moans and shouts transfigured as funk-rock gnarls. For Davis, tonal semantics functioned as a guttural instrument of blues-rock bohemia. Her gruff, jarring sound reflected her commitment to representing working-class black women's sexuality and self-love in an utterly unsentimental manner that recalled blues women's suspicious attitudes toward the ideology of romantic love and its prevailing notions of domesticity.[117] In sum, Davis's pyrotechnics were paralinguistic sketches of black women's lowdown funky realities, which she highlighted with wordless and non-syllabic signification. As the late Barbadian poet Kamau Brathwaite might say, "the sound [was] part of the meaning."

NASTY GAL

"Nasty Gal," the title track of Davis's third album, is perhaps her most profound statement on sexual politics. She examines the contradictions of male privilege and misogyny while excoriating the hypocrisy therein. The song epitomizes funky erotixxx. Davis excoriates "what is libidinous and blasphemous in" black men's misogyny, especially Stallings's "imperialistic" implications "within its social mores and sexual morality." The ironic title reflects the rhetorical method she uses to render her critique. Reminiscent of early blues artists' transformation of the Standard English word "funk," which we discussed in chapter 2, Davis skillfully resorts to symbolic inversion: "any act of expressive behavior which inverts, contradicts, abrogates, or in some fashion presents an alternative to commonly held cultural codes, values, and norms, be they linguistic, literary, or artistic, religious, social, and political."[118]

In "Nasty Gal" Davis uses symbolic inversion to reprise Cox's premise in "Wild Women Don't Have the Blues." Whereas Cox's persona mocks the notion of treating "a man right," Davis's persona describes the shortsightedness and cruelty that contribute to women's cynicism. In particular, there's an intriguing analogy between Davis's song and her complex relationship with legendary trumpeter Miles Davis. Indeed, "Nasty Gal" can be interpreted as an allegorical response to his (mis)representation of her in his autobiography—which is to say, the persona in "Nasty Gal" puts her ex on blast. The song is set in the aftermath of the relationship during which he shamelessly delighted in freaky fetishes with her. Afterward, however, he scandalizes her as nasty and salacious like blues singers, while representing himself as a model of morality and cosmopolitanism. Consequently, Davis historicizes the conflict at the outset of the song, "running it down," so to speak, for context and clarification. The persona cites a litany of his misogynous name-calling: bitch, witch, wench, ho. Yet she remains unperturbed. Like earlier blues personae, she resorts to ironic humor, lampooning his attempt to defame and sully her reputation for the express purpose of expropriating her agency and diminishing her social upstanding.

At issue is the man's conflation of coitus and control. The central conflict involves his unsuccessful attempt to dictate her actions and mold her identity, particularly since he believes that she should cultivate a bearing more in keeping with conventional notions of feminine grace and respectability. At the conclusion of the relationship, he castigates the persona as vulgar, simpleminded, and country. However, she wields an impressive arsenal of rhetorical weaponry and psychological armor, which, ironically, she developed in blues culture—the infamous space he associates with simplemindedness. The persona engages in a fascinating display of rhetorical counterpunches, reminding him repeatedly of his slanderous statements ("you said"). She also uses symbolic inversion. Reminiscent of blues-era comediennes like Moms Mabley and Wanda Page, the persona appropriates her ex's invectives and converts them into brainstorming material. In this way, she transforms his attacks into stinging criticisms of misogyny. Her exposé of racy details about their relationship is central to her methodology. The backstories provide a clear understanding of the contradictions at hand—he's stigmatizing the very qualities he found attractive when they met. Consequently, the persona uses parody to nullify the piquancy of his vilification when she counterattacks: "You used to love it ooh to ride my broom honey." The satire imbued in "honey" is pointed. Davis sings "honey" as "huh-nay," and she sings the line in a playful high note that amounts to a side-eye expression of ersatz sexy sweetness. This is funky erotixxx par excellence.

Yet another example of Davis's funky erotixxx involves the persona's re-deployment of his witch-image, triggering a pattern of comedic flourishes and quick-witted signification. As he castigates her, she deftly converts his statements into call and response. The repartee prompts her to reveal his fetishes and point up his agenda: to deny her individuality and suppress her sexual agency. Of course, his exercise in futility only renders his insults more laughable. When he calls her an alley cat, she quickly reminds him of his captivation when she scratched his back during sex. In boasting about her sexual prowess, the persona elucidates the shifting grounds and glaring contradictions that underlie and characterize the bourgeois ideology that reproduces (black) male privilege. But rather than conceding the contradiction, the man attacks her morality. Here Davis represents the inherent intricacies of sexual desire intermingled with patriarchal power and ideology. The ex adheres to notions of hierarchy that reify his social upstanding, yet he's keenly aware that his public image is incongruent with having a self-proclaimed nasty gal as his lover. As she points out, he sang a different song behind closed doors. Her erotic talents and sexual ingenuity were so captivating that he clutched the bedside by his fingernails after she left the room. Not surprisingly, he still sends her private messages despite her determination to be free.

The persona's criticisms interface with Miles Davis's depiction of Betty Davis in *Miles: The Autobiography* (1989). Since the two artists were married, there are interconnections between her song and Miles's subsequent representations of her as his ex-wife not only in his composition "Back Seat Betty" (1981) but in his autobiography as well. Yet this isn't to suggest that "Nasty Gal" is autobiographical or that Miles listened to the song and responded by seeking retribution in his music and autobiography, although Miles's collaboration with Davis on the poignant song "You and I," which appears on *Nasty Gal*, all but guarantees that he listened to the title track. On the contrary, my argument, pure and simple, is that the three artifacts are interconnected. Miles's characterizations of his ex-wife replicate the language, tropes, attitudes, and hypocrisy that she ridicules in "Nasty Gal." In fact, his representations of Davis reenact the premise of her song.

During an intermission of Davis's Columbia recordings, for instance, Miles is clearly audible, telling her, "That's right, go ahead and sing with the gum in your mouth. Bitch." Likewise, in the interview with John Ballon that accompanies the recording, Davis said that Miles titled his song "Back Seat Betty" as a personal dig at her.

> I know that we recorded "Politician." That was the Eric Clapton/ Jack Bruce song. And at the end of the song I say real sexy, "Get in the back seat." So after my marriage to Miles broke up, I was living in California, and I received a call about 4 o'clock in the morning and this song just started playing. And I said, "This has to be Miles . . ." And he got on the phone and he says, "I'm namin' that song Backseat Betty." And it came from my saying, "Get in the back seat" on "Politician." . . . I said, "Miles, don't call it that." And he says, "Yes, I am." And a couple of writers reviewed the album that this was on [We Want Miles] . . . and they all commented on "Backseat Betty."[119]

The parallels between the conflict in "Nasty Gal" and Miles's assailment of Davis are striking. Miles debases Davis's reputation *after* their marriage and, quite notably, after *Nasty Gal* was released. In his autobiography, Miles's portrayal of Davis is nearly identical to the male character in "Nasty Gal." Miles uses the word "wild" to describe Davis on more than one occasion and alternately labels her "a free spirit," "a rocker and a street woman." But Miles's most damning statement is his description of Davis's sexuality: "She was raunchy and all that kind of shit, all sex, but I didn't know that when I met her—and if I did, I guess, *I just didn't pay much attention.*"[120]

Of course, Miles's statement is a prototypical example of chauvinistic projection—his expletives reek of the raunchiness he projects onto Davis. More fundamentally, though, Miles's portrayal of Davis bears the unmistakable imprint of racial ideology. His statement that Davis was "all sex" invokes the Cartesian mind-body split that has been used throughout American history to impede black women's agency and mythologize their sexuality and subjectivity by caricaturing them as irrational and unintelligent. The inherent contradictions become readily apparent when Miles states that he "didn't pay much attention" to Davis's sexual proclivities before they were married, while admitting that during his marriage "Betty was a big influence on my personal life as well as my musical life. She introduced me to the music of Jimi Hendrix—and to Jimi Hendrix himself—and other black rock music and musicians." Like the ex in "Nasty Gal," Miles makes no complaints about

Davis's sexuality until after their relationship. What really irked Miles and Davis's male character in "Nasty Gal" wasn't black women's sensuality so much as their insistence on determining when, where, and how they expressed it.

POSTLUDE

Davis's marginalization in and eventual exclusion from the music industry were commensurate with her radical sexual politics. She aspired, in both form and content, to abrogate the oversight of black women's sexuality from men regardless of ethnicity—an undertaking fraught with pitfalls. To the extent that funk was coextensive with the Black Power movement, it represented working-class people's interpretations of black aesthetics. But the masculinist orientation of black power and its cultural component, the Black Arts Movement, reified patriarchal concepts of gender that filtered into funk, and conflicting reactions to her art paralleled conflicting meanings of the term "funk." On the one hand, Davis reflected the honesty and integrity that epitomizes blue funk aesthetics. On the other hand, renunciations of her artistry invoked a racialized definition of "funk," e.g., sexual deviance. Such logic harkens back to racial ideology in early American culture when Thomas Jefferson and other like-minded thinkers fused malodor and contamination as a composite trope to cast African Americans as phenotypically ignoble, irrational, and unintelligent in order to normalize the exploitation of slavery. Efforts to suppress Davis's recordings, performances, and her personality drew heavily from Jefferson's ideological framework. And as is often the case with pioneering cultural rebels, the systemic misrepresentation of her as a purveyor of sexual deviance not only impeded her artistic development; it also camouflaged the misogyny that contributed to her illegibility and banishment from the industry.

Today, Davis leads a private life in a modest apartment just outside of Pittsburgh. Her legacy rests on what she calls "three albums of hard funk" that reflected the unruly sensibilities of black women in street culture in the 1960s and 1970s. Her characters were counterparts to black female characters in fictional narratives penned by the most influential black women writers of the period. Like most effective progressive movements, the feminist movement inspired new collectives and broad readerships; and since black women writers were among the vanguard thinkers, their writings were especially appealing to editors and publishers in the literary marketplace. Such was not the case for Davis; the music industry didn't have a comparable infrastructure to accommodate her artistry. Yet she remained committed to changing women's attitudes about sexuality. Davis's recordings and performances were disruptive manifestations of funky erotixxx—which is to say, a distinct version of the black fantastic.

Outro

The story of DJs sampling funk beats in the early days of hip hop is now a twice-told tale. But the question of how the concept of funk remained viable has yet to be examined. Meshell Ndegeocello deserves special mention in this regard. She's cited Prince as an inspiration; and like the singer and multi-instrumentalist extraordinaire, she often plays virtually all the instruments on her albums.[1] More to the point, though, Ndegeocello exemplifies several characteristics associated with funk, including musicianship, contrarianism, eccentricity, and organic intellectualism. As she explained in a 2012 interview with musicologist Tammy Kernodle, her early experiences playing bass in go-go bands formed her musical foundation:

> Everything is based around the drum and percussion so you can dance. And it helped me understand the aspect of groove-oriented aspects of music. . . . I watch[ed] people as I play[ed] to see what their body language [was] showing me in terms of where they [felt] the groove. I just think it helped me tremendously . . . where I fit bass lines and tempos. . . ."[2]

For Ndegeocello, go-go performances provided conceptual introductions to the dynamics of the funk principle. Like earlier blues-oriented musicians, she underscores reading body movement in her approach to music making. In fact, her comments about playing bass are nearly identical to Ohio Players bassist Marshall Jones's approach that we discussed in chapter 1.

A former member of the Black Rock Coalition, Ndegeocello's aesthetic might be described as postmodern blue funk.[3] She incorporates rock, funk, jazz, hip hop, and other styles into her music, and her sound defies categorization. For instance, her album *Cookie: The Anthropological Mixtape* (2002) features guitarist Michael Hampton, otherwise known as Kidd Funkadelic of P-Funk, as well as samples of Angela Davis's speech and recordings of poets

Gil Scott-Heron, Etheridge Knight, and Countee Cullen. And whereas funk musicians usually avoided topics related to homophobia and queer sexuality, Ndegeocello foregrounds these themes. Her music thus takes up where funk music left off. For Ndegeocello, songs are like short stories: creativity as critical analysis. We can briefly observe her organic intellectualism in "Leviticus: Faggot" (1996) which showcases her musicianship, songwriting, singing, spoken word, social commentary, and eccentricity. In the video, the genders associated with Ndegeocello's sexuality, persona, and vocal timbre are indeterminate. She wears a close-cropped haircut and a white undershirt, which were fashionable among young black men in urban areas.

At the same time, Ndegeocello's songwriting includes key elements of blues aesthetics. In the title, "Leviticus" is an ironic Biblical allusion, and "Faggot" evidences symbolic inversion. The Book of Leviticus promotes Christian morality: "you shall love your neighbor as yourself."[4] Ndegeocello excoriates the hypocrisy of black Christians who stigmatize queer sexuality just as blues singers challenged church authorities years ago. The song tells the story of Leviticus, a little boy whose family withholds love from him because they mistake his delicate sensibility for moral deviance. Ndegeocello scrutinizes the parents' fundamentalist attitudes that germinate their myopia—they can't see the virtue in their child's feminine mannerisms. And since Leviticus can't become a "real" man, that is, suppress his queerness and thus conform to the sexual doctrine of the church, his parents reject him unceremoniously. His father kicks him out at sixteen. Ndegeocello uses a variety of vocal styles and pitches in the song, ranging from husky-toned spoken word to slight falsetto. These timbral variations illustrate and vivify an array of emotions and perspectives signified in the lyrics. In this way, Ndegeocello thematizes mistreatment like an old blues singer. Adept at mimicry and parody, she re-presents prototypical sounds and cadences of black urban street men. She even personates their physical gestures when they say, "Stop acting like a bitch."

Yet the music sounds almost idyllic. Though Ndegeocello plays bass on the track, she also plays lead guitar in a low register, embellishing drummer Gene Oliver Lake's steady groove with a pulsating riff that she punctuates with a full-bodied blues-tinged twang, adding soulful tone color to each phrase. Wah Wah Watson complements Ndegeocello with intermittent accents in higher notes on guitar while she and women background vocalists sing the hook: "Save him from this life." When juxtaposed against the gut-wrenching tragedy of Leviticus's life, the tonal collage of rejuvenating rhythm and melodic lyricism accentuates the pathos of the story, which typifies the contrariety of blue funk. The pious rejoicing continues while Leviticus is "crowned queen" with his beaten body. And like classic blues singers, Nde-geocello closes the song with mocking irony. Alluding to "the wages of sin is death" in the Book of Romans, she sings the refrain from "Swing Low Sweet Chariot" as background singers represent Leviticus's voice as he rises like Jesus while "angels dance around [his] soul."

The contradictions underlying the stigmas of queer sexuality, evident in all forms of human degradation, have become more acute in the twenty-first century. At the same time, artists have demonstrated renewed interest in funk. Kendrick Lamar, Erykah Badu, Trombone Shorty, Bruno Mars, Janelle Monáe, Childish Gambino, Nik West, Anderson.Paak, and other contemporary artists have engaged the concept in recent years. This raises the question: why? Given the precepts of funk—unvarnished truth; contrariety; unabashed pleasure; and implicit predilection for reciprocity—such interest may exemplify, on some level, dialectical responses to troubling conditions. American society is increasingly characterized by escalating intolerance related to intensifying contradictions in the political economy and a commensurate lack of philosophical frameworks that generate viable alternatives to reductive logic and crass commercialism. When African Americans say, "Don't fake the funk" or "Keep it funky" to emphasize the importance of truth, they accentuate the meaning of "funk" and demonstrate the significance of the concept in everyday life.

So in this historical moment, when the world is teetering on the brink of fascism, when human value is increasingly assessed in terms of money, power, and status, and when so-called progressive theories are often new-fangled versions of the status quo, there's little wonder why funk remains relevant. When asked why funk resonates with audiences today, Kansas City bassist and singer Jewel "JC" Carter replied, "That's an easy question to answer. We live the funk every day. It's not just the grooves that Earth, Wind & Fire, Parliament-Funkadelic, Ohio Players, the Bar-Kays, and all those other groups played. We *live* the funk, and that's why they respond to it when we express this in our music." For Carter, funk is clearly more than a musical genre. He describes it existentially. "I lost two sons, and I have holes in my heart that will never heal. This isn't about me," he said. "It's about sharing a gift that I have."[5] Such is the ugly beauty of funk.

ᒪotes

INTRO

1. D'Angelo, "A Conversation with D'Angelo Hosted by Nelson George, May 2014," Red Bull Music Academy Festival. http://www.redbullmusicacademy.com/about/projects/festival -new-york-2014. Retrieved June 27, 2017.

2. Greg Tate, "The Electric Miles," in *Flyboy in the Buttermilk: Essays on Contemporary America: An Eye-Opening Look at Race, Politics, Literature, and Music* (New York: Simon & Schuster, 1992), 73.

3. Rickey Vincent, *Funk: The Music, the People, and the Rhythm of the One* (New York: St. Martin's Press, 1996), 28.

4. Richard J. Ripani, *The New Blue Music: Changes in Rhythm & Blues, 1950–1999* (Jackson: University Press of Mississippi, 2006), 7.

5. Ripani, *New Blues Music*, 89.

6. Ripani, *New Blues Music*, 90.

7. Samuel A. Floyd Jr. makes a similar observation about Charlie Parker's seminal bebop composition "Now's the Time" (1944) and Paul Williams's 1949 rhythm and blues hit single "Hucklebuck." Floyd points out that both songs are based on the blues even though the styles and levels of complexity in the songs are markedly different. See Samuel A. Floyd, *The Power of Black Music: Interpreting Its History from Africa to the United States* (New York: Oxford University Press, 1995), 144.

8. Charles Keil, *Urban Blues* (1966; rpt., Chicago: University of Chicago Press, 1991), 32.

9. Maureen Mahon, *Right to Rock: The Black Rock Coalition and the Cultural Politics of Race* (Durham, NC: Duke University Press, 2004), 138.

10. Vernon Reid, "The Vibe Q: George Clinton," *Vibe*, November 1993: 45–46.

11. Mahon, *Right to Rock*, 28.

12. Ripani, *New Blues Music*, 90.

13. Ronnie Reese, "A Message from the Meters," *Wax Poetics*, no. 13 (Summer 2005): 114.

14. John Abbey, "George Clinton," *Blues and Soul*, December 1978. https://www.rocks backpages.com/Library/Article/george-clinton-2.

15. Tony Bolden, "Free Your Mind: Funk Transfigured as Black Cultural Aesthetics," *Journal of Foreign Languages and Cultures* 2.1 (June 2018): 86.

16. Francesca T. Royster, *Sounding Like a No-No: Queer Sounds and Eccentric Acts in the Post-Soul Era* (Ann Arbor: University of Michigan Press, 2012), 15.

17. Royster, *Sounding Like a No-No*, 8.

18. Royster, *Sounding Like a No-No*, 8.

19. Richard Iton, *In Search of the Black Fantastic: Politics and Popular Culture in the Post-Civil Rights Era* (New York: Oxford University Press, 2008), 17.

20. Iton, *In Search of the Black Fantastic*, 16.

21. David Nathan, "Parliament/Funkadelic," *Blues & Soul*, May 1978. https://www.rocks backpages.com/Library/Article/parliamentfunkadelic. Retrieved September 13, 2018.

22. Keith Shadwick, *Jimi Hendrix*, 76. See also booklet notes to Lonnie Youngblood Featuring Jimi Hendrix, *Two Great Experiences* (CD, Empire Musicwerks, 2003).

CHAPTER 1: GROOVE THEORY: LINER NOTES ON FUNK AESTHETICS

1. George Clinton, qtd. in Vincent, *Funk: The Music, the People, and the Rhythm of the One*, 13.

2. Teresa L. Reed, *The Holy Profane: Religion in Black Popular Music* (Lexington: University of Kentucky Press, 2003), 15. See also Mark Anthony Neal, "Sly Stone and the Sanctified Church," in *The Funk Era and Beyond: New Perspectives on Black Popular Culture*, ed. Tony Bolden (New York: Palgrave Macmillan, 2008), 3–9. For an alternative approach, see Scot Brown's analysis of the role that public schools in Dayton, Ohio, played in the development of funk musicians. Scot Brown, "A Land of Funk: Dayton, Ohio," in *The Funk Era and Beyond: New Perspectives on Black Popular Culture*, 73–88.

3. Teddy Pendergrass, *Truly Blessed* (New York: Putnam Adult, 1998), 34.

4. Guthrie P. Ramsey Jr., *Race Music: Black Cultures from Bebop to Hip Hop* (Berkeley: University of California Press, 2004), 13.

5. James "Blood" Ulmer, "Jazz Is the Teacher, Funk Is the Preacher," *Are You Glad to Be in America?* Rough Trade, 1980.

6. James Brown, "Papa's Got a Brand New Bag, Pts. 1, 2, & 3," 1965. *Star Time* (CD box set, Polydor, 1991).

7. Lyn Collins, "Interview," *Mama Feelgood* (CD, Hi & Fly Records, 2006). It's also notable that scholars of go-go music have made similar parallels between go-go and Pentecostal music. See Kip Lornell and Charles C. Stephenson Jr., *The Beat: Go-Go Music from Washington, D.C.* (reprint, Jackson: University Press of Mississippi, 2009). See also Natalie Hopkinson, *Go-Go Live: The Musical Life and Death of a Chocolate City* (Durham, NC: Duke University Press, 2012). According to Hopkinson, "Go-go can feel a lot like a Pentecostal church service. . . . Neither erects a huge barrier between who is performing and who is watching. Both are heavy in call and response" (51). See also Glen Hinson, *Fire in My Bones: Transcendence and the Holy Spirit in African American Gospel* (Philadelphia: University of Pennsylvania Press, 1999).

8. Paul Taylor, "An Interview with Nathaniel Mackey," *Callaloo* 23.2 (Spring 2000): 645.

9. Barbara Christian, "The Race for Theory," *Cultural Critique* 6 (Spring 1987): 52.

10. John Miller Chernoff, "The Artistic Challenge of African Music: Thoughts on the Absence of Drum Orchestras in Black American Music," *Black Music Research Journal* 5 (1985): 2.

11. Vincent, *Funk*, 4.

12. Jonathan David Jackson, "Improvisation in African-American Vernacular Dancing," *Dance Research Journal* 33.2 (Winter 2001–2002): 43.

13. Leon Forrest, *The Furious Voice for Freedom: Essays on Life* (Wakefield, RI: Asphodel Press, 1994), 46.

14. Bruce W. Talamon, *Soul. R&B. Funk. Photographs 1972–1982* (Cologne, Germany: Taschen, 2018), 268.

15. See Olly Wilson, "The Association of Movement and Music as a Manifestation of a Black Conceptual Approach to Music-Making," in *More Than Dancing: Essays on Afro-American Music and Musicians*, ed. Irene V. Jackson (Westport, CT: Greenwood Press, 1985), 9–23. Amiri Baraka makes a similar observation about jazz musician Charlie Parker, stating that "Parker did not admit that there was any separation between himself and the agent he had chosen as his means of self-expression." Amiri Baraka, *Blues People: Negro Music in White America* (New York: Morrow, 1963), 30–31.

16. Kyra D. Gaunt, *The Games Black Girls Play: Learning the Ropes from Double-Dutch to Hip-Hop* (New York: New York University Press, 2006), 59.

17. This cognitive modality was prefigured by the principle of *ase*, which literally means "so be it," in traditional African cultures. For a detailed analysis of this principle, see Robert Farris Thompson, *Flash of the Spirit* (New York: Vintage, 1984).

18. Thomas F. DeFrantz, "The Black Beat Made Visible: Hip Hop Dance and Body Power," in *Of the Presence of the Body: Essays on Dance and Performance Theory*, ed. Andre Lepecki (Middletown, CT: Wesleyan University Press, 2004), 66.

19. DeFrantz, "The Black Beat Made Visible," 66.

20. Gaunt, *The Games Black Girls Play*, 62.

21. Natalie Hopkinson, *Go-Go Live: The Musical Life and Death of a Chocolate City* (Durham, NC: Duke University Press, 2012), 42.

22. Gaunt, *The Games Black Girls Play*, 98.

23. Gaunt, *The Games Black Girls Play*, 98.

24. The dance vocabulary of the Moonwalk has a long history. James Brown distinguishes the Camel Walk from the Moonwalk by pointing out that the latter dance "is really the bicycle, a move Charlie Chaplin used to do. You know how you get on a bicycle and ride it backwards? That's the moonwalk—the Charlie Chaplin bicycle done backwards." James Brown, *The Godfather of Soul: An Autobiography* (reprint, New York: Thunder's Mouth Press, 1997), 55. Brown's commentary notwithstanding, Michael Holman suggests that the basic dance vocabulary of the dance was performed as far back as 1872. Writing about a dance that appeared a generation later, Holman states: "A dance that appeared around the turn of the century in Black minstrel shows called Stepping on the Puppy's Tail also had an amazing resemblance to the moon walk. Stepping on the Puppy's Tail was described as moving each foot alternately backwards 'like a horse pawing the ground.'" Michael Holman, "Breaking: The History," in *That's the Joint!: The Hip-Hop Studies Reader*, eds. Murray Forman and Mark Anthony Neal (New York: Routledge, 2004), 13–20 (33). Other notable examples include Bill Bailey's version in the 1943 film *Cabin in the Sky*. In 1955 Bailey performed an extended version that is nearly identical to Jackson's dance. http://www.YouTube.com/watch?v=y71njpDH3co (retrieved September 29, 2013). Verta Mae Grosvenor's version also comes to mind. Gros-

venor developed hers during her tenure as a dancer with jazz musician Sun Ra's band. She
states, "I developed the Space Walk, the one that Michael Jackson did later and called it the
'moon walk.'" See Tony Bolden, "Theorizing the Funk: An Introduction," in *The Funk Era
and Beyond: New Perspectives on Black Popular Culture*, 20.

25. Many scholars interpret the ability to create dynamic expression while maintaining
an impassive exterior as an aesthetic of the cool. For a detailed discussion, see Thompson,
Flash of the Spirit.

26. Portia K. Maultsby, "Dayton Street Funk: The Layering of Multiple Identities," *The
Ashgate Research Companion to Popular Musicology*, ed. Derek B. Scott (Burlington, VT:
Ashgate, 2009), 268.

27. Jacqui Malone, *Steppin' on the Blues: The Visible Rhythms of African American Dance*
(Urbana: University of Illinois Press, 1996), 95–96.

28. See Howard Spring, "Swing and the Lindy Hop: Dance, Venue, Media, and Tradition,"
American Music (Summer 1997): 183–207. According to Spring, "The first public reference
to the Lindy Hop occurred in 1928, just before the music started to change. This suggests,
at least at the beginning, that the dance set off changes in the music. Once set in motion,
the nature of the process was one of mutually influential feedback between dancers and
musicians . . ." (184).

29. This approach can be found in hip hop as well. As Joseph Schloss points out, "[T]he
value of a groove is often felt in the body through the oft-cited 'head nodding' or through
dance . . ." (143). Schloss then quotes producer Negus I, who correlates dancing with the art
of producing: ". . . I think it also helps to be a dancer, to dance a lot. . . . If you dance a lot, you
know what's going to move you to dance. And so, when you're making a beat, that's gonna
help you a lot. As opposed to something that *sounds* good, something that *feels* good is really important" (143). Although I'm skeptical of the opposition between sound and feeling,
Negus I's comments are nonetheless helpful in understanding how dancing can inform a
musician's approach to sound. There are numerous examples of similar statements by black
musicians. See Joseph Schloss, *Making Beats: The Art of Sample-Based Hip-Hop* (Middletown,
CT: Wesleyan University Press, 2004).

30. Bootsy Collins, qtd. in Thomas Sayers Ellis, "From the Crib to the Coliseum: An
Interview with Bootsy Collins," in Bolden, *The Funk Era and Beyond*, 91. In a recent article,
keyboardist Lisa Coleman made a similar point about the importance of kinesthesia in funk
aesthetics in her recollection of playing in Prince's band The Revolution during his *Purple
Rain* tour: "[A] lot of things didn't happen unless he gave us visual cues. . . . [H]e would do
a slight move of his hand, which would cue a riff or something. You'd have to watch pretty
darn closely. Every once in a while, to cue the end of the song, he'd throw a hankie into the
air, and when the hankie hit the ground, that's when we would stop." See David Browne,
"Prince's Epic 'Purple Rain' Tour: An Oral History," *Rolling Stone*, June 22, 2017. http://www
.rollingstone.com/music/features/princes-epic-purple-rain-tour-an-oral-history-w476429.
Retrieved June 27, 2017.

31. Alan Leeds, qtd. in *Make It Funky*, Yvonne Smith, director and writer (PBS, 1995).

32. Zora Neale Hurston, "Characteristics of Negro Expression," in *The Jazz Cadence of
American Culture*, ed. Robert O'Meally (New York: Columbia University Press, 1998), 302.
Brown's biographer R. J. Smith corroborates the statements by Bootsy Collins and Alan Leeds

in his discussion of drummer Jabo Starks's efforts to learn Brown's show. R. J. Smith, *The One: The Life and Music of James Brown* (New York: Gotham Books, 2012).

33. James Brown, *I Feel Good: A Memoir of a Life of Soul* (New York: NAL, 2005), 80.

34. Brown, *I Feel Good*, 79.

35. Brown, *I Feel Good*, 84.

36. Olly Wilson, "'It Don't Mean a Thing If It Ain't Got That Swing': The Relationship Between African and African American Music," in *African Roots/American Cultures: Africa in the Creation of the Americas*, ed. Sheila S. Walker (Lanham, MD: Rowman and Littlefield, 2001), 167.

37. I'm also reminded here of Kool and the Gang's "Hollywood Swinging," *Wild and Peaceful* (Mercury Records, 1973).

38. Stanley Dance, *The World of Count Basie* (New York: DaCapo, 1985), 157. My italics.

39. Hip hop heads will naturally recognize an affinity between Ellington's liquid metaphor and the concept of flow in MCing. Recently, the singer Gregory Porter employed a variation of this trope in the title song of his album *Liquid Spirit* (Blue Note Records, 2013).

40. Duke Ellington, qtd. in Ken Rattenbury, *Duke Ellington, Jazz Composer* (New Haven, CT: Yale University Press, 1990), 14. Richard J. Ripani repeats Ellington's statement nearly verbatim when he states that "there is no way to accurately write swing using the Western system of notation." Ripani, *The New Blues Music*, 452.

41. Maceo Parker, qtd. in *Make It Funky*, Yvonne Smith director and writer. My italics.

42. Brown, *I Feel Good*, 81.

43. Brown, *I Feel Good*, 87.

44. George Clinton, on *The Tavis Smiley Show*, PBS, July 30, 2011.

45. Robert Farris Thompson, *Flash of the Spirit: African and Afro-American Art and Philosophy* (New York: Random House, 1983), 7.

46. I'm reminded of a statement by Nathaniel Mackey that seems pertinent here. In his interview with Paul Taylor, Mackey finds a correlation between the contrariety of funk music and the epistemological premises of such noted intellectuals as the Guyanese novelist and essayist Wilson Harris and the French philosopher and novelist Catherine Clément. Mackey also discerns an implicit social critique in such contrariety. Having mentioned Harris in the previous sentence, Mackey states, "I was struck . . . by Catherine Clément's discussion, in *Syncope*, of a reversal or distillation of odors, the saint's, the yogi's or the mystic's transformation of the fetid odors of bodily exertion, breakdown or putrefaction into spiced aromas, floral aromas. She in fact says that the saint, the yogi and the mystic are "living perfume bottles." I couldn't help thinking of this in relation to funk, the African American transformation of offensive odor into a canon of approval, aesthetic approbation, an analogously mystical distillation of the otherwise or ostensibly offensive into perfume. There's also a social, cultural critique bound up in this" (649). Paul Taylor, "An Interview with Nathaniel Mackey," *Callaloo* 23.2 (Spring 2000): 645–64.

47. The relative indifference from blacks toward Parliament-Funkadelic during its early years is one of the fascinating ironies of black cultural history. As the drummer Frank "Kash" Waddy recalls, in the early phase of Parliament/Funkadelic, "we had an all-White fan base. Then when funk became a household word, *then* they shipped us a Black act! . . . One guy [from the label] finally told us the truth, and said, 'Hey man, these guys don't want you to

leap over to surburbia, they just want you to do well in urbana."' See Matt Rogers, "Trap Music: Drummer Frankie 'Kash' Waddy Stays on the One," *Wax Poetics* 18 (2006): 96–100.

48. It's also worth noting that the falsetto, a common characteristic in rhythm and blues inherited from the blues tradition, arguably exemplified contrariety insofar as the form encompassed male and female voices.

49. Jimi Hendrix, qtd. in *Jimi Hendrix—Band of Gypsys: Live at Fillmore East*, dir. Bob Smeaton (DVD, Experience Hendrix, 2011).

50. See *Jimi Hendrix*, directed by Joe Boyd and John Head, (DVD, Warner Bros, 1973). Hendrix's brother, Leon Hendrix, has suggested that Hendrix's appeal among blacks may have been underreported. He recalls, "I suspected that the people who complained the most about my brother's music being popular with the white kids probably had his records stashed away somewhere in a closet and still listened to it at home at night" (125). Leon Hendrix with Adam Mitchell, *Jimi Hendrix: A Brother's Story* (New York: Thomas Dunne Books, 2012).

51. Rogers, "Trap Music: Drummer Frankie "Kash" Waddy Stays on the One," 100.

52. Leon Hendrix, *Jimi Hendrix: A Brother's Story*, 184.

53. Greg Tate, *Midnight Lightning: Jimi Hendrix and the Black Experience* (Chicago: Chicago Review Press, 2003), 39.

54. Rickey Vincent, *The History of Funk Show*. https://kpfa.org/program/the-history-of-funk/. Retrieved November 25, 2011.

55. Tate, *Midnight Lightning*, 29.

56. Calvin Simon, qtd. in Dave Marsh, *George Clinton and P-Funk: An Oral History* (New York: Avon Books, 1998), 55.

57. George Clinton, qtd. in Dave Thompson, *Funk: Third Ear—The Listening Companion* (New York: Backbeat Books, 2001), 87.

58. Thompson, *Funk*, 42. My italics.

59. Marsh, *George Clinton*, 82.

60. See Zora Neale Hurston, *Mules & Men* (1935; reprint, Bloomington: University of Indiana Press, 1978), 33–34. I should also note here that this folktale foregrounds contrariety, a key principle in blues culture.

61. Forrest, *Furious Voices*, 45.

62. Jeanette Washington, qtd. in Marsh, *George Clinton*, 101.

63. Toni Morrison, *The Bluest Eye* (1970; reprint, New York: Random House, 1993), 68.

64. George Clinton, qtd. in Vincent, *Funk*, 177.

65. Ishmael Reed, *Mumbo Jumbo* (New York: Scribner, 1972), 5.

66. Reed, *Mumbo Jumbo*, 4.

67. Reed, *Mumbo Jumbo*, 117.

68. It's also worth noting here that Clinton's theory of the funk is remarkably similar to Du Bois's notion of the "frenzy" in his 1903 essay "Of the Faith of the Fathers." Recalling his initial experience of witnessing spirituality in a black southern church, Du Bois notes that the frenzy seized devotees with supernatural joy, and that the shrieks, shouts, and trances he witnessed weren't peculiar to blacks, but that "so firm a hold did it have on the Negro, that many generations firmly believed that without this visible manifestation of the God there could be no true communion with the Invisible." W. E. B. Du Bois, "Of the Faith of the Fathers," in *The Souls of Black Folk* (1903; reprint, Cutchogue, NY: Buccaneer Books, 1976), 140–51 (142).

69. Gaunt, *The Games Black Girls Play*, 5.

70. In positing electricity as a metaphor for the funk, Clinton is employing virtually the same trope as blues and jazz musicians in previous periods. See "Theorizing the Funk: An Introduction," in Bolden, *The Funk Era and Beyond*, 13–29.

71. Greg Tate, *Flyboy in the Buttermilk: Essays on Contemporary America* (New York: Simon and Schuster, 1992), 17.

72. Nelson George, *The Death of Rhythm and Blues* (1988; reprint, New York: Penguin, 2003), 154.

73. Anne Danielsen, *Presence and Pleasure: Funk Grooves of James Brown and Parliament* (Middletown, CT: Wesleyan University Press, 2006), 115.

74. Ramsey, *Race Music*, 11.

75. Duke Ellington, *Music Is My Mistress* (Cambridge: Da Capo, 1976), 100.

76. Brown, *I Feel Good*, 81.

CHAPTER 2: BLUE FUNK: THE UGLY BEAUTY OF STANK

1. George Murphy "Pops" Foster and Tom Stoddard, *The Autobiography of Pops Foster: Jazzman, as Told to Tom Stoddard* (Berkeley: University of California Press, 1971), 16. My italics.

2. Cheryl L. Keyes, "Funkin' with Bach: The Impact of Professor Longhair on Rock 'n' Roll," in Bolden, *The Funk Era and Beyond*, 223.

3. Lerone Bennett Jr., "Soul on Soul," *Ebony*, December 1, 1961, 113.

4. Chris Albertson, *Bessie* (Stein and Day, 1972), 85. It is also worth noting that singer and guitarist T-Bone Walker, who prefigured much of Jimi Hendrix's style by playing the guitar with his teeth and performing the splits while doing so, also recorded a song titled "Funkytown."

5. Gerald Jensen, "Bittersweet," *Waxpoetics* (March/April 2010): 95.

6. James Brown, *The Godfather of Soul: The Autobiography* (New York: Macmillan, 1986), 6.

7. Maceo Parker, *98% Funky Stuff* (Chicago: Chicago Review Press, 2013), 75.

8. Jensen, "Bittersweet," 121.

9. Albert Murray, *Stomping the Blues* (New York: Da Capo Press, 1987), 181.

10. Murray, *Stomping the Blues*, 17.

11. Ralph Ellison, "Little Man at Chehaw Station," in *The Collected Essays of Ralph Ellison*, ed. John F. Callahan (1995; rpt., New York: Modern Library, 2003), 516.

12. Charles Johnson, "A Phenomenology of the Black Body," *Michigan Quarterly Review* 32.4 (Fall 1993): 606.

13. Johnson, "Phenomenology," 606, my italics.

14. Frantz Fanon, *The Wretched of the Earth*, trans. Constance Farrington (1961; New York: Grove Press, 1963), 41.

15. Johnson, "Phenomenology," 607.

16. Johnson, "Phenomenology," 601.

17. Johnson, "Phenomenology," 601.

18. Johnson, "Phenomenology," 601.

19. Fredrika Bremer, *Homes of the New World: Impressions of America* (New York: Harper and Brothers, 1853), 316. See also Teresa Reed, *The Holy Profane: Religion in Black Popular Music* (Lexington: University of Kentucky Press, 2003), 17.

20. See Charles Keil, *Urban Blues* (1966; rpt., Chicago: University of Chicago Press, 1991), 106.

21. Thomas Dixon, *The Clansman* (1905).

22. See Alyn Shipton, *A New History of Jazz* (New York: Continuum, 2001), 671.

23. Johnson, "Phenomenology," 606.

24. Johnson, "Phenomenology," 603.

25. See John Ballon, liner notes, *Nasty Gal* (1975; reissue, Light in the Attic Records, 2009). See also Cheryl L. Keyes, "She Was Too Black for Rock and Too Hard for Soul," in "The Funk Issue," ed. Tony Bolden, special issue, *American Studies* 52.4 (2013): 42.

26. Michael Haralambos, *Soul Music: The Birth of a Sound in Black America* (1974; rpt., New York: Da Capo Press, 1985), 65.

27. Charles Richardson, *A New Dictionary of the English Language, Vol. 1—A to K.* (Philadelphia: E.H. Butler & Co., 1846), 866.

28. See Ned Sublette, *The World That Made New Orleans: From Spanish Silver to Congo Square* (Chicago: Lawrence Hill Books, 2008), 66–67.

29. Robert Farris Thompson, *Flash of the Spirit: African and Afro-American Art and Philosophy* (New York: Vintage Books, 1983), 104.

30. Ned Sublette, *The World That Made New Orleans: From Spanish Silver to Congo Square* (Chicago: Lawrence Hill Books, 2008), 67.

31. Tony Bolden, *Afro-Blue: Improvisations in African American Poetry and Culture* (Urbana: University of Illinois Press, 2004), 39.

32. Dictionary.com, http://www.dictionary.com/browse/funk. Accessed June 16, 2018. Bold print and italics are original.

33. Horace Silver, *Let's Get to the Nitty Gritty: The Autobiography of Horace Silver* (Berkeley: University of California Press, 2006), 102.

34. Larry Neal, "The Ethos of the Blues," in *Visions of a Liberated Future: Black Arts Movement Writings*, ed. Michael Schwartz (New York: Thunder's Mouth Press, 1989), 110.

35. B.B. King with David Ritz, *Blues All Around Me: The Autobiography of B.B. King* (New York: Avon Books, 1996), 83.

36. See "Blues Story: A Documentary," YouTube video posted by Mark Fredell, June 12, 2014. https://www.YouTube.com/watch?v=5qq_qnLHf74. Retrieved June 13, 2018.

37. E. Belfield Spriggins, "Excavating Local Jazz," *Louisiana Weekly*, April 22, 1933: 5. See also Danny Barker, *Buddy Bolden and the Last Days of Storyville*, ed. Alyn Shipton (London: Cassell, 1998), 26; Donald Marquis, *In Search of Buddy Bolden* (1978; rev. ed., Baton Rouge: Louisiana State University Press, 2005), 109.

38. Marquis, *In Search of Buddy Bolden*, 111.

39. Barker, *Buddy Bolden and the Last Days of Storyville*, 26.

40. Marshall and Jean Stearns, *Jazz Dance: The Story of American Vernacular Dance* (1964; rpt., New York: Da Capo Press, 1994), 24.

41. Stearns, *Jazz Dance*, 24.

42. Alan Lomax, *The Land Where the Blues Began* (1993; rpt., New York: New Press, 2002), 321.

43. Lomax, *The Land Where the Blues Began*, 325.

44. Portia K. Maultsby, "Funk," in Mellonee V. Burnim and Portia K. Maultsby, *African American Music: An Introduction*, 2nd ed. (New York: Routledge, 2015), 301.

45. Michel Martin, "Bootsy Collins Brings Back the Funk," "NPR Music," May 19, 2011. http://www.npr.org/2011/05/19/136462443/-bootsy-collins-brings-back-the-funk.

46. I'm indebted to funk scholar Scot Brown for his insight on Bootsy Collins in a recent telephone conversation. A bass player in his own right, Brown has appeared on several panels with Collins and interviewed him several times. I thank him for his contribution.

47. Richard Iton, *In Search of the Black Fantastic: Politics and Popular Culture in the Post-Civil Rights Era* (New York: Oxford University Press, 2008), 14.

48. Iton, *In Search of the Black Fantastic*, 14.

49. Iton, *In Search of the Black Fantastic*, 14.

50. Allison Davis, Burleigh B. Gardner, and Mary R. Gardner, *Deep South* (1941; rpt., Chicago: University of Chicago Press, 1965). See also Haralambos, *Soul Music*, 35.

51. Haralambos, *Soul Music*, 33.

52. Barbara Babcock, *The Reversible World: Symbolic Inversion in Art and Society* (Ithaca, NY: Cornell University, Press, 1978), 14.

53. Amiri Baraka, *Blues People: Negro Music in White America* (New York: Morrow, 1963).

54. Baraka, *Blues People*, 219–20.

55. Nat Hentoff, "Garvin Bushell and New York Jazz in the 1920s," *Jazz Review* (January 1959): 12.

56. Zora Neale Hurston, "Characteristic of Negro Expression" (1934), *The Sanctified Church* (1981; rpt., Berkeley: Turtle Island, 1983), 62–63.

57. Tanya Ballard Brown, "The Origin (And Hot Stank) of the 'Chitlin' Circuit,'" NPR, February 16, 2014. http://www.gpb.org/news/2014/02/16/the-origin-and-hot-stank-of-the-chitlin-circuit.

58. It should be noted that "jazz" was also taboo in many quarters of American society. There was even a movement to abolish the word in 1924. See Gerhard Kubik, *Jazz Transatlantic, Volume 1: African Undercurrents in Jazz Culture* (Oxford: University Press of Mississippi, 2017), 4.

59. Willie King, "Willie's Testament," *I Am the Blues*, (CD, no label, 2000).

60. David Evans, *Big Road Blues*, 18.

61. FunkyKev1, "P-Funk Interview (Part 1 of 2)," includes George Clinton, Bootsy Collins, and Bernie Worrell, early 1990s, YouTube video clip, November 25, 2011. https://www.YouTube.com/watch?v=AspK_BSUor8. Retrieved July 16, 2018.

62. David Evans, *Big Road Blues: Tradition and Creativity in the Folk Blues* (1982; rpt., New York: Da Capo Press, 1987), 31.

63. Amiri Baraka, "The 'Blues Aesthetic' and the 'Black Aesthetic': Aesthetics as the Continuing Political History of a Culture," in *Digging: The Afro-American Sound of American Classical Music* (Berkeley: University of California Press, 2009), 25.

64. Tony Bolden, *Afro-Blue: Improvisations on African American Poetry and Culture* (Urbana: University of Illinois Press, 2004), 39.

65. Jon Michael Spencer, *Blues and Evil* (Knoxville: University of Tennessee Press, 1993), 70.

66. Reed, *The Holy Profane*, 34. The black writer Arna Bontemps's recollection of a blues guitarist who attempted to play on church grounds is also notable. According to Bontemps, "Just as sure as God had his heaven, the devil had his hell. And the box (guitar), as all the older folk know, has always been a special device of the devil's. I can remember what happened to one of these careless minstrels who made the mistake of wandering onto the church grounds . . . back in my childhood. The sisters of the church lit into him like a flock of mother hens attacking a garter snake." See Spencer, *Blues and Evil*, 27.

67. Angela Davis, *Blues Legacies and Black Feminism: Gertrude "Ma" Rainey, Bessie Smith, and Billie Holiday* (New York: Random House, 1998), 123.

68. Davis, *Blues Legacies*, 4.

69. Adam Gussow notes that black preachers had economic motives for castigating blues singers as devil worshippers. According to Gussow, preachers in the Mississippi Delta between 1920 and 1940 "were radically destabilized by the Great Migration and the disastrous diminishment it was wreaking on their membership rolls and collection plates. . . . they were relentlessly focused, in a distinctly this-worldly way, on their repeated failure to deliver the bottom-line numbers they'd been assigned." See Adam Gussow, *Beyond the Crossroads: The Devil and the Blues Tradition* (Chapel Hill: University of North Carolina Press, 2017), 51.

70. Gussow makes a similar argument when he states that preachers' "condemnation[s], in a social environment dominated by the heavy hand of the black church, inevitably helped shape the aesthetic contours of [blues] music as well as the life journeys of those who chose to play it." See Gussow, *Beyond the Crossroads*, 50.

71. Keil, *Urban Blues*, 33.

72. I'm borrowing Olly Wilson's term. See Olly Wilson, "'It Don't Mean a Thing If It Ain't Got That Swing': The Relationship Between African and African American Music," in *African Roots/African Cultures: Africa in the Creation of the Americas*, ed. Sheila S. Walker (Lanham, MD: Rowman & Littlefield, 2001), 159.

73. Keil, *Urban Blues*, 52, my italics.

74. Brenda Dixon Gottschild, *Digging the Africanist Presence in American Performance: Dance and Other Contexts* (Westport, CT: Greenwood Press, 1996), xiv.

75. Gottschild, *Digging the Africanist Presence*, 13–14, my italics.

76. I should acknowledge that some scholars find the word "Africanist" objectionable, and they consider it a misnomer—a noun, not an adjective. Others believe that it minimizes or obscures the diversity of ethnic and cultural traditions throughout the African diaspora. However, the larger point here is that Gottschild's insight into the principles of black dance movements can be informative in a critical discussion about a virtually identical principle in blues musicianship. For her part, Gottschild addresses the issue in her introduction, stating, "In sum, the term denotes concepts and practices that exist in Africa and the African diaspora and have their sources in concepts or practices from Africa." See Gottschild, *Digging the Africanist Presence*, xiv.

77. Gottschild, *Digging the Africanist Presence*, xiv.

78. Gottschild, *Digging the Africanist Presence*, xiv. Evans makes a similar point about contrast in African American music in a nuanced discussion of black musicians' engagement with Western principles: "Dualism also characterizes African-American musical aesthetic terminology. Musical performances can be described alternately as hot and cool, hot and

sweet, clean and dirty (funky), hard and mellow, smooth and rough, low down and high class, up-to-date and old-time. In western thought, however, one of these paired elements is generally viewed as good and its opposite bad or unacceptable." David Evans, "Patterns of Reinterpretation in African-American Music in the United States," in *African Perspectives: Pre-Colonial History, Anthropology, and Ethnomusicology*, eds., Regine Allgayer-Kaufman and Michael Weber (Frankfurt: Peter Lang, 2008), 213.

79. Zora Neale Hurston, "The Sanctified Church," in *The Sanctified Church: The Folklore Writings of Zora Neale Hurston* (Berkeley: Turtle Island, 1981), 91.

80. Michael W. Harris, *The Rise of Gospel Blues: The Music of Thomas Andrew Dorsey in the Urban Church* (New York: Oxford University Press, 1992), 89.

81. Gayle Wald, *Shout, Sister, Shout!: The Untold Story of Rock-and-Roll Trailblazer Sister Rosetta Tharpe* (Boston: Beacon Press, 2007), 22–23.

82. Craig Werner, *Playing the Changes: From Afro-Modernism to the Jazz Impulse* (Urbana: University of Illinois Press, 1994), 297–98.

83. Murray, *Stomping the Blues*, 27.

84. Murray, *Stomping the Blues*, 27.

85. Lindsay Patterson, *The Negro in Music and Art* (New York: Publishers Co., 1967), 56. See also Larry Neal, "The Blues Ethos," *Visions of a Liberated Future: Black Arts Movement Writings* (New York: Thunder's Mouth Press, 1989), 107.

86. Greg Kot, *I'll Take You There: Mavis Staples, the Staples Singers, and the March up Freedom's Highway* (New York: Simon and Schuster, 2014), 42.

87. Nat Hentoff, liner notes to Milt Jackson, *Plenty, Plenty Soul*, recorded January 1957 (LP, Atlantic 1269, 1957). See also Gerri Hirshey, *Nowhere to Run: The Story of Soul Music* (New York: Da Capo Press, 1984), 77.

88. I'm borrowing Teresa Reed's term here.

89. William Russell and Ralph Collins, interview with Bill Matthews, March 10, 1959, in Hogan Jazz Archive, Tulane University. See also Marquis, *In Search of Buddy Bolden*, 100.

90. Jon Michael Spencer, "Towards an Autobiography of a Blues Concept," in *Fertile Ground: Memories & Visions*, eds. Kalamu ya Salaam and Kysha N. Brown (New Orleans: Runagate Press, 1996): 211.

91. Alan Lomax, *Mister Jelly Roll: The Fortunes of Jelly Roll Morton, New Orleans Creole and Inventor of Jazz* (1950; rpt., Berkeley: University of California Press, 1973), 60.

92. Lomax, *Mister Jelly Roll*, 60.

93. Samuel A. Floyd Jr., *The Power of Black Music: Interpreting Its History from Africa to the United States* (New York: Oxford University Press, 1995), 85.

94. Marquis, *In Search of Buddy Bolden*, 32.

95. Marquis, *In Search of Buddy Bolden*, 31.

96. Wilson, "'It Don't Mean a Thing If It Ain't Got That Swing,'" 156.

97. Olly Wilson, "The Association of Movement and Music as a Manifestation of a Black Conceptual Approach to Music-Making," in *More Than Dancing: Essays on Afro-American Music and Musicians*, ed. Irene V. Jackson (Westport, CT: Greenwood Press, 1985), 9.

98. I might note here that all music reflects basic cultural values, regardless of the society or social group. There have also been numerous discussions of how black writers or painters interface with specific stylistic features of blues or jazz. But Wilson is suggesting that un-

derlying principles or philosophical aspects of music are evident in other media. Moreover, in marginalized cultures analyses that elucidate such values take on added significance. An important linchpin of slavery and Jim Crow was that African American culture was itself a mythic notion, and concepts and black music were oxymoronic at best. Music tended to be viewed as entertainment only, and/or musical innovation was seldom examined in relation to philosophical principles that can be observed in other areas of African American culture such as literature and visual art—hence the importance of Wilson's statement.

99. Olly Wilson, "The Heterogeneous Sound Ideal in African-American Music," in *New Perspectives on Music: Essays in Honor of Eileen Southern*, eds. Josephine Wright and Samuel Floyd (Warren, MI: Harmonie Park Press, 1992), 327–38.

100. Spencer, *Blues and Evil*, xxvi.

101. Yusef Komunyakaa, "It's Always Night," in *Blue Notes: Essays, Interviews, and Commentaries* (Ann Arbor: University of Michigan Press, 2000), 22.

102. Douglas Gorney, "The Secret Life of Thelonious Monk," *The Atlantic*, March 29, 2010. https://www.theatlantic.com/entertainment/archive/2010/03/the-secret-life-of-thelonious-monk/38128/. Retrieved May 28, 2018.

103. Frederick Douglass, *Narrative of the Life of Frederick Douglass* (1845; rpt., Mineola, NY: Dover Publications, 1995), 8.

104. Wald, *Shout, Sister, Shout!*, 25.

105. Wald, *Shout, Sister, Shout!*, 24.

106. Wald, *Shout, Sister, Shout!*, 24.

107. Wald, *Shout, Sister, Shout!*, 24.

108. Lenore Kitts, "Toni Morrison and 'Sis Joe': The Musical Heritage of Paul D," *Modern Fiction Studies* 52.2 (Summer 2006): 497.

109. Gottschild, *Digging the Africanist Presence*, 19.

110. Gottschild, *Digging the Africanist Presence*, 14.

111. Ellison, *Invisible Man* (New York: Random House, 1952), 176, my italics.

112. Ellison, *Collected Essays*, 697.

113. Wynton Marsalis, qtd. in *The Art of Romare Bearden*, dir. Carroll Moore (DVD, National Gallery of Art, 2004).

114. Langston Hughes, "The Negro Artist and the Racial Mountain" (1926), in *The Norton Anthology of African American Literature*, 2nd ed., eds. Henry Louis Gates, Jr. and Nellie Y. McKay (New York: W.W. Norton, 2004), 1314.

115. Murray, *Stomping the Blues*, 51.

116. Murray, *Stomping the Blues*, 45.

117. Hurston, "Characteristics of Negro Expression."

118. Malone, *Steppin' on the Blues*, 15–16, my italics.

119. Gottschild, *Digging the Africanist Presence*, 14. Again I acknowledge here that some scholars find the word "Africanist" somewhat questionable. Gottschild addresses this issue in her book. See introduction to *Digging the Africanist Presence*, xiii–xv.

120. Stearns and Stearns, *Jazz Dance*, 13.

121. Kalamu ya Salaam, "the blues aesthetic," in *What Is Life?: Reclaiming the Black Blues Self* (Chicago: Third World Press, 1994), 13–14.

122. Bruce Tantum, "Q&A: Dâm-Funk," *XLR8R*. September 14, 2015. https://www.xlr8r .com/features/qa-dam-funk. Retrieved May 28, 2018.

123. Judith Wilson, "Creating a Necessary Space: The Art of Houston Conwill, 1975–1983," *International Review of African American Art* 6, no. 1 (1984): 50.

124. Wilson, "Creating a Necessary Space," 58.

125. Ellison, *Invisible Man*, 157.

126. Ellison, *Invisible Man*, 581.

127. Stearns and Stearns, *Jazz Dance*, 215.

128. Stearns and Stearns, *Jazz Dance*, 197.

129. Lightnin' Hopkins, qtd. in Marshall and Jean Stearns, *Jazz Dance*, 23.

130. I'm borrowing the subtitle of Jacqui Malone's book *Steppin' on the Blues*.

131. It is also worth noting that even in avant-garde jazz, which relatively few listeners associate with dancing, motion has been vitally important. Ekkehard Jost writes: "One of the important distinguishing features [of AACM] lies in the rhythm, or—more precisely—in those verbally elusive qualities that result from motion and are psycho-physically felt as motion, which form one of the decisive criteria of every kind of jazz, be it swing, bebop or free jazz." See Ekkehard Jost, *Free Jazz (The Roots of Jazz)* (1974; rpt., New York: Da Capo Press, 1994), 173.

132. Murray, *Stomping the Blues*, 189.

133. Black Arts writer Kalamu ya Salaam echoes Murray's point in his essay "the blues aesthetic." What's interesting is that, in many ways, their perspectives on politics and culture are nearly diametrically opposed. Yet Salaam's statement on the centrality of dance in blues aesthetics essentially echoes Murray. Salaam writes, "check out how african american soldiers turn close-order drill into dance, listen to how they call cadence, follow their syncopated shuffle-step variations on the basic martial march. This synchronization . . . is the single most identifiable characteristic of the blues culture." See Kalamu ya Salaam, "the blues aesthetic," in *What Is Life?: Reclaiming the Black Blues Self* (Chicago: Third World Press, 1994), 14–15.

134. Debra DeSalvo, *The Language of the Blues: From Alcorub to Zuzu* (New York: Billboard Books, 2006), 16–17.

135. See Richard Powell, *The Blues Aesthetic: Black Culture and Modernism* (Washington, DC: Washington Project for the Arts, 1989), 16.

136. When I was an English professor at the University of Alabama, I wrote this poem as a tribute to Willie King and his band the Liberators whom I observed regularly at a juke joint called Bettie's Place in Prairie Point, Mississippi, in the late 1990s and early 2000s. King was given a ceremonial key to the city of Tuscaloosa, Alabama, and I was asked to write a commemorative poem.

137. Mack McCormick, "Tradition Rediscovered," *Rhythm and Blues Magazine* 4 (1964): 14–15. See also, Keil, *Urban Blues*, 58.

138. There's been much discussion among scholars about the meaning of "toodle-oo." Several factors, including a chance occurrence, determined the spelling in the title. Ellington pronounced the word "todalo," but Vocalion's printer misspelled it when the company recorded the song in 1926. To compound matters, there seem to be multiple etymologies and meanings related to "toodle-oo." According to Chadwick Hansen, one etymology might be derived from the KiKongo term *to* which refers to someone's buttocks, haunch, or hips. In the

United States, Chadwick observes, the term was sometimes reduplicated as *toto*, probably for added emphasis. The Pinkster festivals in eighteenth-century New York, for instance, featured African Americans performing "toto dances." Likewise, in his 1947 recording of the Creole song "Salée Dame," singer and clarinetist Albert Nicholas, accompanied by guitarist Danny Barker, bassist Pops Foster, and pianist James Johnson, sang the following Afro-French lines: "Salée dame laissez mo' voir / Ton grand noir toto," which loosely translates as "Dirty lady, let me see / Your big black butt." Thus Chadwick suggests that blues singers' use of todalo and toodle-oo may also have been black vernacular reformulations of *toto*. The eroticism in Bessie Smith's 1929 recording "It Makes My Love Come Down" is unmistakable when she sings, "When I get my toodle-oo / It makes my love come down."

At times, "todalo" connoted sexuality and signified dancing low down on the ground, so to speak, like a boogie dance. In the song "I'm Satisfied," for instance, Mississippi John Hurt sings, "First in the country, then in town / I'm a todalo shaker from my navel on down." And Ma Rainey sings the line "I got the toad low blues" on her recording "Toad Frog Blues" (1925). However, the British-based website Phrase Finder posits an Anglophone etymology. Of course, the most familiar definition of "toodle-oo" is the antiquated term for goodbye. But its older meaning is quite similar to Miley's usage of the term: "The British term 'toodle-oo' is a fellow-traveller of various terms associated with walking or departing in a carefree manner—*toddle, tootle* and their extended forms *toddle-off* and *tootle-pip*. . . . *Tootle* is a variant of *toddle*, both meaning 'walk in a leisurely manner.'" The latter etymology seems closest to Ellington's meaning. My understanding of the etymology of "toodle-oo," which appears in the title of Duke Ellington's composition "East St. Louis Toodle-oo," has been enriched by the scholarship of Chadwick Hansen and Mark Tucker. I'm particularly indebted to their etymological analyses and discussions of the KiKongo word *to* and the black vernacular word "todalo" in blues and jazz lyrics. Hansen offers convincing evidence that African Americans used variations of the KiKongo term *to* in different parts of the country, and that "todalo" is a vernacular derivation of *to*. See Chadwick Hansen, "Jenny's Toe Revisited: White Responses to Afro-American Shake Dances," *American Music* 5.1 (Spring 1987): 1–19. For a slightly alternative, and somewhat corrective, response to Hansen, see also Mark Tucker's article "On Toodle-oo, Todalo, and Jenny's Toe," *American Music* 6.1 (Spring 1988): 88–91.

139. Ellington, *Music Is My Mistress*, 106.

140. Kevin Young, *The Grey Album: On the Blackness of Blackness* (Minneapolis: Graywolf Press, 266). Ellington's tribute to Bubber Miley and references to storytelling among blues instrumentalists exemplify Young's brilliant concept of storying, which informs his entire discussion.

141. Jack Cullen interview with Duke Ellington. Station CKNW, Vancouver, Canada, October 30, 1962. Issued on Varèse International recordings (VS 81007). See also Mark Tucker, *The Duke Ellington Reader* (New York: Oxford University Press, 1993), 338–39.

142. Robert Gordon, *Can't Be Satisfied: The Life and Times of Muddy Waters* (New York: Little, Brown, 2002), 109, my italics.

143. See "Blues Story: A Documentary," https://www.YouTube.com/watch?v=5qq_qnLHf74.

144. Alyn Shipton, *A New History of Jazz* (New York: Continuum, 2001), 671. See also Tony Bolden, "Theorizing the Funk: An Introduction," in *The Funk Era and Beyond: New Perspectives on Black Popular Culture* (New York: Palgrave Macmillan, 2008), 15.

145. Dizzy Gillespie with Al Fraser, *To Be or Not to Bop: Memoirs* (New York: Doubleday, 1979), 42, my italics.

146. Ed Vulliamy, "BB King at 87: The Last of the Great Bluesmen," *The Guardian*, October 6, 2012. http://www.theguardian.com/music/2012/oct/06/bb-king-music-blues-guitar.

147. John Cephas, qtd. in Powell, *The Blues Aesthetic*, 16–17.

148. Haralambos, *Soul Music*, 54.

149. Murray, *Stomping the Blues*, 75.

150. Johnson, "Phenomenology," 603.

151. Powell, *The Blues Aesthetic*, 83.

152. Ramsey, *Race Music*, 73–74.

153. See Bolden, *Afro-Blue*, 44.

154. Murray, *Stomping the Blues*, 138.

155. Sherley Anne Williams, "Bessie on my wall," in *Some One Sweet Angel Chile* (William Morrow, 1982), 39.

156. In the Preface of *God's Trombones* (1927), James Weldon Johnson made a similar point in his famous statement that "a trombone . . . possess[es] above all others the power to express the wide and varied range of emotions encompassed by the human voice . . ." (7).

157. Davis, *Blues Legacies and Black Feminism*, 127.

158. Duke Ellington, qtd. in Nat Shapiro and Nat Hentoff, *Hear Me Talkin' to Ya: The Story of Jazz as Told by the Men Who Made It* (New York: Dover Publications, 1966), 224–25.

159. Jeff Todd Titon, "Thematic Pattern in Downhome Blues Lyrics: The Evidence on Commercial Phonograph Records since World War II," *Journal of American Folklore* 87 (1974): 318. See also Bolden, *Afro-Blue*, 45.

160. Leonard "Baby Doo" Caston, *From Blues to Pop: The Autobiography of Leonard "Baby Doo" Caston*, ed. Jeff Titon, JEMF Special Series (Los Angeles: John Edwards Memorial Foundation, 1974), 23. See also Titon, "Thematic Pattern in Downhome Blues Lyrics," 318; Bolden, *Afro-Blue*, 45.

161. Greg Tate, *Midnight Lightning: Jimi Hendrix and the Black Experience* (Chicago: Chicago Review Press, 2003), 39.

162. See Tate, *Midnight Lightning*, 54.

163. BeyeZee, "Roger Troutman on the Talk Box," 1987, Video Soul clip, YouTube, Troutman interviewed by Donny Simpson. March 11, 2011. https://www.YouTube.com/watch?v=L_CBZkd2tGE&list=RDL_CBZkd2tGE&t=15. Retrieved July 9, 2018.

164. AylerGhosts, "Roger Troutman Interview in Tokyo," early 1990s, YouTube, July 11, 2008. https://www.YouTube.com/watch?v=bJhni9kXA5U&list=RDDy7ksl-xUiQ. Retrieved July 9, 2018.

165. Charley Gerard, *Music from Cuba: Mongo Santamaria, Chocolate Armenteros, and Cuban Musicians in the United States* (Westport, CT: Greenwood Press, 2001), 54. Herbie Hancock tells a slightly different version of this story in his autobiography. See Herbie Hancock with Lisa Dickey, *Possibilities* (New York: Viking, 2014), 49.

166. Hancock, *Possibilities*, 205, my italics.

167. Ellison, "The Little Man at the Chehaw Station," 496.

168. Jimi Hendrix, *Starting from Zero: His Own Story* (New York: Bloomsbury, 2013), 21.

CHAPTER 3: SLY STONE AND THE GOSPEL OF FUNK

1. Jeff Kaliss, *I Want to Take You Higher: The Life and Times of Sly and the Family Stone* (Milwaukee: Backbeat Books, 2008), 4. See also Chris Williams, "Freddie Stone discusses Sly and the Family Stone's Stand! on its 45th anniversary," *Wax Poetics*, November 14, 2014. http://www.waxpoetics.com/blog/features/articles/sly-family-stones-freddy-stone-discusses -stand-on-45th-anniversary/. Retrieved September 25, 2018.

2. Robin D. G. Kelley, *Thelonious Monk: The Life and Times of an American Original* (New York: Free Press, 2009), 42.

3. Kaliss, *I Want to Take You Higher*, 46.

4. Kaliss, *I Want to Take You Higher*, 4.

5. Kaliss, *I Want to Take You Higher*, 5.

6. David Henderson, "Sly and the Family Stone," *Crawdaddy!*, September 1, 1967; Rpt., *Paste*, June 9, 2015. Retrieved May 24, 2016.

7. Patryce "Choc'Let" Banks, *Deja View: Memoirs of a Funk Diva* (Los Angeles: Reigno Publications, 2009), 18.

8. Patryce Banks, *A "Choc'Let" State of Mind: Poetry and Short Stories* (Elk Grove, CA: A Motion Publication, 2005), 71.

9. Joel Selvin, *Sly and the Family Stone: An Oral History* (New York: Avon Books, 1998), 64.

10. Reed, *The Holy Profane*, 22.

11. Neal, "Sly Stone and the Sanctified Church," 7.

12. Dalton Anthony, "A.K.A. Sly Stone: The Rise and Fall of Sylvester Stewart," in *Rip It Up: The Black Experience in Rock 'n' Roll*, ed. Kandia Crazy Horse (New York: Palgrave Macmillan, 2004), 42.

13. Olly Wilson, "The Association of Movement and Music as a Manifestation of a Black Conceptual Approach to Music-Making," in *More Than Dancing: Essays on Afro-American Music and Musicians*, ed. Irene V. Jackson (Westport, CT: Greenwood Press, 1985), 20.

14. Wilson, "The Association of Movement and Music as a Manifestation of a Black Conceptual Approach to Music-Making," 20.

15. Johan Nilsson, *Sly Stone: Portrait of a Legend*, YouTube, April 11, 2010, https://www .YouTube.com/watch?v=9cPuiiKt8rs. Retrieved February 9, 2017. Italics added.

16. Vincent, *Funk: The Music, the People, and the Rhythm of the One*, 94.

17. Nikki Giovanni, *Black Feeling, Black Talk/Black Judgement* (1970; rpt., New York: Morrow Quill Paperbacks, 1979), 75. See also Vincent, *Funk: The Music, the People, and the Rhythm of the One*, 124.

18. Wilson, "The Association of Movement and Music," 10.

19. Wilson, "The Association of Movement and Music," 11.

20. Nelson George, *The Death of Rhythm and Blues* (New York: Pantheon Books, 1988), 108.

21. Here I'm borrowing Jimi Hendrix's concept of sky church music. Hendrix, like Stone, Sun Ra, George Clinton, and others, conceptualized music in spiritual terms that, in its full fruition, could stimulate an experience that was akin to a sort of interplanetary communication. But where Hendrix seemed to refer primarily to his music, I use the term here in a broader sense of euphoric collectivity espoused by Stone and the rockers who loved his music.

22. Davis, *Blues Legacies and Black Feminism*, 7.

23. Anthony, "A.K.A. Sly Stone," 49.

24. Matt Rogers, "Hit Man: The Funk Mob's Garry Shider and His Mighty Bop Gun," *Wax Poetics* (August/September 2006): 117.

25. See "George Clinton," *Unsung*, TV One, October 11, 2010.

26. George Clinton, "Preface," in Jeff Kaliss, *I Want to Take You Higher*, xi.

27. Banks, *Deja View*, 18.

28. Sly Stone, liner notes, *Dance to the Music*. Epic Records, 1968.

29. Ricky Vincent, qtd. in "Sly & the Family Stone," *Unsung*, TV One, June 25, 2012.

30. Vincent, *Funk*, 168.

31. Barney Hoskyns, "Looking at the Devil," *The Guardian*, March 19, 2006. https://www.theguardian.com/music/2006/mar/19/urban.popandrock. Retrieved February 12, 2017.

32. Paul Shaffer, qtd. in *Small Talk about SLY: Sly and the Family Stone Documentary*. https://mail.google.com/mail/?shva=1#search/sly+stone/159c9785aed30f12. Retrieved February 9, 2017.

33. Rickey Vincent, *Party Music: The Inside Story of the Black Panthers' Band and How Black Power Transformed Soul Music* (Chicago: Lawrence Hill Books, 2013), 59.

34. "Charlie Wilson Talks Sly and the Family Stone: On the Record (Interview)," Rhapsody TV, YouTube, February 12, 2013. https://www.YouTube.com/watch?v=_ecWamGRr2Q. Retrieved May 25, 2016.

35. RockShorts, "Sly Stone 1976 TV Profile," YouTube, March 3, 2012, https://www.YouTube.com/watch?v=oMiUC9X3UQU. Retrieved February 11, 2017.

36. Cornel West, qtd. in *Small Talk about Sly (Part 31)*. https://www.YouTube.com/watch?v=Rx1mQNALjS8&list=PLE-9fJHthijPoKEk4XnLNmovq9YTBvfk-&index=31. February 9, 2017.

37. Chris Williams, "Freddie Stone discusses Sly and the Family Stone's Stand!," *Wax Poetics*, November 14, 2014.

38. Neal, "Sly Stone and the Sanctified Church," 5.

39. Selvin, *Sly and the Family Stone: An Oral History*, 54.

40. David Henderson, "Sly and the Family Stone," *Paste*, June 9, 2015. Reprint from *Crawdaddy!*, September 1, 1968. https://www.pastemagazine.com/articles/2015/06/crawdaddy-classics-sly-and-the-family-stone.html. Retrieved February 12, 2017.

41. John Hardy, "A whole new thing—Good gracious alive!—It sure is!," liner notes to *A Whole New Thing*, Epic Records, 1967.

42. Selvin, *Sly and the Family Stone: An Oral History*, 40.

43. "Sly & the Family Stone," *Unsung*, TV One, June 25, 2012.

44. Selvin, *Sly and the Family Stone*, 60.

45. Selvin, *Sly and the Family Stone*, 60.

46. Anthony, "A.K.A. Sly Stone," 48.

47. Thefivecount, "Sly and the Family Stone—Larry Graham Interview," YouTube, March 12, 2013. https://www.YouTube.com/watch?v=2D6GlPtaV_o. Retrieved May 25, 2016.

48. Eric Sandler, "Greg Errico: The Backbone to Sly and the Family Stone. Pt 1." revive-music.com. May 9, 2013. http://revive-music.com/2013/05/09/greg-errico/#.WJ8e2vIYHnF. Retrieved February 11, 2017.

49. Vincent, *Funk*, 16.

50. Clinton, Preface, in Kaliss, *I Want to Take You Higher*, xi.

51. Larry Graham, "Sly and the Family Stone—Larry Graham Interview," 2013. https://www.YouTube.com/watch?v=2D6GlPtaV_0. Retrieved May 25, 2016.

52. Selvin, *Sly and the Family Stone*, 28.

53. Tammy Kernodle, "Diggin' You Like Those Ol' Soul Records: Meshell Ndegeocello and the Expanding Definition of Funk in Postsoul America," in "The Funk Issue," ed. Tony Bolden, special issue, *American Studies* 52, no. 4 (2013): 191.

54. *Make It Funky*, dir. and written by Yvonne Smith. PBS, 1995.

55. "Sly and the Family Stone—Larry Graham Interview."

56. "Sly and the Family Stone—Larry Graham Interview."

57. Selvin, *Sly and the Family Stone*, 29.

58. Zycopolis TV, "Marcus—Teaser 2: Marcus Miller & Larry Graham," YouTube, January 15, 2015. https://www.YouTube.com/watch?v=X5gtGgbJKMU. Retrieved February 13, 2017.

59. Selvin, *Sly and the Family Stone*, 41.

60. Miles Marshall Lewis, *There's a Riot Goin' On* (New York: Continuum, 2006), 44–45.

61. Vincent, *Party Music*, 49–50.

62. Joel Selvin, *Sly and the Family Stone*, 22.

63. Henderson, "Sly and the Family Stone."

64. Henderson, "Sly and the Family Stone," my italics.

65. Michael A. Gonzales, "Sly & the Family Stone: Still All the Way Live [interview]," *Ebony*, July 29, 2015. http://www.ebony.com/entertainment-culture/sly-the-family-stone-still-all-the-way-live-111#axzz3hI3mhUiS. Retrieved May 25, 2016.

66. Audre Lorde, qtd. in *Wisdom for the Soul of Black Folk*, ed. Larry Chang (Washington, DC: Gnosophia Publishers, 2007), 114.

67. Baraka, *Blues People*, 30–31.

68. Regarding the laughter, Jerry Martini has commented that members of the band were standing behind Greg Errico while he was laying down the final tracks for "Sex Machine." I don't question Martini's statement; however, the fact that Stone decided to keep this portion of the song suggests that he approved of not only its effect but its implications as well.

69. Neal, "Sly Stone and the Sanctified Church," 5.

70. Professor Groove, "Interview with Marva Whitney." *We Funk Radio*. October 31, 2006. https://www.wefunkradio.com/extra/marva. Retrieved February 13, 2017. My italics.

71. Wilson, "Movement and Music," 10.

72. Clinton, Preface, in Kaliss, *I Want to Take You Higher*, x.

73. Samuel 16:16. The Bible, King James Version.

74. Neal, "Sly Stone," 8.

75. Neal, "Sly Stone," 8.

76. Dalton Anthony argues that "Thank You (Falettinme Be Mice Elf Agin)" reflects the effects of a freebase cocaine high, and that the critique in the song concerns Stone's battle with freebase cocaine. However, although Anthony's argument that the song is a self-referential narrative is certainly credible, it is doubtful that Stone was specifically alluding to freebase cocaine because that form of the drug did not become popular until a few years later. See Anthony, "A.K.A. Sly Stone," 51. Similarly, songfacts.com states: "The lyrics are scathing and mostly directed at Sly himself . . ." http://www.songfacts.com/detail.php?id=4426. Retrieved February 13, 2017.

77. Herbie Hancock, "B notes." Herbie Hancock, *Headhunters*. Columbia Records, 1973. Reissue, 1996.

78. Bolden, *Afro Blue*, 73.

79. Bolden, *Afro Blue*, 72.

80. Selvin, *Sly and the Family Stone*, 70.

81. Selvin, *Sly and the Family Stone*, 70.

82. Selvin, *Sly and the Family Stone*, 78–79.

83. Selvin, *Sly and the Family Stone*, 79.

84. Kaliss, *I Want to Take You Higher*, 73.

85. Neal, "Sly Stone," 7

86. See Michael Wadleigh, *Woodstock: 3 Days of Peace and Music: The Director's Cut*. Warner Bros., 1994. My italics.

87. Stallings, *Funk the Erotic*, 8.

88. It should be noted here that the word "frenzy" is one of the earliest known synonyms for the funk/spirit. Both W. E. B. Du Bois and James Weldon Johnson used it to refer to the psychosomatic phenomenon that is the funk/spirit.

89. Dennis Chambers, qtd. in Dave Marsh, ed., *George Clinton and P-Funk: An Oral History* (New York: Avon Books, 1998), 134.

90. Miles Davis with Quincy Troupe, *Miles: The Autobiography* (New York: Simon and Schuster, 1989), 321.

91. James Mtume, panelist, "'Who Stole the Soul?': Black Music and the Struggle for Empowerment in the Twentieth Century," Association for the Study of African American Life and History Centennial Convention. September 25, 2015. Mtume cited Miles Davis as another "genius," but did not mentioned the third person he knew.

92. Maurice White, *My Life with Earth, Wind & Fire* (New York: HarperCollins, 2016), 77–76. It's important to note that White's statement reprised Joel Selvin's comment: "There was black music before Sly Stone, and there was black music after Sly Stone. Simple as that." See Selvin, *Sly and Family Stone*, xi. Rickey Vincent quotes a similar passage from a newspaper article that Selvin wrote. See Vincent, *Party Music*, 52.

93. Stone's concept of "flashing" also prefigures art historian Robert Farris Thompson's groundbreaking study on spirituality in African diasporic cultures. See Thompson, *Flash of the Spirit*.

94. Rickey Vincent, qtd. in "George Clinton," *Unsung*, TV One, October 11, 2010.

95. Eric Sandler, "Greg Errico: The Backbone of Sly and the Family Stone Pt. 1." revive-music.com. May 9, 2013. http://revive-music.com/2013/05/09/greg-errico/#.WKRtqvIYHnF. February 15, 2017.

CHAPTER 4: SONGBIRD: CHAKA KHAN AS FUNK QUEEN

1. Vincent, *Funk*, 191.

2. Iton, *In Search of the Black Fantastic*, 17.

3. Royster, *Sounding Like a No-No*, 8.

4. Chaka Khan with Tonya Bolden, *Chaka!: Through the Fire* (New York: St. Martin's Press, 2003).

5. Khan with Bolden, *Chaka!*, 50.

6. Royster, *Sounding Like a No-No*, 102.

7. *Tear the Roof Off: The Untold Story of Parliament-Funkadelic*, directed by Bobby J. Brown. DVD, Vision Films, 2016.

8. Amy Nathan Wright, "Exploring the Funkadelic Aesthetic: Intertextuality and Cosmic Philosophizing in Funkadelic's Album Covers and Liner Notes," in "The Funk Issue," ed. Tony Bolden, special issue, American Studies, 52.4 (2013): 147.

9. David Nathan, "Rufus' Chaka Khan: Golden Lady," *Blues and Soul*, December 1975.

10. Vernon Gibbs, "Rufus Featuring Chaka Khan: *Rufusized* (ABCD-837)," *Crawdaddy!*, June 1975.

11. Khan with Bolden, *Chaka!*, 24.

12. Chaka Khan, "Rare Interview '86 Pt 1," https://www.YouTube.com/watch?v=Q1yXLU 1C18A. Retrieved February 18, 2017.

13. Louisa "Blu Lu" Barker. *Wild Women Don't Have the Blues*, directed by Christine Dall. DVD, San Francisco: California Newsreel, 1989.

14. Ramsey, *Race Music*, 4.

15. Khan with Bolden, *Chaka!*, 24.

16. Khan with Bolden, *Chaka!*, 25.

17. Khan with Bolden, *Chaka!*, 25.

18. Khan with Bolden, *Chaka!*, 17.

19. Khan with Bolden, *Chaka!*, 17.

20. Khan with Bolden, *Chaka!*, 17.

21. Khan with Bolden, *Chaka!*, 16.

22. Khan with Bolden, *Chaka!*, 24.

23. Khan's musical background is similar to Jimi Hendrix's. Like Khan, Hendrix grew up listening to his parents' blues records, and began responding to the music as a preadolescent by imitating guitarists such as Robert Johnson and Muddy Waters. Once, when he was supposed to be cleaning up, he strummed a broom so vigorously that its strands were strewn over the floor, prompting his father to purchase his first guitar.

24. Khan with Bolden, *Chaka!*, 39.

25. Khan with Bolden, *Chaka!*, 41.

26. Khan with Bolden, *Chaka!*, 39.

27. Khan with Bolden, *Chaka!*, 66.

28. Khan with Bolden, *Chaka!*, 39.

29. Khan with Bolden, *Chaka!*, 40.

30. Khan with Bolden, *Chaka!*, 42.

31. Khan with Bolden, *Chaka!*, 38.

32. Khan with Bolden, *Chaka!*, 50.

33. Khan with Bolden, *Chaka!*, 37.

34. Khan with Bolden, *Chaka!*, 44.

35. Khan with Bolden, *Chaka!*, 57.

36. Khan with Bolden, *Chaka!*, 57.

37. Khan with Bolden, *Chaka!*, 58.

38. Khan with Bolden, *Chaka!*, 59.

39. John Abbey, "Rufus: Today and Tomorrow," *Blues and Soul*, July 1975.

40. Keil, *Urban Blues*, 31.

41. John Szwed, "Musical Adaption among Afro-Americans," *Journal of American Folklore* 83.324 (1969): 119.

42. Abbey, "Rufus: Today and Tomorrow."

43. Khan with Bolden, *Chaka!*, 125.

44. Iton, *In Search of the Black Fantastic*, 17.

45. Chaka Khan, "Chaka Khan," in *I Got Thunder: Black Women Songwriters on Their Craft*, ed. LaShonda Katrice Barnett (New York: Thunder's Mouth Press, 2007), 64.

46. Billy Holiday, qtd. in *Hear Me Talkin' to Ya: The Story of Jazz by the Men Who Made It*, ed. Nat Shapiro and Nat Hentoff (1955; rpt., New York: Dover Publications, 1966), 201.

47. Khan with Bolden, *Chaka!*, 127.

48. Khan with Bolden, *Chaka!*, 127.

49. Kathy Dobie, "Midnight Train: A Teenage Story," in *Trouble Girls: The Rolling Stone Book of Women in Rock*, ed. Barbara O'Dair (New York: Random House, 1997), 227.

50. Dobie, "Midnight Train: A Teenage Story," 227.

51. Khan with Bolden, *Chaka!*, 59.

52. Chaka Khan, "Chaka Khan: Rare Interview '86 Pt 1."

53. Khan, "Chaka Khan," 68.

54. Stallings, *Funk the Erotic*, 59.

55. Khan, "Chaka Khan," 67, my italics.

56. Ellington, *Music Is My Mistress*, 180.

57. Iton, *In Search of the Black Fantastic*, 8.

58. Khan with Bolden, *Chaka!*, 19.

59. Miss Myasia, "Chaka Khan Documentary 2006," YouTube, December 18, 2016, https://www.YouTube.com/watch?v=05A1s12vu7k. Retrieved March 24, 2017.

60. Khan with Bolden, *Chaka!*, 86.

61. Lydia Hutchinson, "Happy Birthday, Chaka Khan!," *Performing Songwriter*, March 23, 2014. http://performingsongwriter.com/chaka-khan/. Retrieved February 21, 2017.

62. Although "Tell Me Something Good" is credited to Stevie Wonder, Khan claims that the song was unfinished when Wonder introduced it to Rufus. In a 1996 interview, she presages the claim that she makes in her memoir. The details of her two accounts are remarkably similar. See Hutchinson, "Happy Birthday, Chaka Khan!" However, according to songfacts.com, "Stevie Wonder wrote this song and recorded it himself on December 13, 1973—he copyrighted it on January 3, 1974." http://www.songfacts.com/detail.php?id=2283. Retrieved January 6, 2017. However, this information does not necessarily contradict Khan's claim that she collaborated with Wonder on "Tell Me Something Good."

63. Khan, "Chaka Khan," 65.

64. Tony Maiden, qtd. in "Chaka Khan Documentary 2006."

65. Stallings, *Funk the Erotic*, 10.

66. Khan with Bolden, *Chaka!*, 72–73.

67. Scot Brown, "A Land of Funk: Dayton, Ohio," in Bolden, *The Funk Era and Beyond*, 76–77.

68. "Rufus & Chaka Khan—Once You Get Started," YouTube, https://www.YouTube.com/watch?v=7fgKhuqNtxw. Retrieved November 20, 2018.

69. Khan with Bolden, *Chaka!*, 83.

70. Lashonda Katrice Barnett, "Chaka Khan," *I Got Thunder: Black Women Songwriters*, 65.

71. Khan, "Chaka Khan," 68.

72. Tamara Winfrey Harris, "'Oh, girl, get up. You got this': Why the 'strong black woman' stereotype is an albatross," *Salon*, July 3, 2015. https://www.salon.com/2015/07/03/oh_girl_get _up_you_got_this_why_the_"strong_black_woman"_stereotype_is_an_albatross/. Retrieved November 23, 2018.

73. Khan with Bolden, *Chaka!*, 81–82.

74. "Chaka Khan: Intimate Portrait," Season 10, Episode 1. Lifetime. 2003. See also, khari06095, "Chaka Khan Biography (Part 2)," YouTube, January 27, 2009. Recollecting his first time watching Khan sing live with Rufus in 1970, Bob Monaco said, "The girl didn't do eight bars, and I had the goosebumps." https://www.YouTube.com/watch?v=vfNiMVtYZt8. Retrieved February 27, 2017.

75. Eric Gaer, qtd. in, "Chaka Khan," encyclopedia.com. 2004. Music: Popular and Jazz: Biographies. http://www.encyclopedia.com/people/literature-and-arts/music-popular-and -jazz-biographies/chaka-khan. Retrieved February 27, 2017.

76. J. R. Robinson, "Bobby Watson, Bassist with Rufus and Chaka Khan, Michael Jackson, Stevie Wonder," interview segment of "Vinyl Night," *PlayerFM*, December 7, 2016. https:// player.fm/series/vinyl-night/120716-bobby-watson-bassist-with-rufus-and-chaka-khan -michael-jackson-stevie-wonder. Retrieved June 8, 2019.

77. Khan with Bolden, *Chaka!*, 94.

78. Khan, "Chaka Khan," 66.

79. Khan, "Chaka Khan," 67.

80. Khan, "Chaka Khan," 66. It should be noted that Native American artists may well have a different interpretation from Khan's. On the other hand, the history of African American and Native American interactions is complicated. There is also the tradition of the black Mardi Gras Indians in New Orleans who traditionally perform in vernacular elaborations of Native people's costumes in black neighborhoods representing the downtrodden.

81. Matt Rodgers, "From Doo-Wop to Funkadelia: Calvin Simon, Grady Thomas, and Fuzzy Haskins of the Parliaments," *Waxpoetics* (August/September 2006): 55.

82. Young, *The Grey Album*, 56.

83. Young, *The Grey Album*, 56.

84. Nathan, *The Soulful Divas*, 194.

85. Nathan, *The Soulful Divas*, 200.

86. Khan with Bolden, *Chaka!*, 85.

87. Khan with Bolden, *Chaka!*, 84.

88. Khan with Bolden, *Chaka!*, 84–85.

89. Stephen Demorest, "The Truth about Rufus," *Circus*, September 13, 1976.

90. Khan with Bolden, *Chaka!*, 108.

91. Phoebe Neel, "Erykah Badu Picks the Songs That Made Her a 'Child of the Funk,'" *Vulture*, November 16, 2010. https://www.vulture.com/2010/11/erykah_badu_slideshow .html. Retrieved June 10, 2019.

92. Kevin C. Johnson, "Chaka Khan talks about 12 songs—some favorites, some not," *St. Louis Post-Dispatch*, June 15, 2014. http://www.stltoday.com/entertainment/music/chaka

-khan-talks-about-songs-some-favorites/article_c784587c-0400-5f8e-9239-b86da7fb522a.
html. February 23, 2017.

93. Tonya Pendleton, "Phillip Bailey Releases New Memoir about His Life With Earth, Wind
and Fire," blackamericaweb.com. April 14, 2014. https://blackamericaweb.com/2014/04/14/
phillip-bailey-releases-new-memoir-about-his-life-with-earth-wind-and-fire/. February
25, 2017.

94. "Chaka Khan: Intimate Portrait," Season 10, Episode 1.

95. Ntozake Shange, *Nappy Edges* (New York: Macmillan, 1991), 2

96. Curtis Bagley, "Chaka!" *Essence* (January 1986): 69.

97. Divinity Roxx, Twitter correspondence with the author, January 10, 2017.

CHAPTER 5: FUNKY BLUESOLOGY: GIL SCOTT-HERON AS BLACK ORGANIC INTELLECTUAL

1. Sofia M. Fernandez, "Bootsy Collins, Chuck D, Eminem React to Gil Scott-Heron's
Death," *Hollywood Reporter*, May 28, 2011. https://www.hollywoodreporter.com/news/bootsy
-collins-chuck-d-eminem-192895. Retrieved November 25, 2018.

2. Kalamu ya Salaam, "The Last Poets and Gil Scott-Heron," *Black Issues Book Review*,
1.2 (March/April 1999): 21.

3. Marcus Baram, *Gil Scott-Heron: Pieces of a Man* (New York: St. Martin's Press, 2014), 214.

4. Baram, *Gil Scott-Heron*, 147.

5. Baram, *Gil Scott-Heron*, 73.

6. Iton, *In Search of the Black Fantastic*, 16.

7. Langston Hughes, "Songs Called the Blues," *Phylon* 2, no. 2 (2nd Qtr. 1941): 143–44. See
also Young, *The Grey Album*, 152.

8. Robert Palmer, "Funk: Scott-Heron's Songs," *New York Times*, October 28, 1980, C8.

9. Iton, *In Search of the Black Fantastic*, 17.

10. Gil Scott-Heron, liner notes, *The Mind of Gil Scott-Heron: A Collection of Poetry and
Music*, Arista AL 8301, 1978.

11. Scott-Heron, liner notes, *The Mind of Gil Scott-Heron*, 1978.

12. Bolden, *Afro-Blue*, 43.

13. Vincent, *Funk*, 164.

14. Baram, *Gil Scott-Heron*, 78.

15. Don Snowden, "Gil Scott-Heron," *LA Vanguard*, May 21, 1976. https://www.rocksback
pages.com/Library/Article/gil-scott-heron. Retrieved May 6, 2017.

16. Gil Scott-Heron, *Last Holiday: A Memoir* (New York: Grove Press, 2012), 179.

17. Baram, *Gil Scott-Heron*, 47.

18. Vernon Gibbs, "Gil Scott-Heron: The Fire This Time," *Playboy*, July 1976. https://www
.rocksbackpages.com/Library/Article/gil-scott-heron-the-fire-this-time. Retrieved May 6,
2017.

19. Joyce Ann Joyce, "Afterword: Gil Scott-Heron: Larry Neal's Quintessential Artist," in
Gil Scott-Heron, *So Far, So Good* (Chicago: Third World Press, 1990), 79.

20. Baram, *Gil Scott-Heron*, 86.

21. Harmony Holiday, Twitter post, April 19, 2019. https://twitter.com/i/web/status /1112859438568767488. Holiday's tribute is an allusion. See Rahsaan Roland Kirk, *The Case of the 3 Sided Dream in Audio Color*, LP, Atlantic, 1975.

22. Roger St. Pierre, "Gil Scott-Heron: *Pieces of a Man* (Philips 6369 415)," *New Musical Express*, May 12, 1973. https://www.rocksbackpages.com/Library/Article/gil-scott-heron -ipieces-of-a-mani-philips-6369-415. Retrieved May 5, 2017.

23. Baram, *Gil Scott-Heron*, 166.

24. Baram, *Gil Scott-Heron*, 79.

25. John Abbey, "Sister Sledge: We Really Are Family," *Blues and Soul*, June 1979. https:// www.rocksbackpages.com/Library/Article/sister-sledge-we-really-are-family. Retrieved May 6, 2017.

26. Baram, *Gil Scott-Heron*, 75.

27. Baram, *Gil Scott-Heron*, 68.

28. Paul Oliver, *Conversations with the Blues* (London: Cassell & Company, 1966), 164–65.

29. Baram, *Gil Scott-Heron*, 247.

30. Joyce, "Gil Scott-Heron: Larry Neal's Quintessential Artist," 74.

31. See Joyce, "Gil Scott-Heron: Larry Neal's Quintessential Artist."

32. Barbara Christian, "The Race for Theory," *Cultural Critique* 6, The Nature and Context of Minority Discourse (Spring 1987): 52.

33. Gil Scott-Heron, "'The Revolution Will Not Be Televised'—Gil Scott-Heron," YouTube, MediaBurnArchive, April 21, 2010. https://www.YouTube.com/watch?v=kZvWt29oGos. Retrieved May 6, 2017.

34. Frantz Fanon, *Black Skins, White Masks*, trans. Charles Lam Markmann (1952; rpt., New York: Grove Press, 1967), 198.

35. Baram, *Gil Scott-Heron*, 147.

36. Baram, *Gil Scott-Heron*, 36.

37. Baram, *Gil Scott-Heron*, 36.

38. Charles Mills, *The Racial Contract* (Ithaca, NY: Cornell University Press, 1997), 1.

39. Mills, *The Racial Contract*, 11.

40. Mills, *The Racial Contract*, 11.

41. Mills, *The Racial Contract*, 16.

42. Mills, *The Racial Contract*, 81.

43. Mills, *The Racial Contract*, 127.

44. Mills, *The Racial Contract*, 126.

45. Mills, *The Racial Contract*, 129.

46. Mills, *The Racial Contract*, 127.

47. See also Fred Moten's cogent analysis of deviance and the racial contract in his essay "The Case of Blackness," *Criticism* 50.2 (Spring 2008): 177–218.

48. I'm borrowing Michelle Alexander's phrase here.

49. "Spiro T. Agnew, Ex-Vice President, Dies at 77," *New York Times*, September 18, 1996. http://www.nytimes.com/1996/09/18/us/spiro-t-agnew-ex-vice-president-dies-at-77.html. Retrieved May 11, 2017.

50. Michelle Alexander, *The New Jim Crow: Mass Incarceration in the Age of Colorblindness* (New York: New Press, 2010), 43–44.

51. Manning Marable, *Race, Reform, and Rebellion: The Second Reconstruction in Black America* (New York: Macmillan, 1984), 119.

52. Robin D. G. Kelley, "Slangin' Rocks. . . . Palestinian Style: Dispatches from the Occupied Zones of North America," in *Police Brutality: An Anthology*, ed. Jill Nelson (New York: W.W. Norton, 2001), 42.

53. Kelley, "Slangin' Rocks," 44.

54. Gil Scott-Heron, *So Far, So Good* (Chicago: Third World Press, 1990), 46.

55. Charles Mills, *The Racial Contract*, 18.

56. Karl Marx and Frederick Engels, *The German Ideology: Part One*. Third edition (1932; rpt. New York: International Publishers, 1995), 47.

57. Marcus Baram, *Gil Scott-Heron*, 87.

58. What is interesting here is that Scott-Heron's instructions to the audience are nearly identical to Horace Silver's preface to his live recording of "Filthy McNasty" in 1961. Though separated by time and genre, both artist foreground the funk principle, that is, kinesthesia in their remarks.

59. Scott-Heron, *So Far, So Good*, 41.

60. Perhaps a contemporary exemplification can be found in the recent controversy over Michigan's computerized unemployment system. According to a state review, the Michigan Integrated Data Automated System (MIDAS), implemented by Governor Rick Snyder, former President and interim CEO of Gateway Computers, "wrongly accused individuals in at least 20,000 cases of fraudulently seeking unemployment payments." The review found that 93 percent of those people were wrongly accused. Instead of using workers to file people's unemployment claims, Snyder implemented MIDAS. As a result of its malfunctions, some people have been ordered to pay hefty fines. Some people have been fined nearly a hundred thousand dollars. Others have filed for bankruptcy. Meanwhile, Michigan's unemployment contingency fund, which had approximately three million dollars in 2011, has grown to over one hundred fifty-five million dollars. See Ryan Felton, "Michigan Unemployment Agency Made 20,000 False Fraud Accusations—Report," *The Guardian*, December 18, 2016. https://www.theguardian.com/us-news/2016/dec/18/michigan-unemployment-agency-fraud-accusations. Retrieved December 21, 2016.

61. Scott-Heron, *Last Holiday*, 179.

62. Scott-Heron, *Last Holiday*, 179. See also Timo Schrader, "500 Shades of Blues: 'Bluesologist' Gil Scott-Heron's 'H2O Gate Blues' as Meta-Performance," *U.S. Studies Online*, December 14, 2014. http://www.baas.ac.uk/usso/gil-scott-herons-h2ogate-blues/. Retrieved May 8, 2017.

63. Davitt Sigerson, "Gil Scott-Heron: You Won't Be Able to Tune In, Turn On, and Cop Out . . . ," *Black Music*, April 1976. https://www.rocksbackpages.com/Library/Article/gil-scott-heron-you-wont-be-able-to-tune-in-turn-on-and-cop-out. Retrieved May 8, 2017.

64. Sheila Weller, "Gil Scott-Heron: Survival Kit on Wax," *Rolling Stone*, January 2, 1975. "https://www.rocksbackpages.com/Library/Article/gil-scott-heron-survival-kits-on-wax. Retrieved May 8, 2017. It should be acknowledged here that many people probably suspected that President Nixon was involved in the Watergate scandal from the very beginning. James W. McCord, coordinator the Committee for the Re-election of the President, was among the five burglars who were all connected to the CIA. But neither beltway journalists nor self-described radicals made any such claims about Nixon publicly.

65. Scott-Heron, *So Far, So Good*, 49.

66. Sigerson, "Gil Scott-Heron."

67. Mills, *The Racial Contract*, 76.

68. Scott-Heron, *So Far, So Good*, 50.

69. Scott-Heron, *So Far, So Good*, 49.

70. Scott-Heron, *So Far, So Good*, 50.

71. Scott-Heron, *So Far, So Good*, 50.

72. Marable, *Race, Reform, and Rebellion*, 119.

73. Scott-Heron, *So Far, So Good*, 51–52.

74. Baram, *Gil Scott-Heron*, 109.

75. Bienlejos, "Gil Scott-Heron 2/3," YouTube, January 17, 2010. https://www.YouTube
.com/watch?v=DuEpT3Go7rU. Retrieved May 11, 2017.

76. Bienlejos, "Gil Scott-Heron 2/3."

77. Scott-Heron, *Last Holiday*, 177. According to Baram, "[S]omeone had begged [the
doctor] to do the operation and then ratted him out." See Baram, *Gil Scott-Heron*, 112.

78. Scott-Heron, *Last Holiday*, 177.

79. Gerald Davis, qtd. in Tony Bolden, *Afro-Blue*, 72.

80. Joyce, Afterword, Gil Scott-Heron, *So Far, Good*, 73.

81. Iton, *In Search of the Black Fantastic*, 16.

82. Scott-Heron, *So Far, So Good*, 34.

83. Baram, *Gil Scott-Heron*, 124.

84. Gil Scott-Heron, liner notes, *The First Minute of a New Day*, Arista, 1975.

85. Baram, *Gil Scott-Heron*, 110.

86. Scott-Heron, *So Far, So Good*, 33.

87. Iris Berger, "Sources of Class Consciousness: South African Women in Recent Labor
Struggles," *International Journal of African Historical Studies* 16.1 (1983): 54.

88. Gil Scott-Heron, liner notes, Gil Scott-Heron and Brian Jackson, *Bridges, Arista* 4147,
1977.

89. Baram, *Gil Scott-Heron*, 135.

90. Scott-Heron, liner notes, *Bridges*.

91. Marcus Baram, *Gil Scott-Heron*, 164.

92. Gil Scott-Heron, liner notes, *Bridges*.

93. Cliff White, "Gil Scott-Heron: And now, for a fascinating and demanding dialogue
...," *New Musical Express*, March 6, 1976. https://www.rocksbackpages.com/Library/Article/
gil-scott-heron-and-now-for-a-fascinating-and-demanding-dialogue. Retrieved June 21, 2017.

94. White, "Gil Scott-Heron."

95. Howard Kohn, "Karen Silkwood: The Case of the Activist's Death." *Rolling Stone*, January
13, 1977. http://www.rollingstone.com/culture/features/the-case-of-karen-silkwood-19770113.
Retrieved December 19, 2016.

96. Scott-Heron reiterates his premise regarding the incongruence between capitalism and public safety in "Tuskegee," the succeeding track on the album. Here, however, he
situates public safety in relation to the racial contract. The thirty-four-second song calls
attention to the Tuskegee experiment conducted by the U.S. Public Health Service in which

black male subjects were denied treatment for syphilis for forty years. "About the USPHS Syphilis Study." http://www.tuskegee.edu/about_us/centers_of_excellence/bioethics_center/about_the_usphs_syphilis_study.aspx. Retrieved December 19, 2016. It is worth noting that the nuclear meltdown was not the only ecological disaster that "We Almost Lost Detroit" augured. For many residents in Flint, Michigan, located a stone's throw away from Detroit, Scott-Heron's song might bring to mind their horrific experiences with the ongoing water crisis in Flint. A result of what CNN News describes as "cost-cutting measures" implemented by Governor Rick Snyder, residents of the city, which is predominantly poor and African American, were deprived of their clean supply of water, and forced to use water from Flint River, which is contaminated with lead. By contrast, Flint-based General Motors Corporation has access to clean water from nearby Lake Huron. Needless to say, the contradiction is glaring. Michigan Attorney General Bill Schuette has stated, "Very evident during the course of this investigation, there's been a fixation on finances and balance sheets. This fixation has cost lives. This fixation came at the expense of protecting the health and safety of Flint. It's all about numbers over people, money over health."

97. Baram, *Gil Scott-Heron*, 166.

98. Baram, *Gil Scott-Heron*, 168.

99. "Scott-Heron's Message on 'Angel Dust' Awarded," *Variety* (November, 14 1979): 73.

100. Baram, *Gil Scott-Heron*, 169.

101. Charles Mills, *The Racial Contract*, 41.

102. Scott-Heron, *So Far, So Good*, 59.

103. Scott-Heron, *So Far, So Good*, 60.

104. Scott-Heron, *So Far, So Good*, 60.

105. Readers familiar with hip-hop will recognize that Scott-Heron's linguistic practice of inserting the sound of "is" into words prefigured the ways that Snoop and other rappers used this approach to create stock phrases in their songs.

106. Gil Scott-Heron, *So Far, So Good*, 59.

107. Ibid.

108. Gil Scott-Heron, *So Far, So Good*, 10.

109. Davitt Sigerson, "Gil Scott-Heron: You Won't Be Able to Tune, Turn On, And Cop Out . . . ," *Black Music*, April 1976. https://www.rocksbackpages.com/Library/Article/gil-scott-heron-you-wont-be-able-to-tune-in-turn-on-and-cop-out/. Retrieved June 21, 2017.

110. Robin D. G. Kelley, "After Trump," *Boston Review: A Political and Literary Forum*, November 15, 2016. http://bostonreview.net/forum/after-trump/robin-d-g-kelley-trump-says-go-back-we-say-fight-back. Retrieved June 21, 2017.

111. Scott-Heron's language here prefigures George Bush's twenty-four-hour ultimatum to Saddam Hussein on the eve of the invasion of Iraq.

112. Scott-Heron, *So Far, So Good*, 9.

113. Scott-Heron, *So Far, So Good*, 10.

114. James Baldwin, *No Name in the Street* (New York: Dial Press, 1972), 149.

115. Baram, *Gil Scott-Heron*, 242.

116. Baram, *Gil Scott-Heron*, 243.

CHAPTER 6: THE KINKINESS OF TURQUOISE: BETTY DAVIS'S LIBERATED FUNK-ROCK

1. John Ballon, "Liberated Sister," *Wax Poetics* 22 (April/May 2007): 122.

2. Ballon, "Liberated Sister," 122.

3. Cheryl L. Keyes, "'She Was Too Black for Rock and Too Hard for Soul': (Re)discovering the Musical Career of Betty Mabry Davis," in "The Funk Issue," ed. Tony Bolden, special issue, *American Studies* 52.4 (2013): 42.

4. Betty Davis, qtd. in Robin Katz, "Betty Davis: Game Is Her Middle Name," *Sounds* 27 (September 1975).

5. jessica Care moore has played an instrumental role in revitalizing interest in Davis. In 2004 she founded an annual tribute to Davis titled Black Women Rock. In addition to Moore's electrifying performances (she won the talent competition at Harlem's Apollo Theater five weeks in a row as a young poet), the event showcases live performances by black women rock artists. Standout performers have included bass player Kat Dyson, who has played with Prince, George Clinton, and Cyndi Lauper, and Divinity Roxx, who is Beyoncé's bass player in her all-female band.

6. jessica Care moore, "They Say She's Different," in "Poet jessica Care moore Pays Tribute to Funk Pioneer Betty Davis and Her Poem Is a Must-Read!" *Ebony*, March 3, 2016. http://www.essence.com/2016/03/03/poet-jessica-care-moore-pays-tribute-funk-pioneer-betty-davis. Retrieved March 22, 2017.

7. Amiri Baraka, "The Changing Same (R&B and New Black Music)," in *Black Music* (1968; rpt., New York: Da Capo Press, 1998), 180.

8. See Vincent, *Funk*, 103.

9. Keyes, "'She Was Too Black for Rock and Too Hard for Soul,'" 42–43.

10. Maureen Mahon, "They Say She's Different: Gender, Genre, and the Liberated Black Femininity of Betty Davis," *Journal of Popular Music Studies* 23, no. 2 (June 15, 2011): 147.

11. Stallings, *Funk the Erotic*, 33.

12. Vincent, *Funk*, 192.

13. Les Lebeiter, "Mood Isn't Candlelight in Betty Davis's Songs," *New York Times*, June 21, 1974, 28. See also Ballon, "Liberated Sister," 124.

14. Keyes, "'She Was Too Black for Rock and Too Hard for Soul,'" 45.

15. I'm borrowing cultural critic Mark Anthony Neal's concept here. For an intriguing analysis of illegibility in black masculinity, see Mark Anthony Neal, *Looking for Leroy: Illegible Black Masculinities* (New York: New York University Press, 2013).

16. Ballon, "Liberated Sister," 122.

17. Ruth Pointer and Marshall Terrill, *Still So Excited: My Life as a Pointer Sister* (Chicago: Triumph Books, 2016), 66.

18. Tina Turner and Kurt Loder, *I, Tina: My Life Story* (New York: Avon Books, 1986), 154.

19. Maultsby, "Funk," 303.

20. Dave Thompson, *Funk: Third Ear—The Listening Companion* (New York: Backbeat Books, 2001), 87.

21. Keyes, "'She Was Too Black for Rock and Too Hard for Soul,'" 44.

22. Keyes, "'She Was Too Black for Rock and Too Hard for Soul,'" 43. See also John Abbey, "Betty Davis: Filthy But Funky," *Blues & Soul* (August 1975).

23. Vernon Gibb, "Betty Davis: The Bottom Line, New York, NY," *Soul & Jazz Record* (August 1974). https://www.rocksbackpages.com/Library/Article/betty-davis-the-bottom -line-new-york-ny. Retrieved April 24, 2017.

24. Lori Burns and Melisse Lafrance, *Disruptive Divas: Feminism, Identity, and Popular Music* (New York: Routledge, 2002), 3. For an intriguing discussion of literary divas in African American culture, see Aisha Damali Lockridge, *Tipping on a Tightrope: Divas in African American Literature* (New York: Peter Lang, 2012). See also Deborah R. Vargas, *Dissonant Divas in Chicana Music: The Limits of La Onda* (Minneapolis: University of Minnesota Press, 2012).

25. Stallings, *Funk the Erotic*, 10–11.

26. Stallings, *Funk the Erotic*, 10–11.

27. Stallings, *Funk the Erotic*, 10.

28. Stallings, *Funk the Erotic*, 10.

29. Stallings, *Funk the Erotic*, 19.

30. Ballon, "Liberated Sister," 117.

31. Ballon, "Liberated Sister," 118.

32. Ballon, "Liberated Sister," 118.

33. See John Ballon, liner notes, *Betty Davis: The Columbia Years: 1968–1969*, CD, Light in the Attic Records, 2016.

34. Ballon, liner notes, *Betty Davis: The Columbia Years*.

35. Charles Rowell, "'Words Don't Go There': An Interview with Fred Moten," *Callaloo* 27.4 (Fall 2004): 965.

36. June Jordan, "A New Politics of Sexuality," in *Some of Us Did Not Die: New and Selected Essays* (New York: Basic/Civitas Books, 2002), 133.

37. Maultsby, "Funk," 304.

38. Maultsby, "Funk," 304–5.

39. In a recent documentary film, several key members of Parliament-Funkadelic discuss the backstory of the collective. Several women accuse George Clinton of sexual exploitation and manipulating artists with drugs. See *Tear the Roof Off: The Untold Story of Parliament-Funkadelic*, directed by Bobby J. Brown, DVD, Vision Films, 2016.

40. Gibb, "Betty Davis: The Bottom Line."

41. James Baldwin, "The Creative Process," in *The Price of the Ticket: Collected Nonfiction, 1948–1985* (New York: St. Martin's Press, 1985), 316

42. Bolden, *Afro-Blue*, 58.

43. Maultsby, "Funk," 304.

44. James Maycock, "Betty Davis: She's Gotta Have It," *Mojo* (February 2005). https://www .rocksbackpages.com/Library/Article/betty-davis-shes-gotta-have-it. Retrieved April 24, 2018.

45. Merriam-Webster Dictionary, "vamp," retrieved May 3, 2019. https://www.merriam -webster.com/dictionary/vamp.

46. Online Etymology Dictionary, "vamp (n.2)," retrieved May 3, 2019. https://www .etymonline.com/word/vamp.

47. Janelle Monáe, qtd. in Mark Anthony Green, "Janelle Monae Takes a Giant Step," *GQ*, January 13, 2017. http://www.gq.com/story/janelle-monae-takes-one-giant-leap. Retrieved March 9, 2017.

48. Stallings, *Funk the Erotic*, 194.

49. Sue Richards and Bob Weinstein, "Betty Davis: Bawdy Bombshell." *High Society* (October 1976): 93. See also Keyes, "'She Was Too Black for Rock and Too Hard for Soul,'" 44.

50. Ntozake Shange, *For Colored Girls Who Have Considered Suicide/When the Rainbow is Enuf* (1975; rpt., New York: Simon and Schuster, 2010), 11.

51. Alice Walker, "Porn," in *You Can't Keep a Good Woman Down* (New York: Harcourt Brace Jovanovich, 1971), 83. See also Ariane Cruz, *The Color of Kink: Black Women, BDSM, and Pornography* (New York: New York University Press, 2016), 18.

52. Audre Lorde and Susan Leigh Star, "Interview with Audre Lorde," in *Against Sadomasochism: A Radical Feminist Analysis*, eds. Robin Ruth Linden, Darlene R. Pagano, Diana E. Russell, and Susan Leigh Star (East Palo Alto, CA: Frog in the Well, 1982), 68, italics original. See also Cruz, *The Color of Kink*, 35.

53. Cruz, *The Color of Kink*, 45.

54. Cruz, *The Color of Kink*, 57.

55. Maultsby, "Funk," 303.

56. It is well known that marginalized intellectuals sometimes succumb to the temptation of responding to their exploitation by counterattacking on the basis of phenotype. In racial politics, this is sometimes referred to as Manichean aesthetics in which racial groups ascribe intrinsic characteristics to the opposing group, so that they are either good or evil. Davis's songwriting avoids this theoretical pitfall. The fact that she does so can only be appreciated by situating her storytelling in relation to feminist writings, which were almost exclusively devoid of this logic. However, one of Alice Walker's early black male characters arguably reproduces tropes of racial ideology in her phenotypical description: "For John had all the physical characteristics that in the Western world are scorned. John looked like his father. An honest black. His forehead sloped backward from the bridge of his eyes. His nose was flat. His mouth too wide." Undoubtedly, Walker is criticizing racialized self-loathing, but the terms in which she registers her critique are a bit troublesome. Arguably, Walker's parody of racial caricature reiterates the narrative of white supremacy with minimum irony. Innumerable black writers have criticized the sort of interpellation that Walker engages here, but readers have to search long and wide to find similar images of black people in nineteenth- and twentieth-century African American literature. See Alice Walker, *In Love and Trouble: Stories of Black Women* (New York: Harcourt Brace Jovanovich, 1973), 108.

57. Robin Katz, "Betty Davis: Aisles of Miles," *Sounds*, August 2, 1975. https://www.rocks backpages.com/Library/Article/betty-davis-game-is-her-middle-name. March 30, 2017.

58. See also Keyes, "'She Was Too Black for Rock and Too Hard for Soul,'" 47.

59. Ariane Cruz, *The Color of Kink: Black Women, BDSM, and Pornography* (New York: New York University Press, 2016), 37.

60. Richard Iton, *In Search of the Black Fantastic: Politics and Popular Culture in the Post-Civil Rights Era* (New York: Oxford University Press, 2010), 16.

61. Stallings, *Funk the Erotic*, 34.

62. I'm borrowing Shana L. Redmond's critical metaphor here. For a full discussion of the concept and trope, see Shana L. Redmond, *Anthem: Social Movements and the Sound of Solidarity in the African Diaspora* (New York: New York University Press, 2014).

63. See Nikki A. Greene, "The Feminist Funk Power of Betty Davis and Renée Stout," in "The Funk Issue," ed. Tony Bolden, special issue, *American Studies* 52.4 (2013): 61.

64. See Keyes, "'She Was Too Black for Rock and Too Hard for Soul,'" 47.

65. See Toni Morrison, *The Bluest Eye* (New York: Holt, Rinehart and Winston, 1970).

66. For a more comprehensive discussion of this topic, see LaShawn Harris, *Sex Workers, Psychics, and Numbers Runners: Black Women in New York City's Underground Economy* (Urbana: University of Illinois Press, 2016).

67. Joan Morgan, *When Chickenheads Come Home to Roost* (New York: Simon & Schuster, 1999), 77.

68. *Betty: They Say I'm Different*, directed by Philip Cox. UK: Native Voice Films, 2018.

69. Henry Louis Gates Jr. and Evelyn Brooks Higginbotham, eds., *Harlem Renaissance Lives: From the African American National Biography* (New York: Oxford University Press, 2009), 96.

70. "Variety House Reviews: Loew's State Theatre in New York," *Variety* 121.5 (January 15, 1936): 21.

71. Richard G. Dudley, "Being Black and Lesbian, Gay, Bisexual, or Transgender," *Journal of Gay and Lesbian Mental Health* 17, no. 2 (2013): 186.

72. Stephen Roberson, "Harlem Undercover Vice Investigators, Race, and Prostitution, 1910–1930," *Journal of Urban History* 35.4 (2009): 494.

73. Roberson, "Harlem Undercover Vice Investigators," 496.

74. See Chris Albertson, *Bessie* (New York: Stein and Day, 1972), 123.

75. Albertson, *Bessie*, 123.

76. Albertson, *Bessie*, 123.

77. See Sharony Andrews Greene, *Grant Green: Rediscovering the Forgotten Genius of Jazz Guitar* (San Francisco: Backbeat Books, 1999), 121.

78. *Standing in the Shadows of Motown*, directed by Paul Justman (2002; DVD, Santa Monica, CA: Artisan Home Entertainment, 2003).

79. Lottie "The Body" Graves's eroticism was hardly anomalous in blues culture. Shortly after I moved to New Orleans in the 1980s, I was accepted into an independent collective of black writers known as the Congo Square Writers Union. After our workshop sessions, we often went out to a local blues club called Dorothy's Medallion Lounge, which was located on Orleans Avenue and where blues singer-guitarist Walter Washington played regularly. But one of my favorite attractions, regardless of the musician who played, was a nude dancer who performed in the background of the stage. She was well over three hundred pounds, and moved her body effortlessly in sync with the music, undulating slowly and sensuously to the rhythms and melodies behind a thin veneer afforded by a lavender see-through curtain. It was difficult to tell if she was completely naked or wore some sort of transparent body suit; but for all intents and purposes, there wasn't much distinction. Years later, while living in Alabama, I befriended the blues singer-guitarist Willie King and watched him perform countless times in Mississippi at a blue jook joint called Bettie's Place, where women from their mid-twenties up to their seventies danced to King's music. And when the music got good and the funk started rising, many women performed dance moves that were uncommon or nonexistent in nightclubs and dives in such urban areas as New Orleans, Atlanta, or the San Francisco/Oakland Bay Area where people danced to R&B hit singles.

80. Ballon, "Liberated Sister," 119. See also Keyes, "'She Was Too Black for Rock and Too Hard for Soul,'" 45.

81. Jessica Hundley, "Interview with Funk Goddess Betty Davis," Interviews with Icons. February 9, 2011. https://interviewswithicons.wordpress.com/2011/02/09/interview-with-funk-goddess-betty-davis/. Retrieved March 27, 2017.

82. *Betty: They Say I'm Different*. Philip Cox.

83. Ballon, "Liberated Sister," 119.

84. Jesse Thorn, "Betty Davis Interview on the Sound of Young America Podcast," Bullseye with Jesse Thorn. February 22, 2009. http://www.maximumfun.org/blog/2007/06/podcast-tsoya-betty-davis.html. Retrieved March 27, 2017.

85. Abbey, "Betty Davis: Filthy But Funky."

86. Stallings, *Funk the Erotic*, 190.

87. As with the image of Betty Davis performing the high kick, this photo is readily available online. However, it was not included in John Ballon's article on Davis, nor is it posted on Light in the Attic Records' website.

88. Davis's band included three background singers, not two. But the other singer is not shown in the photo. I have not been able to ascertain their names.

89. Maycock, "She's Gotta Have It."

90. See Oliver Wang, liner notes, *They Say I'm Different*, reissue, Light in the Attic Records, 2007.

91. Maycock, "She's Gotta Have It."

92. Stallings, *Funk the Erotic*, 192.

93. Stallings, *Funk the Erotic*, 190.

94. Keyes, "'She Was Too Black for Rock and Too Hard for Soul,'" 45.

95. Keyes, "'She Was Too Black for Rock and Too Hard for Soul,'" Keyes is borrowing Cornel West's term "kinetic orality."

96. Keyes, "'She Was Too Black for Rock and Too Hard for Soul,'" 42. See also John Ballon, liner notes, *Nasty Gal*, reissue, Light in the Attic Records, 2009.

97. Mahon, "They Say She's Different," 152.

98. Charles Shaar Murray, "Betty Davis: Nasty Gal," *New Musical Express*, November 8, 1975. https://www.rocksbackpages.com/Library/Article/betty-davis-nasty-gal. Retrieved March 31, 2017.

99. Banks, *Deja View*, 117.

100. Keyes, "'She Was Too Black for Rock and Too Hard for Soul,'" 44.

101. Geoff Brown, "Betty, First Lady of Funk," *Melody Maker*, September 27, 1975, 47. See also Mahon, "They Say I'm Different," 152.

102. Richard Bauman, *Verbal Art as Performance* (1977; rpt., Prospect Heights, IL: Waveland Press, 1984), 19. See also Bolden *Afro-Blue*, 66.

103. Amiri Baraka, "Dope," in *Selected Poetry of Amiri Baraka/Leroi Jones* (New York: William Morrow, 1979), 329.

104. Amiri Baraka, "Dope," on *Poets Read Their Contemporary Poetry: Before Columbus Foundation*, CD, Folkways Records, 1980.

105. Tracie Morris, "Poetics Statement: Sound Making Notes," in *American Poets in the 21st Century: The New Poetics*, eds. Claudia Rankin and Lisa Sewell (Middletown, CT: Wesleyan University Press, 2007), 210.

106. Geneva Smitherman, *Talkin and Testifyin: The Language of Black America* (Detroit: Wayne State University Press, 1977), 66.

107. Keyes, "'She Was Too Black for Rock and Too Hard for Soul,'" 42.

108. Keyes, "'She Was Too Black for Rock and Too Hard for Soul,'" 48.

109. See Jeff Chang, "A Funk Queen Steps out of the Shadows," SFGate, May 18, 2007. http://www.sfgate.com/entertainment/article/A-FUNK-QUEEN-STEPS-OUT-OF-THE -SHADOWS-Betty-2593729.php. Retrieved March 29, 2017.

110. Keyes, "'She Was Too Black for Rock and Too Hard for Soul,'" 51.

111. Renée Stout, email message to the author, September 20, 2015.

112. Renée Stout, email message to the author, September 17, 2015.

113. See Charles Henry Rowell, "Words Don't Go There: An Interview with Fred Moten," *Callaloo* 27, no. 4 (Fall 2004): 960.

114. Keyes, "'She Was Too Black for Rock and Too Hard for Soul,'" 48.

115. Davis, *Blues Legacies and Black Feminism*, 127.

116. Writing in 1942, Lawrence Hostetler notes that Handy's song and blues music generally "had a pronounced influence on our slow fox-trot rhythms." See Lawrence Hostetler, *Walk Your Way to Better Dance* (1942; rpt., Worcestershire, UK: Read Books, 2013).

117. See Davis, *Blues Legacies and Black Feminism*.

118. Barbara Babcock, *The Reversible World: Symbolic Inversion in Art and Society* (Ithaca, NY: Cornell University Press, 1978), 14.

119. See Ballon, liner notes, *Betty Davis: The 1968–1969 Columbia Sessions*.

120. Miles Davis with Quincy Troupe, *Miles: The Autobiography* (New York: Simon and Schuster, 1989), 304.

OUTRO

1. Alex MacPherson, "'Prince is not a nice person. But I just have to accept that': The universe according to funk shapeshifter Meshell Ndegeocello," *Fact Magazine*, June 14, 2014. https://www.factmag.com/2014/06/14/meteor-shower-the-universe-according-to-funk -shapeshifter-meshell-ndegeocello/2/. Retrieved June 19, 2019.

2. Tammy Kernodle, "Diggin' You Like Those Ol' Soul Records: Meshell Ndegeocello and the Expanding Definition of Funk in Postsoul America," in "The Funk Issue," ed. Tony Bolden, special issue, *American Studies* 52.4 (2013): 186–87.

3. Many scholars have discussed the sexual politics related to Meshell Ndegeocello's prowess as a bass player. For a fascinating in-depth discussion of the history of the bass and the implications of gender and sexual politics related to Ndegeocello's expertise as a bass player, see Tammy Kernodle, "Diggin' You Like Those Ol' Soul Records," 181–204.

4. Leviticus 19:18. The Bible, New King James Version.

5. Jewel Carter, telephone interview with the author. May 19, 2019.

Selected Bibliography

Albertson, Chris. *Bessie*. New York: Stein and Day, 1972.

Alexander, Michelle. *The New Jim Crow: Mass Incarceration in the Age of Colorblindness*. New York: New Press, 2010.

Babcock, Barbara. *The Reversible World: Symbolic Inversion in Art and Society*. Ithaca: Cornell University Press, 1978.

Banks, Patryce. *A "Choc'Let" State of Mind: Poetry and Short Stories*. Elk Grove, CA: A Motion Publication, 2005.

Banks, Patryce "Choc'Let." *Deja View: Memoirs of a Funk Diva*. Los Angeles: Reigno Publications, 2009.

Baraka, Amiri. *Blues People: Negro Music in White America*. New York: Morrow, 1963.

Baraka, Amiri. *Black Music*. 1968; reprint, New York: Da Capo Press, 1998.

Baraka, Amiri. *Digging: The Afro-American Soul of American Classical Music*. Berkeley: University of California Press, 2009.

Baram, Marcus. *Gil Scott-Heron: Pieces of a Man*. New York: St. Martin's Press, 2014.

Barnett, Lashonda Katrice. *I Got Thunder: Black Women Songwriters on Their Craft*. New York: Thunder's Mouth Press, 2007.

Bolden, Tony. *Afro-Blue: Improvisations in African American Poetry and Culture*. Champaign: University of Illinois Press, 2004.

Bolden, Tony. *The Funk Era and Beyond: New Perspectives on Black Popular Culture*. New York: Palgrave Macmillan, 2008.

Bolden, Tony, ed. "The Funk Issue." Special issue, *American Studies* 52, no. 4 (2013).

Brown, James, and Bruce Tucker. *The Godfather of Soul: The Autobiography*. New York: Macmillan, 1986.

Brown, James. *I Feel Good: A Memoir of a Life of Soul*. New York: New American Library, 2005.

Burnim, Mellonee V., and Portia K. Maultsby. *African American Music: An Introduction*. 2nd ed. New York: Routledge, 2015.

Cruz, Ariane. *The Color of Kink: Black Women, BDSM, and Pornography*. New York: New York University, 2016.

Davis, Angela Y. *Blues Legacies and Black Feminism: Gertrude "Ma" Rainey, Bessie Smith, and Billie Holiday*. New York: Vintage Books, 1998.

Davis, Miles, with Quincy Troupe. *Miles: The Autobiography.* New York: Simon and Schuster, 1990.

DeSalvo, Debra. *The Language of the Blues: From Alcorub to Zuzu.* New York: Billboard Books, 2006.

Ellington, Duke. *Music Is My Mistress.* 1973; reprint, New York: Da Capo Press, 1976.

Ellison, Ralph. *Invisible Man.* New York: Random House, 1952.

Evans, David. *Big Road Blues: Tradition and Creativity in the Folk Blues.* 1982; reprint, New York: Da Capo Press, 1987.

Fanon, Frantz. *The Wretched of the Earth.* Translated by Constance Farrington. New York: Grove Press, 1963.

Fellez, Kevin. *Birds of Fire: Jazz, Rock, Funk, and the Creation of Fusion.* Durham: Duke University Press, 2011.

Gaunt, Kyra D. *Games Black Girls Play: Learning the Ropes from Double-Dutch to Hip-Hop.* New York: New York University Press, 2006.

Gillespie, Dizzy, with Al Fraser. *To Be or Not to Bop: Memoirs.* New York: Doubleday, 1979.

Giovanni, Nikki. *Black Feeling, Black Talk/Black Judgement.* 1970; reprint, New York: Morrow Quill Paperbacks, 1979.

Gottschild, Brenda Dixon. *Digging the Africanist Presence in American Performance: Dance and Other Contexts.* Westport, CT: Greenwood Press, 1996.

Greene, Sharony Andrews. *Grant Green: Rediscovering the Forgotten Genius of Jazz Guitar.* San Francisco: Backbeat Books, 1999.

Gussow, Adam. *Beyond the Crossroads: The Devil and the Blues Tradition.* Chapel Hill: University of North Carolina Press, 2017.

Guy, Buddy, with David Ritz. *When I Left Home: My Story.* New York: DaCapo, 2012.

Hancock, Herbie, with Lisa Dickey. *Possibilities.* New York: Viking, 2014.

Haralambos, Michael. *Soul Music: The Birth of a Sound in Black America.* 1974; reprint, New York: Da Capo Press, 1985.

Hendrix, Jimi. *Starting at Zero: His Own Story.* New York: Bloomsbury, 2013.

Natalie Hopkinson. *Go-Go Live: The Musical Life and Death of a Chocolate City.* Durham, NC: Duke University Press, 2012.

Iton, Richard. *In Search of the Black Fantastic: Politics and Popular Culture in the Post–Civil Rights Era.* New York: Oxford University Press, 2008.

JanMohamed, Abdul. *Manichean Aesthetics: The Politics of Literature in Colonial Africa.* Amherst: University of Massachusetts Press, 1983.

Kaliss, Jeff. *I Want to Take You Higher: The Life and Times of Sly and the Family Stone.* Milwaukee: Backbeat Books, 2008.

Keil, Charles. *Urban Blues.* 1966; reprint, Chicago: University of Chicago Press, 1991.

Kelley, Robin D. G. *Thelonious Monk: The Life and Times of an American Original.* New York: Free Press, 2009.

King, B.B., with David Ritz. *Blues All Around Me: The Autobiography of B.B. King.* New York: Avon Books, 1996.

Khan, Chaka, with Tonya Bolden. *Chaka!: Through the Fire.* New York: St. Martin's Press, 2003.

Lomax, Alan. *The Land Where the Blues Began.* New York: New Press, 1993.

Mahon, Maureen. *Right to Rock: The Black Rock Coalition and the Cultural Politics of Race.* Durham, NC: Duke University Press, 2004.

Malone, Jacqui. *Steppin' on the Blues: The Visible Rhythms of African American Dance.* Urbana: University of Illinois Press, 1996.

Marable, Manning. *Race, Reform, and Rebellion: The Second Reconstruction in Black America.* New York: Macmillan, 1984.

Marquis, Donald M. *In Search of Buddy Bolden: First Man of Jazz.* 1978; rev. ed., Baton Rouge: Louisiana State University Press, 2005.

Mills, Charles. *The Racial Contract.* Ithaca: Cornell University Press, 1997.

Mills, David, Larry Alexander, Thomas Stanley, and Aris Wilson. *George Clinton and P-Funk: An Oral History.* New York: Avon Books, 1998.

Morgan, Joan. *When Chickenheads Come Home to Roost.* New York: Simon & Schuster, 1999.

Morrison, Toni. *The Bluest Eye.* New York: Holt, Rinehart and Winston, 1970.

Murray, Albert. *Stomping the Blues.* 1976; reprint, New York: Da Capo Press, 1987.

Nathan, David. *The Soulful Divas.* New York: Billboard Books, 1999.

Parker, Maceo. *98% Funky Stuff.* Chicago: Chicago Review Press, 2013.

Pendergrass, Teddy. *Truly Blessed.* New York: Putnam Adult, 1998.

Pointer, Ruth, and Marshall Terrill. *Still So Excited: My Life as a Pointer Sister.* Chicago: Triumph Books, 2016.

Powell, Richard J. *The Blues Aesthetic: Black Culture and Modernism.* Washington, DC: Washington Project for the Arts, 1989.

Ramsey, Guthrie P., Jr. *Race Music: Black Cultures from Bebop to Hip Hop.* Berkeley: University of California Press, 2004.

Reed, Ishmael. *Mumbo Jumbo.* New York: Doubleday, 1972.

Reed, Teresa. *The Holy Profane: Religion in Black Popular Music.* Lexington: University of Kentucky Press, 2003.

Ripani, Richard J. *The New Blue Music: Changes in Rhythm & Blues, 1950–1999.* Jackson: University Press of Mississippi, 2006.

Royster, Francesca T. *Sounding Like a No-No: Queer Sounds and Eccentric Acts in the Post-Soul Era.* Ann Arbor: University of Michigan Press, 2012.

Scott-Heron, Gil. *So Far, So Good.* Chicago: Third World Press, 1990.

Scott-Heron, Gil. *The Last Holiday: A Memoir.* New York: Grove Press, 2012.

Selvin, Joel. *Sly and the Family Stone: An Oral History.* New York: Avon Books, 1998.

Shadwick, Keith. *Jimi Hendrix: Musician.* San Francisco: Backbeat Books, 2003.

Shange, Ntozake. *for colored girls who have considered suicide / when the rainbow is enuf: a choreopoem.* New York: Macmillan, 1977.

Shange, Ntozake. *Three Pieces.* New York: St. Martin's Press, 1981.

Shapiro, Nat, and Nat Hentoff. *Hear Me Talkin' to Ya: The Story of Jazz by the Men Who Made It.* 1955; reprint, New York: Dover Publications, 1966.

Spencer, Jon Michael. *Blues and Evil.* Knoxville: University of Tennessee Press, 1993.

Springer, Robert, ed. *The Lyrics in African American Popular Music.* New York: Peter Lang, 2001.

Stallings, L. H. *Funk the Erotic: Transaesthetics and Black Sexual Cultures.* Champaign: University of Illinois Press, 2015.

Standing in the Shadows of Motown. directed by Paul Justman. DVD, Santa Monica, CA: Artisan Home Entertainment, 2002.

Tate, Greg. *Flyboy in the Buttermilk: Essays on Contemporary America: An Eye-Opening Look at Race, Politics, Literature, and Music.* New York: Simon & Schuster, 1992.

Tate, Greg. *Midnight Lightning: Jimi Hendrix and the Black Experience.* Chicago: Chicago Review Press, 2003.

Tate, Greg. *Flyboy 2: The Greg Tate Reader.* Durham: Duke University Press, 2016.

Turner, Tina, and Kurt Loder. *I, Tina: My Life Story.* New York: Avon Books, 1986.

Vincent, Rickey. *Funk: The Music, the People, and the Rhythm of the One.* New York: St. Martin's Press, 1996.

Waksman, Steve. *Instruments of Desire: The Electrical Guitar and the Shaping of Musical Experience.* Cambridge, MA: Harvard University Press, 1999.

Wald, Gayle F. *Shout, Sister, Shout!: The Untold Story of Rock-and-Roll Trailblazer Sister Rosetta Tharpe.* Boston: Beacon Press, 2007.

Werner, Craig. *Playing the Changes: From Afro-Modernism to the Jazz Impulse.* Urbana: University of Illinois Press, 1994.

White, Maurice. *My Life with Earth, Wind & Fire.* New York: HarperCollins, 2016.

Williams, Sherley Anne. *Some One Sweet Angel Chile.* New York: William Morrow, 1982.

Young, Kevin. *The Grey Album: On the Blackness of Blackness.* Minneapolis: Graywolf Press, 2012.

Index

About the Author

Credit: Aldon Lynn Nielsen

Tony Bolden is editor of *The Langston Hughes Review,* and teaches courses on African American culture at the University of Kansas. His previous books include *Afro-Blue: Improvisations on African American Poetry and Culture* and *The Funk Era and Beyond: New Perspectives on Black Popular Culture.* He is currently completing a book manuscript tentatively titled "Knee-Deep: The Kinetic Aesthetic in Black Expressive Culture."

CPSIA information can be obtained
at www.ICGtesting.com
Printed in the USA
BVHW071529020821
613134BV00003B/8